COLOR AND RACE

THE DÆDALUS LIBRARY

Published by Houghton Mifflin Company and
The American Academy of Arts and Sciences

A New Europe?, edited by Stephen R. Graubard
The Professions in America, edited by Kenneth S. Lynn
The Woman in America, edited by Robert Jay Lifton
Science and Culture, edited by Gerald Holton
Utopias and Utopian Thought, edited by Frank E. Manuel
The Contemporary University: U.S.A., edited by Robert S.
    Morison
The Negro American, edited by Talcott Parsons and Kenneth
    B. Clark
Creativity and Learning, edited by Jerome Kagan
Fiction in Several Languages, edited by Henri Peyre
Conditions of World Order, edited by Stanley Hoffmann
Toward the Year 2000: Work in Progress, edited by Daniel Bell
Religion in America, edited by William G. McLoughlin and
    Robert N. Bellah
Color and Race, edited by John Hope Franklin

COLOR AND RACE

EDITED AND WITH AN INTRODUCTION
BY JOHN HOPE FRANKLIN

HOUGHTON MIFFLIN COMPANY BOSTON
1968

Second Printing R

Copyright © 1968 by The
American Academy of Arts and Sciences

Library of Congress
Catalog Card Number: 68-8526

The introduction by John Hope Franklin, "Color and Race in the
Modern World," and "The Problem of Polarization on the Axis of Color,"
by Talcott Parsons, are here published for the first time. The other
essays in the book originally appeared in the Spring 1967 issue of
Dædalus, the Journal of the American Academy of Arts and Sciences.

Printed in the United States of America

CONTENTS

CONTENTS

JOHN HOPE FRANKLIN

Introduction: Color and Race in the Modern World

I

At the present time, when the world is so unsettled, we know all
too little about the factors that affect the attitudes of the peoples
of the world toward one another. It is clear, however, that color
and race are at once among the most important and the most enig-
matic. We also know that while studies of the subject tend invariably to focus on the United States, where color and race can often
be observed in some of its most dramatic—and violent—forms, it
must be recognized as a phenomenon that, in one degree or another,
is almost universal in its manifestations. As *The Economist* pointed
out shortly after the Los Angeles riots of 1965:

> People still talk as if the racist conflict in America was in a category of its
> own; or as if the only significant race confrontation was the one between
> black and white men. . . . The week of the Los Angeles riots was also
> the week when Malaysia broke apart because brown men could not con-
> trol their dark suspicions of yellow men, and when black and brown men
> resumed their efforts to slug it out in southern Sudan. All the evidence is
> that there is potential trouble wherever people of different colours rub
> shoulders uneasily together. The history of the black-brown dividing line
> in independent Africa in the last five years—with splits opening up in
> Sudan, Mauretania, in Chad and between Somalia and Kenya—makes a
> man's heart sink into his boots.

The participants in the Copenhagen Conference on Race and
Color in 1965 met just days after the Los Angeles riots to present
and discuss the papers that were to constitute the basis for this
volume. Each member of the conference had an authority's view
of one dimension or another of the problem, and all were willing to
speculate on the significance of recent events. Some of them, by
training and experience, were able to take a larger view of the problem of color and race and recognize its far-flung ramifications. Only

after listening to the papers and the discussion were they able to appreciate fully the profound implications of their findings. They had learned that the specter of color and race haunts every nook and corner of the world, consuming an inordinate amount of mankind's energies and attention that are so desperately needed to solve the major problems of peace and survival.

Some of the papers prepared for the conference were for the purpose of stimulating discussion, and they achieved that objective admirably. Others were for publication in this volume, and they benefited greatly from the observations and criticisms that the participants generously offered. When it became clear that major areas or aspects of the subject had not been covered by the papers, several authorities were commissioned to prepare papers on those subjects for this volume. Because The American Academy of Arts and Sciences has already published an extensive study on the Negro American, this volume does not dwell in any considerable way on that subject, but the substance of many of the papers in this volume is clearly relevant to the situation in the United States. It would be impossible, within the space of a few hundred pages, to treat all areas of the world where there is a problem of color and race. Nor is it possible to touch on all aspects of the problem. This volume presents a selection of the most pressing aspects of color and race that are relevant to a consideration of the problem in a worldwide context.

II

The pervasiveness of color and race, both in time and space, is of special interest to our contributors. Some, but not all, believe that the consciousness of color and the emergence of antagonisms based on color are as old as human society itself. Professor Shils observes that human beings have needs that are so deep and fundamental as to constitute a primordial quality. And he identifies religious sensibilities and color identification as prime examples. Other needs or other vehicles of self-identification may tend to recede with time and events; but color, as a basis of attack or of defense—or a justification for it, persists to a degree that suggests indestructibility.

One may or may not subscribe to the view that consciousness of color was among the earliest sensibilities of men. The persistence of this quality over most of human history is however, an inescapable fact. The history of human relations has involved all too frequently the confrontation and, consequently, the conflict of peoples of different colors and races. The result invariably has been the humiliation, insult, and injury of one by the other. As Professor Shils says:

Military conquest and alien rule, cultural derogation and individual affront, political suppression, military repression, and almost every other kind of coercion form an important part of the history of the colored peoples resident in the once-colonial countries or descended from them, and they are bitterly remembered. Color is the shorthand that evokes all these griefs and grievances.

If color and race constitute the basis or the justification for conflict between peoples of different areas and races, it also constitutes the basis for differentiation and preference *within* a given society or even within a racial group. If Freud was correct in his theory that the overriding pleasure instinct first becomes gratified within one's own body, then it may be argued that even within a society a person will be attracted to those who most resemble himself. If, in addition to this, people of the same or similar color share common experiences such as the achievement of a superior social or economic status or their relegation to a degraded status, it merely serves to intensify color affinity. Even where there is only a slight tendency in this direction, any segmentation has the effect of underscoring what had been, at the outset, only minimal differences. As Professor Gergen points out, "Once such segmentation occurs, not only within-group similarity but also dissimilarity across groups may increase at a rapid rate." This makes possible not only the development and enforcement of a system of *apartheid*, but also a remarkable hierarchy of color differentiation within a given racial group.

Nowhere is the pervasiveness of color more dramatically illustrated than in the matter of semantics. Since color describes certain characteristics of an object, rather than the object itself, it is easy to react emotionally to a description in which color is the principal attribute. Professor Gergen observes that people of highly dissimilar cultural backgrounds react similarly to a given color; he indicates that studies of color symbolism have concluded that blackness elicits, on the whole, unfavorable responses, while whiteness evokes favorable responses. There are notable exceptions, and it should be observed that people in advantaged positions tend to ascribe to those of a different color those traits that justify or explain their disadvantaged position. In the Caucasian-dominated culture of the West, moreover, color symbolism has served to reinforce the assumptions that whiteness connotes virtue and purity, while blackness connotes wickedness and defilement. As Professor Bastide makes abundantly clear, the implications of such symbolism for religion and for everyday relations in a society dominated by white men seem obvious.

It was inevitable that, under the circumstances, any effort to neutralize or to end world domination by white men would be accompanied by a large-scale rejection of Western values. In the development of an ideology of equality—or even superiority—the darker peoples of the world have confronted the color symbolism of the white world and have rejected it altogether. In Africa, the rejection has found expression in the concepts of *negritude* and the African personality. In the United States, it has found expression in the concepts of black nationalism and black power. "The resentment of Asia, Africa, and, to some extent, Latin America at past behavior and at all present assumptions of superiority is an actuality," says Philip Mason. In the United States, the black militants who reject the values of the white man "dress unaffectedly and wear their hair *à la mode Africaine*," in order to emphasize their identification with "black values." Even more important, as Professor Eric Lincoln observes, "The synonym of nationalism is black ethnocentrism, and ethnocentrism always implies a suspicion of some other peoples' integrity, their values, and their truths."

This rejection of Western values and the growing consciousness of group identity have, in turn, stimulated the movement toward self-determination and self-government. First, it involved the reestablishment of the black man's history, in which color and race were rejected as delimiting factors in achievement. Darker peoples had once been self-governing, and if they could throw off the economic and political domination of the white man, they would govern themselves again. Fired by a sense of their own past and by the urgency of the present, the darker peoples of both Asia and Africa took the giant step toward self-government. Meanwhile, black power in the United States, intent on the glorification of blackness, looks toward the achievement of economic and political power based on group identity and loyalty. Harold Isaacs sees in this, as Frantz Fanon does, a transition from nationalism to chauvinism to a new racism. He says:

The same newness marks the relationships just beginning between the black man, whether African or other, and other non-whites elsewhere in the world. On this score it now seems somberly reasonable to predict that color will continue to be a more critical factor for the black man than for any other kind.

III

There was a time when the view that race was a decisive factor in determining individual and group achievement was widely accepted. As Professor Isaacs observes, "Racial mythologies built around differences in skin color and physical features were among the prime tools of power used in the era of the Western empires." In the United States, it was around the Negro's blackness and its concommitant characteristics that the white world built up its rationale for reducing him to a less-than-human status. In Asia and Africa, it was the "innate backwardness" of the darker peoples that lent respectability as well as justification to their exploitation and domination by Europeans for centuries. While these myths have been largely demolished and while political independence has become almost world-wide, the effects of long years of acceptance and practice remain. Europeans and Americans have difficulty in becoming accustomed to the new non-subordinate status of darker peoples, and they betray the rigidity of their own feelings in a dozen different ways: in their insistence on continuing their cherished distinctions based on color and race and in their condescending and patronizing concessions that under their chaperonage the backward races are moving toward adolescence.

Whether awareness of color is a primordial quality suggested by Professor Shils or the carefully inculcated attitude claimed by Professor Isaacs, in the old world and in the new it remains an essential fact of daily life. Professor Wagatsuma tells us that long before any sustained contact with either white Europeans or dark-skinned Africans or Indians, the Japanese valued white skin and deprecated black skin. Later contact with the white world, whose industrial and economic prowess the Japanese wished to emulate, merely strengthened their view that whiteness was synonymous with beauty. But in a country such as Japan where self-identity is secure and where its own history glorifies a distinctive racial and cultural tradition, a certain ambivalence is evident. Thus, the Japanese view the Caucasian skin as "ugly" in texture and quality, therefore maintaining a Japanese skin supremacy, "while at the same time admitting the better appearance of the refined Caucasian facial structure."

In India the problem of race and color is complicated by the infinitely more perplexing problem of caste. Nevertheless, as Professor Béteille indicates, sharp physical differences exist. North Indians, for example, have a "vague prejudice" against South Indians on account of their dark skin color. In many Indian languages, the words *fair* and *beautiful* are often used synonymously. "The ideal bride, whose beauty and virtue are praised in songs sung at marriages, almost always has a light complexion." Anyone who has examined the matrimonial columns of Indian newspapers is impressed with the frequency with which a light skin is mentioned as a desirable quality in a bride. Even so, few if any places in India have experienced any significant conflict between "racial" or "color" groups. Perhaps the great overlap between adjacent segments and the absence of any real polarity in color are explanations for this relative peace.

Professor Brown has suggested that color is not important in determining the relationships of North Africans to one another or even to the blacks of the South. The unifying factors in North Africa—Islam, the Arabic language, economic organization, architecture, cuisine, and even dress—minimize color considerations. There is, as in India, the absence of polarity in color. When darker Africans from the South migrated to the North, they were not segregated or deprecated in some specific manner. If this movement continues and if the competition for jobs becomes more intense, it remains to be seen if the North Africans will maintain the kind of color indifference that has characterized their attitude in the past. There is also the question of whether North Africans will become more closely identified with the movement for African unity that emphasizes, at least in part, the importance of the solidarity of darker peoples.

As one surveys the old world and the new, it becomes quite clear that in no other country of the world is color more important than in South Africa. It is, as Colin Legum says, the sole determinant of power there. Power and privilege go hand in hand, and whites enjoy them exclusively. White supremacy has become white tyranny; and this has been accompanied by the view that force is necessary to maintain it. Conversely, the blacks—both in South Africa and in other areas of the continent—have increasingly embraced the view that the tyranny can be overcome only by violence. This was confirmed by the emergence of Rhodesia as a new state based on white tyranny and the manifestation on the part of the rest of the world of utter hopelessness and helplessness in the face of it. This, Mr. Legum believes, has set South Africa on a collision course that will lead to an unprecedented bloody racial conflict unless "prophylactic action becomes possible." At the present time, such intercession cannot be foreseen, and it is in South Africa and Rhodesia that the prospects for racial peace are at present the dimmest.

Only in recent years—after World War II—have Europeans experienced the problem of race and color to any considerable degree. An increasing number of French Africans and West Indians have taken up residence in France; and although they suffer no crude forms of segregation or discrimination, their sense of alienation is, nevertheless, real. Dr. Raveau observes that Negroes living in France are made marginal by their color. The problem of adjustment, even in a relatively congenial environment, has been, at best, difficult.

It is Britain, however, that has experienced the greatest problem in adjusting to the influx of hundreds of thousands of black people from Africa and the West Indies and many brown people from Pakistan and India. Most Britons, with the possible exception of some who had worked in the colonial service, had no previous experience with darker peoples and would have resented any suggestion that they harbored prejudices or even reservations regarding them. They were very much like many whites in the northern part of the United States who had enjoyed both their insulation and their theoretical views of racial equality until they confronted the situation in their own communities. The influx of large groups of darker peoples into their midst put the views of both Britons and northern whites in the United States to a severe test. Many of them discovered for the first time that they had their own prejudices and that they were not prepared to accept their darker brothers as equals.

The experience of a colored immigrant in trying to gain acceptance in Britain can be as searing as that of the southern Negro in New York or Boston or Chicago. As E. R. Braithwaite has observed, the high visibility of the colored immigrant "is a constant reminder of his earliest relationship with them—slave to owner, subject to sovereign, conquered to conqueror, and man to master." There is small wonder that as the numbers of colored immigrants in Britain increased, the reaction ranged from the crude sloganizing of "Keep Britain White" to the more subtle and effective forms of discrimination in housing and employment. Conflicts and fear of greater conflicts in the future have forced the major political parties as well as the government to take cognizance of the problem and to seek ways to solve it. Parties, however, have been more concerned about counting votes than about facing the problem. Professor Little observes what is even more important: "Even in official circles little apparent attention has been paid to the sociological issues that lie beneath the surface of what is oversimplified as a black-white confrontation."

There was a time when the view prevailed that were it not for the presence of Europeans in the West Indies racial harmony would prevail there. Even before the movement that led to the overthrow of colonial rule, it was clear to the careful observer that such was not the case. Perhaps because of the legacy of certain values that was a result of long years of European domination or perhaps because of other factors, including all the problems inherent in a multiracial society, most of the West Indian islands continue to be plagued by racial tensions and conflict in one degree or another. Color and racial distinctions persist without the sanction of law, and Mr. Lowenthal fears that in some respects West Indian race relations have actually deteriorated. Even if race and color do not define West Indian classes, color is frequently the crucial determinant of status; and consciousness of color is always close to the surface. In the face of this reality the submerged masses, most of whom are black, have the most serious doubts that their opportunities to move up in the social and economic scale are unlimited.

The situation on the mainland of Central and South America is essentially the same. There are no serious Negro-white conflicts, but the matter of Indian-white relations is frequently overlooked. In Panama and the Andes, as well as in Brazil, the very idea of segregation based on color is generally repulsive. Professor Pitt-Rivers observes, however, that there is a high degree of social differentiation, and at times it is associated with physical characteristics, including skin color. He points up the difficulties in reaching any definitive conclusion about the problem of race and color on the mainland when he observes that "ethnic classification is the end product of the most elusive social processes that endow not only words, but feelings and perceptions with a special significance." Professor Fernandes argues that in Brazil successful Negroes have broken through the barriers behind which historical stereotypes had consigned them and have been supported in their new status by those whites who believe in tolerance and equality. Even in a relatively favorable situation such as exists in Brazil, however, Professor Fernandes recognizes that as long as the past is a part of the present, the favor won by individual Negroes presents no final solution of the problem of color and race.

IV

The relationship of color and race to the peace of the world has increasingly become a central issue in international relations during the last century. The competition for Africa among the Western nations and the racial factor in the struggle for power that culminated in World War I indicated how impossible it was to neglect the question. If there was any doubt about the matter, it was dispelled when Japan, the first non-white nation to achieve the position of a world power, sought unsuccessfully at the Peace Conference to have a provision for racial equality written into the Covenant of the League of Nations. The matter would not die, and the growing conflict in Asia, the problem of maintaining European control in Sub-Saharan Africa, and the brewing crisis in the relations of Italy and Abyssinia all had the most serious racial implications. The racist dogmas espoused by the Nazis before and during World War II were a culmination of the development that brought the matter of race to a closer relationship with the problem of peace.

The new states that emerged after World War II were largely non-white, constituting more than one fourth of the world's population. While there was no overtly articulated sentiment against the "rising tide of color" or a "yellow peril," there were, nevertheless, numerous African and Asian states that had to be reckoned with. They were important forces in the United Nations and in regional arrangements, such as the Organization for African Unity and the Southeast Asia Treaty Organization. As nations, they stood in relationship to the white nations as black and brown and yellow peoples stood in relation to the white world. They were, for the most part, poverty-stricken, underdeveloped, and uneducated. The white nations had difficulty in adjusting to the new status of the darker nations as free and independent. And the attitudes of condescension and impatience of the former merely served to increase their sensitivity and to widen the gap between the two groups.

As Robert K. A. Gardiner has observed, these movements of rejection and of self-assertion have had significant political repercussions. The Bandung Conference indicated that an Afro-Asian group was resolved to stand together against what it considered to be the persistent determination of the white nations to dominate the world. Later, in their search for some resolution of the problem posed by the great powers, all of whom were white, the Bandung conferees concluded that color as a basis for a common cause was transitory and elusive. This view was further eroded by the realization of some darker peoples that religion, namely Islam, was more important than race and that geography was more important than color. It was also marked by what Mr. Gardiner calls the dilemma of the Chinese Communists "of whether to opt for the mantle of the true heir of Marx and Lenin or for that of leader of the 'non-white' world."

None of these alternatives or solutions seemed to constitute a sound basis for solving the problem of color and race. In the concluding article for this volume, Professor Parsons explores the problem of polarization in terms of color in the context of the whole development of Western society and its relations to the rest of the world. While he concedes that the most serious possibility for the emergence of a new polarization is clearly the axis of color, he argues with force that it will fail to crystallize as the major basis of division in the world.

Even if Professor Parsons' cautious prognostication is correct, there remains the difficult task of solving or at least coping with one of the most perplexing and persistent problems that mankind has ever faced. Perhaps Mr. Gardiner was correct in saying:

The greatest challenge to mankind is how to foster adjustments in conventional outlook and in minimum standards of behavior in a fragmented world moving toward unity. Unity must not be confused with uniformity. It would be as absurd to expect a standard human type as to expect a uniform world culture. A world of free men must be a world of diversity.

COLOR AND RACE

EDWARD SHILS

Color, the Universal Intellectual Community, and the Afro-Asian Intellectual

I

IN ITSELF color is meaningless. It is not like religion, which is belief and entails either voluntary or hereditary membership in a community of believers and therewith exposure to an assimilation of a tradition of beliefs. It is not like kinship, which is a tangible structure in which the individual has lived, which has formed him, and to which he is attached. It is not like intellectual culture, which is belief and an attitude toward the world (or particular parts of it). It is not even like nationality, which is a superimposition of beliefs about a community of culture upon a common primordial existence of that community in a given territory. The designation of a person as being of a particular religious community or of a particular school of thought or even of a given nationality is a statement about that person's mind, about the pattern of meaning by which he interprets reality. His participation in the interpretation of reality according to that pattern of meaning might be hypocritical, it is undoubtedly intermittent and vague. All this notwithstanding, the involvement of the mind is a major though not the sole component in the definition of the person in question. It is not this way with color.

Color is just color. It is a physical, a spectroscopic fact. It carries no compellingly deducible conclusions regarding a person's beliefs or his position in any social structure. It is like height or weight—the mind is not involved. Yet it attracts the mind; it is the focus of passionate sentiments and beliefs. The sentiments color evokes are not the sentiments of aesthetic appreciation. Nor does color have any moral significance; color is not acquired or possessed by leading a good or a bad life. No intentions are expressed by color; no interpretations of the world are inherent in it; no attachments are constituted by it. The mind is not at work in it, and it is not a social relationship. It is inherently meaningless.

1

Why, then, has this inherently meaningless property of man come to assume such great importance in the self-image of many human beings? Has only a historical accident of an unequal distribution of power and wealth between two differently pigmented aggregates of human beings led to this cleavage between those called white and those called colored? Or have sentiments of injury and anger implicated in the consciousness of being colored developed because those called white have so often used their greater power to injure those called colored in ways beyond what is intrinsic in the exercise of power?

One of the simplest and most obvious reasons why color is a focus of passionate sentiments is that it is an easy way to distinguish between those from the periphery and those from the center of particular societies and of the world society. Differences of pigmentation symbolize or indicate contemporaneous differences between present wealth and power and present poverty and weakness, between present fame and present obscurity, between present eminence in intellectual creativity and present intellectual unproductiveness. It is correlated with past events too—above all, with past events of humiliation, injury, and insult. Military conquest and alien rule, cultural derogation and individual affront, political suppression, military repression, and almost every other kind of coercion form an important part of the history of the colored peoples resident in the once-colonial countries or descended from them, and they are bitterly remembered. Color is the shorthand that evokes all these griefs and grievances. Is it more than that?

Conquest and maltreatment were not first brought to Asia and Africa by the European imperial powers. Long before, Asians had conquered other Asians; Arabs had exploited and enslaved black Africans, often with the aid of other black African rulers. Still, it is the European conquest that is remembered. It is remembered most vividly because it is the most recent, extending well into the memory of all living adults and many young people. It is also remembered because it was experienced more painfully than previous imperial conquests. The greater painfulness stems, in part, from the vividness of freshly remembered events. Moreover, this more recent dominion—imperial and internal—inculcated moral, political, and intellectual standards for its own criticism, a practice previous imperial rulers had not employed. The acquisition of the standards implicit in the religious and political culture that the whites brought to Asia and Africa and that they preached and partly observed in

their own countries made the discrepancy between those standards and their own action and presence in Asia and Africa and their
conduct toward colored peoples in their own countries uncomfortable to bear.[1] There seem to be some other reasons as well. The
European conquerors came from far off, they were not expanding
neighbors, and they were of a different color.

Tyranny is always painful, but tyranny exercised by the ethnically alien, whose ethnic alien-ness is underscored by the most
easily distinguishable color difference, is especially repugnant. In
Asia and Africa, the illegitimacy of an ethnically alien tyranny is
almost all gone now. Why does it still rankle so much in the hearts
of Afro-Asian intellectuals? They are no longer being exploited,
maltreated, or insulted by white men in their own countries. Why do
they still feel the slights directed against their fellow-colored in the
few parts of the world still under colonial rule or in the United
States or in the United Kingdom?[2]

Their feeling of being excluded from the center, of being
treated contemptuously as inferiors, of having their weakness
"rubbed in" comes to a tormenting focus in their awareness of the
differences in color between themselves and the "white" men at the
center. The injurious actions explicit in policy and custom, the
studied insults implicit in policy, and the random insults of individuals are wounding to those who experience them and to those
who identify with the wounded.

II

There is certainly much truth in the explanation of color identification that points to the coincidence of patterns of color distribution and patterns of the distribution of power and wealth. The
coincidence of color with inferior positions in the various distribu-
tions in colonial societies, in predominantly white societies, and in
world society reinforces—some would say, generates—the interpretation of "color identity" as a variant of "class identity." There is
truth also in the proposition that color identification arises in part
from the assimilation by the colored periphery of the dominant
white center's use of the categories "whiteness" and "coloredness."
But these hypotheses, valuable though they are, do not provide an
exhaustive explanation. Another element should be mentioned not
as an exhaustive alternative explanation, but as a complementary
one that deals with a vital phenomenon otherwise excluded from
consideration. It is this: Self-identification by color has its origins

3

in the sense of primordial connection with which human beings find it difficult to dispense.

The prominence and ubiquity of self-identification by kinship connection and territorial location are well-known, but they tend to be taken for granted and even neglected in the study of modern society. Because they are taken for granted, they are seldom reduced analytically to man's need to be in contact with the point and moment of his origin and to experience a sense of affinity with those who share that origin. The need for connections or relationships of a primordial character will be endemic in human existence as long as biological existence has a value to the individual organism. Ethnic identification, of which color identification is a particular variant, is a manifestation of this need. Traces of the sense of affinity and of shared primordial properties occur also in the phenomenon of nationality.

Self-identification by color seems to entail some reference to a common biological origin that is thought to establish ties of affinity, sometimes obligation and solidarity among those who share it, and of separation from those who do not. In its crudest form, it denies the membership of those of other colors in the same species.

There are great interindividual differences in this sense of affinity with those who share a putatively common origin, just as there are great interindividual differences in the need for contact with divinity. The need, where it is weak, is often powerfully reinforced by the cultures and social structures generated by color identification and by those that parallel it. A weak disposition toward color identification can be strengthened by class—or national —identifications that are congruent with color boundaries.

Decrease in the dominance of primordial attachments of kinship and locality has been accompanied by an increase in the importance attributed to ethnicity and color. The latter two represent a broadening of the scope of particularistic primordial identification. Ethnicity in numerous cases—color in very few—has yielded precedence in many respects to nationality, which verges toward civility while retaining much of a primordial, often pseudo-ethnic basis.

In nationality, the primordial element begins to recede. It yields to an "ideal" or "ideational" element—a "spirit," an "essence"— that is recognized as involving the mind. It is not accidental that a common language—the most widely shared of cultural objectivations—has so often been regarded as a crucial element in nationality.

The primordial is one focus of man's disposition to attribute

4

sacredness to particular entities or symbols. It was a great accomplishment of the human race to have relocated the sacred from the primordial to the ideal, from biological and territorial properties of the self and the kinship-local group to entities apprehensible by thought and imagination. But it has done so only very falteringly. Its failure to accomplish it entirely is a source of many of mankind's miseries. The shift occurred in both Judaism and Buddhism, although the Jews retained the primordial ethnic element in a central position. It reached a high development in Christianity and in Islam. Nevertheless, in none of the cultures in which these religions have become established has the sacredness of the primordial been anything more than diminished. Still, it has been displaced to some extent, as the development of religion and politics testifies. The sacred—both primordial and "ideal"—is capable of attenuation and dispersion. The growth of modern society is the history of this attenuation and dispersion—with numerous relapses into intensification and concentration. There is, however, a major primordial property that has been very reluctant to yield its sacredness to attenuation. This is color.

The self-identification by color common among Asians and Africans of wide horizon—and the Afro-Asian intellectuals, in particular —is not attributable exclusively to its primordial quality. Nor is color the sole or always dominant criterion of this self-identification. Color plays a considerable, if indeterminate, part in their self-identification because it symbolizes many other properties of the Africans' and Asians' position in their own societies—both in colonial times and in the world since independence. For intellectuals, additional factors—such as their position in the world-wide intellectual community and their own societies, and the relation of these societies to those of the once-ruling imperial powers and the other advanced countries—coincide with the color self-identification and accentuate its force. When these other factors diminish, the intensity of the total self-identification by color will diminish too. But what of the primordial root of the color-identification? Will color yield some of its power in the formation of the self-image of Asians and Africans? Will it yield some of its power over the intellectual's self-image and its influence on his response to intellectual things?

III

I should now like to turn away for a moment from color as a focus of self-identification and consider possible changes that might enter into the self-identification of intellectuals—literary men, journalists, scientists, and scholars. First of all, their focus on nationality and civility might grow if the new states become consolidated internally as integrated national societies. They might also identify themselves as members of intellectual communities which transcend the boundaries of states and the limits of regions and continents.

The intellectual community, in its territorial scope and its criteria of admission, is the most universal of communities. Its adherents are scattered over the world's surface. To be a member of it, a person must either be engaged in intellectual activities or be in the state of mind that intellectual actions express and engender. In principle, no primordial properties, such as connections of kinship, locality, tribe, or territory, are valid in the assessment of the qualifications for membership in any of its constituent institutions or for advancement in its corporate or honorary hierarchies. (Of course, in practice, primordial properties are sometimes operative in governing admission to membership in particular corporate institutions, but those who apply them know that they are contravening the rules of the intellectual community—unarticulated and amorphous though these are.) The intellectual community is universalistic because it applies criteria of universal validity, criteria generally acknowledged throughout the world as true and relevant by those who have been exposed to them by education and training. Sometimes the intellectual community might seem to have no reality, to be only a figurative name for a class of actions and states of mind, to be, in fact, no community at all. It certainly lacks a corporate structure, although it has many subsidiary corporate structures, such as international scientific and professional associations. It lacks a formal structure of authority, although it has many subsidiary structures of authority, such as universities, research institutions, periodicals, and professional associations. It lacks formal articles of faith, but it has many quite specific actions and beliefs that define membership. Indeed, as a single community, it scarcely exists, and yet it would be excessively and prejudicially toughminded to deny its existence altogether. Its subsidiary, more specialized spheres certainly have more reality; they are more easily apprehensible.

The world scientific community is one of these. It is the community of those who do scientific research, the real science that is practiced with efficacy in teaching and research in many parts of the world. Its members communicate easily with one another—partly because the subject matter of each substantively specialized subsector is common to all its members wherever and whoever they are, partly because the symbols and notations used are universally uniform, and partly because science, particularly scientific research, uses one or a few common written languages.

The international scientific community has three major lines of internal differentiation. The first, differentiation by substantive spheres of knowledge, is so pronounced that members of some sectors are frequently unable to communicate about their substantive interests and results very efficiently with members of other sectors, even those within the same country or university. The second, differentiation according to the quality of individual and collective performance, results in an approximation of a hierarchy of individuals and institutions (departments, universities, laboratories). The third, which follows from the second, is a territorial differentiation and hierarchy within a larger territory; it is intranational and international. In the international intellectual community, entire countries become the units for assessing the merit of performance or the basis of the average of accomplishment of particular intranational institutions. (In both, the assessment of the merit of collectivities is a precipitate or average of the assessment of the work of individuals; as a result, the ranks of particular individuals, their institutions, and their countries are only imperfectly correlated with one another.)

Yet despite these vertical and horizontal lines of differentiation and separation, the international scientific community does exist. Specialized scientists, blocked from communicating with one another about what they know best by the specialization of their knowledge, regard one another as "scientists." They consider themselves as having very important, although ordinarily unspecified, things in common. Regardless of their special subjects, they have the same heroes—Galileo, Newton, Darwin, Mendel. They believe that they belong to a common group because they perform and are committed to the performance of certain types of action and to the maintenance of certain states of mind that bring them together and set them apart from other human beings. They accept in common the discipline of scientific procedure, the unconditional value of truth, and the worthwhileness of striving for it. From this mutuality grows an attachment to one another, not as persons but as the bearers of an outlook.

7

The members of the scientific community are, of course, members of other communities as well, many of them authoritatively elaborated, with specific and specifiable obligations. Citizens of states and municipalities, administrators of laboratories and university departments, they are also members of political parties, churches, clubs, and civic and professional associations. They have different nationalities and religious beliefs. None of these properties or characteristics is, however, allowed in principle to contaminate the obligations scientists acknowledge themselves to have as scientists or to impair the affinity they sense among all scientists. In assessing the results of another scientist's research, a scientist permits none of these other obligations to stand in the way of his overwhelmingly preponderant obligation to observe, to think, and to judge as a scientist. In activities that are more secondary within the scientific community, these other obligations and loyal ties sometimes play a greater part, although there, too, it would ordinarily be denied that this is so in particular cases, and it would be emphatically denied in principle.

In the social sciences, with the exception of economics, there is much less common culture among the practitioners. Whereas economic theorists and economists speak to one another out of a knowledge of a common set of problems and a common body of literature, sociologists and political scientists diverge markedly after sharing but a few common elements in their disciplines. They have relatively fewer common symbols and notations. The data of the various social sciences, being largely descriptive of particular situations, are more intimately related to the various territories in which they were gathered and from which the social scientists come. The problems many social scientists study are, moreover, more intimately involved in their own particularistic attachments, even though they seek and often attain a high degree of detachment. Insofar as this detachment becomes more or less articulated in a general theory or in specific techniques, it gives them a common universe of discourse and thereby confers membership in an international community. Nevertheless, the international communities of social scientists are not as unified nor as integrated as those of the natural scientists. The social scientist's self-identification is more affected by his particularistic attachments than is that of the natural scientist.

The humanistic disciplines, except for general linguistics and certain classical subjects, are even more parochial than the social sciences. Much of the work of the humanistic disciplines is concerned with the establishment, precision, and interpretation of the national or regional (continental or otherwise territorial) cultural inheritance in the form of history, modern languages, literary, religious, philosophical, and artistic works. Much of the work done in these fields is only of interest to nationals of the countries in which it is done, and this not primarily because of linguistic barriers. Some of the scholarship in history and sociology is part of the consensus and dissensus of the various national societies in which it is carried on, and it entails relatively little transnational self-identification.

The practice of the social sciences and the humanistic subjects has nonetheless a considerable internationality. For one thing, the study of the society and the culture of a particular country is not confined to nationals of that country. Oriental and African studies —history, religion, society, literature, and languages—link European and American social scientists and humanistic scholars with scholars indigenous to the countries being studied. These studies, too, have their disciplined techniques, their heroes, and their classics, which are commonly shared by scholars wherever they are. The world communities of scholars in the social sciences and humanities are patchier and less integrated than the world community of natural scientists, but they are international communities nonetheless.

Literature has not the common institutional (largely academic) foundation, nor the compact, systematically unfolding tradition of the academically cultivated branches of science and scholarship. The diversity and lack of connection among traditions are greater. Nevertheless, the novel in both English-speaking and French-speaking Africa is and must be viewed in the larger context of the English and French literary traditions. Independent oral and written literary traditions enter into the creative work of Asian and African prose writers, but the great European models toward which the novelists outside Europe orient themselves help to form and guide the work of novelists in the Asian and African countries. Poetic creation shows these latter characteristics to an even greater extent. Shakespeare, Hugo, Yeats, T. S. Eliot, and Rimbaud are influences all over the world and create a sense of unity among poets.

IV

The world-wide intellectual community is neither dense, continuous, nor highly organized. Its coverage is very imperfect, and it does not have a complete consensus. Nonetheless, members of the various communities in the major areas of intellectual life evaluate intellectual performance with little or no reference to nationality, religion, race, political party, or class. An African novelist wants to be judged as a novelist, not as an African; a Japanese mathematician would regard it as an affront if an analysis of his accomplishment referred to his pigmentation; a British physicist would find it ridiculous if a judgment of his research referred to his being "white."

Every community has a center in which its highest values are symbolized and represented, from which authority is exercised on behalf of these values, and to which deference is given. Intellectual communities are no different from primordial communities and communities of religious belief in this regard. The centers of the modern intellectual communities are largely in the West—in the United Kingdom, Western Europe, and North America. The Soviet Union has recently become more of a center than Tsarist Russia was—except in literature—and Japan is beginning to become one. These two newer centers are handicapped because their languages are not so widely known outside their borders as those of the Western European and North American centers. They have also come forward more recently, and they have not entered so much into the modern cultures of Asia and Africa as have the older centers. The metropolitan cultures are still the centers for much of the modern intellectual life of the new states for such obvious reasons as the facility offered through the language introduced by the former ruler and the relatively low cultural productivity, in modern works, of the new states. The increased demands for intellectual products in the new states—books, periodicals, services of intellectual institutions, results of research and scientific surveys—have placed a burden on local or indigenous intellectual powers which they cannot yet accommodate.[3] The result is dependence on the most easily available source—which is, in most cases (except Indonesia), the culture of the former ruler. Pride, realism, and the competition of the great powers in seeking the approval of the new states have altered the pattern somewhat, but not fundamentally.

The institutional structure was organized on the assumption—by both parties—that the colonies were, insofar as they had a modern intellectual life, peripheral to the metropolitan centers. Where they had universities, they were formed on the metropolitan pattern. Many who taught in them, indigenous and expatriate, were

10

trained in the metropolitan universities. The books on sale in bookshops came from the publishers in the metroplitan countries, since the publishers were organized to supply the colonial market, such as it was; the same was true for periodicals. The young men who were trained either in the metropolitan universities or in the governmental or missionary institutions acquired the culture of the metropolis. If they became creative and productive, they did so as members of an intellectual community that had its center in the metropolis.

With relatively small differences, these conditions still exist in the new states of Asia and Africa. One of the constitutive differences between the center and the periphery in the intellectual community is that the scholars and the scientists of the center are more widely known. Exceptional individuals at the periphery are accepted as equals at the center because of their accomplishments and regard themselves more or less as equals. They share the standards of the metropolis and judge themselves in that light; they appreciate that their own accomplishments put them in a position equal to that of the leading persons at the center and superior to that of the more mediocre practitioners at the center. The weight of the awareness of peripherality or provinciality persists, however, even among those who have become creative, because their accomplishment has not yet been attended by an intellectual infrastructure of institutions and products. They have not yet succeeded in changing the map that members of the intellectual communities in their own country and abroad carry in their minds.

This might not make much difference within a single country with a common language and culture. When center and periphery are located in different countries, however, it is quite another matter. The intellectual centers are more powerful economically and militarily, more famous, and more populous intellectually. The volume of their production is richer and is taken more seriously, not only because it is superior intellectually but also because the countries in which it is produced are more powerful and more famous. Moreover, the metropolitan cultures are the cultures of the former rulers or of those who are somehow associated in the minds of those on the periphery with their former rulers. All this strains the self-esteem of the intellectuals at the periphery. At the same time, the modern culture of the countries at the periphery of the international intellectual community is discontinuous with the indigenous culture of the peripheral areas.

As if to symbolize the whole thing, the inhabitants of the countries at the periphery are of a different color from those at the center.

Within an intranational intellectual community, there are strains of inferiority and superiority. It is not pleasant to adjudge oneself to be mediocre, to be intellectually dependent on others, and to see the world's praise directed toward them. Yet in addition to the usual mechanisms that preserve failures and near-failures from extremes of distress, belonging to a culture with a high position in the intellectual hierarchy also reduces the stress of failure—just as membership in a common nationality alleviates to some extent the distress of inequality.

The situation is more complicated and less favorable for the intellectuals of Asia and Africa. They are not members of this broader national community of culture of the center. They have their own national and regional cultures in which their own dignity is involved and which they do not share with their intellectual confreres of other nationalities and countries. This cuts them off to some extent from those intellectual confreres and reduces the solidarity of the ties of intellectual affinity. Their own national and regional cultures are, furthermore, like all human creations, subject to assessment. The criteria for the assessment of a complex culture of many strands and a long history are more qualified and more ambivalent than are the criteria of accomplishment and worth in the intellectual communities. Given the particularistic attachments that individuals have to their own cultures, bound up with them as they are through kinship ties and early experience, judgments about them are likely to be more "relativistic" than those about accomplishments in the various fields of modern culture, where the criteria are more consensual. Nonetheless, intellectuals in the new states are affected by the order of worth assigned to their culture by those at the centers of the international intellectual communities. They feel this way, although the centers' pre-eminence within any particular field of intellectual work does not qualify them for comprehensive judgment.

Cultures are assessed, in part, on grounds of their "modernity." Since the criteria of intellectual worth, being so vital to modernity, form such a large ingredient in the criteria of national worth, there is a tendency for national cultures as a whole to be ranked very roughly and approximately in accordance with the level of intellectual eminence.

In the more delimited realms of modern science and scholarship, the present-day nullity of the traditional inheritance of the African and Asian countries seems unchallengeable.[4] This consensus between center and periphery breaks down, however, when attention is shifted to the broader fields of culture, to religion and ethos. There is something substantially contemporaneous in these realms; societies have lived by them over long stretches of time, reaching into the present. They have become incorporated into works of thought and art, some of which have held the attention and aroused the admiration of the center in ways unparalleled by anything else in the social structures and cultures of the African and Asian countries.[5] They are, moreover, objects of genuine primary attachment for many intellectuals in these countries. Even where they are not, they are something to fall back on as evidence of past creativity, of greatness in human accomplishments and quality. They are, thereby, worthy of respect before a universal audience; by that token, they enhance the dignity of those who participate in or are otherwise associated with them and who are also part of a world-wide intellectual community and share some of its standards. The indigenous traditional cultures offer the simulacrum of an alternative center to which the intellectuals of Asia and Africa are drawn.

V

The need for a counter-center has a widely ramified origin. The Asian and African intellectuals are more than intellectuals participating in some manner in the universal intellectual community. They are members also of territorially limited but more than local societies, delimited nationalities, and a subspecies of the human race with pigmentation different from that of those in ascendancy.

Their conscious identification of themselves by these classifications is partly a product of their assimilation into the world-wide intellectual community. They came to transcend the narrowly local and ascended to the national, regional, and continental through participation in the universal intellectual community. Through modern education and training at home, through experience with the metropolis while being educated and trained in metropolitan institutions or in domestic institutions formed on their model, through sojourns in the metropolis, they became aware that they were something different from what they had been and what they were becoming. They became aware that they belonged to the colonial peoples, that they belonged to distinctive continents; they

13

came to perceive themselves as having nationality, which they defined as coterminous with the area over which the authority they rejected ruled. The self-definition was a negative one; it was the product of a process of distinguishing the self from the powerful, oppressively dominating center.

One major primordial property symbolizes through its concentration of all differences their differences from the metropolis. This is skin color. The awareness of differences in skin color heightens awareness of other differences. It does so not just by symbolizing those differences, but by serving as a focus of self-identification as a member of a species with a distinctive biological origin and separateness.

VI

The conflict between the primordial realm and the realm of the mind is especially pronounced in the intellectual, who—by virtue of what he is—is, in a way, the custodian of things of the mind for his society. Intellectual activity is the cultivation of the "ideational" realm. A change in the African or Asian intellectual's relations to the center of the international intellectual community might diminish the intensity of his color identification. The provinciality of his present position in the intellectual community is one of the distractions from which he suffers. This is only aggravated by the structural handicaps, both institutional and social, of his own country and the world.

When many more African and Asian intellectuals become productive and creative in the natural and social sciences, in humanistic scholarship, and in literature, their position will begin to change, and so will their self-identification by color. As individuals in the universities and towns of Africa and Asia begin to produce works that commend themselves to the intellectual appreciation of their colleagues at the centers in other parts of the world, and as they begin to produce some of their own succession, they will emerge from provinciality to centrality. This has already happened in certain fields and in certain places—for example, in statistics and economic theory in Calcutta and Delhi. Once these achievements begin to take deeper root by reproducing themselves and expanding their influence within India, the diminution of Indian intellectual peripherality will be under way. Similar processes are readily imaginable for other parts of Asia and Africa. They are not likely to occur in a very short time, but as they do, the strain of an inferior position in the international intellectual community will be reduced. A sense of genuine equality will then join to the sense of shared standards an awareness of shared accomplishment.

In emerging as new centers in the network of creative centers of the international intellectual community, African and Asian intellectuals will cease to feel so urgently the need for a counter-center, of which color is one of the foci of identification. The argument for a counter-center is only a largely contrived surrogate for the real thing. The counter-center could never be successful in attaining the end these intellectuals seek—the dignity of creative achievement.

The impetus to the "revolt against Western values" will weaken. The values will cease to be Western, except in the sense that in their more recent history they have been most cultivated in the West. They will become more fully what they are already patchily and unevenly—the universalistic values of a world-wide intellectual community.

The enhancement of the quality of civility in their societies will likewise work to diminish the force of the color identification. The closely connected sense of nationality will differentiate the "world of color," and will thereby reinforce the factors shifting the need for "serious" attachments away from color to alternative foci of *la vie sérieuse*.

As these changes occur—and it is reasonable to expect them to occur—the primordial attachment to color will still remain, but it will be deprived of its extraneous supports; it will no longer act so powerfully on the sentiments. Like ethnic, kinship, and local primordial attachments, it will survive but not so strongly as to deflect the intellect and imagination from their appropriate activities. Just as the rule of law and political equality have become established in areas once dominated by primordial attachments and the particularistic standards they dictated, so will the intellectual communities and their universalistic standards constrict the loyalties nurtured by the self-identification of color. This identification will become fainter and fainter.

REFERENCES

1. Cf. the dedication of Nirad C. Chaudhuri's great book, *The Autobiography of an Unknown Indian* (New York, 1951).

2. In a statement concerning the recent British legislative restrictions on Com-

monwealth immigration, a great Indian public servant, one of the most rational and modern of men without the slightest trace of xenophobia, demagogy, or revivalism in his mental make-up, writes:

"Sadly it must be recorded that Britain, the mother of parliaments, the originator of democracy and the rule of law, the home of liberty and fair play, the refuge of the persecuted and the oppressed, has fallen far below her high degree. She has now publicly declared herself a country riddled with colour consciousness. She needs constant replenishment of her labour force but she will take care to see that most of the new workers have white skins. They need not belong to the Commonwealth. Better by far total strangers politically, Portuguese and Greeks and Spaniards and South Irish than West Indians and Nigerians and Indians. . . .

"The Labour politicians, whatever and however strong their moral convictions in this matter, have discovered, perhaps to the dismay of some of them, that the voter, the ordinary Briton, feels strongly on this subject. He does not like the coloured man, black or brown, and he does not want them near him. They fear the political party which will not keep the coloured out will lose votes, and what after all are principles, moral or other, in comparison with votes? . . . A party led by a statesman and with a few statesmen in it might well have resisted the impact of the alleged general dislike and decided to educate the electorate rather than give way to its prejudice, but the last British statesman was Churchill, and puny are the men of Westminster today.

"So much for the British side. More important for us, our proper attitude to this declaration of national dislike. Not a few of us have come across some instance of colour-prejudice on our visits to England. (The writer can remember experiences on his first visit in 1921 and his last in 1962.) We have however put them down to aberrations on the part of an individual or a small section. No indictment most of us have felt like drawing up was against the British people as a whole. But now proposals in Parliament put forward by Her Majesty's Government in all seriousness and with all solemnity assure us that we were wrong, that the whole British people cannot tolerate us because of the colour of our skins. This is a serious situation and the answer to it from us must be equally serious.

"Since it is obvious that no self-respecting person thrusts himself into company where he is not wanted, all brown and black people should refrain from going to Britain for any purpose whatever. This may entail some loss in the matter of education, but there are many countries now in which quite as good, or even better, training can be obtained than in Britain. Business connections with Britain should be reduced as much as possible, nor should undue friendliness be shown toward British officials and businessmen in black and brown countries. After all reserve in place of cordiality is the least retort to deadly insult. A special effort must be made to refrain from looking at the world through British eyes, a practice to which educated Indians are in particular addicted. There is no real reason for regarding what happens or is thought in Britain as specially important to us, for keeping up with life there through the *Times, The Guardian, The New*

Statesman, etc. Britain after all today is a small island off the West Coast of Europe, not the centre of the world.

"We wish Britain no harm; in the hearts of those of us who knew the best of her people and hold many of her sons and daughters our friends, there will always be a warmth for them and her, but the clear implication of the measures her government proposes we must realize. No special relationship is possible, no special cordiality can be sustained, with those to whom the colour of your skin is anathema. Let the coloured doctors and nurses, so notably welcomed because so emphatically useful, remember this. They are sought as mercenaries. Will they be mercenaries, sell their souls for a mess of pottage to those who scorn the people of their colour, but have no objection to using for their own benefit, as the Roman patrician used the Greek physician slave, the skill they in particular have acquired at the cost of people of that colour?" ("Alas for Britain," *Opinion* [Bombay], Vol. 6, No. 15 [August 17, 1965], pp. 3-4.)

3. Indeed there is no good reason why local resources or persons should be expected to provide all that is needed when it is available from abroad; to do so would not only be wasteful of scarce resources but also beyond the powers of the underdeveloped countries.

4. The situation is quite different as regards the remotely past accomplishment of India, China, and the Islamic Middle East in science and mathematics.

5. It is interesting to speculate on the influence of Max Müller and other Western Indologists on the renewal of Hinduism in the last part of the nineteenth century, and of the European appreciation of African sculpture on African self-esteem in the twentieth century.

ROBERT K. A. GARDINER

Race and Color in International Relations

I

"SEVENTY-FIVE years ago," a contemporary historian notes, "the political map of Asia and Africa was drawn by statesmen in London, Paris and Berlin"; a Russian general could haughtily announce that "Far Eastern affairs" were "decided in Europe."[1] Long before, the famous Dr. Samuel Johnson had described the Americas as "a new world" given by Columbus to European curiosity.[2]

Even during the mid-nineteenth century, the height of Europe's influence, the process of Europe's decline as leader of the world had already begun. This loss of authority could be seen in the breakaway of the Latin American countries, in the birth of modern Japan, in the stirrings inside China against the Manchu dynasty, and in the rising power of the United States and Russia. It culminated in the twentieth century in two world wars.

Even while Europe's pre-eminence lasted, it was far from monolithic. The clash of the separate nationalisms was seen most clearly in what has been described as "the scramble for Africa." But one feature applied to all of Europe. The expansionist and colonizing powers were white men ruling a world of colored men. The colored peoples soon began to notice that the thrustful foreigner who dominated the evolution of their world with his superior fire-power and his superior organization was always a white-skinned European. Once articulated, this realization was to affect profoundly the development of international relations in the twentieth century.

War has proved to be the great catalyst of modern international relations. Even apparently inconclusive wars, such as the contemporary conflicts in Southeast Asia, do more to change the

18

relations between nations—and not only those nations that are directly involved—than any other known phenomenon. This generalization is certainly true of World War I. Even though radical change in the configuration of international affairs had begun before World War I—and indeed helped to bring it about—nothing in international relations was ever the same after the war. Japan had already established itself as a force in world affairs, a fact explicitly recognized by Britain in 1902 when the two countries entered into an alliance, and underlined for all the world to see when Japan defeated Russia in 1905. Lancelot Lawton, writing in 1912, put the rise of Japan into sharp racial perspective when he said:

Japan leads the van in the march of Asia towards the attainment of her ideal, the recognition of equality with the nations of the West. The civilization of Japan may be superficial, but it is a militant civilization. The danger to the West lies in the existence of a state of indifference which may find unpreparedness when the time arrives for the inevitable conflict with the nations of the East. . . . Unless the West awakens to the imminence of danger, the predominance of the white over the yellow races will cease.[3]

Before World War I ended, it was clear that the "European Age" was coming to an end. Symbolic of the changed state of affairs was the United States' decision to enter the lists in 1917, after having pursued a policy of non-involvement in international conflicts during the nineteenth century. The concept of the "balance of power" had been rooted in the assumption of European dominance in world affairs; in 1917 President Woodrow Wilson served notice that the world had ceased to be an arena reserved for the elaborate acrobatics of European power politics. America's intervention—in the First, as in the Second World War—can be seen as a direct result of the recognition that its own security could be threatened by any grave disturbance of the *status quo* in Europe.[4]

Moreover, the United States was acutely aware that the Pacific was going to loom larger and larger in world affairs. "The empire that shifted from the Mediterranean," said Theodore Roosevelt in 1903, "will in the lifetime of those now children bid fair to shift once more westward to the Pacific." And again:

The Mediterranean era died with the discovery of America, the Atlantic era is now at the height of its development and must soon exhaust the resources at its command; the Pacific era, destined to be the greatest of all, is just at its dawn.[5]

19

By the time that Roosevelt spoke, the United States had become a Pacific power. Its annexation of the Philippines and Guam at the end of the nineteenth century was perhaps a turning point. In 1899, when American Secretary of State John Hay issued his famous "open-door" declaration on Western dealings with China, he was announcing to the European powers—who had been proceeding on the assumption that they could carve up Asia among themselves as they had carved up Africa—that Asia was, indeed, a very different situation. American interests in China and in the Far East in general had now become a vital element in the world power equation. This left no room for the European technique of extending the balance-of-power game beyond Europe, as had been done by the partition of Africa.

Just as the emergence of the United States, Russia, and Japan as Pacific world powers ended the long period of Europe's unquestioned dominance in world affairs and transformed the character of international politics, so, too, the American entry into World War I and the Russian Revolution introduced the beginnings of a new pattern. The United States and Russia had been on the periphery of the international power struggle; they now appeared at the center, armed, moreover, with the beginnings of universal ideologies that were essentially revolutionary in character. With their ideology of "the self-determination of peoples," Wilson's Fourteen Points, says K. M. Pannikar, were "acclaimed as a doctrine of liberation" in Asia. On the other hand, "imperialism meant something totally different after Lenin's definition of it as the last phase of capitalism, and his insistence that the liberation of subject peoples from colonial domination was a part of the struggle against capitalism."[6]

While "the European civil war" of 1914-18 was destroying both Western solidarity and Europe's image outside the West, the peoples who had for so long been the victims of Western dominance were being offered new concepts of their own rights. In the year 1919 alone the "Fourth of May Movement" arose in China, the Destour Party was born in Tunisia, and the first Pan-African Congress was held in Paris. By 1919 the nationalist movement in Indonesia had expanded to an organization of some two and a half million people calling for complete independence from the Dutch.

Up to this time, the race element in international conflicts had remained unexpressed. When, however, Japan, admitted as a full participant to the Peace Conference at Versailles in 1919, proposed that racial equality be written into the Covenant of the League of Nations, race came out into the open. The proposal was out-voted, but the point had been made.

The Japanese move did not, of course, spring from a purely altruistic concern for the world's non-whites. Japan had its particular axe to grind: Japanese immigration to the West Coast of America had been drastically curtailed in the years preceding World War I. A direct presidential initiative had been needed in 1907, for example, to rescind a 1906 decree by the San Francisco School Board stipulating segregated schools for Japanese children.

The whole question of non-white immigration into white areas has very wide implications for relations between the white and the non-white worlds. Of the two major demands made by Japan at the Versailles Peace Conference, one was for title to its conquest of German-held territory in China's Shantung province, and the other for explicit recognition in the Covenant of the principle of racial equality. It was the property, not the principle, that Japan won.

After the sounding of this initial warning-bell, race was not destined to play an overt part in the working of the League of Nations, although it was impossible to be unaware of its brooding presence in the background of the Italo-Abyssinian conflict. The League itself was, with the exception of Liberia, Ethiopia, China, and Japan, an all-white and predominantly European affair.[7] That this should be so was never questioned even by the more far-sighted. As late as 1926, Sir Frederick (later to be Lord) Lugard could write of "the so-called awakening of the colored races."

What was significant in the evolution of this new attempt at organized and regulated confrontation among the nations of the world was the emergence of group alignments within the League —something that is usually described as the "bloc" system. Five such blocs have been identified in the assemblies of the League: the Latin American, the Commonwealth, the Scandinavian (with the occasional adherence of the Netherlands), and a group comprising Germany, Austria, Hungary, and, later, Italy; looser groupings of Balkan states also appeared from time to time.

The blocs operated as pressure groups or lobbying mechanisms for elections to the Council and to committees of the League. A Nominations Committee was finally established in an attempt to cut down on lobbying, and at the same time to meet the demands of the smaller nations, for whom bloc voting and lobbying had represented a certain "democratic" protection against the power and influence of their larger fellow-members. This committee functioned only during the last three years of the League's existence. The bloc system was to come into its own again when the United Nations Organization was created after World War II.[8]

The League's Permanent Mandates Commission was to have tremendous importance for the political development of colored peoples. The establishment of the mandate system—with its implicit guarantee of eventual self-determination—and the explicit power of the League of Nations to intervene in the exercise of the mandate by the mandatory power introduced a new concept into relations between the dominant white Westerners and the colored subject peoples. The decision of the International Court of Justice on the case of South-West Africa is still topical, as is the subsequent resolution of the U.N. General Assembly revoking South Africa's mandate. With this exception, whenever a League mandate was created, the path to eventual independence, passing through the post-World War II freeway of the Trusteeship Council, has been clear and unimpeded.

Thus, while the League was not precisely a major factor in the evolution of international relations during the twenty-odd years that separated the two World Wars, its influence in the area of dealings with dependent—and mostly colored—peoples was real and lasting.

II

Churchill had perceived that within less than a year of the ending in Europe of World War II, "from Stettin in the Baltic to Trieste in the Adriatic an iron curtain" had descended. Europe was no longer the center of the world but, rather, a continent caught in the middle of a conflict between two non-European super-powers—Russia and the United States. The "dwarfing of Europe"[9] was progressing on another level as well, the demographic—a process that had begun, according to some students, toward the end of the nineteenth century.

Demography is not all. Although Europe still maintains the inherent advantages that its technological superiority conferred upon it (as is witnessed in the rapid recovery of Western Germany in the postwar years), this technology is no longer beyond the reach of non-European and non-Westernized countries. Russian, Japanese, and, to a lesser extent, Communist Chinese examples demonstrate this. It is unlikely that the two thirds of the world's population that inhabit Asia and Africa, given the advantage of modern technology and their clearly growing preoccupation with making that technology their own, will remain permanently in thrall to the less than 30 per cent known as "the West."

The ideological clash that divides the world into "East" and "West" may, of course, be pursued to the point of the final holocaust that nuclear warfare threatens. But, for the purposes of this discussion, one must assume that mankind will spare itself this suicidal denouement and, predicting survival, try to assess realistically the probable significance of these new facts of the contemporary world.

Demographers maintain, indeed, that for a considerable time to come the rate of growth of the colored two thirds of the world will be higher than that of the white minority. There will very likely be, therefore, increasing pressure from the world's population—and particularly the colored population—on available land space. Probable pressure points and trouble spots are not difficult to pick out. As long ago as the beginning of this century, the "white Australia" policy was introduced to protect what one writer called "a population less than the depleted population of Scotland" against "the congested millions of colored peoples just across the sea."[10] Only recently has legislation been introduced in the United States to mitigate some of the effects of previous laws, the unequivocal purpose of which had been to limit severely the immigration of those same "congested millions of colored peoples." About the same time that this legislation was being passed in the United States Congress, a Socialist government in Britain was preoccupied with measures to control the immigration of colored peoples.

The new states that have come into being since the end of World War II account for one quarter of the world's population; current estimates place the populations of the new Asian states alone at four times that of the European Economic Community. Granted the eventual acquisition of "Western" technology, a radical change has taken place in the world order. There are the beginnings, at least, of a shift of concern to what has been called the "Third World," whose populations are largely non-white. It is a long way from the days when the "Yellow Peril" was the white man's bugbear—when fear of Oriental competition was couched in purely racial terms. The emergence of the new states has provided a new kind of political education for the older members of the international community, and the new states themselves have been learning many of the sobering realities of statehood. Above all, the confrontations between the "Third World" and the old European world provide opportunities for bridging what may be described as the "cultural gap" between them. The very conventions and rituals of legal and diplomatic procedures serve to offer the scope needed for hammering out understanding and respect among nations.

The new nations have in common their relative poverty, their underdevelopment; they all possess a technical and organizational capacity inadequate for exploiting their natural and human resources. One cannot strictly say that they have their color in common; yellow-skinned, black-skinned, or brown-skinned people, the bond they share is the fact that they are not white. This negative similarity has become a strong rallying point for them simply because of the experience of recent centuries when the white Westerner became increasingly conscious of himself as white and confidently assumed that his whiteness was a guarantee of his political, technical, and military pre-eminence.

The non-white, non-Western peoples, overwhelmed by the superior efficiency of European technology, accepted at first the white man's estimates—not only of himself, but of themselves also. Later, disillusionment, disgust, and a renewed self-respect set in, and the white man's standards were vehemently rejected. At Bandung in 1955, Jawaharlal Nehru spoke of this reaction when he said:

Has it come to this, that the leaders of thought who have given religion and all kinds of things to the world have to tag onto this kind of group or that, and be hangers-on of this party or the other. . . ? It is an intolerable thought to me that the great countries of Asia and Africa shall have come out of bondage into freedom only to degrade themselves in this way. . . . I will not tie myself to this degradation . . . and become a camp-follower of others.[11]

In Africa the same motives have given rise to the concept of "the African Personality," which is both a rejection of "Westernization" and a reassertion of the values and separate identity of Africa's own cultural heritage.

These movements of rejection and of self-assertion have had, as was to be expected, political repercussions as well. The most famous of these, the Bandung Conference of 1955, had its roots in the emergence of a fairly coherent Afro-Asian group at the United Nations during the Korean crisis of 1950. During the period immediately after World War II, the new nations gradually realized they had at least a number of negative reasons for making common cause in their international relations. President Sukarno said at Bandung: "This is the first intercontinental conference of colored peoples in the history of the world." While there may be several interpretations of the significance of this fact, that it was a fact cannot be disputed. The road from Bandung led to Belgrade, where many of the Bandung nations discovered they could make common cause with nations neither Asian nor African nor colored. It also led, in 1965, to the fruitless Algiers meeting, ruined by an ideological split in the Communist world, by a geographical argument about who is and who is not Asian, and by China's dilemma of whether to opt for the mantle of the true heir of Marx and Lenin or for that of leader of the "non-white" world.

III

Though there is some community of interest among the non-white states, it is not a hermetic one. It cannot be hermetic because each of its single components is a country with its own history, culture, and, for the most part, language. The meetings of new partners usually must be conducted in languages not their own, languages borrowed from—or imposed by—former Western rulers; the radical African leader may feel closer to and find it easier to make contact with a Parisian than a Djakartan. One commentator suggests that "for many participants the [Bandung] conference seems to have been attractive as an emotional herding together for mutual reassurance in a puzzling world."[12] When even those nations best equipped in wealth and experience visibly flounder from crisis to crisis, it is not surprising that the new countries—uncertain of their direction, uncertain sometimes of the choices that may exist—should have tried to turn to one another for moral support and enlightenment.

But coherent co-operation between sovereign countries must be based on more than urgent impulses. Nothing less than self-interest will do—or, at least, what is imagined to be self-interest, under whatever guise it may appear, and ideology is perhaps one of its most popular contemporary guises. A variety of impulses has then combined to produce meaningful alignments among the newly emerged nations, just as in postwar Europe a mixture of national motives produced the Rome treaties of 1957.

These new alignments—the Arab League is the oldest, the Organization of African Unity, the youngest—came into being as a result of economic or political or politico-economic imperatives. That regional groupings would and should exist has been explicitly recognized in two twentieth-century attempts to regulate the world order by international organizations. The Covenant of the League of Nations did not affect "the validity of international engagements, such as treaties of arbitration or regional understandings . . . for securing the maintenance of peace"; Article 52 of the Charter of the United Nations makes very much the same provisions.

The workings of what have been called the "caucuses" within the United Nations constitute a separate study in themselves.[13] One school of thought condemns the "bloc" or "caucus" system on the ground that it involves a complicated and sometimes unprincipled process of vote-swapping which frequently leads to issues being neither debated nor voted upon according to their real merits. Another school contends that in a large organization such as the United Nations this kind of arrangement actually facilitates the process of negotiation and compromise which is an unavoidable element in international relations once the possibility of coercion is removed. It can also be argued, with some cogency, that the presence of many such groups in an international organization could obviate any tendency toward excessively rigid divisions on major issues. Flexibility and real regard for the different nuances in any given question would, thereby, be increased, resulting in greater possibilities of solution or compromise. This is a very significant thought which, logically extended, may be helpful in examining some of the directions international relations may take in the future.

In the context of the postwar world, one of the most striking multinational groupings is the Commonwealth of Nations. Starting life under the aegis of the Westminster Statute of 1931 as a loose association of Anglo-Saxon states, individually called dominions but collectively retaining the style of empire, this group now boasts an embryonic full-time Secretariat headed by an American from Canada and an African from Ghana.

The turning point for the "British" Commonwealth came in

1947, when the former imperial domain of India became the two independent states of India and Pakistan. Strains on the imperial concept, though of a significantly different sort, had, however, already begun to be felt in the first decades of this century. In the process of growing into their own sovereign personalities, Australia, New Zealand, and Canada, once the purest of imperial outposts, had learned that the essential problems of their independence could no longer be regulated from London; that the demographic pressures of the Far East and the geopolitical realities of life for an independent state in the Pacific were not European; that they must, on balance, be more sensitive to what was happening in the White House than to what was happening in Whitehall. Thus, the Commonwealth was one of the first political entities to reflect the weakening of European world hegemony.

When independence was granted to India and Pakistan, a new era decisively began. How new was even then not clearly visible; the lessons of Australia, New Zealand, and Canada had not been interpreted as pointing to an ultimate breakup of the Commonwealth. A Labour member of Parliament, Mr. Patrick Gordon-Walker, said in 1947 that while Mr. Churchill might "throw away" the Empire as George III had done with the American colonies, the Labour Government's aim was to "save it" by giving the colonies self-government. "If this plan comes off, the empire will be a very powerful idea indeed."[14] Mr. Gordon-Walker's idea was one of a multiracial community of free nations. In this sense, the British Commonwealth represents an experiment of capital importance for mankind, crowded together as it is on one planet.

The independence of Pakistan and India differed in quality from that which the "white dominions" had enjoyed up to that time. These countries were not tied to Britain by bonds of race; how was it, then, that despite the geopolitical pressures, despite the lack of racial affinity, these countries opted to remain in association with the former imperial power? The answer is complex, and possibly not fully known, though self-interest obviously played a role in this development.

The postwar Commonwealth has proved again that race is not the indispensable cement of international groupings. It has proved this positively, by the adherence of India and other republics— plus one independent federation, Malaysia. The 1965 war between India and Pakistan is negative proof of the fragility of racial bonds.

While the Commonwealth was fumbling along on its pragmatic path, theorists in continental Europe were at work. "Imagine," they said to themselves, "if 220,000,000 Africans and 200,000,000 Europeans could get together into an economic unit. With Europe's skills and techniques, and Africa's raw materials, one could create potentially the most powerful single bloc in the world."[15] The origins of the Eurafrica concept go back some forty years. Vernon McKay cites a book published in 1933 by a French writer, Eugene Guernier, entitled *L'Afrique—Champ d'expansion de l'Europe.* This work argues that a "longitudinal" view of geopolitics would make of Europe and Africa, after the immigration of fifteen to twenty million Europeans into Africa, one of these intercontinental units. Germany, too, got into the act; one German publicist cited by McKay called, in 1952, "for a strong Franco-German nucleus of a European community, without Britain, for the common exploitation of African resources." Europeanists in the United States seemed to subscribe to this idea on the assumption that Latin America was the special responsibility of the United States, and that Africa should be a special sphere of interest for Europe.

Several versions of this concept became current after World War II. They all had one thing in common: Europe came first; Africa, second. Africa was to be "Europe's dowry," a means of redressing Europe's losses "without the burdens of the colonial relationships."[16] Strategic considerations also came into play. "Africa is the natural complement of, and is vital to the defense, life, and subsistence of Europe," wrote a French commentator in 1957.

The French Community, inaugurated under President de Gaulle's Fifth Republic and buttressed by the association of former French dependencies with the European Common Market, provided a combination of the ideas of Eurafrica with the basic assumption of the British Commonwealth. First, Guinea chose independence outside the Community; not long after, the other eleven African members took the same road. Present trends are toward regional co-operation, with accompanying regional consciousness and regional pride, as expressed in the Organization of African Unity. But an association of Franco-phone countries is still an aspiration shared by France with her former dependencies. There is, therefore, the possibility of a world-wide French-speaking association based on historical and cultural links. African states that were former British or French dependencies must somehow reconcile their belonging to a British Commonwealth or a world-wide Franco-phone organization with their allegiance to the O.A.U. In a way, Britain and France face the same problem: how to be European states while belonging to non-European communities.

IV

Contemporary history throws a somewhat ambiguous light on the relationship between race and international affairs. At a given time, in a given situation, race will seem to have been a major consideration in the actions of nations. Yet in situations where the racial factor might be expected to dominate, nations are often guided by quite different considerations. Indeed, it is sometimes impossible to determine where to draw the line between race considerations and the ties of history and culture which can bring nations together.

This is illustrated by the case of white Australia. The European-settled subcontinent has recognized that its destiny is a Pacific destiny. In the past, Australia never thought of seeking an accommodation or understanding with its Pacific-Asian neighbors. Rather, Australia and New Zealand sought first the protection of the powerful British navy and then turned their eyes toward the United States. Were they appealing to their "kith and kin," or were they drawn by affinities of culture and history? What explains the near-panic at the turn of the century that led to the introduction of the "white Australia" policy? The sense of isolation in a "yellow sea" must have exacerbated the natural wish to have the protection and support of the "like" and to fend off what may have seemed the inevitable "swamping" of their country by "yellow hordes." Fifty years later, when the ANZUS security pact was signed by the United States, Australia, and New Zealand, was it not possible to detect undertones of white solidarity in the face of the "yellow masses" pressing on the Australasian subcontinent? It is hard to say; a similar treaty was signed with the brown-yellow Philippines. Also, the allies of the United States in the current Viet-Nam war consist of brown-yellow Southeast Asians as well as the white dominions.

Clearly it is difficult—sometimes impossible—to draw the line between economic, political, and military motivations. The European Economic Community faces Comecon in an ideological as much as an economic confrontation. The Alliance for Progress was as much a political as an economic initiative. The growing disparity between the rich and the poor nations plays an important part in the ideological and power contest between the two megaliths of East and West. The economic contest has produced its own set of alignments. Aid has become a potent weapon in the struggle for allegiances, and the poor countries are gradually organizing themselves to ensure that they get from it the greatest benefit and the least harm, and avoid external economic, military, or ideological domination.

At the same time one cannot ignore a persistent feature of the age—the growing economic interdependence of communities. In the words of Thorsten Veblen, "As things stand now, no civilized country's industrial system will work in isolation. . . . As an industrial unit, the nation is out of date." The case may be a little overstated, but it is true that industrial technology knows no borders and contains within itself the dynamic of internationalism. These developments, together with the growth of trade, are gradually but relentlessly forcing nations and races toward interdependence. Although the world is still very far from Gunnar Myrdal's dream of a "world economy," the volume and scope of contemporary international trade and its growth carry implications of greater and greater international contacts and relations. Because of this interdependence, it is permissible to look at the rules and regulations that govern international trade as a sort of universal "social contract."

There is also evidence of a trend toward an epoch of what can only be called universalism, some aspects of which are sometimes described as the "Americanization" of the world. Its overt forms are addiction to American ideas in dress, in the popular arts, in commercial design, and even in speech and mannerisms copied from film stars. This is effect. Two of the main causes would seem to be the tremendous material preponderance of the United States in practically every area of life in this century, and the revolutionary developments that have taken place in international communications.

One cannot escape, however, the conviction that these are not more than the mechanics of the matter. Behind the mechanics there must be some quality in human nature that craves assimilation with its like. That the craving has so far found its satisfaction only in the more restricted groups of family or tribe or nation is an accident of geography and history. The economist's concept of the demonstration effect that applies equally within societies as among societies is a recognition of this tendency to imitate. In the past, the model, not the will, has been lacking, a lack which contemporary technologies have finally filled. Indeed, it is only partially accurate to speak of Americanization in this context. The victories of American soft drinks and blue jeans are easily matched by the conquests of the espresso machine, Zen Buddhism, the Calypso, and judo.

In the field of scholarship, institutions of higher education are now springing up in all parts of the world. The world of learning is, therefore, becoming truly universal. Guided by the principles of scientific objectivity, its members will appeal "neither to prejudice nor to authority," nor will they "confuse . . . the subjects [about] which they argue with race, politics, sex, or age."[17] These principles have been so conscientiously observed that Professor Jacob Bronowski is able to say: "A scientist who breaks this rule . . . is ignored. A scientist who finds that the rule has been broken in his laboratory . . . kills himself."[18] This is not only a comfort in a bewildering world but grounds for hope that the realization of world peace through the rule of law is not utopian.

The world is without doubt now approaching a stage where the rapid social and intellectual assimilation of all its inhabitants into a world community will be possible. Within this community there will be differences. One shall continue to observe a distinction but not a contradiction between the spirit of the community (*Volkgeist*) and the spirit of the age (*Zeitgeist*). It is also reasonable to accept that there will be a world outlook (*Weltanschauung*) all peoples can share.

There are some who hold the view that racism can ultimately be eliminated only through a process of wholesale miscegenation. This is, essentially, a sentimental analysis that both denies the countless crossings of the race barriers humane people have accomplished throughout history and ignores the occurrence of civil war, not to mention fratricide. The mixture of races is not a necessary precondition to international understanding. At the same time, the intermingling of all the strands of the human race would seem a natural outcome of the spreading of the media of mass communication and the speed of modern transportation.

The late President Kennedy drew attention to the common lot of man in the twentieth century when he said in his address to the General Assembly of the United Nations in 1961:

A nuclear disaster spread by wind and water and fear could well engulf the great and the small, the rich and the poor, the committed and the uncommitted alike. . . . We in this hall shall be remembered either as part of the generation that turned this planet into a flaming funeral pyre or the generation that met its vow to save succeeding generations from the scourge of war.[19]

Now that at least one non-white country has joined the ranks of nuclear powers—and others have the technology to do likewise —President Kennedy's words have an even more urgent ring. "Colored" and "white" both have their hands on the nuclear trigger. In the midst of these inexorable and irreversible processes, race or color scarcely qualifies as a decisive agent.

If I am optimistic about the long term, I am far less so about the short term. In what I call the short term—say, the next twenty-five years—the world will have to face the realities of the situations in Rhodesia and in South Africa. These will remain matrices of conflict between white and non-white nations. Battle lines will be drawn, roughly, along the emplacements of the now nearly ended colonial struggle. Added to this are the new tensions of race or tribe to be seen in some of the newly independent African countries and in certain parts of Southeast Asia. These are such bitter and dangerous conflicts that it is sometimes difficult to see them in the proper light and context.

The world is being obliged, through its increasing mastery over its resources and its increasing knowledge of itself, to regard itself as "one." Separate groupings of nations are more and more becoming just one aspect of a world society. This process of becoming "one" calls for action at various levels and in many spheres. It is of paramount importance that within states or communities discrimination be eliminated—especially in education, employment, housing, and the administration of justice. Between states, two steps have already been taken toward the building of a society of nations: the acceptance of the principle of self-determination of peoples and the respect for the sovereignty of states, however weak or poor. Efforts of communities to meet their daily needs in the economic field are both facilitating and making necessary the development of "one" world. The physical threat to the survival of the human race is terrifying. The greatest challenge to mankind is how to foster adjustments in conventional outlook and in minimum standards of behavior in a fragmented world moving toward unity. Unity must not be confused with uniformity. It would be as absurd to expect a standard human type as to expect a uniform world culture. A world of free men must be a world of diversity.

REFERENCES

1. Geoffrey Barraclough, *An Introduction to Contemporary History* (London, 1964), p. 88.

2. Quoted in Arthur P. Whitaker, *The Western Hemisphere Idea* (Ithaca, 1954), p. 6.

3. Lancelot Lawton, *Empires of the Far East* (London, 1912), cited by C. Northcote Parkinson, *East and West* (New York, 1965).

4. Cf. Grayson Kirk, "World Perspectives, 1964," *Foreign Affairs* (October, 1964).

5. Barraclough, *An Introduction to Contemporary History*, p. 70

6. K. M. Pannikar, *Asia and Western Dominance* (London, 1953), pp. 199-200.

7. Philip W. Quigg, *Africa: A Foreign Affairs Reader* (New York, 1964), p. 6.

8. Cf. Thomas Hovet, Jr., *Bloc Politics in the United Nations* (Cambridge, 1960), pp. 1-3.

9. Cf. Barraclough, *An Introduction to Contemporary History*, pp. 69ff

10. James Marchant, *Birth Rate and Empire* (London, 1917), quoted in Barraclough, *An Introduction to Contemporary History*, p. 76.

11. Laurence W. Martin, *Neutralism and Non-Alignment* (New York, 1962), p. 8.

12. *Ibid.*, p. xiv.

13. Cf. Hovet, *Bloc Politics in the United Nations.*

14. Quoted in Vernon McKay, *Africa in World Politics* (New York, 1964), p. 27.

15. Cf. *Ibid.*, pp. 124-37.

16. *Ibid.*

17. Jacob Bronowski, *Science and Human Values* (London, 1958), p. 64.

18. *Ibid.*

19. Quoted in Arthur Schlesinger, Jr., *A Thousand Days: John F. Kennedy in the White House* (New York, 1965), p. 427.

ROGER BASTIDE

Color, Racism, and Christianity

SARTRE HAS brought out quite well the part the eye plays in racial attitudes, but he does not go far enough. The eye has its substitutes. Some time ago, we discovered in talking to blind persons that they recognize immediately the race of persons whom they meet—without any mistake—by smell, by the texture of the skin, and especially by the voice. On the basis of this sensory information, they react exactly as the sighted do: with antipathy or aloofness if they are racially sensitive, or with a kind of physical attraction if they are not. This shows that any kind of perception can serve as a stimulus to racial attitude. Color is neutral; it is the mind that gives it meaning.

What is important is not so much the ability to see but the ability to see what others see. It is not so much my eye as the eyes of those who surround me. A blind person knows that he is seen. The voice—high-pitched or hoarse—of anyone who speaks to him releases instantly the reactions that society has built up in him. These reactions are the same as those of the sighted. Colors are not important in themselves as optical phenomena, but rather as bearers of a message.

The blind people whom we interrogated were Brazilians. They belonged to a country in which prejudice is based not on race but on color, where discrimination varies in direct proportion to the blackness of the skin. The ideal woman is not a blond or a fair-skinned woman but a brunette or dark-skinned woman and especially a "rosy-tinted" mulatto woman.[1] A blind Brazilian replaces the entire gamut of color tints by shades of voice, and he reacts in the same way as a person who can see. He performs immediately the transposition from one register to another and finds in the sonorities recorded by his ear the message that the sighted attach to color.

34

This experiment led us to concentrate our attention on the symbolic perception of color and of differences in racial attitude in the various Christian faiths.

To study these particular dimensions, the Christian religion must be disassociated from the churches. While religion "transcends" the world, the church itself is very much in the world. It always finds itself in a particular social situation, and its reactions are determined by its environment. The church, whose history began in the Pentecost, may deserve and try to be in Tertullian's phrase a *genus tertium,* a third race over and above the conflict between the "Greeks" and the "Barbarians." It is, nevertheless, established in a world of Babel, a world of disunity and discord.

Although the most liberal Christians of South Africa recognized, for example, the brotherhood of men before God, they were willing to accept segregation of worship if providing the same church for the white and black natives—the Afrikaners and the Bantus—were considered harmful to the cause of Christ among the Christians. René Ribeiro describes in this connection a rather curious case that occurred in Brazil[2]: A Protestant pastor from North America, serving in Recife, Brazil, showed himself to be extremely tolerant and unbiased while there. The moment he stepped on the airplane to return to the United States, however, all his southern prejudice immediately returned. He had not changed his faith; he had simply found himself in a different social situation.

Sociologists have shown that the Negro churches were, above all, instruments of self-expression for the colored community as a separate community. As is the case with the Muslim faith today, they were instruments of protest and of racial revolt. They were in essence more social than religious. But we do not wish to place ourselves in this article in the field of sociology of human—only too human—institutions, but rather in the field of religious feeling and experience (phenomenology).

I

Christianity has been accompanied by a symbolism of color. This symbolism has formed and cultivated a sensitivity to color that extends even to people who claim to be detached from religion. It has created a "backwash" of fixed impressions and attitudes difficult to efface.

Racial hatred has not evolved solely from this Christian symbolism; nor can it be fully explained by economic causes alone. Its roots extend much farther and deeper. They reach into sexual complexes[3] and into religion through the symbolism of color. In human thought every gulf or separation tends to take the form of a conflict of color. This holds not only for concrete obstacles of tribal separation—as between the Indians of the plain and the ancient Mexicans—but also for obstacles between men—as in the social structure of ancient Egypt or the castes of India. Christianity has brought no exception to this very general rule.

There is a danger of confusing in Christianity that which belongs to the scope of rationalization—that which can, as in all ideology, be explained in the final analysis by the economic infrastructure—and the symbolism of color, which falls within the scope of pure religion. When Christians tried to justify slavery, they claimed black skin was a punishment from God. They invoked the curses cast upon Cain, the murderer of his brother, and upon Ham, son of Noah, who had found his drunken father naked in his tent. Against the background of this symbolism, they invented causes for the malady, intended to justify in their own eyes a process of production based upon the exploitation of Negro labor. Later, other rationalizations and counter-rationalizations got woven around the same symbolism.

The Christian symbolism of color is very rich. Medieval painting makes full use of it. Some colors are, however, more pertinent to this discussion than others. The color yellow, or at least a dull shade of yellow, has come to signify treason. When Westerners think of Asiatics, they unconsciously transpose this significance to them, converting it into a trait of ethnic psychology. Consequently, they treat Asiatics as persons in whom they cannot have confidence. They can, of course, give excellent reasons in defense of their behavior: the closed or uncommunicative character of the Japanese, the smiling impassiveness of the Chinese, or some historic case of treason—but these are all reasons invented after the fact. If Westerners could have prevented themselves from being influenced by a symbolism centuries old, they could just as easily have found reasons to justify an impression of the yellow race as loyal and affectionate.

But the greatest Christian two-part division is that of white and black. White is used to express the pure, while black expresses the diabolical. The conflict between Christ and Satan, the spiritual and the carnal, good and evil came finally to be expressed by the conflict between white and black, which underlines and synthesizes all the others. Even the blind, who know only night, think of a swarm of angels or of devils in association with white and black—for example, "a black soul," "the blackness of an action," "a dark deed," "the innocent whiteness of the lily," "the candor of a child," "to bleach someone of a crime." These are not merely adjectives and nouns. Whiteness brings to mind the light, ascension into the bright realm, the immaculateness of virgin snow, the white dove of the Holy Spirit, and the transparency of limpid air; blackness suggests the infernal streams of the bowels of the earth, the pit of hell, the devil's color.

This dichotomy became so dominant that it dragged certain other colors along with it. Celestial blue became a simple satellite of white in painting the cloak of the Immaculate Virgin, while the red flames of hell became a fit companion for the darkest colors. Thinking is so enslaved to language that this chain of associated ideas operates automatically when a white person finds himself in contact with a colored person. Mario de Andrade has rightly exposed the evils of this Christian symbolism as being rooted in the very origins of the prejudice of color. In America, when a Negro is accepted, one often says, in order to separate him from the rest of his race, "He is a Negro, of course, but his soul is white."

II

Although Christ transcends all questions of race or ethnology, it must not be forgotten that God incarnated himself in a man of the Jewish race. The Aryans and the Gentiles—even the most anti-Semitic—worship their God in a Jewish body. But this Jewish body was not white enough for them. The entire history of Western painting bears witness to the deliberate whitening or bleaching effort that changed Christ from a Semitic to an Aryan person. The dark hair that Christ was thought to have had came to be rendered as very light-colored, and his big dark eyes as blue. It was necessary that this man, the incarnation of God, be as far removed as possible from everything that could suggest darkness or blackness, even indirectly. His hair and his beard were given the color of sunshine, the brightness of the light above, while his eyes retained the color of the sky from which he descended and to which he returned.

The progressive Aryanization of Christ is in strict accordance with the logic of the color symbolism. It did not start, however, until Christianity came into close contact with the other races—with the African race, in particular. Christian artists began to avoid the darker tints in depicting Christ in order to remove as much as possible of their evil suggestion.

The Middle Ages did have their famous Black Madonnas which were and still are the object of a devotion perhaps even deeper than that which is dedicated to many of the fair-complexioned images of the Holy Virgin. But the Black Virgin represents to her devotees not so much the Loving Mother as a sorceress, a rain maker, a worker of miracles. She has the magnetism of the strange, smacking of Gypsies and Moors; she stirs the heart as if a bit of magic—even a near-diabolical sorcery—were involved in her miracles. She is not the beloved mother who clasps the unfortunate to her white breast and comforts them with her milky white arms, drying their childish tears with the fair tresses of her bright-colored hair, but a mysterious goddess endowed with extraordinary powers. The symbolism of her dark color is not eliminated in the cult; it is only repressed—and badly repressed—because it infiltrates into the prayers that are directed toward her. Nevertheless, the Black Virgin helps one to understand the appeal used by Catholicism in its efforts to convert pagan peoples to the faith.

References must again be made to painting. The Three Kings or Three Wise Men who came to worship the newborn child were depicted as white men at first. They later came to represent the three great continents: Europe, Asia, and Africa. Balthasar was the Negro King who came to bring his tribute to the fair-haired child amidst the golden straw. He was pictured behind the other two Magi and even sometimes kneeling closest to the Babe, but never between the other two—that would have been equivalent to ignoring his color. Racism subsisted in the disguised form of a patronizing attitude in this first attempt to remove the demoniac symbolism from the black skin.

A similar effort can be seen in the creation of colored saints intended for races other than the white race. St. Mauritius, a commander of the Roman legions in Egypt who was martyred there, was originally depicted as white but then as a Moor, and finally in the thirteenth century as a Negro.[4]

Such changes were exploited for purposes of evangelism as the frontiers of the known world extended farther. The church long ignored St. Benedict of Palermo, known as St. Benedict the Moor, but finally officialized him with the development of missions in Africa and of slavery in the Western Hemisphere. This case illustrates another rationalization on the part of the church intended to break the nominal chain of symbolism. In order to escape from feminine temptations, St. Benedict prayed to God to make him ugly —so God turned his skin black.

To see only symbolism in these cases would, however, be a mistake. Because the symbolism is merely repressed, it returns from another angle. From the mystical, it is converted into the aesthetic. Evil takes the form of ugliness. Above all, the colored saints—St. Mauritius, St. Benedict the Moor, St. Iphigenia the Mulatto, and St. Balthasar the Negro King—are only intermediaries, well below the Virgin Mary and Christ, who stayed white. They express more the difference, the abyss, between people of different races than the unity. They stand for stratification in a multiracial society.[5] The color black found only a subordinate place in the hierarchy descending from white to black.

In the desire of the church to become universal, the color black became detached from its symbolic significance only to be subsumed in an ideology. This ideology reflected the religious dimension of the paternalism white Catholic masters felt toward Indian serfs and African slaves. When color became a part of an ideology, it was obvious that colored people would react by a counter-ideology. Mulattos prayed to white saints to show that they belonged to the race of the masters. According to folk rumor, a mulatto in Brazil would put the portrait of his Negro mother in the kitchen and that of his white father in the parlor. He would shun colored saints and invoke only the aid of white saints, even though these were claimed by pure white people to belong exclusively to them. The mulattos invented the brotherhood of the Cord of St. Francis in order to enter, by the back door so to speak, the aristocratic church of the Franciscans and to mingle with the white people there.

Negroes whose skin was entirely black set out to reverse the values of the traditional Catholic iconographic system. They first invented black angels with kinky hair and flat noses. Then, prompted by a sentence in the Gospels referring to the Holy Virgin, *Niger erat sed pulchra* ("Black she was, but beautiful"), they conceived of a Black Virgin. This happened only in comparatively recent times, however. Furthermore, Christ himself was left untouched, as though to make him black would have been a sacrilege. Paternalism was still too strong for the hierarchy of color to be upset entirely.

39

Only in a country where segregation became the rule, as in Anglo-Saxon, Protestant North America and African colonies, did the revolt of the Negro go so far as to create a Black God and a Black Christ. In the African colonies, Messianism represented an effort on the part of the Africans to free themselves from the dominance of the white missions and to establish Black Messiahs as saviors of their own rejected, downtrodden, and exploited race.

Systems of imagery can never do more than reflect the social and economic infrastructure in a form that can never be entirely reversed. This color imagery represents only the reactions of the church to a social situation imposed upon it from without. This imagery could not, therefore, abolish the more powerful pressure of the underlying symbolism.

Catholic Latin America, with its racial interbreeding which it considers an expression of racial democracy, offers a new chain of associations between the color black, the devil, and sin. Anyone wishing to study the manifest content of these associations need only consult the work of Baudelaire, who was profoundly steeped in Catholicism in spite of—or because of—his taste for "Le Fleurs du Mal." Indeed, Baudelaire actually sought in his colored sweetheart the sensation of sin through carnal love with a woman whose color suggested the flames of Hades.

These sensations, although less clearly evident in the cult of the Black Venus in the Tropics, are there in the essence. South Americans are deeply branded by Catholicism. Sin occupies a larger place in South American literature than in European. A distinction is always made between a white woman, the object of legitimate courtship and marriage who is worshiped like the Holy Virgin, and the colored woman, the mistress who is an object of pleasure. A woman of color is considered to be a person of sheer voluptuousness. The slightest gesture she makes, such as the balanced sway of her body as she walks barefoot, is looked upon as a call of the female sex to the male. On the other hand, the white woman is desexualized, if not disincarnated or at least dematerialized.

In Latin American society, marriage limited to one's own color led to a mystic transposition of the wife before the altar of God. The symbolism of the color white played a preponderant role in this transposition. A too carnal enjoyment of the wife would have taken on the aspect of a kind of incest, degrading to both the white man and the white woman. White signified purity, innocence, and virginity. A woman whose skin was not entirely white suggested the carnal merely by her color. She became, therefore, the legitimate object of enjoyment.

The South American perhaps does not realize so fully as Baudelaire did the workings of this symbolism. It does, nevertheless, operate to the detriment of physiological reality. When, for instance, the antislavery poet Castro Alves wanted to express his reaction against the stereotyped mentality anchored in the symbolism of color, he found no other resource than to cast his colored heroine into a waterfall where thousands of brilliant drops created a white bridal veil around her dusky skin.

III

The Protestant's association of the color black with the devil and sin was as strong as the Catholic's. But the Protestant, feeling sure that his soul would go straight to hell, placed the bulwark of Puritanism between himself and the temptation of the woman with color-tinted skin.

Puritanism served to strengthen and deepen the roots of the symbolic association by arousing the idea that the contagiousness of color was associated with contagiousness of sin. The mere presence of a non-white woman was sufficient to sully the eyes and mark the flesh of the white man. Without the grace of God, man was considered to be feeble in the face of worldly temptations. Satan wielded such power over the emotions that every contact with women of the African race was to be avoided. They who bore the color of the infernal master had to be fought against by building up defense reactions of an aesthetic nature.

A white man had to convince himself that colored women were ugly and had an unbearable odor and an oily skin. By maintaining that they had none of the qualities of the ideal woman, a white man could establish a moral protection. When fear was not sufficient, barricades of an institutional nature were established: segregation by color in trains, streetcars, theaters, post offices, and other public places. The schools, where Satan could most easily work his evil influence by giving white children the habit of playing with colored children, were segregated.

Rationalizations about the practical effects of mixed marriages can, of course, camouflage the action of the symbolism: Sin was defined as a stain or pollution, the white person becoming blackened. Religious doctrine was expressed by measures of spiritual hygiene accompanied by the anguish of never having taken quite all the precautions necessary. No matter how careful a person was, he might be stricken by madness in spite of himself, as if a colored woman exuded sin by her mere presence. Over and above any historical or economic factors, the roots of segregation are to be found in the idea of contagiousness of sin through color.

Thus, in the field of religious ideas, the association of the color black with sin was expressed by different behavior patterns in the Catholics and the Protestants. The Catholic brought to the New World the heritage of medieval culture. This culture was characterized not only by the taboo of the white woman, who had been elevated when knighthood was in flower to the almost inaccessible rank of a Madonna, but also by the so-called right of the feudal lord to women of lower rank. The Protestant brought with him, on the other hand, the characteristics of the middle-class culture that was coming into being in the Western world at the time of the discovery and colonization of the New World—a culture characterized by strict family morals and a stern Puritanism. This was, in particular, the culture of the Anglo-Saxon, Dutch, and Calvinist middle classes; the Italian upper-middle class had adopted the ethics of the old medieval nobility.

An examination of Calvinism unveils other impressions in which the symbolism of color is firmly entrenched. Calvin believed that "the knowledge of God was deeply rooted in the minds of men," be they pagan or Christian. This knowledge could, however, be stifled by superstition, which blinded the intelligence, or by sin, which corrupted the senses. Contrary to any concept of racial hatred, Calvin considered reason to be proper to all men whether pagan or Christian. Concomitantly, all men were sinners. Because the pagans had not been able to trace nature back to its Creator, they had stifled the knowledge of God. They had reduced the sacred to phenomena of the senses. Even if they were moral in conduct, they deviated from the true objective of morality—the honor of God, not the glory of man.

Throughout the *Institutes,* Calvin grounds sin in human nature. Ignorance of Christ did not automatically acquit the pagans who had never heard of him. Their souls, too, were made of mud and filth. When the Calvinists came to America and found themselves in the presence of pagan Indians, it was perfectly natural that they should set about with missionary fervor to destroy the corrupt nature of these pagans. They had not come to the New

World with any racial attitude, but, on the contrary, with an idea of essential equality. Indians and colonists were equal—equal in sin on the lowest level and in divine grace on the highest. This theoretical equality could be made actual. The Indian had only to give up his natural liberty, which was anarchical, troublesome, and diabolical, and bow to the superior law of the Christians as laid down in the Good Book. Unfortunately, the Indian preferred his liberty to servitude and his diabolical practices to the rules of Holy Writ. This was, in the eyes of the Puritan, an infallible sign of negative predestination, the unavoidable damning of the Indian's soul.

Although the judgment of God regarding these Indians remained a mystery, their perseverance in diabolical practices proved to the Calvinists that God had refused to shed his grace upon them.[6] What a spectacle the Indian presented to the white colonizer. The tyrannical rule of the tribal chief instead of democracy, wretched poverty happily accepted instead of economic prosperity—all evidence of a diabolical persistence in sin that doomed the Indian to eternal damnation. The association of the darker color of the skin with a parallel blackness of the soul became for the Puritans arriving in the New World a fact of experience. The symbolism of color was confirmed as an obvious truth.

As Max Weber has shown, success in life was, for the Calvinists, a sign of selection:

The Lord God in multiplying his graces upon his servants and conferring upon them new graces every day shows thereby that the work that they have begun is agreeable to him and he finds in them the matter and the occasion to enrich and increase their benefits. . . . To him who has it shall be given. . . . I therefore confess that the faithful shall expect this benediction, that the better they have used these graces of God the more shall other new and greater benefits be added to them every day.[7]

Some curious passages in the *Institutes* take on a special significance when the problem of the religious origins of racism is considered. Man is assailed from all sides by temptations and living in a doubtful world; Calvin includes in the dangers that threaten man life among the savages and the pitfalls of country life.[8] Although he condemns racism, he maintains that the precept of salvation must be limited to those who have some alliance or affinity with Christians.[9] He adds in his *Commentary on Mat-*

thew that God esteems more highly the small company of his own than all the rest of the world.[10]

These ideas—the danger of pagan contagion and the priceless value of the small flock—constitute the religious basis for the "frontier complex" or restricted-group sentiment. South Africa has institutionalized this attitude in the form of *apartheid*.[11] White culture becomes identified with defense of the faith. The white community feels itself to be a community elected by God to make fertile a land that the non-Europeans could not exploit. The natives have cast themselves away from divine election because they have not used properly the talents God has given them.

In some cases, the natives have even made perverse use of the gifts of God. For example, the white people strove to perfect a race of cattle that could furnish great monetary wealth to the Africans. The Bantus, however, preferred quantity. They made the number of cattle a sign of wealth and used them as the price of women in marriage, not as objects of productivity. The white people tried to teach the natives the value of saving money and the use of capital, their Calvinist standard of ethics for labor, morals, and divine vocation, but the natives worked only for the needs of immediate consumption and spent the surplus in feasts—feasts which in the eyes of the whites were always of a licentious or erotic nature.

Thus, the Calvinists reached the same conclusion about the African natives as they had about the Indians. The Calvinist missionary had given the Bantu the opportunity to enter into the economy of salvation, but he had refused. He preferred to continue living in his diabolical manner. Even when converted, the African mixed into his Christian ideas a whole series of superstitions. He interpreted the Christian dogma he was taught according to the dictates of his pagan mentality, inventing prophetesses and messiahs.

The community of the whites had no sense of loss when it came to consider itself as the small flock of the select. Its economic success was proof of divine grace, just as the situation of the blacks was the sign of their rejection. The "frontier complex" or restricted-group feeling rests, therefore, in the final analysis upon the Calvinist idea of predestination and visible signs of divine election.

In this way, dark skin came to symbolize, both in Africa and in America, the voluntary and stubborn abandonment of a race in sin. Contact with this race endangered the white person's soul and the whiteness of his spirit. The symbolism of color thus took on one of the most complicated and subtle forms, in both Protestantism and Catholicism, through the various steps through which darkness of color became associated with evil itself.

IV

The ramifications of this symbolism must now be traced through the double process of secularization in America and of de-Christianization in Europe. Western culture, even among atheists, still remains profoundly steeped in the Christian culture of the past. The symbolism of color continues, therefore, to be effective even when it goes unrecognized. Secularization and de-Christianization do involve, however, new phenomena that cannot be overlooked.

With the coming of independence to America, the philosophy of the European Enlightenment replaced to a great extent the Puritanism of the early colonists. It was first espoused by the aristocratic class of the South, of which Jefferson was the representative figure, and then by the hard-working classes of New England. American democracy is still undoubtedly colored by religion, but Americans tend more and more to retain only that part of Christianity which is based on reason, which is something quite close to what the philosophers used to call "natural religion."

Ralph Barton Perry, in his book *Puritanism and Democracy*, explains well the significance of this transition from Calvanism to an acceptance of the philosophy of the Enlightenment: Puritanism taught that men should distrust their own inclinations and their natural faculties, seeking both their origin and their salvation in a supernatural order. It was a religion of misanthropy. The philosophy of the Enlightenment, on the other hand, was human, optimistic, and eudaemonic.

Such a revolution of thought and feeling should have been marked by a revision of racial values. It was, in fact, the philosophy of the Enlightenment that precipitated the abolition of slavery. Why, then, was there no serious attack upon the symbolism of color, since it was no more founded upon reason than the social institution of slavery which got carried away by a tidal wave of thought and reason?

First of all, Calvinism still remained just under the surface, ready to be revived at the slightest opportunity. The migration toward the West, as Perry has also pointed out, was considered to be further proof corroborating the idea that the Puritans and founders of American democracy had formed of their destiny. The pioneering success was interpreted as a sign of divine grace. The Puritan felt sure that he was among the chosen few when he succeeded in standing up under adversity and triumphing over obstacles.

With the consolidation of national groups in the Western world and the triumph of the spirit of Enlightenment, nothing remained of Calvinism except the barriers forged by the "frontier complex" or restricted-group-boundary concept. The positive elements of Calvinism ceased to exercise their dynamic effect with the rise of secularization and the transition from the old Christianity to a rational religion of democracy. Nevertheless, the barriers fostered by Calvinism still stood as signs of distinction between white men and colored men.

The worst was to happen when the descendants of the slaves finally assimilated North American values and gave themselves over to a "white narcissism." They could see no other way to demonstrate their identification with America than by adopting a kind of Puritanism. The introduction of this factor into Negro Protestantism defined the religion of the colored middle class. By introducing into its religion a factor historically linked to the condemnation of the Indian and the Negro as inveterate savages, the Negro middle class introduced also its own condemnation. The Christian symbolism of color, interiorized in the Negro, gave rise to the neuropathic character, marked by a guilt complex, of the Negro middle class.

It must not be thought, however, that Catholic Latin America did not experience similar phenomena. But interracial sexuality was accepted there, and the drama found its solution in the mingling of blood. White blood acted as a tonic both physically and morally for the Negro, in a process Brazilians call "purging the blood." The progressive whitening of the African race was coupled with its progressive spiritualization.

In Europe, while capitalism had sources in Calvinism, as has been brought out by Max Weber, its development was destined to destroy the Calvinistic code of ethics. The multiplication of productive power could not maintain its pace without the parallel multiplication of needs. This gave rise to an ethic of consumption and finally to materialism. Moreover, scientific thought was undermining the supernatural foundations of the religious concept. The universe was becoming a system of laws that human reason could discern. Capable of being expressed in equations, it was consequently devoid of everything sacred.

The Africans whom the white man was to meet in the colonies had neither this materialistic concept of life nor this rational concept of the universe. Tribal life continued, even after contact with the white man, to follow the ancestral norms. It took no account of the value of time or money.[12] The schools introduced by the colonizers had no other purpose than to change the mentality of the African, to prepare him to become a good worker in the service of the white man's plantations and factories and a good consumer capable of buying the white man's products. It destroyed the African's concept that everything is penetrated with something sacred and implanted a more materialistic view of life.

This change of perspective ought to have caused the Christian symbolism of color to disappear entirely. But the change in the African mentality did not come about as rapidly as was anticipated by the founders of the lay schools. Money was not used in accordance with Western standards but lavishly for the purchase of wives and the prestige of family groups. The relations of the African with his employer still followed the archaic pattern of familial or tribal relationships, and not that of the modern contractual ethic of industrialization. In short, it appeared to the white man that the native remained alien to the materialistic approach of the capitalistic economy and also to the rational spirit of science, which had become the new religion of that economy.

Thus, in the symbolic association of color which we have been discussing, some of the elements have disappeared. Associations with the devil and sin have no place in the concept of the universe introduced in the late-nineteenth century. But the "frontier complex" between two conflicting mentalities has held firm. Black and white have taken on other meanings: These meanings still follow, however, the basic antithesis founded centuries before on the white purity of the elect and the blackness of Satan. Because this symbolism became secularized, it survived the collapse of the old Christian code of ethics and the advent of another system of ideas. The Christian tree had been uprooted, but had left root fragments that continued to creep obscurely under the surface.

Mircea Eliade has taught us to discover in the present the remnants of primitive archetypes, such as the nostalgia for Para-

ROGER BASTIDE

dise Lost and the Center of the World. It is not surprising, then, that a symbolism of color associations could survive the disappearance of its mystical Christian roots. A change of polarization is taking place today, however. The conflict between light and dark is not so much expressed by the two colors—white and black—as by a chain of experience of white men in their relations with races of non-European stock. A black or dark color has come to symbolize a certain social situation, class, or caste. There still remains, even in this process of secularization, something of the antithesis of darkness and light—the brightness of the sky and the darkness of anguish.

REFERENCES

1. Brazilian films are typical of this point of view. In Europe, a blond is usually the heroine, and a brunette the dangerous woman. In Brazil, the dark woman is loving and faithful, while the blond is the vamp who leads a man to ruin.

2. René Ribeiro, *Religiaõ e Relaçoẽs Raciais* (Religion and Racial Relations; Rio de Janeiro, 1956).

3. Roger Bastide, *Sociologie et Psychanalise* (Sociology and Psychoanalysis; Paris, 1951).

4. Wolfgang S. Seiferth, "St. Mauritius, African," *Phylon*, No. 4 (1941), pp. 370-76.

5. St. Benedict became the Saint of the Indians and Negroes. Most statues of him are to be found in homes, and it is there that his Saint's Day or Feast Day is celebrated. There may be, however, a special chapel for him in churches where numbers of Indians or Negroes worship. For illustrations from Venezuela, see R. Olivares Figueiroa, "San Benito en el folklore occidental de Venezuela," *Acta Venezolana*, Vol. 2, Nos. 1-4 (St. Benedict in the Western Folklore of Venezuela; 1946-47).

6. Juan A. Ortega y Medina, "Ideas de la Evangelización anglosajona entre los indígenas de los Estados Unidos de Norte-America," *América Ingigena*, Vol. 18, No. 2 (Ideas Used in the Anglo-Saxon Evangelization of the Indians in the United States; 1958).

7. Jean Calvin, *Institution de la religion Chrétienne*, ed. F. Baumgartner, Vol. 2, Part 3 (The Christian Institutes of Calvin [author's translation]; Geneva, 1888), p. 11.

8. *Ibid.*, Vol. 1, Part 17, p. 10.

9. *Ibid.*, Vol. 2, Part 8, p. 54.

10. *Ibid.*, Vol. 9, pp. 37-38.

11. Concerning this frontier complex and its various dimensions, including the cultural aspects which are generally the most stressed but which we consider' as only derivatives of the first, see Kenneth L. Little, *Race and Society* (Paris, 1952). The reader may be surprised that we have quoted here two passages from Calvin which the Afrikaners do not use in their justification of *apartheid* and that we have not quoted the passages of Calvin (*Works,* Parts 36-51, pp. 400-803; Commentary on Jeremiah, Part 24, p. 2; Sermon on the Ephesians, Part 6, pp. 5-9) which the South Africans do use for that purpose. These latter passages are utilized as rationalizations of the racial situation and therefore after the fact, deforming Calvin's thought. (Cf. Benjamin J. Marais, *Colour, Unsolved Problem of the West* [Cape Town, n.d.], pp. 300ff.) The passages that we have quoted appear to have been stimuli acting upon both the conscious and the subconscious mind of the Dutch pioneers long before the advent of the *apartheid* situation.

12. Concerning this development of Calvinism in regard to science and its impact on the blacks, see Michael Banton, *West African City: A Study of Tribal Life in Freetown* (London, 1957).

PHILIP MASON

The Revolt Against Western Values

THAT THERE are biological differences among different human
populations is self-evident. In primitive times many of these differences probably had value for survival. With increasing control
of the environment in modern times, the differences have become
considerably less relevant. Although opportunities for mental development are hardly ever equal between members of one population and those of another, the nearer they approach equality, the
more likely it is that the two populations will produce in about the
same proportions individuals over about the same range of intellectual potential.

In the nineteenth century, cultural differences were great between those of European stock and the other populations. The
form of social organization and the technical advantages of the
European group enabled it to establish a dominance over the
others exemplified and symbolized in two institutions: colonialism
and slavery. The dominant group was physically different from the
groups dominated, particularly in their skin color, called by
an odd convention white. Color became the most permanent of
distinguishing badges.

Slavery and colonialism are now virtually ended, but the so-
called white nations are, on the whole, rich and the non-white,
poor. The gap between them is growing wider. Social structure is
changing everywhere, while the growing speed of communications
makes possible comparisons that would not have occurred to the
tribesman of fifty years ago. His grandson wants what the rich na-

---

This paper is an abridgement of an article written for the Copenhagan Conference, which met September 5-12, 1965. The article was completed, therefore, before the death of Malcolm X and the coming into prominence of
Stokely Carmichael.

tions have and he has not—education, hospitals, old-age pensions. The cultural gap is still real, and understanding difficult.

Past memories of slavery and colonialism arouse non-white resentment at the contrast between excessive wealth and poverty; all are associated with one physical difference—color. Stories of social exclusiveness, prejudice about color, arrogance, and resulting humiliation continue to reach the new nations from the old colonial countries and the United States.[1] Strong emotions are linked with physical difference—in no way important except as a badge. These emotions are a factor in world politics. Many white people associate with non-whites poverty, inefficiency, and backwardness, while non-whites, looking at the whites, remember colonialism and slavery, think of riches and power and their selfish misuse. Each attributes to the other cruelty and sexual maladjustment.

In the heyday of their power, the white peoples had to reconcile their own ideals of freedom and democracy with the practice of slavery and colonization. This imperial predicament presented itself to Athens in the fifth century B.C. as much as to France and Britain in the nineteenth century A.D. For the latter, an obvious solution was to assume that the subject peoples were not only different in culture and control of the environment, as they manifestly were, but also somehow inherently and permanently different. It was like Aristotle's justification for slavery: Some people, he thought, were slaves by nature. To affirm this had become by the end of the nineteenth century a corporate need of the community. This need fused with an individual psychological need of much longer standing.

Distrust of strangers and loyalty to the group must have had some value for survival in the earlier stages of man's development. Today these linked attitudes of loyalty and aggression survive—sometimes in a rational form with value to society, sometimes in forms that are innocuous if juvenile, but sometimes in atavistic forms harmful to society. Nearly all who leave the tribe feel the need for the security of corporate unity. Loneliness is a characteristic danger to modern man. And the more insecure the individual feels, the stronger this need is liable to be. The same is true of the complementary tendency toward aggressiveness. Everyone has been forced by living in society to repress some aggressive tendencies. The more insecure a man is, the more likely he is to look for some safe target at which to direct these aggressive tendencies.

Man is a creature of inner conflict. Few do not feel that they fall short, either of their own high standards or of receiving the proper admiration of their fellows. One remedy is to escape from loneliness by merging one's individuality in a tribe, a majority, a nation, and from the feeling of inadequacy by projecting on to someone else shortcomings detestable in oneself, or vices secretly envied but not practiced for fear of the consequences. Thus men—particularly the unsuccessful and dissatisfied—have a personal need for a devil, a universal enemy. It is convenient to personify him in a member of another group—national, religious, or racial.

This personal need has been felt in the colonial nations at least since early Christian times. The devil is seen in the form of a Negro in many records of the medieval period. The Western color symbolism of good and evil, joy and mourning, has helped to establish this identification. By the late-nineteenth century, the personal need could fuse with the corporate need to justify economic exploitation of non-whites. Moreover, for a brief period a misunderstanding of Darwin's theory of natural selection supported the racist dogma of an inherent inferiority.

Such prejudice issued in widespread exclusion, humiliation, and exploitation by the whites. A similar phenomenon occurred more dramatically in Hitler's Germany. The scapegoat mechanism was used against the Jews to unite the nation in a militancy that seemed to be the only remedy for frustration and defeat. Prejudice has not, however, been universal in the colonial nations and the United States. Among educated and successful people, the personal need for a scapegoat is slight. The corporate need has often been met by a benevolent paternal liberalism that envisaged change. Today this paternalism seems complacent and its assumptions humiliating.

Sir Theophilus Shepstone, Administrator of Nepal, wrote in 1850: "The injunctions of our religion compel us to recognise in the Natives the capability of being elevated to a perfect equality, social and political, with the white man." Or again, consider Mountstuart Elphinstone, Governor of Bombay from 1819 to 1827. An exceptionally humane and farsighted man, Elphinstone introduced public education in Bombay before there was any state contribution to education in Britain. He constantly opposed "colonization" in India (by which was understood the introduction of large numbers of English people) because it would mean that "the people of India would sink to a debased and servile condition resembling that of the Indians in Spanish America." He believed it to be a duty to educate: "I do not perceive," he wrote, "anything we can do to improve the morals of the people except by improving their education." In general, he looked forward to an end to British rule in India, when "the improvement of the natives" reached "such a pitch as would render it impossible for a foreign nation to retain the government."

The aim, then, was to "improve," and it was assumed that "improvement" meant becoming more like the Victorian English. This assumption was implicit in the British "reforms" in India from 1919 onward and later in Africa. The subject peoples would be led step by step to a form of constitution based on the English. As the opportunity for governing themselves was graciously conceded, they would imitate, with becoming eagerness, the English way. Even more clearly and explicitly was it the intention of French colonial rulers in the nineteenth century to assimilate their colonial subjects.[2] Until recently similar assumptions lay behind most writings on the Negro American. This is *paternalism,* a word that has taken on in this context a specialized sense; it implies above all things the father's delusion that his son will want to be the man his father was—though he will perhaps never quite succeed.

In *An American Dilemma,* Gunnar Myrdal makes the double point that the white majority has made the Negro what he is, and that the Negro himself characteristically wants to be what the white majority wishes to be. Since the Negro has accepted white values, America's problem is to persuade the whites to extend the hand of friendship. In his introductory chapter, Myrdal has a section headed "A White Man's Problem." It contains these words:

It is thus the white majority group that naturally determines the Negro's "place." All our attempts to reach scientific explanation of why the Negroes are what they are and why they live as they do have regularly led to determinants on the white side of the race line.[3]

And again he writes:

In his allegiances the Negro is characteristically an American. He believes in the American creed and in other ideals held by most Americans, such as getting ahead in the world, individualism, the importance of education and wealth. He imitates the dominant culture as he sees it and insofar as he can adopt it under his conditions of life.[4]

These words were published in 1944. Are they still valid? Is it still true to say that the Negro American wants total integration? There is an intense impatience with gradualism and a determination to have "Freedom now," but this does not mean that the goal of integration has changed. Some Negroes, as yet a small minority, loudly proclaim, however, that there is no hope of justice from white men. They claim the Negroes must keep themselves uncontaminated from degenerate white blood and corrupt white ideals. Many Negro intellectuals and members of the Negro middle class reject certain tenets of the Black Muslims and similar movements. Nevertheless, even those who reject most strongly still feel in certain moods emotionally sympathetic with a rejection of white ideals.

The white assumption that the Negro "wanted in" was more complete and inclusive in America than it was in France and Britain, because in America the Negro had lost his own culture. The rejection of white culture by the Black Muslims is, consequently, violent and dramatic. Though extreme, the Black Muslim movement is a symptom of more general unrest.[5] Its essence is the desire for an identity of one's own, a rejection of something second-hand. This is surely an element in much that happens today in Ghana. Ghana's very name is an attempt to borrow from a past that is African. Its speeches at the United Nations and national robes flamboyantly proclaim a determination to be itself.

I. *The Black Muslims*

In 1965, *The Annals of the American Academy of Political and Social Science* devoted a special number to the Negro protest. The authors seem, to an outside observer, to fall into two camps—those who emphasize the progress made in the last twenty years, and those who emphasize the inequalities that remain. In general, there is little about the Black Muslims. They are not, of course, entirely ignored. Arnold Rose suggests that "group identification may become so strong that Negroes, like American Jews, may not want full integration."[6] Jane and Wilson Record suggest, on a similar note, that an increasing number of Negro leaders "redefine racial protest in pluralist rather than in liberalist terms."[7] But the unstated assumption is usually the other way; probably most thoughtful Americans, and several of these writers, would agree with Tilman C. Cothran's judgment that the recent demonstrations suggest "a validation of Myrdal's hypothesis that the race problem in America . . . is a problem in the minds of white people."[8]

At the time Myrdal wrote, millions of white people avoided conscience qualms by taking refuge behind the myths of "white superiority" and

"Negro satisfaction." Science does not support the racial-superiority myth, and non-violent direct action has shattered the "Negro satisfaction" or "good race relations" myth.[9]

Many assume that the Negro will want to come into the citadels when they have fallen. The assumption, not confined to whites, is strongly held by many middle-class Negroes who have made progress at getting "in." It is an assumption reasonable in itself and hard to dispel because it is welcome to those who make it. But to spend even a few hours studying the works of James Baldwin, Richard Wright, and Ralph Ellison is to begin to wonder whether the assumption is safe.

The evidence in its favor is strong. It is common not only to the older protest groups—the N.A.A.C.P. and the Urban League— but to the activist groups—the Congress of Racial Equality, the Southern Christian Leadership Conference, the Student Nonviolent Co-Ordinating Committee. Their stated aims embody it; they want equality, not separation. Jane and Wilson Record write: "With few exceptions, notably the Garvey movement of the 1920's and the Black Muslims of today, modern Negro protest organizations have been nonseparatist; moreover, they have been nonracial, aimed at acceptance within the existing politicoeconomic system."[10] This is, of course, true. What is significant, on the other side, is the intensity and special quality of the feeling among Black Muslims. The movement's psychological background arouses widespread emotional sympathy even among those who cannot intellectually accept its dogmas.

The Black Muslims are symptomatic; their particular response to the situation is less important than the situation itself and the sympathy felt with certain aspects of their reaction. The whole movement as it actually exists is based too personally on Elijah Muhammad and may easily collapse. There are already signs that it is less strong than it was. Nevertheless, its significance as a symptom remains. In any case, the Muslims are not the only symptom. Howard Brotz has recently described the Black Jews of Harlem[11]; they are reacting in a similar way to the same situation. The content of their dogma is quite different from that of the Muslims, but the psychological background is the same. C. Eric Lincoln mentions in his book on the Black Muslims that "more than twenty bodies in New York City operate in the name of black solidarity."[12] The same kind of emotional stress has produced symptoms which resemble one another, both in the United States and elsewhere.

The Black Muslims owe something to Garveyism, to the many black lodges and fraternity societies of the South, and, more and more directly, to the Moorish Science Temple of America. Garveyism was born in the years immediately after World War I, a period when American race relations reached perhaps their nadir. Seventy Negroes were lynched in the year after the war, some still in the uniform of the U.S. Armed Forces. In 1919, there were twenty-five race riots. Garvey wanted a king, a president, a government—in short, a nation—for black men; he was a West Indian and his movement was international, a kind of African Zionism proclaiming freedom and independence for the "400,000,000 Negroes of the world."

The black lodges and fraternities of the South are a less direct influence. The members, ignorant and unorganized, have sought isolated Biblical texts in order to show that God is black, to identify themselves with Israel, to demonstrate that their oppression is the result of a curse that will end. "I am black" (Jeremiah 8:21) is the word of God; the Ethiopian eunuch who helped Jeremiah to get out of the cistern (Jeremiah 38:7) is glorified; many passages are quoted about serving a strange nation in a far land (for example, Jeremiah 5:15-17). The Moorish Science Temple, a much more direct influence, was founded in 1913 by Timothy Drew, who later called himself Noble Drew Ali. These movements clearly proceed from the same psychological causes.

The essence of the doctrine, from the point of view of this essay, is that a man must have a nationality before he can have a God. The so-called Negroes of America, having been robbed of nationality, religion, name—everything—by white men, must recover their identity as a nation, their personal identity, their names. Noble Drew Ali gave each of his followers—who, he taught, were really Moors—a personal identity card; the Prophet Fard gave each convert his "true" name, a name that had been lost but was now revealed by Allah. The convert is born again and accepts a very high standard of personal puritanism. There must be no sexual irregularity, no smoking, no drinking, no gluttony. A member can be disciplined for being overweight. Disallowed also are cosmetics, personal display, and conspicuous spending. Very substantial almsgiving is required, the proportion being fixed at one third of a member's yearly income.

It could be said that a member must at all costs avoid confirming the white stereotype of the Negro. He must cut himself off from white people in every way; he must "buy black" and avoid contributing to white wealth. Black Muslims must make themselves economically self-sufficient by saving and by joining co-operative societies. Every Muslim should be ready to die defending his women from the lustful assaults of white men. Above all, the Muslim must never mingle with white people in marriage; he must reject their degenerate blood as well as their corrupt morals. The whites have had their day—why integrate with a dying man?

In the beliefs of the Black Muslims, as in those of various other protest groups, there are absurd elements that are not likely to appeal to the educated. (That Muslims are linked by blood to all non-white people and that the rule of white men will end in 1984 are examples.) Nor does it seem likely that very serious attempts will be made to learn Arabic, which is singularly unrelated to the needs of modern Americans. There are, however, two more permanent elements—the cluster of forms of behavior repudiating the white stereotype of the Negro and the cluster of beliefs repudiating white good intentions.

The determination not to "act like a nigger" imposes very severe discipline. Regulations help the devotee to build up his self-respect and to regard with contempt the corrupt and luxurious race that has humiliated his people. This is a feature common to many protest movements.

The repudiation of white good will is more specific to the Muslims. Had "the white man" really wanted to be just, they argue, he could have been so at any time during the last three hundred years. While undisputed ruler of the world, he never spoke of "integration; now [that] he has seen his empires crumble, he is willing to throw his faithful dog the driest bone he has, hoping that dog will once more forget the past and rush out to save his master."[12] But that "dry bone" means integration at the bottom.

A Muslim can trust no white man. Christianity kept the "so-called Negro" subservient to the white man; Christianity lynched Negro men and raped Negro women. Unless the Muslim—all so-called Negroes are Muslims whether they know it or not—rids himself of the slave mentality and all remnants of Christianity, he will share in the distintegration of a corrupt and dying world.

This, of course, is crude racism, as crude as anything put out by the Ku Klux Klan or the Nazis. (That the provocation to which it is a response is much greater is beside the point.) "The white man" and "Christianity" are thought to be monolithic blocks and their substance uniform throughout. The act of one is taken as the act of all, which is almost a definition of group prejudice. The response of the Negro to the "group identification" of the white is a "group identification" of his own. Already there are dangerous manifestations of familiar themes. The defense of female purity is shared with the white Southerner. There is also a militant inner circle of storm troopers, known as the Fruit of Islam, who discipline the unruly. The Muslims are a social movement with economic objects riding a religious vehicle. Its true political aims are still undefined. It seems clear, however, that the atmosphere is not likely to be favorable to a tolerance of a variety of opinions, to a liberal individual democracy. Black racism is very like white racism.

If it is to be understood and properly evaluated, it must be related to a much wider area of expectant emotion. Eric Lincoln writes:

Today's generation of Negro youth . . . are determined to change the Negro's status *now*—by nonviolent action if nonviolence will work. So long as they have a vestige of faith in the white man's latent decency, their strength will be exerted through integrative organizations. . . . But if that flickering faith is allowed to perish, black nationalism may feed sumptuously on their despair.[13]

This impatience of the Black Muslims needs to be seen against the wider background expressed by Negro imaginative writers.

The principal figure in Richard Wright's *Native Son* starkly embodies a myth come true in human flesh

To Bigger and his kind white people were not really people; they were a sort of great natural force, like a stormy sky looming overhead, or like a deep swirling river stretching suddenly at one's feet in the dark. As long as he and his black folks did not go beyond certain limits, there was no need to fear that white force. But whether they feared it or not, each and every day of their lives they lived with it.[14]

In *Notes of a Native Son*, which contains a perceptive critique of Wright's novel, James Baldwin writes:

And there is, I should think, no Negro living in America who has not felt, briefly or for long periods, with anguish sharp or dull, in varying degrees and to varying effect, simple, naked and unanswerable hatred; who has not wanted to smash any white face he may encounter in a day, to violate, out of motives of the cruelest vengeance, their women, to break the bodies of all white people and bring them low, as low as that dust into which he has been and is being trampled.[15]

Here is another of the main strands in the psychological background of the Muslims. It explains the attraction the Negro intellectual feels toward the Muslims, even though he is repelled by the absurdities in their creed. The feeling is directed with an added irritation at the white liberal, whose good intentions make it more difficult to hate all white men without reserve.

A third strand—and not the least important—is the search for identity. This is the phrase that is generally used, but what is really sought is a cultural and intellectual pedigree. It is expressed in the visiting cards of Noble Drew Ali, the new name given to the reborn Muslim, the official designation as "The Black Nation of Islam," or the recurring phrase "The Lost-Found Nation of Islam." This, too, is a constant theme for the Negro writers, among whom there was a period of romantic nostalgia for an exotic African home, a land of golden fruits and brilliant flowers, beautiful black women and mysterious black kings.

This wistfulness could not survive contact with reality. Langston Hughes was as disillusioned with Africa[16] as V. S. Naipaul was more recently with India.[17] Ralph Ellison saw that to expect in Africa a homeland with which he would find himself linked as though by instinct was to identify race and culture. James Baldwin fled from a United States in which he was rejected to Paris and Switzerland. Baldwin could not, however, honestly identify himself with European culture. He discovered that he was American after all, even though he was denied a "lousy cup of coffee" in America. "In this long battle," he writes, "the white man's motive was the protection of his identity; the black man was motivated by the need to establish an identity."[18]

Impatience is one strand in the rope; resentment at oppression, at ostracism, at indifference, at patronage, a second; the search for identity, a cultural pedigree, a third. All three are shared by Black Muslims and intellectuals alike. What is still rejected by most Negro Americans is the tactic of separatism. One cannot hate all the time—as Baldwin admits—and what is the use, when the odds are so heavy? Like the Afrikaner, the Negro American has nowhere else to go. He must live with this situation. Besides, there is much that he admires. He is an American, as more than one writer has stressed—perhaps the most American of all Americans. James Baldwin, looking at Chartres Cathedral, feels he is less a part of the Western heritage than is a white American. He cannot find refuge in Europe; he must return to his American-ness.

But what tactic can the Negro adopt? Until recently the Negro in the South was confronted with a social system that he had to accept, avoid, or rebel against. It was easiest to bow to it. It was possible to escape for a time in the Negro church, in a lodge or fraternity, or, more permanently, in the North. In the end there was only disillusion; escape could not be permanent. Revolts occurred but were suppressed. Most of the time, revolt was perceived to be hopeless, and the Negro was therefore dubbed submissive.

Today, these three ways of dealing with the social situation—acceptance, avoidance, aggression—are all felt to be insufficient. Even in the South, acceptance of the old system has surely ceased except outwardly as a temporary tactical device. Avoidance cannot be a permanent answer to an honest man, as Baldwin discovered. Rejection of the old system must be, by now, almost complete among northern Negroes with any education, but this does not mean rejection of the values of the dominant group. The northern Negroes are poised expectantly, still ready to be Americans. But we will not have integration on the white man's terms, they say. Then on what terms?

Myrdal was clearly right; the whole nation must change if "the problem" is to be solved. It was an error to think that only the Negroes had to change. It is surely also an error to think that only the whites must change; the Negroes will be changing at the same time, but in what direction?

The Black Muslims have made explicit a distinction that is ultimately destructive, searingly antiseptic; they have proclaimed the impossibility of continuing to believe in a religion of love that rejects the Negro, and a politics of equality that judges him to be inferior.

The importance of the protest has been established. "We shall overcome" has been the theme song of the integrative, activist organizations. If they do not overcome, the likelihood seems to be that one American in six will fiercely reject the American ideal.

II. *Millenarian Cults*

The Ras Tafaris of Jamaica are one of the non-white protest groups that are not building on an ancient culture of their own but either constructing from an imaginary past or stealing from another culture. They are not dissimilar to the Negro lodges or fraternities of the South, combining in one institution their protests against two predicaments: that of the ex-slave in a color-conscious society and that of the unemployed and uneducated urban laborer recently divorced from a rural background. They, too, search the Old Testament for divine inspiration. Jeremiah 8:20 tells them that God is black and that Negro women have been abused by white men; Jacob, the chosen son, was smooth and, therefore, black; Esau, the rejected, was red and hairy and, thus, the first white man. (Others believe that the first white man was Gehazi, the leper white as snow, of II Kings 5:27.) Like the Black Jews of Harlem, the Ras Tafaris believe they are descended from Ethiopians; like the Garveyites, they plan to return to Ethiopia—or originally planned; latterly they have become a trifle disillusioned.

Their theology is primitive and irrational, but they have the same emotional need as the Black Muslims and even James Baldwin. They refuse to accept any longer the values of a society that despises them and are searching for an identity of their own. They seek escape in a community that despises, or pretends to despise, the lighter-skinned. The ostensible, outward target of their resentment is a class, the rich and the established, usually people of lighter skin. ("The white man" in Jamaica sometimes means a well-to-do person who behaves as though he came from Europe and would often not be classed as "white" in the United States.) There is, of course, another target—their own failure and frustration.

The cargo cults of the Pacific islands are also protest movements against a world in which white people have benefits that non-whites lack. They differ, however, from the Ras Tafaris in ways that are illuminating. The identifying mark of a cargo cult is an expectation of wealth in the form of Western goods coming from overseas in a ship or airplane; this is not exactly rejection of Western values, but it is a hope for a simplified magical escape from intolerable stress. Raymond Firth writes of these cults:

[They arise] as a resultant of several factors in operation together: a markedly uneven relation between a system of wants and the means of their satisfaction; a very limited technical knowledge of how to improve conditions; specific blocks or barriers to that improvement by poverty of natural resources or opposed political interests. What constitutes a cult is a systematized series of operations to secure the means of satisfaction by non-technical methods.[19]

As in the movements previously discussed, there is usually an anti-European element in the cargo cults, an attempt to be rid of foreign domination, of all the bewilderment and frustration arising from contact with a more technologically developed culture. There are usually features intended to sharpen identification with the group—a flag, a uniform, or a badge. There are, however, wide differences in the degree of reliance on magic among the movements classified as cargo cults.

The kinds of protest movement that we have been considering can be illuminated by placing them in a spectrum, or on a ladder, between two extremes. There would be not one but a number of such "ladders."[20] They would range from the use of pure magic to a rational technical attempt to obtain the ends desired; from the traditionalist to the radical revolutionary; from the need to glorify the group's own past to wholesale borrowing from another culture; from emotional forms of expression to a quiet withdrawn ritual. The ladder is not always a useful metaphor because it has only two ends. Nevertheless, a movement, to be understood, must be given a place within a series of frames of reference. Another such frame is the degree to which a movement's aims emphasize economic, social, political, or spiritual benefits. There are too many such frames of reference for any simple taxonomy to be revealing.

A preliminary and fairly clear-cut distinction can, however, be made. Although some movements may engross a person's whole time for many years, they can be entirely excluded from the class of movement presently being considered because they have limited and relatively defined objectives. The Anti-Corn Law League is an example from English history of such a movement. The kinds of protest movement this paper discusses may be called protest cults. They aim (or expect) to change the whole life of their adherents. They believe that certain benefits will follow from these changes. They must, as Raymond Firth says, aim to some extent at achieving their ends "by non-technical methods." Moreover, if they are to be truly cults, there must also be a certain spiritual totalitarianism in their aims.

The cargo cults differ greatly. In some the rational element dominates; in others the magical is predominant. Peter Worsley has suggested that the cargo cults have certain features in common with some African millenarian cults.[21] All of them involve, in varying degrees, rejection or re-interpretation of the Western values that have produced the stress. This combines with some break with the traditional past. The cults seek to unite their members under one leadership—even though there are often different groups or tribes represented in the cult.

Members must be born again in order to make a new start. Further, they must be committed; there can be no turning back. Commitment may be celebrated by obscene or blasphemous oaths or ritual. Mau Mau is an obvious example; the obscene practices charged against the Templars had perhaps the same purpose of committing the participants body and soul to the brotherhood. A break with the past, apart from its obvious value to a leader in fostering unity and commitment, has a deeper significance. The cult is a protest against a total situation in which two social systems are at variance. It is a protest against both; it is a dissatisfaction with the self as well as with the solution offered from outside.

English writers have argued that what used to be called the Indian Mutiny was mainly military rather than national, and that the underlying feeling was reactionary. One of the declared objects, for instance, was to restore the custom of burning widows alive. The motives for this historical emphasis are obvious. Indian writers, for reasons equally obvious, have stressed the wider nature of the rising and, perhaps more doubtfully, its forwardness of outlook. Both have found ample evidence to support their views.

This disparity becomes intelligible in the light of the present discussion. The military leaders were in simultaneous protest against a present of which they were themselves a part and a future in which they feared they would be Westernized. They restored *sati* more because Europeans had forbidden it than because they were fanatical believers in Hindu custom; indeed, some were Moslem. The Mutiny served a double purpose: a defiance of European rule and a joint commitment in something that could not be undone. This was a political rising, not a millenarian cult, but it does share other features with the cults; for example, the extremely widespread belief that the bullets of the British and their Punjabi and Gurkha allies would turn to water.[22]

The break with the past as well as the future, combined with a sacrificial act of commitment to the cult, can be seen most clearly in a well-known episode in South African history. On the instructions of their prophetess, many sections of the Xhosa killed all their cattle on the day the new age was to begin.[23] In several cargo cults, the devotees throw away their money—the sole, if inadequate, means available for getting the goods they desire. In 1942 in India, seed stores were the first things the peasants destroyed in a rising that, on the level of explicit utterances, the British could rightly define as pro-Japanese. The Indian National Congress could, perhaps more profoundly if without much evidence, diagnose the uprising as a result of the stress between nationalism and the imperial power.

The literature on the Negro American commonly maintains that the Negro churches have provided the main opportunity for leadership. They have also acted as a means of escape, as "an expression of internal solidarity and a means of differentiation against other groups."[24] They have been, in short, the best means the southern Negro has had of asserting his identity in a form of which he can be proud. For him to reject the Negro churches is to cut himself off from the past. He thus refuses the only source he has had in the past for benefits he is still seeking, declaring it inadequate. He is like the cargo cultist who throws away his money. This is exactly what the Black Muslim does when he angrily denounces Christianity as a dead religion of lies and slavery, when he associates the cross with the symbol of a Negro hanged by lynch law.

It is, therefore, certainly a mistake to call the Black Muslims a "nativistic" cult, a term that is used of a movement "designed to revive or perpetuate selected aspects of a society's culture."[25] Indeed it seems doubtful whether this term is really of very wide application. The cults and movements considered have all had a dual aspect: protesting against an imposed culture, but seeking a new way out; asserting some aspects of the old culture more in defiance of the alien than for any intrinsic worth, but at the same time bitterly repudiating some aspects of the "native" culture.

Worsley has suggested that it is normal for a cult to progress from a strong emphasis on magic to a more orthodox political position. The magic of the millenarian cult is almost bound to produce disillusion. When the cult's nature changes or disappears, the whole scene becomes altered—old beliefs have been shattered, previous assumptions destroyed, former rivalries submerged. It is worth considering, in the light of this trend, certain pentecostal sects among West Indians living in Britain. These resemble the Negro churches of the old South more than they do the Black Muslims. Far from rejecting Christianity, the pentecostal sects regard themselves as the only true Christians.[26] They are as puritanical as the Muslims in regard to drinking, smoking, gambling, wearing make-up; they are almost as generous in subscribing to common funds. They, too, feel they have escaped from a hostile world. They have been born again to find a new self-respect and happiness in a new world.

Followers are usually recruited from poor and ignorant people. Those who are attracted by the discipline and the fellowship of the sects are not, however, the idle and the improvident. They correspond to the skilled and semiskilled "serious" people who formed the backbone of English nineteenth-century nonconformist support for John Bright and Richard Cobden. They reject white society not as white but as non-Christian. Although their psychological and historical background has many affinities with that of the Negro in the southern United States, they have so far found a positive answer to society's rejection. The question is whether their children will reject their answer and turn to bitter protest against what the West has offered.

III. *The New Countries*

The protest cult is an extreme choice of action. It is, perhaps, seldom adopted unless there are economic pressures that reinforce the emotional situation. It is not, of course, a choice confined to human populations of any particular skin color; Nazism, the Ku Klux Klan, and the Afrikaner Broederbond have markedly cult-like features. Those more trained to analytical use of reason than most Black Muslims usually reject attachment to a cult as intellectually unsatisfying. Deeply concerned with their search for an identity, they often experience, however, the same emotional forces as the Muslims. The Black Muslims are the symptom of a tension that spreads far beyond their membership, far beyond America. Many Negro American writers alternate between an angry rejection of what has rejected them and an unhappy return to an Americanism that is all they have. It would be interesting to compare in detail these American writers with the French writers on *négritude*. It will have to be enough to say that the concept of *négritude* begins as a negation; it is inevitable to refer at this point to Aimé Cesaire's famous poem:

> Eia pour ceux qui n'ont jamais rien inventé
> pour ceux qui n'ont jamais rien exploré
> pour ceux qui n'ont jamais rien dompté

The poem goes on to proclaim something deeply felt but not intellectually definable and, then, to state something positively African rather than black.[27]

Negro intellectuals share the emotional response of the masses

65

to past white superiority and the associations that have linked color to colonialism, slavery, and poverty. Their emotional response is identical, their intellectual dilemma more agonizing. While the intellectuals will not give formal assent to the dogmas of a cult, they may be expected occasionally to react emotionally as though they were members of a cult. This applies not only to the spokesmen for national minorities, but also to the leaders of recently independent nations, who are equally in search of a lost identity.

This point is borne out in the thought of contemporary African leaders—in, for instance, Julius Nyerere's description of African socialism. Unlike European socialism, African socialism is not based on the overthrow of capitalism by means of class war. It rejects this negative approach and is based rather on "familyhood." There is an ancient tribal unity of the extended-kinship system within which every kinsman must be helped. Everyone has his work to do; there are no parasites and no exploiters—a tribal Garden of Eden. The only modification needed is the extension of the concept of kinship to include everyone in the nation and, eventually, all mankind.[28] This perhaps Utopian vision is further illuminated by D. K. Chisiza's well-known paper on the African outlook. He writes:

We of Africa belong neither to the East nor to the West . . . We excel neither in mysticism nor in science and technology but in the field of human relations. That is where we can set an example to the rest of the world.

He goes on to describe "the African" as tolerant of other people's ideas, hospitable, and deeply committed to family and personal relations.

With us, life has meant the pursuit the happiness rather than the pursuit of beauty or truth. We pursue happiness by rejecting isolationism, individualism, negative emotions, and tensions on the one hand; and by laying emphasis on a communal way of life, by encouraging positive emotions and habitual relaxations.

And he adds later: "God knows we are not kind because we are fools but because He ordained that we should be kindness-drunk rather than pride-drunk."[29]

It is easy to say that this is highly idealized and that all Africans do not always behave exactly like this; Shaka, for instance, behaved much more like the African stereotype of a European. But the criticism is not valid. No group lives up to its own ideals. If Christians had really been Christian, there would be no Black Muslims.

Importantly, Africans are here rejecting emphatically anything borrowed and constructing ideals of conduct that are altogether theirs. These ideals must not be Western, but recognizably linked with an ideal vision of the closed tribal system in which Africans once lived. Moreover, the system must be new as well as African: "Through co-operatives, a clan can translate the old tribal structure into the modern money economy," writes Tom Mboya in *Freedom and After.*[30] A hundred such sentences could be found. The need for an African philosophy[31]—an African system of values—is felt universally. Not surprisingly, the African Personality, African Socialism, and Pan-Africanism operate in some of the new African states as the dogmas of a creed. This becomes almost a cult, and all those who play a part in public life must give emotional assent to it.

Frantz Fanon expresses this mood:

The unconditional affirmation of African culture has succeeded the unconditional affirmation of European culture. On the whole, the poets of Negro-ism oppose the idea of an old Europe to a young Africa, tiresome reasoning to lyricism, oppressive logic to high-stepping nature, and on one side stiffness, ceremony, etiquette, and scepticism, while on the other frankness, liveliness, liberty and—why not?—luxuriance; but also irresponsibility.[32]

African nationalism under colonial rule was forced to begin as rejection. To be successful in establishing independence from colonial rule, it had, almost always, to recognize and make use of emotions similar to those of a protest cult. There were usually features reminiscent of the Black Muslims, the Nazis, the Afrikaner Broederbond. Much depended on how acute was the need for unity and how intransigent the situation. In the 1950's, for instance, there was much less need for sacrificial commitment to an almost desperate cause in Tanganyika than in Kenya. There was no call for Mau Mau in Dar es Salaam.

But there was always some sense of struggle, of need for commitment, some feeling that everything must be put aside till freedom was won. This sense of commitment is always highly intolerant. It could hardly be expected that it would vanish overnight with independence. The old war against poverty and ignorance remained. There was the new need to make a nation from a group of tribes. All these factors were reinforced by the intellectual's dilemma, the search for an intellectual and emotional pedigree. This explains why cult-like features may well persist long after

67

independence—indeed, long after the need for them may seem, from the outside, to have largely disappeared.

The emotional background in the ex-colonial countries of Asia is very different, but not quite so dissimilar as it seems at first sight. Cultures with written languages were ancient in Asia long before Europeans came on the scene. But at the time of the first contacts, these cultures were uniformly quiescent and, in some cases, decadent. The Europeans quickly established an ascendancy. Further, they made the same arrogant assumption in Asia as they had made in Africa and America—that the "improvement of the native" meant becoming more European.

In India during the early stage of contact with Europe, certain noble and progressive Indian minds, such as Raja Ram Mohun Roy, sought to borrow all they could from the new culture. This stage was followed by one of revulsion, and all that could be connected with the Vedas was glorified. The two traditions, indeed, overlapped and continued side by side. There were representatives of both in the Congress Party until and after independence in 1947. Hindu orthodoxy, in a pure and intolerant form, was then and has remained a minority politically. The majority party still contains, however, the modernizing, borrowing element and also another element whose followers still look—in thought, if not in dress or manners—to the ancient scriptures.

The best-known of these scriptures is a debate—staged on the battlefield in the presence of the enemy—as to the advisability of fighting, indeed of any action at all. The debate ends with the conclusion (the word is actually inappropriate; there can be no conclusion to such thought) that man should perform his function. This carries to a Western mind an inescapable implication that the function is allotted. Nothing could differ more from the spirit of Ajax and Hector. Pure extroverts, they do not argue about whether they should fight. Each boasts that he will win.

The spirit of the Gita is not wholly removed from another Western influence, exemplified in the Epistles attributed to John. But the substructure of Indian traditional thought is immensely foreign even to this strand of Western culture. Deeply ingrained is a readiness to look at every action *sub specie aeternitatis*. The Gita seems to a foreigner to have more bearing on the conduct of government and business in India than *The Imitation of Christ* has in Europe.

India then faces, in perhaps the most acute form of all the

Asian countries, not only immense problems of food, poverty, and population, but a double spiritual crisis. Traditional religious ideals are estranged from current business and politics; at the same time, India must find a way of fusing two cultures and creating a new identity of its own.

The resentment of Asia, Africa and, to some extent, Latin America at past behavior and at all present assumptions of superiority is an actuality. How far is this resentment likely to lead to a rejection of Western values? It would be a mistake to think of Western values only in terms of things wanted. Most of the world does unquestionably want a number of things that originated in the West—though now often easily obtainable from Japan—such as bicycles and sewing machines and transistor radios. No one is going to refuse a camera because he resents colonialism. But are Western ideals likely to be rejected because of colonialism and the association of color with slavery and oppression?

In a passage already quoted, Gunnar Myrdal identifies certain American ideals, namely, "getting ahead in the world, individualism, the importance of education and wealth." Of these, individualism is widely rejected, often consciously by Africans, more hesitatingly by Asians. Education all seek with eagerness and mixed expectations. On the importance of wealth, there is in all cultures a gap between expressed ideal and practices. All seek wealth while proverbially and ideally despising it; not all give it equal emphasis. The new nations do tend to reject still other ideals, largely because of the West's own failure to live up to them.

They recognize as yet no common intellectual authority with whom appeal can be lodged. Christianity many of them have never accepted; its association with the West has made it suspect to all. Lip service is paid to "democracy," but this term is very diversely interpreted. There is little allegiance to the creeds of Locke, the Encyclopedists, and the American founding fathers. Freedom of speech, liberty to express unpopular views, freedom of the press and the judiciary—all these fight a losing battle. The world has known systems—Rome, Islam, medieval Christendom—within which a single ethical code prevailed. The world of today, with its immensely swifter physical communications and its interlocking trade and currencies, has no common cultural or religious code, only the feeblest beginnings of an international legal system, only the vaguest foundations for an international code of morality.

This may be due partly to modern Western man's vivid sense

of failure, which has largely replaced the sense of sin. It is popularly expressed as a failure of the system of morality under which he was brought up—a failure of the church, of Christianity, of democracy. It is, of course, really his own failure to bring closer the ideal systems of his religion and the practical assumptions by which governments and businesses function.

However expressed, the consciousness of failure is real. How can the remnants of Western Christendom—the white nations—expect anyone else to be enthusiastic about ideals they themselves have so lamentably neglected? These ideals do basically form one system. Although the English Revolution of 1688, the thought of the American founding fathers, and the Enlightenment were a conscious protest against medieval Christendom, they grew from it; they were the child of the Christian system of faith that in so many ways they challenged. It would be disastrous if this whole rich evolutionary development of thought were rejected because of the aberration of racism.

Is this an imaginary danger? Frantz Fanon writes:

But every time Western values are mentioned they produce in the native a sort of stiffening or muscular lock-jaw. During the period of decolonisation, the native's reason is appealed to. He is offered definite values, he is told too frequently that decolonisation need not mean regression, and that he must put his trust in qualities which are well-tried, solid and highly esteemed. But it so happens that when the native hears a speech about Western culture he pulls out his knife—or at least he makes sure it is within reach. The violence with which the supremacy of white values is affirmed and the aggressiveness which has permeated the victory of these values over the ways of life and of thought of the native mean that, in revenge, the native laughs in mockery when Western values are mentioned in front of him. In the colonial context the settler only ends his work of breaking in the native when the latter admits loudly and intelligibly the supremacy of the white man's values. In the period of decolonisation, the colonised masses mock at these very values, insult them and vomit them up.[33]

But, it may be argued, Fanon was an extremist, writing after frightful experiences in Algeria. Some of the British may console themselves with the paternalistic thought: "Our Africans don't feel like this." White Americans are comforted to think that the Negro still "wants in." But the evidence suggests that there are times when every non-white person feels as Fanon's "native" feels. International affairs seem likely to be influenced for many years by such emotions. Because the West has failed to live up to the ideals of

70

Christianity and democracy, of freedom and tolerance, a sharp tendency to reject them has arisen.

But it may still be hoped that national minorities, particularly the Negroes, will accept a national code. This seems to depend not only on the working out of internal problems—automation and unemployment, poverty and housing, as much as human rights—but also on international race relations.

The rejection of Western values has frequently taken on various aspects of cultism. Cultism is not basically a racial reaction; people of a subordinate group are likely to behave in this way when faced with a situation that seems hopeless. But where the dominant group is a different color, there is an added permanence to the situation, a hopelessness that makes the occurrence of cultism more likely. The racial features of cultism are of the West's making; they have appeared in the Black Muslims because the Negro was rejected. They appear for the same reason in the new nation states. If there is no easing of world racial tensions, internal tensions will be more difficult to solve and cult-like behavior more likely to recur. The loyalty of national minorities in the United States and Britain may, in that case, be drawn on racial lines rather than national. The nightmare presented by the phrase "a line-up of rich white nations against poor non-white nations" would be succeeded by something worse—"a line-up of white persons against non-white."

Perhaps this is too crude and too gloomy a picture. In a recent essay, James Q. Wilson has pointed out that the Negro in politics can be effective with allies, but hardly in separate parties. Yet he adds, "the white liberal, in the eyes of Negro radicals, makes the fatal error of believing that meaningful change can be accomplished within the present political, social and economic system."[34] Most human beings are deeply ambivalent. Perhaps political behavior based on alliances within the present system is to be expected, even though there are increasing signs of "wanting out" in literature and thought and emotion. It would be unwise to ignore the almost invariable pattern of subordinate groups in other situations who at first "wanted in" but whose loving turned to hating before the superordinate were ready to receive them.

Perhaps in the international sphere, too, the nightmare is cruder than it need be—yet it is alarming. The defeat of Communism or the prevention of its spread is an objective of American and, to a lesser extent, British foreign policy. What is the assumption behind this? Although seldom formulated, it surely assumes that in the area thus saved there will be common standards of accepted international behavior—that, broadly speaking, the governments this side of the Iron Curtain will behave more and more like those of Scandinavia and Canada.

The trends observable by the student of race relations suggest that this is improbable. Associations with color and racism smear the positive aspects of Western ideals. There is wide agreement on certain objectives. Many governments have signed the Declaration of Human Rights, which proclaims a variety of liberties seldom enjoyed in the past, seldom enjoyed today. But even if governments paid them more lip service, a chill negative note about these liberties would still remain. They are the product of the Enlightenment and lead, at best, to the theoretical equality of *laissez-faire* liberalism. Such equality is not enough. Neglect and exploitation have to be succeeded not by equality but by benevolent discrimination. Until there is world government, this is unlikely to be forthcoming in a form and to a sufficient extent capable of modifying the resentments here described.

This is a depressing if realistic note to sound. It may well be that it hopelessly underestimates the vigor and optimism of the American people, their ability to manage their own affairs successfully and to give leadership to the world. Talcott Parsons has written:

Just as successful Negro inclusion will put the seal on the Marxian error in diagnosing American society, so the United States, with strong Negro participation, indeed leadership, has the opportunity to present a true alternative to the Communist pattern on a world-wide basis, one which is not bound to the stereotype of "capitalism."[35]

He is entirely right in linking the problems and stating the challenge. If the challenge is not successfully accepted, the dangers will be many.

REFERENCES

1. I understand that in Swahili the word *kalaba* ("color-bar") has come to mean any act of injustice or oppression.

2. In the twentieth century, assimilation ceased to be the official aim. To one who is not French, however, the new ideal does not seem very different.

3. Gunnar Myrdal, *An American Dilemma* (New York, 1944), p. li.

72

4. *Ibid.*

5. It does not really affect my argument if the Black Muslims have, in fact, passed their zenith. If the emotion they express is as important as I suspect, Elijah will find an Elisha.

6. Arnold Rose, "The American Problem in the Context of Social Change," *The Annals of the American Academy of Political and Social Science: The Negro Protest,* Vol. 357 (January, 1965), p. 5.

7. Jane Cassels Record and Wilson Record, "Ideological Forces and the Negro Protest," *ibid.,* p. 95.

8. Tilman C. Cothran, "The Negro Protest Against Segregation in the South," *ibid.,* p. 72.

9. *Ibid.*

10. Record and Record, *ibid.,* pp. 94-95.

11. Howard Brotz, *The Black Jews of Harlem* (New York, 1964).

12. C. Eric Lincoln, *Black Muslims* (Boston, 1961), p. 33.

13. *Ibid.,* p. 246.

14. Richard Wright, *Native Son* (New York, 1964), p. 109.

15. James Baldwin, *Notes of a Native Son* (London, 1964), p. 41.

16. Harold R. Isaacs, "Five Writers and Their African Ancestry," *Phylon,* Nos. 3 and 4 (1960).

17. V. S. Naipaul, *An Area of Darkness* (London, 1964).

18. Baldwin, *Notes of a Native Son,* p. 163.

19. Raymond Firth, "The Theory of Cargo Cults," *Man* (September, 1955).

20. Marion W. Smith, "Towards a Classification of Cult Movements," *Man* (January, 1959).

21. Peter Worsley, "Millenarian Cults in Melanesia," *Human Problems in Central Africa* (March, 1957).

22. For a Freudian explanation of this, see O. Mannoni, *La Psychologie de la Colonisation* (Paris, 1950); translated as *Prospero and Caliban* (London, 1956). The belief is reported from Tanganyika in the Maji rebellion, Matabeleland, Burma, New Guinea, Kenya, New Zealand.

23. W. M. Macmillan, *Bantu, Boer and Britain: The Making of the South African Native Problem* (London, 1929); or any South Africa history.

24. E. U. Essien-Udom, *Black Nationalism: A Search for an Identity in America* (Chicago, 1962), p. 334.

25. William A. Shack, "Black Muslims: A Nativistic Religious Movement Among Negro Americans," *Race* (November, 1961).

26. Malcolm Calley, *God's People: West Indian Pentecostal Sects in England* (London, 1965).

27. See, for instance, another poem by Aimé Césaire:

> Ma Négritude n'est pas une pierre, sa surdité
> ruée contre la clameur du jour
> ma Négritude n'est pas une taie d'eau
> morte sur l'oeil mort de la terre
> ma Négritude n'est ni une tour ni une cathédrale
> elle plonge dans la chair rouge du sol
> elle plonge dans la chair ardent du ciel

28. Julius Nyerere, "Ujamaa: The Basis of African Socialism," *Africa's Freedom* (London, 1964).

29. D. K. Chisiza, "The Outlook for Contemporary Africa," *Journal of Modern African Studies,* Vol. 1, No. 1 (1963).

30. Tom Mboya, *Freedom and After* (London, 1963).

31. See, for instance, Kwame Nkrumah's *Consciencism* (London, 1964), an attempt to supply Africa with just that new philosophical background of its own.

32. Frantz Fanon, *The Wretched of the Earth* (London, 1965), p. 172.

33. *Ibid.,* p. 35.

34. James Q. Wilson, "The Negro in Politics," *Dædalus,* Vol. 94, No. 4 (Fall, 1965), p. 963.

35. Talcott Parsons, "Full Citizenship for the Negro American? A Sociological Problem," *ibid.,* p. 1049.

HAROLD R. ISAACS

Group Identity and Political Change: The Role of Color
and Physical Characteristics

I

NOTHING MARKS a man's group identity more visibly or more permanently than the color of his skin and his physical characteristics.
Men have used these primary symbols of what has been called
"race" as a basis for their self-esteem or their lack of it. Skin color
has served as the badge of master and subject, of the enslaved and
the free, the dominators and the dominated. Of all the factors
involved in the great rearrangement of human relationships taking
place today, skin color is the most glandular. Hence none is more
sensitive, more psychologically explosive, or more intimately relevant to each individual's involvement in the process of political
change.

This matter of "race" has invested much of current political
change with its deepest kinds of emotional violence, a greater and
deeper and less easily appeased violence than one discovers or experiences in confrontations across lines that are more simply economic, social, or even cultural. It underlies the stronger passions
more commonly aroused in national collisions, especially where
these are also ethnic in character. Around it swirl all the rationalizations, self-deceptions, mythologies, and mystifications by which
men have patterned their stores of pride or debasement, of elevation or rejection of others or of self. It colors the images in which
men have made their gods.

By current political change I mean, to begin with, the great and
obvious ones—the shift from colony to nation, the collapse of the
power systems of the last two or three centuries, and the rise of
new ones at national, regional, and intercontinental levels. These
changes have brought or have begun to bring other less obvious
or less visible transformations in their wake. With the collapse of

the power structures came the collapse of the superstructures, mythologies, assumptions, and styles of behavior that had governed the patterns of relationships between groups of people within the power systems in the past. The plainest of these are the superiority-inferiority patterns of races and cultures and most especially the myth of white supremacy established and maintained during the era of Western white world dominance. Much that was "given" in these matters for so long has now been taken away; much of the present turmoil comes out of this disorderly re-ordering of human experience.

Under the pressure of these massive displacements, the relative place of virtually every group of people on earth has been shifting in some way. All the lights, angles, shadows, and reflections by which people see themselves or are seen by others have moved or are moving; all the postures and styles of behavior are ceasing to be what they were, and more or less convulsively becoming something else. In this kaleidoscopic process, color and physical characteristics have, of course, been highly visible, more so perhaps than much else that might be of equal or greater importance. Political and economic change is most heavily subject to considerations of geography, resources, technology, power, social organization. Nothing in this paper will suggest that the element of skin color or "race" is coequal with any of these in the determination of human affairs. But it is present in them all. It varies in importance, but is nowhere unimportant.

The "racial" mythologies built around differences in skin color and physical features were among the prime tools of power used in the era of the Western empires. Virtually all of the seventy-odd new nations carved out of these empires since 1945 represent transfers of political power from whites to non-whites. The end of the political system supporting the idea of white supremacy on a world scale inevitably forced the liquidation of that same idea as practiced in the United States. The "racial" issue has been central to the substantial changes that have taken place or begun to take place in the American society during this period.[1] The single element of color or "race" clearly never stands alone. Its place and relative importance can be fixed only by examining the particulars of every particular case; and the same goes for its relative place in the shifting patterns of the many group identities of people living through the experience of change. We know a great deal more about "race" than we did. Scientists have by now killed off the most egregious myths built up around it. But these myths, though demolished in the scientific journals, remain largely intact in the actuality of everyday life among great masses of people and still govern much human behavior. They continue to figure in major ways in all current affairs and will clearly continue to do so for quite some time. Most broadly seen there are two such ways: The first is the great ongoing rearrangement of mutual attitudes and behavior between whites and non-whites. The second, coming much more newly into view, is the appearance of tensions and conflict between and among non-whites of many different kinds.

II

The first presents the vastly complicated business of liquidating or at least mitigating or converting the legacy of the two or three centuries just past. This involves working out the terms on which whites and non-whites are to live with each other in a world where the power to maintain white supremacy has disappeared but where its remnants and its effects will persist for a long time to come. Rear-guard battles for the maintenance of white supremacy will go on for quite a while in places like South Africa and Rhodesia and in parts of the American South. The issue will also flare up in new ways, as it has in northern cities in the United States, where ghetto tensions aggravated by the uneven pace of change have produced riots and the confrontation of black- and white-racist extremisms, as well as the broader and more complicated emotions of the so-called "blacklash," the resistance of unreconstructed whites to the pressure of newly-emancipated Negroes. The issue may flare up in new places, as it has in England, where a virulent white racism has appeared among lower-class Englishmen who face for the first time substantial numbers of non-white immigrants on their home ground. This "new" phenomenon has been marked by violent collisions in English cities, the emergence of white-racist extremist groups, and the injection of the race issue into British politics. It replaces the older and more genteel kinds of racism that could be practiced by middle- and upper-class Englishmen in the past days of British power when they totally controlled the conditions of the encounters with non-whites, whether they were dealing with small numbers of transient colonials at home or with the larger masses of colonial subjects at a great distance.

The "racial" issue carried over from the past remains a potent weapon in the continuing world-power conflict, as its use by Communist China shows. It adds all kinds of imponderables to a future already quite sufficiently clouded by other grim possibilities. These carry-overs and new consequences make the burden heavier and more complicated, but even without them, it would be foolish to think that this great re-adjustment in human affairs could take place without great pain and spasms of violence.

The political underpinnings for the practice of white racism can be bulldozed away rather quickly, as the abrupt collapse of most of the colonial system has showed. Legal support for it can be soon liquidated, even with deliberate speed, as the experience in the United States during the last ten years has proved. These are great changes in themselves, sufficient to transform social situations and to create wholly new conditions in the lives of individuals. Still, much else waits to be more slowly transformed. Whites have to lose the habits of mastery. Non-whites have to lose the habits of subjection. These are deeply imbedded not only in each individual but in the economy, in the society, in the whole culture. The gap between white and non-white is also in great measure a gap between have and have-not. Indeed, as the history of empire and the slave trade shows, racial mythologies were first used largely to help create, widen, maintain, and rationalize this gap. It will not be quickly or easily closed, as everyone now knows who has had any contact with the intractable problems of development in the former colonies or the hardly less formidable problems of overcoming poverty at the lower levels of American and other Western societies.

But the gap is not economic alone. The habits of mind created by this long history of mastery and subjection are part of the culture itself in all its many manifestations. Conscious and unremitting effort will be needed to free the culture of the many gross and subtle ways in which it has shaped whites and non-whites to these patterns. This effort begins in the political, legal, and economic systems, but then must move into society's educational systems and religious establishments, its great bodies of sacred and profane literature, folklores, and languages and vernaculars. Social mechanisms are only now beginning to bend themselves to this effort—more so in the United States today than anywhere else in the world. Meanwhile, all the great numbers of individuals formed by this culture must live through this time of change, each one experiencing it in his own acutely personal way, each one bruised or cut or wounded, terrified or enraged, by the jagged edges of a social order being torn apart. The old order of things produced its sets of deformities; the process of correction produces its own. These may give way in due course to some more commonly tolerable condition for all—a world in which people will hate or despise one another for different or less idiotic reasons. But right now and for some unpredictable length of time, whites and non-whites will be suffering from all kinds of astigmatic distortions as they struggle to refocus their views of themselves and of others.

Among the whites, there are rear-guard racist diehards or, much more numerously, members of the great generality of people who share the common mindsets and behavior patterns of their culture and will not easily abandon or change them. Some may fight desperately to hold on to the receding power of their whiteness. Many more cling passively to the belief that their whiteness is superior. Still others insist on preserving their own tribal separatenesses. As between former white imperial master and non-white colonial subject, the nationalist overturns have, of course, produced this separateness, at least for the latter; the migration of non-whites to post-imperial England has created one of the "new" situations in which white separateness becomes an issue in a place where it never had come into question before. Just how "whiteness" may serve as a basis for a separate group identity in some future pluralism remains to be seen. What is clear now is that it will not again be possible—certainly not in the American society—to maintain white privilege by denying non-whites their share of the common rights of all. It is an irony worth noting that while American democratic ideology is at long last imposing itself on white tribalism in America, the same kind of white tribalist behavior is breaking again and again in Communist Russia and other European Communist countries through the restraining façade of Communist ideology. In Communist theory, any kind of racism is, like anti-Semitism and other oppression of minorities, a social disease produced only by exposure to capitalist exploitation. In Communist fact, white-racist behavior, like anti-Semitism and all kinds of restraints on minorities, has become embarrassingly visible, especially in the friction between local whites and non-whites—particularly African students and, by Peking allegations, also Chinese. Without either minimizing American or Western-European white tribalism or exaggerating the Russian, it will obviously take some time before white people generally come more fully to terms with the new non-supreme terms of their whiteness.

On the other hand, it may be even harder for non-whites to get used to the new non-subordinate status of their non-whiteness. Great numbers of the present adult generation of non-whites are products of their long history of subjection to whites. The characteristic pattern has been one of internalization of all the downgrading or debasement of their kind, especially among those who had moved up as far as they could toward the levels occupied by their white masters. They have in one degree or another accepted the white world's image of them, defending themselves against it through devices of imitation or attempted assimilation, of weakness or dependency, or—in fewer cases—through the passions of a counter-racism. These styles of coping with adverse circumstances were built into their lives from their earliest breathing moments. Many political and economic factors came into play in the re-making of these relationships, but it was this condition of mind and spirit among the subject peoples that had to be somehow transmuted and overcome in the nationalist movements of the last forty years or so and in their counterpart in the much older protest movement among Negroes in the United States. These struggles were waged primarily in the political arena, but were all accompanied by some form of defensive counter-self-assertion of pride in the more remote past, in the nation, in culture, in "race."

Among black men, this has taken the form of the effort, mainly made by Negro American writers and scholars, to re-establish the black man's history, always accompanied, as in the work of W.E.B. DuBois, by the theme of reassertion of respect for one's own blackness or Negro-ness. The flame of militant "blackism" or "black nationalism" has flickered for a long time at the edges of the Negro rights struggle. It has flared up when fueled by great frustration, as in the Garvey movement of the 1920's or in the more recent Black Muslim movement. Banked and smothered when hope for a more successful American pluralist solution rises, it emerges as this hope wanes. The unbearable slowness with which things move produces despair as it has currently among those who cry for "black power" or turn to insensate violence. Perhaps the most explicitly racialist of all these counter-assertions was the idea of *négritude* born in the work of Aimé Cesaire, a black poet of Martinique, who sought to raise and arouse the self-esteem of black men by telling them that there were mystically universal characteristics, connected with joy and beauty, in blackness itself. A less poetic version, much more politically conceived, was advanced by Kwame Nkrumah, an American-educated, British African politician who raised the slogan of an "African personality" to promote a new unity among black men.

For the Negro American (and, in varying degrees, for black men elsewhere) the element of color and physical characteristics remains the core of a deep and profound group identity crisis. It was precisely around the Negro's blackness and his Negroidness that the white world built up its rationale for reducing him to a less-than-human status. Around these characteristics, too, the black man built up his own ways of surviving, submitting, and resisting. In all its aspects this mutual process was woven into the fabric of our culture and into the personality-types it helped to create. Ripping it out or reweaving it has become part of the major new business of our time, and it is proceeding vigorously, at least in the American society. Ceasing to be the subhuman the white man made him has become the Negro's new business, and the white man's new business has become ceasing to be the superman that his subjection of the Negro allowed him to think he was.[2]

Among whites and non-whites alike, the present adult generation was raised largely on the old terms of conditioned relationship, has gone through the experiences of the power shift that has produced such great changes in the last decade or so, and is now struggling to see itself in new terms in the new setting. Just behind it is a newer generation of younger adults who have been seeing themselves in all the years of their growth in these revised or partially-revised conditions, but who still live in a world that is not yet all new or wholly of their making. Coming up now in their teens and twenties are young people who have never known anything but the present environment of kaleidoscopic change. Children are being born who will come up into a world in which they will discover themselves in some new way from the very beginning of their lives. The terms of a new kind of relationship between white and non-white are being drawn. What their shape might be and what they might become from place to place, no one can yet clearly see, for too much besides color or "race" is involved in any such projection.

Of all the "new" racial situations created by the new politics, one of the most striking and possibly the least foreseen has come about in Israel. Israel itself presents one of the more remarkable examples of the interaction of political change and group identity. Jews are attempting in the most explicitly political way—by creating their own state—to erase their marginality and outsider-ness. They are seeking to give unambiguous national form to the ambiguities and varieties of the Jewish identity as it was shaped during twenty centuries of dispersion throughout the world. For Jews in Israel as well as for Jews everywhere, the question of questions has become: Who and what is a Jew? The answer bears on the Jew's culture, history, and nationality. If this were all, it would have been more than sufficient. To an unforeseen degree, however, in Israel it also bears on his color and physical characteristics.

The flow of Jews into Israel, about a million and a half in the last twenty years, has come in two main streams, the first from eastern and central Europe, the second from the West Asian or North African countries—Yemen, Iraq, Egypt, Morocco, Tunisia, Algeria, Tripolitania. The people of these two streams, the "Western" or "European" and the "Eastern" or "Oriental," are now approximately equal in number in Israel's present population. This is what has begun to be called "the two Israels." Many consider that it raises the most critical of the formidable problems the new Jewish state faces. It carries with it the most decisive implications not only for what kind of cultural being but also what kind of physical being the *Israeli* is going to be.

Under the mantle of a largely-undefined common "Jewishness," in a tiny, crowded land facing all the tasks of rapid development under conditions of constant external threat, there is now a confrontation that sweeps out widely from the more specifically Jewish division between *Ashkenazi* and *Sephardi,* and becomes an encounter between European and non-European, Western and Eastern, modern and traditional, industrialized and non-industrialized, skilled and unskilled, educated and uneducated—and also "white" and "non-white." As anyone who stands on a street of an Israeli city can observe, the ingathering of the long-wandering tribes of Israel has dramatically shown the extent to which Jews have become not only the cultural but also the physical products of the cultures in which they lived as "outsiders" for so long. The European Jews appear in all the ethnic varieties of Europeans, and "Oriental" Jews appear in all the shades of "whiteness" to "semi-whiteness" to "non-whiteness" of skin common among the people of the countries in which they lived. Jews seeking to regain homogeneity in Israel now not only have to bridge all the great differences of culture and civilization that separate peoples of industrialized and non-industrialized societies, but also have to close the gap of color. These cultural and "racial" differences among Jews will have a large and perhaps critical role in all Israeli affairs. Unless they are blunted and ultimately resolved by some new synthesis, some new process of mutual accommodation and absorption, they could generate painful and perhaps destructive tensions and conflicts in Israeli society. Assuming the best of all possible outcomes, the successful integration of the "two Israels" will mean the emergence of Israel's own kind of modernized society. It will also have to mean, as the generations pass, the effective intermingling of these different ethnic strains. Out of this will come an Israeli who will be not only some different kind of Jew, but also a different physical type, a remingling of whatever it was that Jews retained or acquired during their long sojourns among others. This will make Israelis a very different kind of people indeed from, for example, the other great mass of Jews pursuing *their* own distinctive development in the United States.

III

In a memorable cartoon some years ago, Peter Arno drew a drunk pounding his fist on a bar and proclaiming: "I hate *everybody*, regardless of race, creed, or color!" This was brought to mind by a passage in a newspaper article soon after the June 1965 coup in Algiers:

The Egyptians saw the Algerians as somewhat boorish upstarts who lacked national traditions. "If I had known what these people were like," said an Egyptian doctor working in Oran to a friend recently, "I would have been against their independence." Algerians, for their part, spoke privately of Egyptians as haughty and overbearing.[3]

This mutual view among "friends" illustrates again that neither kinship nor common creed nor ideological or political bonds can keep people from despising one another. Besides being full of venom against the ex-dominant Europeans, lighter-skinned Algerians and lighter-skinned Egyptians also share feelings of superiority over their darker-skinned compatriots and, by all accounts, something closer to contempt for their black African counterparts south of the Sahara. In isolating here some of the evidences of the "new" upcroppings of "racial" antipathies, I do not mean to suggest that "racial" differences are the only or even the main reasons for the general absence of brotherly love, but simply to point out that they are also present and have their own peculiar and important part in this common human condition.

What is "new" or, rather, newly apparent is the extent to which the "race" or color issue has shown its presence in the "non-white" world. It appears with varying intensity along the entire color spectrum, among all shades of men who have attached values to "lightness" and "darkness" of skin in almost every culture and place. These attitudes were submerged for a long time in the common subordination of all non-whites to the whites. Now that non-whites have regained political power and the mantle of white supremacy has been removed, many of these older designs are coming into view again, either in the forms they had long possessed or in new forms created by the new circumstances. We are becoming more and more aware of the many ways in which people outraged by the superiority patterns imposed on them by the whites now impose similarly based (or baseless) patterns of their own on the many shades of color differences among themselves.

This is partly a legacy from the era of white domination, though just how large a part, it is difficult to say. Submission to total white power led people of many different kinds to internalize, to accept as true the myths of white superiority. In sections of virtually every society and culture over which white men made themselves masters during the last two or three hundred years, non-white people adopted the going "white" standards of beauty and value. This "yearning after whiteness" produced color-caste systems with whiteness or lightness at the top and blackness or darkness at the bottom. Although black men in the Americas were perhaps most deeply damaged by this process, they shared its deformities with people in every part of the world where white domination was practiced in its various styles by the aloof British, the more supple French, the tepidly paternalistic Dutch, and the remarkably literal Spanish. The colonial color bar generally operated through strong but informally maintained codes, but in Spain's colonies the higher status of whiteness was doled out in precise degrees by law, with explicit distinctions in the legal rights assigned to each fractional measure of whiteness. The half-castes or mixed bloods rose to a unique degree to the top of the local colonial social scale in Spain's dominions, including the Philippines. They fell just under the pure Spaniards (locally born and home born, in that order) instead of falling into the limbo that mixed-bloods came to occupy in the colonies of Britain, France, and, to a slightly less extent, Holland.

In all its forms, the weight of this part of the legacy of European rule lies heavily on all ex-colonial societies today. The "yearning after whiteness" that stems from the era of white domination persists in the form of color-caste attitudes still strongly held by people in the ex-colonies, not only among the elite but among the masses as well. This makes it relatively easy for some ex-colonial subjects to hold white ex-rulers responsible for the patterns of racialism that have now come into view among them.

This view is more valid in some instances than in others. Among Filipinos, for example, there is an almost obsessive preoccupation with color and physical characteristics. It appears in almost every aspect of everyday family life, in dating and mating, in the raising of children, and at every point of contact between people of varying groups and kinds in the population. The most relevant words and a long string of vernacular equivalents or variations crop up with great frequency: fair-skinned, dark-skinned, high nose, low nose, "chinky eyes." Where this preoccupation fits into the patterns of Filipino group identity is not easily or precisely fixed. Bits of evidence suggest the presence long ago of high value on light skin color among the brown-skinned Malay peoples from whom the modern Filipinos are derived. This is now laced into a fine and complex mesh, into all the ways Filipinos have of perceiving their ethnic and cultural mixes—their Malay, Chinese, Spanish, and American layerings—and the ways in which these get expressed in their regionalisms, social relations, languages, religion, national consciousness, and political style. Filipinos inherit their attitudes about skin color from every part of their past. These attitudes are incorporated in what they have become and must be included in whatever definition they will now make of the meaning of being Filipino.

In quite a different form, the responsibility of the colonial rulers for new racial conflicts in some ex-colonies is especially plain in situations the Europeans actually created in the first place. One example is the confrontation in Malaysia between Malays and Chinese, most of whom are there because Chinese were brought in as contract laborers to work in British mines. Another is the collision in Guyana between descendants of Africans brought to the colony in British slave ships and descendants of East Indians brought in, also by the British, as indentured laborers. Similar or related examples of European-created situations can be found in Trinidad and Fiji, and in African countries like Sierra Leone or Gambia, where Creole minorities have become the new ruling classes over masses still mainly black.

Valid as it may be in many instances, the charge of European white responsibility for current racial patterns in the ex-colonies is valid only up to a point. In many places, this point is quickly reached. The white imperialists did raise the value of white over dark, but they rarely created the value in the first place. They exploited antagonisms based on differences of color and kind; they did not originate them. It is convenient to hold the ousted white imperialists responsible for it all, and it is never wholly false to do so; nor is it ever wholly true, and sometimes it has nothing to do with the truth at all. It often tends to be the self-punitive view of white liberals overburdened with guilt for the sins of their colonialist fathers or the self-aggrandizing view of ex-colonial subjects. It is a way of converting the less-than-human into more-than-human. The guilty white liberal is only too glad to assign all virtue to the oppressed; the oppressed is usually only too ready to accept this gratuitously offered halo. The Asian or African nationalist was often glad to see himself not only as winning power back from the Europeans but also as restoring the human spirit to the higher levels from which only European malevolence had cast his people down. Great struggles were waged and sacrifices made in the name of this belief or this pretense. It has been difficult to maintain, however, in what has followed. Both Asian and African nationalism adopted the ideas or at least the rhetoric of European liberal or radical humanism. The "freedom" won turned out to be something considerably less than freedom in the political sphere, while in the "racial" sphere it has often meant, as Frantz Fanon mournfully acknowledged, displacement of European white racism by a non-European non-white racism. This is a matter still too little explored by too many, but there is much to indicate that unmistakable patterns of what we would call "racialism," and especially attitudes about skin color, formed part of many of these cultures long before their exposure to the power of the conquering white Europeans.

In Africa only some of these new outlines are now dimly seen. Two main "new" patterns of relationship come into view. One appears in black Africa itself among the many tribes of people who live south of the Sahara; the other lies between the people of black Africa and non-black or Arab Africa north of the Sahara.

In black Africa people are divided into a multitude of tribes clustered in several large groups, some marked off by language types, some by physical differences. For a long time the main business of modernization in Africa is going to be bringing these groups into some new kind of coherence based on new political and economic development. This is going to be a complex and formidable undertaking for tribal divisions exist within each of black Africa's thirty-five new nation-states and cut across the new national boundaries. The friction can be explosive, as eruptions of conflict have shown in the Congo, in Ruanda and Burundi, in Somalia, Kenya, and Uganda.

The differences are heavily matters of geography, culture, history, levels of development, and social organization, all coming under the pressure of the new national and international politics. At certain points, tribal differences are also physical, sometimes spectacularly so, as in the case of the tall Hamitic Watusi and the shorter Bantu Bahutu who engaged in some massively bloody clashes in late 1963 and 1964, fighting and raiding across the borders of several newly-created states. There are differences of color and feature, from brown to black, from Hamitic aquilinity (in which the Ethiopians, like the Watusi, take such haughty pride) to Negroid broadness in which there are also variations. We are still vastly ignorant about the quantity and quality of these differences and will have to wait to learn more both about their nature and their impact on the new history of emergent Africa as it unfolds.

The new relations coming into being between black Africans south of the Sahara and non-black Africans north of it are somewhat more visible. Between these there are at least one strong link and at least one deep chasm. The link is Islam, the religion of Northern Africa and of perhaps as much as a third of the black population in the South. The chasm is deeply cleft and no easier to cross than the Sahara; it is the historic memory of Arab enslavement of black men, an activity in which Arabs, Berbers, and others of the North were engaged long before they had to begin sharing their profits with the slavers arriving later from Europe. Both of these elements in North-South African relationships have come strikingly into view in the recent new politics of the continent. Nasser's abortive bid to shape and lead a new pan-Africanism was at least partly based on the appeal to a new and greater Islam— including the claim that Islam's professions of brotherhood among men are more fully practiced than Christianity's. Pan-Africanism itself, in all its mooted shapes, has stumbled upon regional, national, and tribal divisions in the new Africa; Nasser's pretensions in particular have stumbled upon the contrary pretensions of other African leaders. Just how Islamic influence will come to bear in the reshaping of emergent Africa remains to be seen.

Meanwhile, the Arab past in black Africa has been most directly invoked in the process of countering Nasser and of keeping Arab influence in general at desirable distance. Moise Tshombe provided possibly the bluntest example of this after his humiliation in Cairo. Following Nasser's refusal to let him attend a conference of African leaders in October 1964, Tshombe mobilized powerful emotional support from crowds of cheering Congolese in Leopold- ville by reminding them that the Arabs had been slavers before and would now become slavers in new form if black men allowed them to be. He staged a show in a stadium in which a band of "Egyptians" raided a village, beat the women, shot some of the men and tied the rest to a long rope by which they were led forth. At this point a Congolese army came dashing in to the rescue, slaying all the "Egyptians" and freeing the slaves. "The real Africa is our Africa, black Africa," shouted Tshombe to the crowd. "We are the Africans of Africa, not the Arabs."[4] The same deeply-imbedded emotions also surfaced last year in the Sudan. Light-skinned Arab Moslem pro-Egyptian northerners used pitiless force to crush a rebellion of the black non-Moslem southern Suda- nese minority. A report from Khartoum observed that the insur- rection, whose "root cause is racial, has pitted African against Arab, reviving the deep racial hatreds of the Arab slave trade among the Negro peoples of the southern Sudan a century ago."[5]

The late Frantz Fanon, a Martinique black man and French- educated psychoanalyst who joined the Algerian war against the French and became one of its most eloquent tribunes, wrote in 1961 with a certain anguish of the "commonest racial feelings" he found among Algerians and Arabs, proud of their "thousand-year- old tradition of culture" while "Black Africa is looked upon as a region that is inert, brutal, uncivilized, in a word, savage" and black men as a people who are "impervious to logic." In what he called "white Africa," meaning Arab Africa, he wrote, black men were insulted by being called "Negro" by children in the streets while African students suffered various embarrassments at the hands of their Arab hosts. Meanwhile, in many of the new states of black Africa itself, wrote this passionate black revolutionist, "from nationalism we have passed to ultra-nationalism, to chauvinism, and finally to racism." The new leaders, whom he scorned as "bourgeois," and the new governing parties were in many places "falling back toward old tribal attitudes, and, furious and sick at heart, we perceive that race feeling in its most exacerbated form is triumphing."[6]

The new chapter in the story of racism that is being written in Africa has only just opened. The same newness marks the relationships just beginning between black men, whether African or other, and other non-whites elsewhere in the world. On this score, it now seems somberly reasonable to predict that color will continue to be a more critical factor for the black man than for any other kind.

Peoples in Asia had varying kinds of experience with white domination. India and most of the countries of Southeast Asia became colonies of Europe, China was semicolonized, and Japan never colonized at all. The Chinese met the arriving Western white man with an attitude of disdainful superiority and the Japanese met him with contemptuous hostility; they both went through the experience of subjection or subordination to white power or white superiority as a galling ordeal. In India, much more fragmented and with a much less coherent sense of any common history or identity among its many peoples, the response was much weaker and more ambivalent. In every case, however, where responses to Westerners took place in racial terms, they were superimposed upon strongly-rooted attitudes about race and skin color that long antedated this encounter. These included powerful race chauvinism, like those of the Chinese and Japanese, social and caste differences accompanied by color differences, as in India, and—almost universally—notions of beauty linked to whiteness or lightness of skin.

The Chinese were beaten into submission by Westerners in the nineteenth century. As a result many Chinese did to some degree accept the white man's view of white superiority, especially in the matter of military power. Only a few Chinese accepted the Western religion that this power supported, but toward the end of the century many modernizing intellectuals did embrace Western social and political ideas in a belated effort to catch up with Western advances. But even while they submitted and sought to emulate, most Chinese retained their great self-pride, rooted in their sense of race and culture, in their identification with a long and great past. Almost alone, indeed, this sustained them during the century and a half of their humiliating subordination to Western barbarians. It burst forth again with explosive vigor when the time finally arrived for Chinese self-reassertion in the revolutionary upheavals of the last few decades.

The Japanese, for their part, reacting more convulsively to the first Western blows a century ago, moved much more quickly than the Chinese to acquire a countervailing power of their own. Their first great success against the West, their defeat of Russia in 1905, was not only a major event in the history of the struggle for power in Asia but also a great turning point in the hitherto one-sided contest between white and non-white, and it was clearly and explicitly seen as such throughout the white-dominated world. Before the Japanese were through, they nearly succeeded in conquering China and replacing the West's empires in Asia with their own. In the course of this effort, they used the racial theme to the full, both in appealing to their fellow "Asiatics" and in depicting Westerners, especially Americans, as white racists under whom no one in Asia could live a self-respecting life. The Japanese offered instead what they proved quite unable to deliver: a self-respecting life under the aegis of Japan. They failed at this, in part at least, because they could not help trying to become the master race of Asia themselves. This Japanese drive was defeated, and the Japanese thrust for self-assertion had to begin all over again and to seek new forms. The Japanese bring to this process a view of themselves and of others that is rooted no less deeply than that of the Chinese in physical as well as historical and cultural self-images.[7]

When Japan fell, it became China's turn at last to seek once more through its new and aggressive Communist regime to erase all the humiliations the Chinese had suffered at the hands of the West for so long. Behind the high and wild emotional drive of this Chinese self-assertion, it is necessary to see the whole history of Western white behavior in China during the last hundred and fifty years. But in looking for its sources, one also has to look beyond this history into the deep pools of Chinese cultural and racial chauvinism.

The strong belief in the superiority of the race of Han and the view of all non-Chinese as "barbarians" are well-known features of the standard Chinese self-image. They go back to the remotest antiquity. "I have heard of making Chinese out of barbarians," said the great sage Mencius nearly 2,500 years ago, "but I have never heard of making barbarians out of Chinese." From those most ancient times, Chinese terms for non-Chinese of almost any kind were characteristically derogatory. They almost always either referred to some physical characteristic or attributed to non-Chinese some beast-like character or non-human origin.

Virtually all non-Chinese were *kuei-tze*, "ghosts" or "devils," inhabitants of the nether world beyond and below China where civilized human beings dwelled. Peoples around the fringes of ancient China were usually described by words representing animals—foxes, wildcats, wolves, apes, and varieties of insects. *Hsiung-nu*, the name for the "Huns" beyond northern China's borders, means literally something to do with slaves, but a history of the Wei period also tells us that the *Hsiung-nu* were the result of the union of a barbarian chieftain's daughter and an old wolf. "That is why," the *History of Wei* goes on to explain, "these people like to stretch their necks and utter long cries, like wolves howling." The Turks are similarly recorded as the outcome of a union between a female wolf and a young boy.

Skin color rarely appears among these descriptions, but does figure sharply in passages about the *"kun-lun* slaves" brought to China by the wide ranging Chinese traders from islands in the southern seas during the Tang and Sung dynasties. Usually called "'devil slaves" or "black devils," they were apparently seen more as beasts than as humans. In the nineteenth century, the "black devils" reappear in the shape of Indian troops brought in by the invading British. Chinese writers of the time describe the English as the "green-eyed devils"—like the fiercest and most evil of the dragons of the spirit world—and their "slave soldiers" as "black devils." "The white ones were cold and dull as the dead ashes of frogs," wrote a poet, "the black ones were ugly and dirty as coal."

How and when the Chinese were introduced to the European idea that they were members of the "yellow race" and how they

91

received the news are all matters still apparently waiting a closer look at the relevant literature of the past century or so. Much waits to be found, as a letter written by a Chinese scholar in the closing years of the Manchu dynasty indicates:

Of the five colors, yellow is the color of the soil, and the soil is the core of the universe. Westerners identify Chinese as a yellow race. This implies that from the beginning, when heaven and earth were created, the Chinese were given the central place. When Westerners laugh at Chinese egotism, why can we not explain it by this reasoning?[8]

In the Chinese classical tradition—as in the Japanese that so largely stemmed from it—the celebration of whiteness as a criterion of feminine beauty is a familiar theme. A poet of the fourth century B.C. celebrated a bevy of beauties for their "black-painted eyebrows and white-powdered cheeks." Of Yang Kuei-fei, the most celebrated beauty in Chinese history, the Tang poet Po Chu-i wrote: "So white her skin, so sweet her face / None could with her compare." Hands and arms of "dazzling white" move gracefully through endless reams of ancient Chinese poetry. The most common metaphor for feminine skin was white jade, and references to all the visible surfaces of jade-colored female skin abound in poets' songs. Chinese folk songs are similarly filled with the whiteness of generations of beloveds: "My sweetheart is like a flower," sings one, "Please, do not let the sun burn her black." In story after story Chinese writers of the 1940's were still quivering at the "snow-white" or "pure white" necks and arms of their heroines.[9] There is some evidence that these standards have prevailed not only among effete upper-class Chinese but among rude villagers as well.[10]

Although Chinese racial and cultural chauvinism is a well-known fact, its particulars have been little studied. It has always figured in the long and complex history of Chinese relations with non-Chinese peoples within China itself, continuing into the present Communist era. Chinese overseas have intermarried freely with many other kinds of people but not without creating certain strains or areas of separateness between mixed Chinese and the unmixed, a condition not difficult to discover in places like Hawaii and the Philippines.

Some suggestion of the Chinese style in these matters turns up in their vocabulary in conflict situations. In the conflict between Chinese and Malays in Malaysia, for example, the racial issue—

and any expression of it bearing on skin color, in particular—is quite marginal compared to the cultural, historical, economic, and political issues that lie between the two groups. But even so the powerful and highly chauvinistic Chinese cultural self-image reinforces itself by views of others expressed, as Chinese feelings so often are, in physical terms. While the most common local Chinese term for Malays is probably *malai-kwai* or "Malay devils," another common one is *bla-chan*, literally a "prawn paste," a way of referring to the Malays as "brown" with the additional suggestion of dark and unattractive. The Chinese term for Indians in Malaysia is *tousee-kwai*, *tousee* meaning a kind of black bean, the literal rendering thus becoming "black bean devils." This is like a Shanghai term for Indians, *hei-tan*, which means simply "black coal." The common Malay vernacular retorts to the Chinese in kind, its word for the Chinese being *mata-sepek*, which means "slit-eyes."

Chinese racial attitudes have come into public or semipublic view only rarely, as they did in 1945 when Chiang Kai-shek's government in Chungking tried to keep Negro American troops from entering China over the Burma Road which they had just done more than anybody else to reopen. Much more recently, an African student in Peking has described Communist Chinese mentors as filled with "the idea of the superiority of Yellow over Black."[11] On the larger scene of the Sino-Soviet conflict in recent years, the Chinese Communists have made strenuous efforts to win friends among Asians, Africans, and Latin Americans by stressing the solidarity of non-whites against whites. In public print, this has always been done by euphemism, the Chinese stressing the "European" character of the Russians in order to keep them out of all-Asian or Afro-Asian enterprises. In their corridor politicking, they have been described as using the racial theme bluntly and crudely in their attempt to win friends for themselves and to alienate others from their Russian foes. There has been some impression but little information about the extent to which their own racial behavior has helped to defeat these Chinese efforts, especially among Africans. Chinese Communist propaganda in general now bestows on Americans all the beast-like features traditionally attributed to all barbarians. They are the offspring of wolves, like the *Hsiung-nu* of long ago, and like the early-arriving Portuguese explorers of four centuries ago, they are depicted as devourers of children.[12]

In India, skin-color attitudes are almost pervasively present in

93

the contemporary culture. They can be traced all the way back to Indian prehistory, to the relationships said to have been established between light-skinned conquerors (the "Aryas") and the dark-skinned inhabitants of the country (the "Dasyas"). These attitudes, identified with the shaping of the Hindu society over the millennia, persist today in the entwining of color with caste. The Sanskrit word for the large caste groups, *varna*, means color, and the word *caste*, from the Latin via the Portuguese, means purity connected with biological lineage, or something very close to and including color. In classical Hindu texts there is an association of colors with the main caste groups—white with the Brahmins at the top, black with the Sudras at the bottom, red or bronze and yellow with the middle groups of Kshatriya and Vaishya. Although there is much denial that these assignments of color values bear directly on skin color as such, there is enough in the past and present actuality of Hindu society to make it plain that skin color is related in important ways to hierarchies of status in the Hindu system.[13]

Although mountains of literature have been produced about Hindu caste, this aspect of it has not been overstudied. Some modern Indian writers argue heavily against the presence of color implications in the caste system without being able to make the fact of color caste in Indian society go away. Highly explicit color values are found in the elaborate criteria that figure in beauty standards and marriage preferences—as anyone can discover any week in any Indian newspaper's matrimonial advertisements—and other choices, relations, and attitudes along the spectrum that shades from the light-skinned northerners to the still-dark-skinned southerners.

These values, vivid in Indian life, have of course been reflected in some of the new relationships created by recent political change. Indian attitudes about color have obviously had much to do with relations between Indian and Africans in Africa. These might be seen, again, as a product of European-created circumstances in which Indians (particularly in Kenya, Uganda, and South Africa) occupied the position of middlemen-traders sandwiched between the ruling whites and the ruled blacks. They naturally identified themselves as far as they could with the dominant whites keeping as detached as possible from the lowly blacks. Gandhi began his life's struggle in South Africa, but it was a struggle to win rights for the Indians there, not for the blacks.

In the past decade, Indian-African antagonisms, rooted in their economic relations, have more than once erupted into violence, mostly in the form of African attacks on Indians. Indians, for their part, have been attempting in these recent years to find common political ground and greater acceptance among Africans, not only among those who have now gained power, as in East Africa, but among those who are still far from doing so, as in South Africa. These efforts have had very limited success. The new nationalist India, intent on winning and influencing African friends, has extended facilities including scholarships to African students for study in India. In India, unhappily, many of them have encountered the Indian color system in which the dark-skinned person is held in the least esteem and the black person in no esteem at all. This, too, has erupted embarrassingly into print. As far back as 1955 a group of African students in New Delhi publicly complained that they had found "the prejudice of Indians almost as bad as that of South African Europeans."[14] These complaints touched off a flurry of mortified and deeply-felt disclaimers and explanations from their Indian hosts.

India's 65,000,000 Untouchables—or, legally, ex-Untouchables—have their own share of these common patterns of Indian color differences and attitudes. Through their experience of recent change,[15] India's color patterns are irregularly sliced. Untouchables are commonly thought to be darker than most other Indians. This is reflected in some of the terms used by caste Hindus to describe Untouchables, the most mortifying ones employed in Kerala, for example, being *karumpan,* "black fellow," or *karumpi,* "black girl." Although more Untouchables may be darker than lighter in color, there are also black or near-black Brahmin or other caste Hindu southerners, and lighter brown Untouchable northerners. A popular folk rhyme dealing with personality attributes of different groups of people includes the following lines: "Beware of a black colored Brahmin and the white colored Chamar (Untouchable leather worker); they can only be handled with shoe in hand"—meaning that they only understand a forceful or threatening attitude. The implication, according to one explanation, is that the transposed skin colors in these castes came about only through bastard birth and that bastards are always crooked and need punishment. The extent to which the line of pollution and Untouchability in India is a color line is, like almost everything else in the Hindu setting, unclear and ambiguous.

These examples could be multiplied almost indefinitely. About each one much waits to be learned of what is past, much needs to be more closely scrutinized in the present. At the very least, they suggest that the issues of "race" and color among men have not been reduced as a source of conflict, only shifted to new places on the crowded stage of current affairs. Every individual, wherever he may be located on this chaotic landscape, has to shape or re-shape his sense of the content and meaning of his identification with his primary group, the group in which he finds himself by virtue of where, when, and to whom he is born. In this set of his identifications, his "race" or the color of his skin will continue to have special meaning to him and to all to whom he relates. Neither homogenization nor the brotherhood of men being in near view, the minimum conclusion is that racial and color differences will continue to figure, more often abrasively than not, in the re-shaping of political and social patterns and relationships that will go on during the remaining years of this century and beyond it into the next.

REFERENCES

1. The relationship between world affairs and race relations in the United States is examined at some length in the opening section of Harold R. Isaacs, *The New World of Negro Americans* (New York, 1963).

2. The complexities and particulars of this are endless. I have examined some of them at some length in *Emergent Americans, a Report on Crossroads Africa* (New York, 1961); *The New World of Negro Americans.* See also "Blackness and Whiteness," *Encounter* (July, 1963); "The Changing Identity of the Negro American," *The Urban Condition* (New York, 1963).

3. *The New York Times,* June 30, 1965.

4. *The New York Times,* October 20, 1964.

5. *The New York Times,* November 22, 1964.

6. Frantz Fanon, *The Wretched of the Earth* (New York, 1965), pp. 127-28, 131.

7. See Hiroshi Wagatsuma's paper, "The Social Perception of Skin Color in Japan," in this volume of *Dædalus.*

8. For this and other citations relating to the Chinese, I am indebted to Mr. Alan P. L. Liu of the M.I.T. Department of Political Science.

9. All quotations from specific references in memorandum by Alan P. L. Liu.

10. An anthropologist has reported some Yunnan villagers' idea of female beauty: "The lighter her skin and the rosier and smaller the mouth, the better. A high-bridged, narrow, pointed nose was preferred." The skin of the ideal man, he added, "was expected to be darker." In the village, he reported "complexions varied somewhat and a lighter color was considered preferable to a dark. The noses of boys and girls were pinched to make the bridges higher, a form which was considered particularly attractive." Cornelius Osgood, *Village Life in Old China: A Community Study of Kao Yao, Yunnan* (New York, 1963), pp. 253-54, 273-74.

11. Emmanuel John Hevi, *An African Student in Red China* (New York, 1963).

12. Alan Liu quotes from an account published by an overseas Chinese traveler in Communist China: "In every nursery school or kindergarten, the following questions-and-answers were often heard:
   " 'Who are the villains?'
   'The American wolves!'
   'Why have the Americans turned into wolves?'
   'Because the Americans have the wolf's heart and dog's lung.' "
Classrooms were described as being decorated with pictures showing American soldiers killing, cooking, and eating children. The soldiers were usually depicted with "their skin full of black hair . . . face painted light blue, long teeth protruding from their mouths" (from Lin Tae, *Ta-lu Chien-wen* [What I Saw on the Mainland; Hong Kong, 1954]).

13. Pulin Garg, "Notes on Importance of Skin Color in India" (Unpublished memorandum, 1965).

14. Harold R. Isaacs, *Scratches on Our Minds: American Images of China and India* (New York, 1958), pp. 280-90.

15. Harold R. Isaacs, *India's Ex-Untouchables* (New York, 1965).

FRANÇOIS RAVEAU

An Outline of the Role of Color in Adaptation Phenomena

BOTH TRADITIONAL societies and those more advanced have always maintained, and in varying degrees still maintain, a certain prejudice against the "foreigner." This xenophobia manifests itself through archetypal clichés to be found not only in the national language—stingy as a Scot, lazy as a Negro, drunk as a Pole—but also in social institutions—prohibition of, or at least bias against, mixed marriages, limitation of economic activity, and non-access to certain offices.

There remains the problem of defining the foreigner inside the boundaries of a country. By what label, both easy to impose and easy to read, can he be kept within the confines assigned to him by the community? This is also a way of fostering the transition of latent aggressiveness to an overt state, which is the inevitable pattern of xenophobias buried in the collective and individual subconscious.

Historically, societies have attempted to mark those who do not belong by many means: measures concerning clothing, adornment, designation of reserved quarters. The flimsiness of external characterizations of the foreigner has often been perceived by peoples who have been quick to give anthropometric observation an important role, elaborating type systems of "the barbarian," "the other." Ancient Rome produced a very accurate literature in this field; for Cicero, the Gaul could not be mistaken for the German, nor the Petchenegian for the Greek, thanks to an abundance of often very subtle notations. The brachycephalic and the dolichocephalic, the long-limbed and the short-limbed, the morphology of the nose and the ear did not escape a Tacitus, and were the forerunners of physiognomy.

But what could be more striking than the color of the skin? All other distinctions fade before this basic one. A black, yellow,

98

or white man immediately stands out in an environment where people have skins of a different color. This definitive barrier cannot be bridged by any artifice. Skin color transforms the human being into a sandwich man perpetually subjected to the gaze of those of a different racial origin. Moreover, since others perceive him as different, he sees himself as such in the eyes of others. At this point, several reactions are possible. Whether the attitudes are firmly established or less fully developed, they are lived out in terms of solutions based on escape, exaggerated self-assertiveness, or simply negative behavior.

The black minority in a white environment may react to this situation in numerous ways. Several factors can affect the total picture. A Negro American will cope with his skin color somewhat differently than an African traveling in Europe. While John Dollard and others are exploring adaptation phenomena in the United States, multidisciplinary research is being conducted at the Centre de Psychiatrie Sociale in Paris under the direction of Professor Roger Bastide, whom I assist. Within the scope of the École Pratique des Hautes Études at the Sorbonne, this work brings together ethnologists, psychologists, sociologists, and physicians of diverse specialities. Various groups in a condition of adaptation are being studied. Among them are Africans from the French-speaking republics.

Since these countries have been granted independence, France has, of necessity, had to accelerate the formation of cadres for the young states on the administrative as well as the technical and economic levels. The development of these new potential elites poses a number of problems; each of them constitutes a subject of study at the Centre.

It is possible to extract from this global approach a number of considerations relative to the role color plays in the process of adaptation. Although our purpose is to isolate this theme, we have not done so in such a way as to ignore other factors—biological, social, and climatic—which enter into the phenomena of adaptation.

To date, the Centre has studied nine hundred Africans in contact with a French environment. About one third has finished the course of adaptation, another third is in the midst of the process, and the last third is just starting. The subjects range in age from nineteen to thirty-eight, with the average being twenty-six.

The pathological cases were studied first, since illness often magnifies the symptoms and psychological aspects hidden most deeply within the sick person. The inductions of hypotheses thus obtained were then verified in terms of the normal. Much smaller test groups composed of natives from Haiti, Martinique, and larger ones from the Malagasy Republic were formed in order to verify and supplement the initial results obtained through intensive study of Africans.

Much of the evidence that will be related may appear elementary; at the level of daily life, however, such situations are loaded with pathos for those who experience them. A black man who comes to a country of whites very often undergoes an initial shock when he faces large numbers of white men and women. In his native country he may have thought about what it would be like to be surrounded by a majority of whites, but the actual experience of being alone in so different a crowd is always felt as something extremely new. His position has been reversed; once one of the dominant group, numerically speaking, he now belongs with the minority.

In Africa, the white man is often identified through his position of authority, wealth, and prestige as a powerful quasi-paternal person, toward whom the African feels unmistakably hostile. He serves both as a model for and an obstacle to personal advancement. The processes of identification leading to the realization of this model presuppose that the model itself will disappear. The dialectic between the colonizer and the colonized, an age-old relationship very much alive in the minds of the young elites of these developing nations, is instrumental in focusing latent aggressiveness on the white man.

The African, therefore, resents the white world as doubly hostile: first, because it is unfamiliar to him, and as such a source of fear; and second, because, through a classic pattern of projection, his own feelings of hostility will be transferred to the receiving environment, and subsequently will turn around and be directed against himself.

The African travels to France to acquire a useful technique, a new knowledge often materialized by a diploma awarded by whites whose demands he generally overrates and whom he fears as more efficient competitors. These various stresses, added to the bioclimatic shock, weaken the African's defenses and result in intense anxiety—the prime symptom of those subjects seen thus far at the Centre.

The anxiety neurosis of one of our first cases gravely interfered with his social adaptation shortly after his arrival in France.
Upon being requested to make a note of his dreams, he remarked
that it was strange to write with a black pencil on white paper,
rather than with a white pencil on black paper. This was a statement of a major symptom of his neurosis. He accused any whiteness of depersonalizing him, of assaulting his mental integrity.
Hence, he developed a series of defense mechanisms such as refusal to travel by subway (oppressive by the white majority) and
repeated sexual failures with white partners because their too-
white nakedness froze him to impotence.

At this point, we suggested that he translate his vision of this
new anxiety-ridden world into drawings and colors. He developed
a series of pictures, different from one another but always showing
faces whose long-term purpose was the reconciliation of black
and white, an evidence of the eradication of the anxiety by the
discovery of faces of other colors—such as green or red. More than
three hundred pictures testify to his evolution, to his progress under
psychotherapy. They faithfully reflect first the anxiety, then the attempts at taming nonpathogenic colors, and finally the conquest
of his fears. The last pictures are banal insofar as the very clear
initial symbolism is hidden by a poor painting technique, but the
latest canvas is sufficiently expressive to mark a reconciliation of
his black color with the white color of some of his fellow men.

From nineteen of these pictures we shall extract a certain
number of themes pertaining to this subject but often found in the
histories of other neuroses. We will distinguish several stages in
the subject's case history. In a way, the subject's work, like that of
any painter, will be characterized by specific stylistic periods, each
having its particular meaning. The order of study is, naturally,
chronological, and we will take our examples from groups of ten
to thirty canvases or drawings. We do not propose to discuss the
psychiatric problem in depth but, through the symptoms of a slice
of history, to delineate the importance that the perception of a life
history can assume.

It is a little paradoxical to write of color when the illustrations themselves are much more representative of reality, but
publishing imperatives prevent us from reproducing here the
twenty or so examples chosen for the conference in Copenhagen.

The first works evidence a period of ambivalence. There is a
desire to be white and thereby to transcend the level of the color

that sets the patient apart. This means identifying himself with another being who looks, notices, and rejects. Finally, it means becoming an anxiety-ridden white man. The rendering gives a strong impression of fear stemming from the awareness that there is no possible solution. A hybrid being is looking out at the patient. The eyes are black; the contours are strongly delineated and suggest an African morphology. To the subject, this means the oneiric possibility of becoming white, but all the time he knows that, within himself, he is really black and that the gaze of others will pierce through him—hence, the burden of anxiety before the impasse.

All the problems of identification with a model are present here. Moreover, these difficulties occur at a formative age, which for these young Africans set apart is one of assimilating a white culture, a process often symbolized for many by attempts to dress in the Western manner. The subjects strive, by typical dress or a uniform, to identify themselves with the function they are going to occupy: diplomat, financier, and so forth. Much has already been written on the theme of the concern for appearances: English-speaking Africans tend to adopt the Oxfordian image as it is stereotyped in the movies, whereas the French-speaking try to identify themselves with the high-ranking civil servants of the Quai d'Orsay. With Africans, this attempt becomes more perceptible, thanks to cosmetics and other aids to feminine beauty. A content-analysis of the advertising in the American magazine *EBONY* shows how great are the temptations for a Negro woman and man to modify their color by means of various artifices. Recently, some beauticians have opened shops in Paris, specializing in this kind of activity.

This is, however, quite often the beginning of a guilty conscience. Africans are free citizens of African republics. They must, therefore, come into their own both politically and nationally. This is much easier for them than for the Negroes of the United States, for instance, who are caught in the clutches of a culture that defines them by exclusion. This contradiction has been used as a means of protection by some of the Centre's test groups from the Antilles and from the Malagasy Republic. During their period of adaptation in France, colored Haitians recognize and assert their color, which they claim as part of their being of another nationality and, therefore, different. By virtue of this, they enjoy a greater freedom of movement within the hostile situation. On the other hand, those from Martinique are simply black and fully French by virtue of the political situation of their island. Hospital statistics on more than eighty cases have shown that the Martiniquans' mental pathology is the most assertive on the racial theme of all the colored men living in France. A similar phenomenon has been observed in the case of the Malagasis. Men from the high plateaus who encounter definite signs of discrimination because of the color of their skin during their stay in France justify this behavior by remembering their own discriminatory attitude at home toward their darker compatriots of the coast on the "Grande Ile." The latter, on the other hand, are more vulnerable; with their backs to the weak wall of their recent nationality, they must fight the struggle demanded by the awareness of their being different.

Let us now return to the patient, who at this initial stage insists on the importance of the black line to delineate the human form in drawing. In the course of psychotherapeutic sessions, he naïvely develops many of the familiar themes of *négritude* extolled by Senghor and Césaire, of whom he has not even heard. This style of expression marks the beginning of his attempt to fix the value of color. Thus, he argues, "Without the black stroke, there is no white shape. Hence, the stroke is the most important and therefore only the black counts." This is part of a long litany that, in addition to discovery, has the value of self-assertion before the white therapist. It is the start of a sincere, and therefore violent, contact—aggressive, but indispensable to the patient's free expression of his psychological conflicts. It develops much more markedly in the third part of the iconography.

There appear then the first attempts to introduce true colors—white and black not being colors in the strict sense of the word. The problem of form and color is thereby quite naturally posed, emphasizing the profound gap that can exist between the morphology of the face and body and their color. What is significant for the subject is not the form of a nose, of lips, of hair, but their color value. He later attempts to modify form but essentially at the symbolic level—hastening the change of skin color in an almost ritualistic manner.

At first the subject applies colors not to bodies but to the objects surrounding them. One leitmotiv is the sun in the shape of a red star accompanied by flames—an explicit assertion expressing a wish for the annihilation of the white man by Africa. The bodies are hidden by white fabrics. In daily life the patient expresses his aggressiveness by violent street fights, acts of rebellion, and perpet-

103

ual criticism of his professional milieu. Worn out by the rebuffs brought on by his behavior and analyzed during psychotherapeutic sessions, he makes attempts at reconciliation in a new series where black and white shake hands under a flowing shroud. The African can be recognized by a red tone, the French by "neutral" blue tone, yet this attempt at amnesty would be a failure in both the subject's real world and that of his phantasms. For that purpose, he identifies red with Africa and suffering. He sees no solution in flight. Disguise in white clothing, thereby becoming a white man even though in traditional African dress, is inoperative. The subject must, then, live with white people while remaining black himself. This awareness represents important progress for it will lead him to a reality that will consist of a beneficial struggle for stability.

The young man dreamed a great deal during this period. It is important to stress without too much analysis the identity of the content of his dreams and his pictorial productions. The dreams are hallucinatory episodes in which black and white confront each other, in which Africa and France are closely intermingled. In one dream, for instance, the subject enters a Parisian subway train in Africa, is crushed by a white mob, struggles, and awakes terrified. In another, his home village is inhabited only by anonymous white people who chase him, drown him, or expel him. These color-oriented dreams are important in the psychotherapeutic treatment of such cases for they reveal interacting tensions and attest accurately to their development. Many of the patients studied have dreamed of the aggressive, crushing subway. It underscores a kind of claustrophobia they feel when among whites. The treatment of the subway dream undergoes continuous modification, progressing toward an integration of Africa. For example, a red subway fills up with black men in Paris and arrives, after a long trip, in the native country of the subject. This return to a happy childhood that had been reconciled with the new adult patient is progressive as is shown by the second dream, the theme of which is the journey from France to the village in an aircraft. This is always a nightmare because the white aircraft, peopled with whites, is unable to land and crashes. Progressively, the aircraft—after being colored in various manners—succeeds in landing, and the subject walks out to the land of his fathers, but then he sees that he is white and dies. In the dream's next stage, he can go on living but as a white stranger in his village, recognized by none of his family. Finally, it becomes a pleasant dream. His return is greeted with joy by his black friends and relatives. Sometimes the psychotherapist accompanies him like a brother and is welcomed as such, but he then changes color and becomes black without disturbing the harmonious unfolding of the dream.

The pictorial expression, thus, often meets this other production of the subconscious, the dream, to settle it. But it is no longer the moving picture that remains, simply static images drawn from a particular moment. The patient discovers that a face can be other than white or black—green, for example. He then creates chaotic pictures strongly imbued with exciting color, the eyes white and red for they are looking at the white world that must be mastered in suffering. In time, his palette is enriched with new tubes of color; his evolving technique comes to the rescue of expression. It is no longer necessary to delineate with black the faces that are green, yellow, or pink. We then are under the impression of being in the presence of waking dreams where the mastery of means of expression is responsible for the evolution of the neurosis.

At this point in the evolution of the patient, an important event occurs. African friends, aware of the difficulties of his life and thinking they have found a solution to his torment, procure a white prostitute for him. The nakedness of the woman and the surprise of the experience freeze the young man, preventing him from having successful intercourse with her—even though he has had precocious sexual intercourse in Africa with various women of his own color. Hence he relapses into anxiety. This episode, although dangerous for the evolution of the treatment as it puts us back months, offers one positive element: the discovery that white skin is rather pinkish. Accordingly, the sheet of white paper is no longer the reflection of a race, nor is the blackness of pencil lead. This is the recognition of an old semantic treason, the analysis of which acquires a liberating effect.

At this stage the evolution in regard to faces becomes more crystallized. The faces painted are no longer anxious but expressionless under the green color. The patient defines them as "different from me and from you, at an equal distance from opposed men."

The tunic put over the bodies reminds us, however, of that of Nessus, all of suffering; it is symbolized by red and is thereby Africa. At that moment he integrates into the chest of his creation a plant of the Yucca type, a dark image of the anxiety that grips him, that grows within him, black and white.

Then a new way of viewing reality seems to lure him on; he develops a series of self-portraits, spending much time before the mirror to assure a likeness. Suffering—emphasized by red eyes that are "witnesses" and by lips that "express"—still plays an important role. Ever present is the strong solar theme, a permanent protest against the paleness of the sun in the temperate zone, which accounts for the whiteness of the country, felt to be dull, cold, and joyless.

With the other portraits attesting to narcissistic aims, we find a phase of "integration." With his identification of resemblance in the world, the subject assimilates the colors green, blue, orange, and red. At the same time, a real improvement appears in his relationships with others. The isolation is less evident, the professional pragmatism clearly transformed. His existence is made bearable as his anxiety abates. This is the period when dreams begin to have happy endings—glad return to his country, promise of success in the qualifying tests. This canvas remains a key document of the reconciliation through color which the palette affords his anxiety. His dress is also affected in that he gives up his attempts at resemblance with the various types of middle-class Frenchmen. He now dons pastel-colored shirts, over-bright ties, and buys a mauve jacket. Faced with this polychromism in his dress, we cannot but evoke the vivid dress of the black populations of America—the United States in particular. Would there not be in this positive attraction for violent colors an attempt to disguise a situation where the duality of black and white is resented as being frustrating? Here again, the subconscious, consulted by means of the dream, reveals in many other cases oneiric histories— veritable orgies of extreme colors. One of the patients would see the streets of Paris red under a green sky. Another reported dream scenes where the Parisian crowds were green and the streets golden yellow. This is probably an attempt to compensate for the failures of a world of white dullness which Césaire evokes in his poems.

This narcissistic period is, however, also a period of actual suffering. The subject, whose behavior has greatly improved, places himself deliberately in wounding situations in order to expose himself to hurts which will maintain him in a state of discomfort. This is the classic phase of masochistic exploitation of the secondary benefits of neuroses. Driven by a missionary spirit, he considers taking a trip to the United States (which he eventually does two years later) in order to mix with the crowds protesting against racial discrimination. Let it be noted that permission of free expression of aggressions in the face of authentically frustrating situations does, in fact, dispel anxiety by casting it into the mold of action. Thus it is that incidents in the United States during the campaigns of school integration, amplified by certain extremist press media in France, have found a large audience among the Africans in Paris, causing various violent manifestations and huge protest meetings. We have verified in all the patients participating in these various movements a total abatement of their anxieties which, of course, reappeared when the agitation no longer had any *raison d'être*. Certain patients, aware of this passing improvement, have tried to maintain it by campaigning feverishly in movements they sought out and have even gone so far as to create incidents justifying the action that thus became a substitute for therapy.

Without assuming a caricatural aspect, many of the subject's canvases attest to such a troubled period; the faces are still black and brown, but superimposed blonde or red hair evidences the white preoccupations that the world in which he lives imposes on him. At this time, the solar symbol in the shape of a huge star, until then bright red, becomes dulled and appears as very gray. This theme disappears because "the Africa of the sun is dead." One can see here a sign that adaptation is on the way to success insofar as Africa becomes blurred as a point of reference.

Furthermore, a symbolic analysis of the shapes and backgrounds in terms of color enables us to localize the various cultural Franco-African antagonisms. The improved condition of the subject at this time permits the expression of his libido which introjects his sexuality; he becomes more daring with white women and openly admits being attracted to them.

There appears then in the production of this case the beginning of transcription of transference (in the psychoanalytic meaning of the term)—the emergence of a figure at last admittedly that of a white man whose function may be therapeutic; hence, the possibility of apprenticeship in a different world. One canvas shows a dark-skinned face with a stroke of black but with very blue eyes on a very red background of "Africa." This is a synthesis portrait. The blue eyes signify strangeness to the race of the patient, the beard is a beginning of the personification of the therapist—ourself—who belongs to the other world and has a fringe of a beard (an involuntary way of facilitating means of personification). This brings out an important question: Can a Negro with an adaptation neurosis be treated effectively by a white doctor? In the light of case histories, it would appear that the doctor-patient relationship under such circumstances will be fruitful, although it may take time to become established, only if the psychiatrist gives proof of his understanding, of a benevolent and non-ethnocentric neutrality. By means of this different face, the patient will be able to tame a new environment; he will be soothed by this therapeutic picture of the doctor whom he invests with the function of ambassador from the hostile world.

In the patient's dreams the therapist often appears in fully conflicting situations. For instance, the subject dreams that he has a date in a café with a white woman. She comes in and walks smilingly toward him at the back of the room; at the last minute she veers and sits down at a neighboring table; at that moment he recognizes the therapist. There are many variations to this: The young woman may be black, the surroundings becoming modified according to the dynamics already met in connection with the means of transportation. In a symmetrical dream the café is very Parisian but located in Africa, and the patrons are black men. The dream has a happy ending; it is no longer anxiety-laden when the patient evokes it in psychotherapy and analyzes it in detail.

The long series of portraits of the psychotherapist shows the detailed evolution of the existing relationship. The doctor is at first a redoubtable figure for the patient. He is invested with the insignia of authority (aging of the image) because he is recognized as the censor of the patient's behavior. Here, too, Africa and France are intermingled by the confusion of the attributes at the level of shape and color. There is also the transfer of certain characteristics of the face (self-portrait) to the image of the therapist, in a way a privileged man in the white world. Actual anxiety no longer shows on the face of the patient but on that of the therapist who remains very much African (dark). But then a turning point appears in the attitude of the patient toward the therapist. Our portraits become very good likenesses. The subject has liquidated his aggressions and develops a very real sense of humor to picture himself and describe situations that used to be filled with conflict for him.

At this point, we try to see the patient at greater intervals and advise him to use on his own those key elements of analysis that he has acquired in the treatment. He throws himself into professional activity. Because of his application and his qualities of thinking and decision-making, he is selected to become the sole distributor for a prominent make of French cars in his country of origin. His artistic activity develops also; he takes courses in drawing and painting in ateliers and visits museums.

After a long summer vacation, he reappears at the Centre in a rather anxious state. He has met a blond girl of Polish origin. Because of her surname, he told us, she has never felt really French; she has revolted against her family environment and is working as a secretary. They are involved in a serious love affair. His hostility and his various anxieties tend to reappear and can be checked only with difficulty. He has come in search of help. In his painting, he has produced a series of canvases portraying white women who have nothing in common with the young Pole except coiffure. He then sketches and paints a woman of whom he is afraid, for he finds himself in a dreaded situation, in the very heart of the problems created by a young Negro's keeping company with a young white woman. By showing off with a Negro, this girl has lowered herself in the eyes of other whites, who look down on her (in much the same way as he despises a young Negro woman who has sexual relations with a white man). She has become a "nigger's girl," a harlot trying to find herself by putting herself in the place of others. The result is a series of portraits showing a *femme fatale* of the variety found in the comics of the 1930's: long spread-out blond hair, large tired green eyes, a heavily reddened mouth turned down at the corners. The skin is greenish with splashes of pink.

That this young girl is marginal in France through her Polish origins attracts him; they have the same perception of the milieu since they stand out in it. At the same time this also repulses him insofar as she is not like all the other white girls of France, whom he thus gives up knowing. It is only after he has established an intimate relationship with the young girl (whom he considers highly because of her virginity) that he decides to marry her. He asks us to meet her so that we may explain to her in his presence his neurotic past, the reasons for it, and the drawbacks this might represent in the future. On the day of that meeting, he brings a canvas (the largest of all, 32" x 20") showing the face of a young woman in blue-black with European features on a background mottled with large brush strokes of blue, green, yellow, red, and black. He points out that although his fiancée is very blond, this is the way he sees her. Starting from the polychromism of this highly competent canvas, he develops the theme of the future: the children to come who will be "mottled because they are half breeds." This perspective is extremely agonizing to him.

The Polish girl, not much of an intellectual and highly emotional, is concerned only with the immediate difficulties of a mixed marriage and draws up a list of obstacles to be overcome (family, nationality, occupation, and so forth), as well as measures that should be taken to solve these problems. Once the problems have been pinpointed and are in the process of being resolved, she asks her fiancé to paint her portrait—"but a good likeness this time." He succeeds, but confesses that he prefers to paint her "after the vacation, when she is sun-tanned." His fiancée shows a certain pride in his artistic talents, but still hopes that they will not prevent him from giving his all to his profession, an honorable and lucrative way of life.

Today they are a mixed couple who, for the last two years, have untangled rather brilliantly many difficulties. Each time he travels to France on business he comes to see us. Unmistakable progress has been made in his painting technique, but he has lost the genius of his neurosis. Here is his own commentary on his latest work:

The carnival-clad character is me. I am no longer black, and I am not white, but a new fellow who must every day learn how to behave and how to think. This is hard because I cannot imitate someone before me. Fortunately, there are gestures which are always the same, like loving a woman petal after petal, like a flower.

Actually, this painting is a composition on a quite impressionistic background with well-blended tones à la Renoir, very harmonious and soft. To the left is a large white flower, a kind of daisy. The right side is occupied by a harlequin with dark skin, black hair, and a dark-yellow coat. He has a white collarette and plucks a petal from the white flower that is scaled to his size.

Such a psycho-affective example of acculturation is rare. The role of color, which is here expressed by privileged means, has appeared to us ever latent in the study of the most banal cases.

Not the mixed marriage but the patient's approach to it is important here. The subject has been brought to it by the long road of neurosis to settle in success, whereas generally this attempt—as lived by those who have the same handicap to start with—only enhances the problems, as is emphasized by Professor Roger Bastide in "Black Apollo and Dusky Venus."

Thus, in the course of his journey on the long road of adaptation to the world of the whites, the colored man makes the apprenticeship of his being different and at the same time of the environment in which he lives. Depending on the strength and the richness of the elements making up his personality, he may or may not integrate the various problems this poses for him. In a certain way his personality will be challenged to secrete protective antibodies that will be furnished by the basic culture. Let us note here that for certain blacks like the French Martiniquans the initial milieu supplies these antibodies only with difficulty and brings on more easily the pathology of color.

Neuroses and psychoneuroses will, therefore, be fed by this color symptom while being expressed, by choice, through its exuberant richness. One understands then how this double resonance can make up an important chapter of the social psychopathology of men made marginal by their color.

KENNETH J. GERGEN

The Significance of Skin Color in Human Relations

ONE OF the most compelling features of Japanese Haiku poetry is its capacity to provide in a few brief lines an image of almost universal proportions. In the lines

> Now my loneliness
> After the fireworks
> Look, a falling star

the reader finds himself in a moment of interrupted solitude and, at the same time, perceives that the contrast between excitement and isolation is common to all men. What would his reaction be, however, if the poet had added color to certain words of the poem? Would the thoughts and feelings about the experience or the broader implications of the poem be any different if the words *loneliness, fireworks,* or *star* appeared in pink as opposed to deep blue? A number of recent experiments have shown that the coloration of words has a powerful impact on one's feelings about and interpretation of poetry.[1] Light shades produce different reactions than dark shades, and blues elicit different associations than reds, although the words and form of the poem remain unchanged.

If colors have such a substantial impact when associated with the written word, is it not also possible that the pigmentation of skin may affect a person's feelings about other people and his interpretation of their actions? In particular, is it possible that color differences may play a divisive role in social relationships? The question is an intriguing one inasmuch as the major work on race prejudice and social conflict has used color simply as a way of designating the battle lines.[2] Much less attention has been paid to the possibility that color may be partially responsible for the battle itself.

112

Color and Social Separation

There are numerous physical dimensions, such as height and weight, along which people within any society vary. For the most part, such dimensions may be characterized in two ways: First, they lend themselves to making fine distinctions, and second, the distribution of people along each dimension is roughly normal. For example, a person's height and weight are subject to very precise specification, and for varying purposes people may be sensitized to slight differences in musculature, manifestations of aging, or girth size. At the same time, for each of these dimensions there is a single norm within a society, and fewer and fewer cases exist as one moves away from this norm. While there are the very tall and the very short, the majority of the population falls within the mid-range. Likewise, populations are not often composed solely of the lean or the heavy.

In the case of skin color, neither of these population characteristics generally holds true. Although fine gradations in skin pigmentation can be made, social traditions normally disregard them. People are classified as white, black, yellow, and so on. To be sure, the classification of "high yellow" or "mulatto" is sometimes used, but at least for members of white society those who fall into such categories could just as well be jet black.[3] The reason for these rather indiscriminate categories may be traced, in part, to the distribution of skin characteristics within a society. Unlike the physical dimensions discussed above, skin color is not normally distributed within most contemporary societies. Rather, the distribution tends to be multi-modal, with the result that several different sub-groupings are commonly recognized. Thus, the common perceptual tendency is to treat as equivalent all those who fall within a given sub-distribution; the person's major problem is in deciding into which of the available sub-groupings a person is to be placed.

In an extensive series of investigations, Charles Osgood and his associates have found that the categories used to classify objects or people take on certain connotative meanings.[4] The primary connotation is evaluative in nature; any category or its exemplars will elicit feelings that may be placed somewhere along a "good-bad" or "pleasant-unpleasant" dimension. The latter two dimensions of connotative meaning are "potency" and "activity." In effect, the person will subjectively estimate the power or strength of various objects and identify them as to their degree of passivity. In-

113

vestigations in this area have found .these same meaning-dimensions to exist in many diverse cultures and to pertain regardless of the particular object being classified.

Inasmuch as one major way of classifying people reflects the various pigmentation groupings, the major question emerges as to whether there may be compelling reasons for negative evaluations to become associated with members of groups other than one's own. Given no other information about persons whose skin differs from one's own, are there psychological processes that tend to cause one to evaluate such persons in a less than favorable way? Evidence from a number of domains suggests an affirmative answer to this question.

From a historical viewpoint, Sigmund Freud played perhaps the first significant role in thinking about this question.[5] On the basis of extensive case studies, Freud theorized that the overriding pleasure instinct first becomes gratified within one's own body. In the life of the infant, libidinal energy becomes attached to the person himself prior to its finding suitable fulfillment in the external world. This narcissistic inclination was felt to be a universal condition, and generic to the individual's later choice of love objects. The adult person would be attracted to those people who most resembled some aspect of his own being.

While many are unsympathetic to Freud's particular statement of the case, contemporary work in the field of social learning tends to bear Freud out in certain respects. It has been shown that a person will seek out and associate with persons who provide gratification or reinforcement. If the initial source of gratification is not available, the person will base his choice of an alternative on the extent to which the potential alternate resembles the initial source. If, for example, a youth has been raised in such a way that he is extremely dependent on his mother for food, affection, or other forms of gratification, he might be expected to choose a wife who resembles his mother in some gross respects. From this point of view, one may generalize to say that self-love will eventuate in love for others who resemble self. In addition, to the extent that the person's major gratifications have been received within a social group delineated by a particular skin color, his future choice of friends, colleagues, or compatriots may be expected to fall within the same category.[6] His evaluation of persons outside the category will be much less positive. Such work suggests that the roots of ethnocentrism may be exceedingly deep.

114

Research on perception leads to similar conclusions. Perceptual tendencies to group objects in the physical world according to their geographical proximity and similarity have long been noted. More recently, Fritz Heider has developed a number of postulates connecting these perceptual tendencies to people's feelings toward one another.[7] He has theorized that people will feel more comfortable if similarity is accompanied by mutuality in feeling. People who perceive themselves to be similar to each other tend to feel the same about each other. Inasmuch as positive feelings are less burdensome to most people than negative ones, similarity is said to breed mutual attraction. We can all perhaps attest to the inclination to feel friendly toward "one of our kind."

Support for Heider's notions rests, however, not only on common observation, but on a voluminous set of research findings.[8] In study after study, it has been shown that people who are similar to each other—be it in terms of attitudes, interests, values, personality, or social characteristics—feel more positively toward each other than those who are dissimilar. While there may be alternative ways of explaining such findings, the implications of this line of investigation seem quite clear for the present purposes. Attraction may be a normal outgrowth within groups that resemble each other in physical characteristics such as skin color. The color line may mark the termination of such tendencies. If persons within a particular color grouping perceive that members of another group tend to be cohesive or internally unified, they may also feel potentially threatened. In this case, the stage is set for the outgrowth of active hostility.

In connection with the similarity-attraction hypothesis, it is also interesting to note the reactions to persons differing in skin color of various explorers or adventurers whose previous experiences with such differences had been limited.[9] In describing his travels with Magellan, Francisco Pigafetta likens the "black people" of Brazil to "enemies of Hell."[10] William Lithgow, the Scottish adventurer, wrote after his voyage to Africa in 1615 that nature "had set a fairer stamp on my face than theirs, which oft I wished (because of the menacing reactions of the natives) had beene as blacke as their ugliness."[11] In 1910, the colonialist Putnam Weale was even moved to write, "the black man is something apart—something untouchable."[12]

A third way in which skin color differences may engender alienation is related to Gordon Allport's supposition that visible differences imply underlying differences.[13] A major share of the socialization process is involved with teaching the child a category system that will enable him to behave differentially toward various objects or events in his environment. He may be taught that certain objects are edible, and that those objects which do not visibly fall into this class are non-edible. Learning an extensive and particular category system may indeed be considered a stamp of membership within a given society. The vast majority of these learning experiences, and thus one's category system, are based, however, on visible differences existing in the environment. When the individual is later exposed to visible differences among people, he would tend to infer that different reactions are necessitated. Skin-color differences do not appear to be immune from this tendency. Indeed, the apparent ease with which people stereotype those of other races seems to lend considerable support to the thesis. Discussion cannot, however, be concluded here. To assume that those who are not visibly similar are basically different is not to assume that they are bad.

To understand the development of alienation in this case, one must appreciate what it is for the individual to encounter another who, on the face of it, appears to be "different." Such situations are almost universally threatening. The other appears strange, alien, and unknown. He suggests to the individual that the relevance of his long-standing styles of relating to others is in severe question; his security in knowing how to act adaptively is shaken. The same reaction often accompanies one's encounter with the mentally ill. As soon as another is categorized or identified as mentally ill, one can no longer assume that one's structured ways of behaving are functional. The common reaction to the unknown, the unpredictable, or the strange is aversion. This reaction has recently been dramatically underscored by a plethora of social psychological studies that have demonstrated the aversive nature of inconsistency.[14] In one investigation, by altering the predictability of a person's behavior, it was found that people became more friendly when the other was predictable, but hostile when they were unable to comprehend his actions.[15] In essence, when skin color differences imply behavioral patterns different from one's own, antipathy may result.

One major way of offsetting the tendency to reject those whose skin differs from one's own would be to generate factual evidence of similarity over and above pigmentation differences. If persons were aware that pigmentation was all that differentiated them from other racial groups, the climate for generating positive relations would be vastly improved. Once the wheels of psychological process are set in motion, the outcome may, however, serve only to sustain the basic tendencies. Avoidance of or aversion to those who appear different tends to create social segmentation. Persons may choose their friends, associates, marriage partners, and places of residence on the basis of perceived similarity. Once such segmentation occurs, not only within-group similarity but also dissimilarity across groups may increase at a rapid rate. Mores, customs, habits, traditions, and languages develop within cultural groupings. These indigenous patterns only serve to accentuate what may have been at the outset minimal differences among groupings.[16] One might conclude that at least within any single culture the continued enforcement of an *apartheid* system over time tends only to reinforce itself. Minimal differences among persons spiral with segmentation.

While some of the processes described above may decrease affiliation across color lines, they do not all actively promote hostility. Moreover, there are other differentiating features within society that do not appear to engender prejudicial feelings. Although sex differences,[17] certain religious vestments, and uniforms may serve a differentiating function, hostility is not a normal component of one's reaction to those who are dissimilar to oneself in these respects. One might also ask why certain racial groups seem to suffer more from such tendencies than others. The moderately rapid assimilation of the Chinese into Western culture can, for example, be contrasted with the arduous path faced by Negroes. Each of these issues leads headlong into the problem of color semantics.

Color Symbolism

Colors, like words or gestures, have substantial currency in the semantic domain. While words are most often used denotatively (for example, to refer to specific objects or events in the real world), color is more often used to communicate on a connotative level. Colors lend themselves to this type of communication because they lack concreteness. Color, like dimensions of shape and size, is perceived as a characteristic of an object, rather than as the object itself. Thus, while seldom denoting objective content, colors have the capacity to elicit directly certain types of feelings or emotions. Artists have long used this assumption to advantage. Within recent times interior designers, advertisers, architects, human engineers, and fashion designers have systematically begun to investigate the impact of color in communication.

How do colors come to have this semantic value, and what feelings do various colors communicate?[18] Some have argued that the connotative meanings of various colors are related to innate physiological structure. For example, certain colors stimulate a greater number of receptor cells in the retina of the eye and, thus, in the central nervous system; these same colors absorb less heat and may, therefore, be cooler to the touch. While this notion may account for certain reactions to color brightness and saturation, it does not account for the many differences produced by the all-important dimension of hue. Nor does this theory explain the range of different emotions that may be elicited by the same color over time. A more reasonable explanation may be derived from principles of associative learning.

Within this latter framework certain environmental events are observed to possess the inherent capacity to produce various emotions. A full stomach may provide the newborn child with a pleasurable sensation, while a loud and unexpected noise may produce fear. Various aspects of the environment to which the initial response has been neutral may come to be associated with these more basic forms of arousal. If a mother's caress has been associated with physical satisfaction, her presence on subsequent occasions may be sufficient to elicit some form of pleasure. While colors may initially be effectively neutral for the developing child, they are constant aspects of his environment. If a given color is usually present when the child is frightened or sad, through processes of associative learning such a color may come to elicit such feelings at later points in time. These associations may develop prior to linguistic abilities; unless extinguished, they may continue through the individual's life.

While the learning hypothesis may largely account for the emotional or connotative significance of various colors, the question of "what" colors communicate remains at bay. This issue also presents an intriguing enigma. Not only do differing colors register differentially on a symbolic level, but the emotional significance of certain colors may be common both within and even across cultural boundaries. If, indeed, primary reactions to colors are learned, it is

118

a matter of some amazement that peoples with highly dissimilar cultural backgrounds should react similarly to a given color.

After careful study of color symbolism in the Western tradition, Matthew Luckiesh lists the following as most commonly associated with black: woe, gloom, darkness, dread, death, terror, horror, wickedness, curse, mourning, and mortification.[19] Walter Sargent adds to this list the attributes of defilement, error, annihilation, strength, and deep quiet.[20] From his studies, Faber Birren concludes that "despair" is the major association elicited by black.[21] Such attributes stand in marked contrast to those associated with white: triumph, light, innocence, joy, divine power, purity, regeneration, happiness, gaiety, peace, chastity, truth, modesty, femininity, and delicacy.[22] Studies of color symbolism in the Bible, the works of Chaucer, Milton, Shakespeare, Hawthorne, Poe, and Melville also reveal a major tendency to use white in expressing forms of goodness, and black in connoting evil.[23]

In terms of the above discussion of connotative meaning, it might be said that white tends to elicit a positive evaluative reaction and black a negative one. Several direct and well-controlled tests of this relationship have been made within Western culture. All convincingly demonstrate the differential evaluative reaction to black versus white. One of the more outstanding of these studies demonstrated not only that white is rated more positively than black, but that both Negroes as well as whites feel similarly in this regard (though whites are more extreme in their differential evaluation of the colors). Furthermore, black is rated by both racial groups as more potent but less active than white.[24] These latter findings are particularly intriguing inasmuch as they coincide with the popular Western stereotype that Negroes are "strong" but "lazy."

While the homogeneity of meaning within the Caucasian-dominated culture of the West is impressive, the possibility that color symbolism may be common across cultural boundaries is even more challenging. The evidence in this case is, of course, much more sparse, and one must be tentative. A systematic examination of a randomly selected group of cultures does reveal, however, many interesting observations: For the Chiang, a Sino-Tibetan border people, a sacred white stone is a leading feature of worship. The anthropologist studying this culture notes the people's basic tendency to equate white with goodness, and blackness with evil.[25] Among the Mongour, descendants of the Mongols, black is the color of mourning, and white betokens good fortune. The Chuck-chees of Siberia utilize black to symbolize the *Kelets*, or evil spir-its. Germaine Dieterlen has observed that for the Bambara, a West African Negro tribe, white is used to symbolize wisdom and purity of the spirit.[26] A piece of white cloth is sometimes hung over the door of a home where the inhabitants have just made a sacrifice; white is also the regal color. The dark tones of indigo, on the other hand, connote obscenity, impurity, and sadness. Black is also iden-tified with the North and the rainy season. Similarly, Negroes of Northern Rhodesia are observed to associate good luck with clean-ness and whiteness. A hunter smears a white substance on his forehead to invoke the powers of fortune; a person who has met with disaster is said to be "black on the forehead." In Nigeria, the Nupe tribe represents bleak or frightening prospects, sorcery, or evil by black, while white implies luck and good prospects. The Yorubas, also in Nigeria, wear white when worshiping, as they be-lieve the deities prefer white. Among the Creek Indians of North America, white betokens virtue and age, and black implies death. Although the present examination did reveal irregularities, these were extremely few and limited largely to instances in which white was associated with funeral rites. In short, the major volume of the evidence suggests widespread communality in feelings about black and white.

Before the significance of these findings for human relation-ships can be examined, the apparent existence of communality must be reconciled with the theory of color learning developed above. If the connotative meanings of colors are primarily learned, why is there not dramatic variability in the emotional impact of various colors from one cultural context to another? One clear rea-son for uniformity in association obviously derives from cultural diffusion. Meanings common within a culture may be passed on to others as a simple result of cross-cultural interaction. Such an ex-planation would not, however, account for the germination of such associations or for their common existence in somewhat isolated areas of the world.

More compelling is the possibility that the emotional response to at least the experience of black and white is established at a very early age, and as a result of almost universal experiences. Two such experiences seem especially germane: the meaning of night versus day for the child, and the training he receives in cleanliness. Night is often a period in which the child is in isolation, without comfort or bodily gratification. Moreover, night is a perfect screen on which he can project his worst fears. Any phantom, no matter how formidable, can exist within the amorphous cover of blackness. In Wallace Stephen's poem "Domination of Black," one finds the following reaction to chaos and disorder:

> I saw the night come,
> Come striding like the color of the heavy hemlocks.
> I felt afraid.

With the coming of daylight, family and environment are again visibly present, and sustenance and touch available. It is also much more difficult to project one's fears onto the compelling properties of visually apparent objects. John Dollard and Neal Miller have perhaps best outlined the profound significance of cleanliness training in the life of the child.[27] It is unnecessary to review the details of their arguments to appreciate that for most children immersion in dirt or other dark substances is ultimately reprehensible, and unsoiled skin rewarded.[28]

Are the basic emotional reactions triggered by various colors generalized to the domain of social interaction? Will, for example, the person whose emotional reaction to black is negative also feel antipathy for people whose skins are dark? In theory, such a possibility is highly plausible, and research has shown that emotions generated by color can be generalized to objects continuously paired with color.[29] But when one turns to the factual domain, the evidence is far from conclusive. The existence of anti-Negro sentiments among whites is subject to a host of explanations that do not involve color experience. More compelling, and yet unsettling, are incidents in which Negroes themselves seem negatively predisposed toward those among them with dark skin. Some of the most dramatic cases of this kind are found in the literature on mental illness among Negroes. Investigators have noted the great frequency with which the desire to be white recurs in dreams and delusional states of hospitalized Negroes. Such patients believe that they are really white, but that their skin is dirty, dyed, or painted. Some even think that they have eaten foods that have caused their skin to darken.[30] Other investigators have found that Negroes' self-esteem may be greatly impaired as a result of such feelings, and that accompanying self-hatred may be generalized to hatred for the entire Negro race.[31] Such feelings do not seem to be limited to psychotic patients. Among normal groups, one study has shown that three out of five Negroes feel that black is the worst color to be.[32] Among Negro college students, light-skinned Negroes are considered more attractive.[33] On the broad social level, Negroes with lighter skin have more education and hold jobs with higher status.[34]

In studies of adults it is, of course, difficult to rule out the impact that the attitudes and treatment received from whites have had on Negro feelings toward self. It would also be a mistake to attribute all these various findings to simple assimilation of white attitudes. Somewhat more convincing with regard to our initial supposition are studies of elementary and preschool children. Even in the second grade, Negro children will prefer white children as friends.[35] The Clarks have found that three-year-old Negro children will notably prefer a white doll to a brown one, feeling the white doll is nicer, looks better, and has a better color. Further studies show that preschool nursery children will fail to identify themselves as Negro and will prefer to see themselves as white.[36]

The supposition that attitudes toward color generalize to attitudes toward people, and in this case working toward the detriment of the Negro, gains further credence when one peruses various accounts of experiences in non-Western cultures. The classic case is the capitulation of the Aztec civilization to Cortez and his small band of soldiers, an event some have thought to be the result of the Aztec association of whiteness with divinity. There are also the accounts of Captain James Cook's explorations in New Zealand, where he found that the more prestigious natives of the tribes were of a whiter cast.[37] Melville's description of the Marquesan islanders is also à propos. Upon the arrival of the first white woman to the island, the "islanders . . . gazed in mute admiration at so unusual a prodigy, and seemed inclined to regard [her] as some new divinity." The Marquesan women were also known to take great pains to whiten their skin in order to appear more beautiful. In India, varna, the word for caste, originally meant "color." While the color of the highest caste, the Brahmins, is white, the color associated with the Sudras, the lowest caste, is black.

Although hardly conclusive, the above evidence suggests that whenever there are distinctively different color lines within a society, there will be a pronounced tendency toward strife between the light and the dark. Further, alterations in laws or social structure, loosening of economic biases, and reduction of prejudice within any period of time will not serve as a trans-historical panacea. Rather, each new generation may have to learn anew the irrational basis of their antipathy. While race prejudice may to some extent be learned, persons may also have to be taught *not* to be prejudiced. The often noted tendency for the dark-skinned to feel inferior may have an initial basis in color symbolism. Such feelings may serve to reinforce exploitation by the lighter skinned, and thus diminish further the self-esteem of the dark. Again, an extended process of relearning may be entailed.

Skin Color in the World of Everyday Relations

A person tends to categorize other people on the basis of overt physical differences and to invest these categories with certain connotative meanings. When such investments take place on a denotative level, they are often called stereotypes. The common tendencies to perceive Negroes as lazy, Jews as mercenary, and Japanese as shy have received keen attention inasmuch as they exemplify indiscriminate modes of thinking. There are also culturally shared stereotypes based on differences in clothing, club or group affiliations, and so on. People feel they know something about a person because he wears the uniform of a policeman or a soldier; the personalities of those affiliated with extreme-right versus left-wing political groups are commonly supposed to differ. Such stereotypes may have subtle but far-reaching influences on human relations. They tend to dull one's sensitivities to the truly individual qualities of the single other. Encountering another, people typically search for information that will allow them to act adaptively toward him. Once it has been found that the person can be stereotyped, the search for and sensitivity to more refined facts concerning the person may be sharply reduced. Thus, color-based categorization and resulting stereotyping can deter what may be termed "personalistic" encounters.[38] In addition to reducing sensitivity, categorization also promotes *object* relations as opposed to *person-centered* relations. Rather than being engaged as a unique individual, the person who is marked as an exemplar of a group becomes an object. He will be identified first of all as Chinese or Negro; the difficulties in breaking through such categorizations to engage the man are considerable. In Buber's terms, the person who is classified on the basis of skin color becomes an *It* rather than a *Thou*.[39]

For the person who may potentially be discriminated against

because of his skin color, additional liabilities may accrue.[40] Being treated as a member of a category, rather than as an individual, one tends to behave in ways that are consistent with the assigned category. If the person feels that others expect him to act diffidently, for example, the path of least resistance is to act in the prescribed manner. In this sense, stereotyping may tend to reinforce itself. In addition, unlike a uniform or group affiliation, skin color cannot be donned or doffed as the situation may demand. The person is thus placed at an important disadvantage because he must always present to others information about his racial background. In essence, he is disadvantaged with regard to information control in the situation. Lest this be taken lightly, one might envision a typical member of white society living out his public life with the words "middle-class suburbanite," "less than a high-school education," or "I was 4-F" emblazoned on his forehead.

As a result of this uncontrolled presentation of information, the person is also forced to attend to its consequences. At the outset of relationships with persons of another racial grouping, he will be forced to seek cues as to the other's assessment of him. In essence, the internal logic might go, "He sees I am Negro"; then, "What does he think of Negroes?" Once the search for cues has commenced, he is forced into an almost schizoid position. He must discriminate between reactions to his skin color as opposed to those relevant to him as a person. He cannot be certain, in effect, whether a warm smile or a cold remark is a reaction to his racial category or to his more individual personage. Persons with wealth or power are faced with parallel problems. They cannot be certain whether their acceptance by another is personal or prompted by their position in life. Such persons are at an advantage, however, in that they often have greater control over the information available to others.

In a society where race prejudice exists, the above problems are only exacerbated. In such cases the person carries with him a constant reminder of his limitations, disadvantages, and diminished opportunities. These constant reminders serve only to support the low-self-esteem syndrome referred to above. The description of some Negroes as being "color struck" may be quite apt. For the strong at heart, skin color may produce overcompensation. Feeling others' discrimination, the Negro may strive all the harder to achieve or gain power. But the seeking of power, whether economic or otherwise, on strictly retaliatory grounds may have unfortunate consequences within a society. Moreover, skin color serves as an easy scapegoat for the person who tries and fails. Rather than asking rational questions calculated to overcome past errors, the person may simply blame his failure on his skin color and ask no further questions. In all too many cases, however, the person's skin color may simply inform him that trying itself is fruitless.

The hurdles of racial equality may be high ones, indeed, and great preparation may be needed for the jump. The most direct mode of offsetting many of these problems may reside in programs of learning. Increased knowledge concerning persons of other races should serve to ameliorate many of the above conditions. In particular, knowledge of basic similarities is at a premium. Such similarities are most likely to be manifested prior to intensive subgroup acculturation, and thus the period of childhood is most strongly implicated as a teaching context. Discrimination learning in the area of color symbolism may also play an important role. Both this type of training as well as training in breaking down stereotypes work against the inertia of imprecise thinking. The ultimate solution may reside in the domain of racial homogenization.

REFERENCES

1. Susan Hole and Kenneth Gergen, "Color and Communication: The Effects of the Hue and Saturation on Reactions to Poetry." Paper presented at the 1966 Meetings of the American Psychological Association.

2. While it must be recognized that within anthropological circles skin color alone is not considered a technically valid yardstick for assessing racial membership, the traditional social distinctions will be adhered to for the present purposes.

3. Some have also ventured that sensitivity to differences in skin shade is much greater within a color grouping than across it. Thus, for example, Negroes may be much more sensitive to lightness of skin among Negroes than are whites.

4. C. E. Osgood, G. H. Suci, and P. H. Tannenbaum, *The Measurement of Meaning* (Urbana, Ill., 1957).

5. Sigmund Freud, "On Narcissism: An Introduction (1914)," *Collected Papers*, Vol. 4 (New York, 1959).

6. John Dunne, whose critical comments have been exceedingly valuable during the preparation of this paper, has suggested in this regard that

attitudes of whites for whom a Negro domestic has served as a mother surrogate may be of special empirical interest.

7. Fritz Heider, *The Psychology of Interpersonal Relations* (New York, 1958).

8. A summary of this literature may be found in Kenneth J. Gergen and David Marlow (eds.), *Personality and Social Behavior* (Reading, Mass., in press).

9. While of interest, these accounts are certainly not intended to be conclusive evidence of the processes at stake. Many alternative explanations can be made. Untangling the processes involved in historical accounts is an almost impossible task.

10. Francisco A. Pigafetta, *The First Voyage Round the World by Magellan,* ed. Lord Stanley of Alderly (London, 1874).

11. William Lithgow, *The Totall Discourse of the Rare Adventures and Painefull Peregrinations (of Long Nineteene Yeares Travayles from Scotland to the Most Famous Kingdomes in Europe, Asia, and Affrica)* (Glasgow, 1906; original, 1632).

12. Putnam B. L. Weale, *The Conflict of Colour* (New York, 1910).

13. Gordon W. Allport, *The Nature of Prejudice* (Cambridge, Mass., 1954).

14. Cf. Jack W. Brehm and Arthur R. Cohen, *Explorations in Cognitive Dissonance* (New York, 1962), for a general discussion of inconsistency.

15. Kenneth J. Gergen and Edward E. Jones, "Mental Illness, Predictability, and Affective Consequences as Stimulus Factors in Person Perception," *Journal of Abnormal and Social Psychology,* Vol. 67 (1963), pp. 95-104.

16. In cases where upward socioeconomic mobility is possible, one offsetting tendency is for the disadvantaged to imitate the customs, dress, and behavior of the advantaged. This tendency had been noted as early as 1903 in the writings of Gabriel Tarde, cf. *(The) Laws of Imitation,* trans. Elsie Parsons (New York, 1903).

17. Sex differences may be a debatable example in this instance. In terms of mobility and autonomy, females are in many respects more disadvantaged than members of racial minorities.

18. This discussion will treat "black" and "white" as colors, although arguments to the contrary could be made on technical grounds.

19. Matthew Luckiesh, *The Language of Color* (New York, 1918).

20. Walter Sargent, *The Enjoyment and Use of Color* (New York, 1923).

21. Faber Birren, *Color in Your World* (New York, 1962). While "strength" and "deep quiet" are exceptional within the group of associations to black, it is not clear that they fall along an evaluative dimension. More will be said below concerning the other connotative dimensions related to black.

22. Birren and others also equate white with death, but the referent here seems

126

to be to the pallor sometimes accompanying death and to the spiritual domain related to the theme of the hereafter.

23. Cf. Harold R. Isaacs, *The New World of Negro Americans* (New York, 1963); Harry Levin, *The Power of Blackness* (New York, 1960).

24. Cf. J. J. Jenkins, W. A. Russell, and G. J. Suci, "An Atlas of Semantic Profiles for 360 Words," *American Journal of Psychology* (1958) for an overview of the subject. The experiment alluded to was conducted by John E. Williams, "Connotations of Color Names Among Negroes and Caucasians," *Perceptual and Motor Skills*, Vol. 18 (1964), pp. 121-31.

25. Thomas Torrance, "The Basic Spiritual Conceptions of the Religion of the Chiang," *Journal of the West China Border Research Society*, Vol. 6 (1933), pp. 31-48.

26. Germaine Dieterlen, *An Essay on the Religion of the Bambara*, trans. Katia Wolf (Paris, 1951), pp. 1-293.

27. John Dollard and Neal Miller, *Personality and Psychotherapy* (New York, 1950).

28. With the lack of viable evidence, it is difficult to know whether this argument would hold on a cross-cultural basis. In addition, for Negroes with very dark skin, dirt may often have the effect of lightening their skin.

29. S. P. Harbin and J. E. Williams, "Conditioning of Color Connotations," *Perceptual and Motor Skills*, Vol. 22 (1966), pp. 217-18.

30. John Lind, "The Color Complex in the Negro," *Psychoanalytic Review*, Vol. 1 (1914), pp. 404-14.

31. Henry Myers and Leon Yochelson, "Color Denial in the Negro," *Psychiatry*, Vol. 11 (1948), pp. 39-46. For further analysis of Negro self-hatred, see Thomas F. Pettigrew, *A Profile of the Negro American* (Princeton, 1964).

32. Charles H. Parrish, "Color Names and Color Notions," *Journal of Negro Education*, Vol. 15 (1946), p. 13.

33. E. S. Marks, "Skin Color Judgments of Negro College Students," *Journal of Abnormal and Social Psychology*, Vol. 38 (July, 1943), pp. 370-76. It will be interesting in this case, as well as the others, to assess the effects of the "black power" movement on Negro evaluation of skin shades. The present tendency could possibly reverse itself.

34. Howard E. Freeman, David Armor, J. Michael Ross, and Thomas Pettigrew, "Color Gradation and Attitudes Among Middle-Income Negroes," *American Sociological Review*, Vol. 31 (1966), pp. 365-74; St. Clair Drake and Horace R. Cayton, *Black Metropolis*, Vol. 2 (New York, 1962), pp. 496-500.

35. Helen Koch, "The Social Distance Between Certain Racial, Nationality and Skin Pigmentation Groups in Selected Populations of American

School Children," *Journal of Genetic Psychology*, Vol. 68 (1964), pp. 63-95.

36. Kenneth B. Clark and Mamie P. Clark, "Racial Identification and Preference in Negro Children," *Readings in Social Psychology*, eds. T. M. Newcomb and E. L. Hartley (New York, 1947), pp. 169-78. Also see Mary Ellen Goodman, "Evidence Concerning the Genesis of Interracial Attitudes," *American Anthropologist*, Vol. 48 (1946), pp. 624-30.

37. Captain James Cook, *The Voyages of Captain James Cook Round the World* (London, 188?).

38. Kenneth J. Gergen, "Interaction Goals and Personalistic Feedback as Factors Affecting the Presentation of Self," *Journal of Personality and Social Psychology*, Vol. 1 (1965), pp. 413-24.

39. Martin Buber, *I and Thou*, trans. Ronald G. Smith (New York, 1958).

40. For an additional treatment of these types of phenomena see Erving Goffman, *Stigma* (Englewood Cliffs, N. J., 1963).

HIROSHI WAGATSUMA

The Social Perception of Skin Color in Japan

LONG BEFORE any sustained contact with either Caucasoid Europeans or dark-skinned Africans or Indians, the Japanese valued
"white" skin as beautiful and deprecated "black" skin as ugly.
Their spontaneous responses to the white skin of Caucasoid Europeans and the black skin of Negroid people were an extension of
values deeply embedded in Japanese concepts of beauty.[1] From
past to present, the Japanese have always associated skin color
symbolically with other physical characteristics that signify degrees of spiritual refinement or primitiveness. Skin color has been
related to a whole complex of attractive or objectionable social
traits. It might strike some as curious that the Japanese have traditionally used the word *white* (*shiroi*) to describe lighter shades
of their own skin color. The social perception of the West has been
that the Chinese and Japanese belong to a so-called "yellow" race,
while the Japanese themselves have rarely used the color yellow to
describe their skin.

I

"White" skin has been considered an essential characteristic of
feminine beauty in Japan since recorded time. An old Japanese
proverb states that "white skin makes up for seven defects"; a
woman's light skin causes one to overlook the absence of other
desired physical features.[2]

During the Nara period (710-793), court ladies made ample
use of cosmetics and liberally applied white powder to the face.[3]
Cheeks were rouged. Red beauty spots were painted on between
the eyebrows and at the outer corners of both the eyes and the
lips. Eyelids and lips were given a red tinge.[4] Both men and
women removed their natural eyebrows and penciled in long, thick

129

lines emulating a Chinese style. The custom of blackening teeth spread among the aristocratic ladies.[5] In the next period (794-1185), when the court was moved to the new capital of Heian (Kyoto), countless references were made in both illustration and writing to round-faced, plump women with white, smooth skin. Necessary to beauty was long, black, straight hair that draped over the back and shoulders without being tied.[6] One can illustrate this conception of white skin as a mark of beauty from *The Tale of Genji* by Lady Murasaki, a romance of the first decade of the eleventh century:

Her color of skin was very white and she was plump with an attractive face. Her hair grew thick but was cut so as to hang on a level with her shoulders—very beautiful.

Her color was very white and although she was emaciated and looked noble, there still was a certain fulness in her cheek.[7]

In her personal diary, the same author depicted portraits of several court ladies:

Lady Dainagon is very small but as she is white and beautifully round, she has a taller appearance. Her hair is three inches longer than her height.

Lady Senji is a small and slender person. The texture of her hair is fine, delicate and glossy and reaches a foot longer than her height.

Lady Naiji has beauty and purity, a fragrant white skin with which no one else can compete.[8]

Writing about the year 1002 in essays called *The Pillow Book*, the court lady Sei Shōnagon described how she despised "hair not smooth and straight" and envied "beautiful, very long hair."[9] In *The Tale of Glory*, presumably written in 1120 by Akazome Emon, a court lady, two beautiful women of the prosperous Fujiwara family are depicted: one with "her hair seven or eight inches longer than her height," and the other with "her hair about two feet longer than her height and her skin white and beautiful."[10] From the eighth to the twelfth century, the bearers of Japanese cultural refinement were the court nobility who idled their lives away in romantic love affairs, practicing the arts of music and poetry. The whiteness of untanned skin was the symbol of this privileged class which was spared any form of outdoor labor. From the eleventh century on, men of the aristocracy applied powder to their faces just as the court ladies did.[11]

In 1184, the warriors took the reins of government away from the effete courtiers and abruptly ended the court's rather decadent era. To protect the *samurai* virtues of simplicity, frugality, and bravery, the warriors set up headquarters in the frontier town of Kamakura located far away from the capital. The warriors maintained Spartan standards, as is evidenced in the many portrait paintings showing rather florid or swarthy countenances. Women still continued, however, the practices of toiletry established previously in the court. In 1333 the warriors' government was moved from Kamakura back to Kyoto, where the Ashikaga Shogunate family emulated court life and re-established an atmosphere of luxury among the ruling class.

Standards of feminine beauty still emphasized corpulence of body, white skin, and black hair, which in this period was worn in a chignon. Preference was voiced for a woman with a round face, broad forehead, and eyes slightly down-turned at the corners.[12] By this time, the old court custom of penciling eyebrows and blackening teeth had become incorporated into the puberty rites practiced for both boys and girls. Such rites were principally held by the warrior class but were later adopted by commoners.[13] The writing of Yoshida Kenkō, a celebrated poet and court official who became a Buddhist monk in 1324, exemplifies the continuing preoccupation this period had with the white skin of women. Yoshida wrote the following in his *Essays of Idleness:*

The magician of Kume (as the legend runs) lost his magic power through looking at the white leg of a maiden washing clothes in a river. This may well have been because the white limbs and skin of a woman cleanly plump and fatty are no mere external charms but true beauty and allure.[14]

Following a chaotic political period, the Tokugawa feudal government was established in 1603. It was to last until the modern period of Japan, more than two hundred and fifty years. Changes occurred in the ideals of feminine beauty during this period of continuing peace. Gradually, slim and fragile women with slender faces and up-turned eyes began to be preferred to the plump, pear-shaped ideal that remained dominant until the middle of the eighteenth century.[15] White skin, however, remained an imperative characteristic of feminine beauty. Ibara Saikaku (1642-1693), a novelist who wrote celebrated books about common life during the early Tokugawa period, had the following to say about the type of female beauty to be found in Kyoto and Osaka:

A beautiful woman with a round face, skin with a faint pink color, eyes not too narrow, eyebrows thick, the bridge of her nose not too thin, her mouth small, teeth in excellent shape and shining white.[16]

A woman of twenty-one, white of color, hair beautiful, attired in gentleness.

Thanks to the pure water of Kyoto, women remain attractive from early childhood but they further improve their beauty by steaming their faces, tightening their fingers with rings and wearing leather socks in sleep. They also comb their hair with the juice of the *sanekazura* root.[17]

Another author, depicting the beauties of the middle Tokugawa period of the 1770's, wrote: "A pair of girls wearing red-lacquered thongs on their tender feet, white as snow, sashes around their waists, with forms as slender as willow trees."[18] Tamenaga Shunsui (1789-1843), an author of the late Tokugawa period, never forgot to mention white skin when describing the beautiful women of Edo (Tokyo):

Her hands and arms are whiter than snow.

You are well-featured and your color is so white that you are popular among your audience.

This courtesan had a neck whiter than snow. Her face was shining as she always polished it with powder.[19]

The use of good water and the practice of steaming the face were thought to make skin white and smooth. Rings and socks were worn in sleep to stunt excessive growth of limbs since small hands and feet were valued attributes of feminine charm. The juice of the *sanekazura* root was used to straighten the hair. These practices all confirm the continuous concern with white skin and straight hair. They also suggest, however, the possibility that many women were lacking in such standards of feminine beauty. The following quotation describes what was considered ugly:

Disagreeable features for a woman are a large face, the lack of any tufts of hair under the temple, a big, flat nose, thick lips, black skin, a too plump body, excessive tallness, heavy, strong limbs, brownish wavy hair and a loud, talkative voice.

These were the comments of Yanagi Rikyō, a high-ranking warrior of the Kōriyama fief, who was also a poet, artist, and noted connoisseur of womanhood in the late-eighteenth century. He contrasted these objectionable features with "the amiable features of a woman, a small and well-shaped face, white skin, gentle manner, an innocent, charming and attentive character."[20] One might speculate that the supposed Polynesian or Melanesian strains, sometimes thought to have entered the Japanese racial mixture, would be responsible for flat noses, thick lips, or brownish, wavy hair. Such features are certainly not rare among Japanese, although they run directly counter to the Japanese image of beauty.

Because Mongoloid skin shows a very quick tendency to tan and to produce "black" skin, the Japanese can maintain lightness of skin only by total avoidance of sunlight. Not surprisingly, Tokugawa women made constant use of parasols or face hoods to hide their skin from sunlight and assiduously applied powder to face, neck, throat, and upper chest.[21] In order to increase the whiteness and smoothness of their skin, women "polished" it in their baths with a cloth bag containing rice bran or the droppings of the Japanese nightingale. Application of other grains such as millet, barley, Deccan grass, and beans was also considered to have some "bleaching" effect on the skin. Juices taken from various flowers were also used for the same purpose,[22] and many medicines were sold that promised "to turn the skin as white as the snow found on the peaks of high mountains."[23]

When a woman's constant care of her skin achieved desired results, she would enjoy such praise as "Her face is so smoothly shiny that it seems ready to reflect," and "Her face can compete with a mirror," or "Her face is so shiny as to make a well polished black lacquered dresser feel ashamed."[24]

From the beginning of the nineteenth century, the Kabuki actors set the standards of men's beauty. A rather feminine type of male with a slender figure, well-formed face, white skin, black hair, and red lips became a favorite object of feminine desire. Men possessing these elements of attractiveness would enjoy such a flattering remark as "You should be a Kabuki actor." By the middle of the nineteenth century, these characteristics began to be considered effeminate. A man with a more dusky skin and a piquantly handsome face became the preferred type.[25]

The word *white* repeatedly used in the quotations taken from these various sources is the same Japanese word *shiroi* that is used to describe snow or white paper. There was no intermediate word between *shiroi* ("white") and *kuroi* ("black") used to describe skin color.[26] When distinctions were made, there would be recourse to such words as *asa guroi* ("light black").

II

Not long after the first globe-circling voyages of Magellan, Westerners appeared on the shores of Japan. Dutch, English, Portuguese, and Spanish traders came to ply their trade in Japanese ports. Both Spanish and Portuguese missionaries sought to establish Christianity in Japan. Before the Tokugawa government sealed off Japan from the West, the Japanese had ample opportunity to observe white men for the first time. In these early contacts, the Portuguese and Spaniards were called *nanban-jin* or *nanban* meaning "southern barbarians," words adopted from the Chinese who had names to designate all the "inferior savages" living to the north, south, east, and west of the Middle Kingdom. The Dutch were called *kōmō-jin* or *kōmō*, "red-haired people."

In several of the colored pictures of the day[27] that included both Japanese and Europeans, the Japanese artists painted the faces of the Portuguese, Spanish, and Japanese men in a flesh color or light brown, but depicted the faces of Japanese women as white in hue. In a few other pictures, however, some Portuguese are given white faces like Japanese women, while other Portuguese are given darker faces. Seemingly, the Japanese artists were sensitive in some instances to some form of color differential among the foreigners. Many Portuguese and Spaniards were actually not so white-skinned as northern Europeans, and after the long sea voyage to Japan, they undoubtedly arrived with rather well-tanned skins. The Dutch in the pictures, on the other hand, seem to be given invariably either gray or white faces. When contrasted with the Japanese women near them, the Japanese feminine face is painted a whiter hue than that of the Dutch.

The differences between the Japanese and the Europeans in these old prints are clearly depicted in hair color and facial characteristics. The Portuguese, Spaniards, and Dutch are all taller than the Japanese and are given somewhat unrealistically large noses. Their double eye folds and their bushy eyebrows and mustaches seem slightly exaggerated. The Portuguese and Spanish hair is painted brown although a few are given black hair. The Dutch hair is usually depicted as either red or reddish-brown in color.[28] Written and pictorial descriptions indicate that the Japanese were more impressed with the height, hair color, general hairiness, big noses and eyes of the foreigners than with their lighter skin color.[29] Some pictures include portraits of the Negro

134

servants of the Portuguese and Dutch. The faces of Negroes are painted in a leaden- or blackish-gray, and their hair is shown as extremely frizzled. The physiognomy of the Negroes is somewhat caricatured and in some instances closely resembles the devils and demons of Buddhist mythology.

Some Japanese scholars of Dutch science seem to have had a notion that the black skin and frizzled hair of Negro servants were the result of extreme exposure to heat and sunshine in the tropical countries in which they were born. In 1787, such a scholar wrote of what he had learned from his Dutch friends about their Negro servants:

These black ones on the Dutch boats are the natives of countries in the South. As their countries are close to the sun, they are sun-scorched and become black. By nature they are stupid.

The black ones are found with flat noses. They love a flat nose and they tie children's noses with leather bands to prevent their growth and to keep them flat.

Africa is directly under the equator and the heat there is extreme. Therefore, the natives are black colored. They are uncivilized and vicious in nature.[30]

Another scholar wrote:

Black ones are impoverished Indians employed by the Dutch. As their country is in the South and the heat is extreme, their body is sun-scorched and their color becomes black. Their hair is burned by the sun and becomes frizzled but they are humans and not monkeys as some mistakenly think.[31]

After the closing of the country by the Tokugawa government in 1639, the only contact of Japanese with Westerners, aside from the Dutch traders, would occur when shipwrecked Japanese sailors would occasionally be picked up by Western ships and taken for a period to a Western country. The reports about the English, Russians, and Spaniards made by these Japanese sailors upon their return commented much more on the hair and eyes of the Occidentals than upon the color of skin.[32]

In 1853 Commodore Perry of the United States Navy came to Japan with his "black ships" and forced Japan to reopen her ports to foreign vessels. When Perry visited Japan for the second time in 1854, there were two American women on board. It was reported in a Japanese document:

On board is a woman named Shirley, 31 years old and her child Loretta, 5 years old. Their hair is red. They have high noses, white faces

135

and the pupils of their eyes are brown. They are medium in size and very beautiful.[33]

The portraits of Commodore Perry and five principals of his staff drawn by a Japanese artist show the Americans with noses of exaggerated size, large eyes, and brownish hair. Their faces are painted in a washed-out, whitish-ash color. In other pictures, however, both American and Japanese faces are painted with an identical whitish-gray, although the Americans are given brown hair and bushy beards. In some pictures showing the American settlements in Yokohama and Tokyo of the 1860's, the faces of both American and Japanese women are painted whiter than those of American and Japanese men. It may well be possible that the American men's faces were more sun-tanned and exposed to the elements during the voyage than the faces of the women who, observing canons of beauty much like those held by Japanese women, may have kept themselves out of the sun. Also, the artists may have simply resorted to convention by which women's faces were painted white.[34]

In 1860 the Tokugawa government sent an envoy with an entourage of eighty-three warriors to the United States to ratify a treaty of peace and commerce between the United States and Japan originally signed in 1854. Some of the members of the entourage kept careful diaries and noted their impressions of the United States during their trip to Washington. Upon meeting the President of the United States, one *samurai* wrote: "President Buchanan, about 52 or 53 years of age, is a tall person. His color is white, his hair is white." The *samurai* leaders were surprised to attend formal receptions at which women were included and to find that American men acted toward their women as obliging servants. They were impressed with the daring exposure afforded by the décolletage of the formal evening gowns worn by women at these balls and receptions. In their diaries they noted their appreciation of American beauty, although they continued to express their preference for black hair:

The women's skin was white and they were charming in their gala dresses decorated with gold and silver but their hair was red and their eyes looked like dog eyes, which was quite disheartening.

Occasionally I saw women with black hair and black eyes. They must have been of some Asian race. Naturally they looked more attractive and beautiful.

Another man expressed his admiration for the President's niece,

Harriet Lane, in true *samurai* fashion by composing a Chinese poem:

> An American belle, her name is Lane,
> Jewels adorn her arms, jade her ears.
> Her rosy face needs no powder or rouge.
> Her exposed shoulders shine as white as snow.[35]

This American belle and her friends had asked another *samurai* at a party which women he liked better, Japanese or American. The *samurai* wrote in his diary:

I answered that the American women are better because their skin color is whiter than that of the Japanese women. Such a trifling comment of mine obviously pleased the girls. After all, women are women.

After seeing about a hundred American children aged five to nine gathered at a May festival ball, another warrior wrote of his admiration of their beauty:

The girls did not need to have the help of powder and rouge. Their skin with its natural beauty was whiter than snow and purer than jewels. I wondered if fairies in wonderland would not look something like these children.

On the way back from the United States, the boat carrying the Japanese envoy stopped at a harbor on the African coast, and the *samurai* had a chance to see the black-skinned Africans inhabiting the region. They noted with disapproval their impression of Negroid features:

The black ones look like devils depicted in pictures.

The faces are black as if painted with ink and their physiognomy reminds me of that of a monkey.[36]

III

In the early Meiji period, the Japanese began their self-conscious imitation of the technology of the West. Less consciously, they also began to alter their perception of feminine beauty. In their writings, they referred with admiration to the white skin of Westerners, but noted with disapproval the hair color and the hairiness of Westerners. Wavy hair was not to the Japanese taste until the mid-1920's. Curly hair was considered to be an animal characteristic. Mrs. Sugimoto, the daughter of a *samurai*, writes in her autobiography that, as a child with curly hair, she had her hair dressed twice a week with a special treatment to straighten it properly. When she complained, her mother would scold her, saying, "Do you not know that curly hair is like that of animals? A *samurai's* daughter should not be willing to resemble a beast."[37]

The body hair of Caucasian men suggested a somewhat beastly nature to Japanese women, and, probably for reasons of this kind, Japanese women of the late-nineteenth century refused or were reluctant in many instances to become mistresses to Western diplomats.[38]

By the mid-1920's the Japanese had adopted Western customs and fashions, including the singing of American popular songs and dancing in dance halls. They watched motion pictures with delight and made great favorites of Clara Bow, Gloria Swanson, and Greta Garbo. Motion pictures seem to have had a very strong effect in finally changing habits of coiffure and attitudes toward desirable beauty. During this period many Japanese women had their hair cut and, in spite of the exhortations of proud *samurai* tradition, had it waved and curled. They took to wearing long skirts with large hats to emulate styles worn by Greta Garbo. The 1920's was a time of great imitation. Anything Western was considered "modern" and, therefore, superior. This trend lasted until the mid-1930's when, under the pressure of the ultra-nationalist, militarist regime, the ties with Western fads were systematically broken.[39]

Already in 1924, Tanizaki Junichirō depicted a woman who represented a kind of femininity that was appealing to "modern" intellectuals of the time. She was Naomi in *The Love of an Idiot*, and her physical attractiveness had a heavy Western flavor. She was sought after by a man who "wished if ever possible to go to Europe and marry an Occidental woman." Since he could not do so, he decided to marry Naomi, who had such Occidental features. He helped her refine her beauty and educated her so that she would become "a real lady presentable even to the eyes of the Occidentals." She became, instead, a promiscuous, lust-driven woman who turned her mentor-husband into a slave chained to her by his uncontrollable passion. An important aspect of Tanizaki's depiction of this Occidental-looking girl is the whiteness of her skin:

Against the red gown, her hands and feet stand out purely white like the core of a cabbage.

Her skin was white to an astounding degree. . . . All the exposed parts of her voluptuous body were as white as the meat of an apple.

138

There is a most interesting passage in this book, however, in which Tanizaki, with a note of disappointment, compares Naomi with a real European woman, a Russian aristocrat living in exile in Japan.

[The Russian woman's] skin color . . . was so extraordinarily white, an almost ghostly beauty of white skin under which the blood vessels of light violet color were faintly visible like the veining of marble. Compared with this skin, that of Naomi's lacked clearness and shine and was rather dull to the eye.[40]

The subtle, not fully conscious, trend toward an idealization of Western physical features by the Japanese apparently became of increasing importance in the twenties. It remained a hidden subcurrent throughout the last war while Japan, as the "champion of the colored nations," fought against the "whites." In spite of propaganda emphasizing the racial ties between Japanese and other Asians, the "yellowness" of the Japanese was never quite made a point of pride. The rapidity with which Western standards of beauty became idealized after the war attests to the continuous drift that was occurring in spite of ten years of antagonism and military hostilities.

IV

Older Japanese who have lived overseas have been astounded upon visiting postwar Japan. The straight black hair of the past is all but gone. Even most geisha, the preservers of many feminine traditions, have permanents and wave their hair. Among ordinary women, one periodically sees extreme examples of hair that has been bleached with hydrogen peroxide or, more commonly, dyed a purplish or reddish hue. Plastic surgery, especially to alter eye folds and to build up the bridge of the nose, has become almost standardized practice among the younger movie actresses and, indeed, even among some of the male actors. There were examples of plastic surgery to be found before the war, but its wide popularity is something new.[41]

Contemporary Japanese men interviewed in the United States and Japan all agreed in valuing the "whiteness" of skin as a component of beauty in the Japanese woman.[42] Whiteness is very often associated in their minds with womanhood ("Whiteness is a symbol of women, distinguishing them from men"), with chastity and purity ("Whiteness suggests purity and moral virtue"), and

139

motherhood ("One's mother-image is white"). Linked with concerns for the skin's whiteness are desires that it also be smooth with a close, firm texture, a shiny quality, and no wrinkles, furrows, spots, or flecks. Some informants mentioned the value of a soft, resilient, and subtly damp surface to the skin. This quality, called *mochi-hada* ("skin like pounded rice") in Japanese, has an implicit sexual connotation for some men.[43]

Although many young men accept the primary preference for white skin, they also admit that sun-tanned skin in a young woman is of a "modern" healthy attractiveness. Some men contrasted such healthy charm to that of a "beautiful tuberculosis patient whose skin is pale and almost transparent," a type of helpless beauty that represented tragic charm during the 1930's. Associated with brownish, sun-tanned skin as a beauty type are large Western eyes, a relatively large mouth with bold lips, a well-developed body, and an outgoing, gay personality.

Such a creature with "Western" charm was held in direct contrast to the more traditional femininity of white skin, less conspicuous physique, gentle manner, and quiet character. One finds these contrasts and stereotypes juxtaposed in popular contemporary fiction. There is some ambivalence about light-colored skin in men. Light skin suggests excessive intellectualism, more effeteness, individuals who are impractical and concern themselves with philosophical questions of life, love, and eternity, and those who are unduly ruminative and lack the capacity to act.

Among the women interviewed, there was a general consensus that Japanese women like to be "white-skinned," but that there is a type of modern beauty in women with sun-tanned skin. The women believe that such women, however, when they marry and settle down, "stop being sporty and sun-tanned. Such a girl will take care of her skin and become white."[44]

Several informants with working-class backgrounds said that, as children, they heard their mothers and other adult women talk about the "fragile, white-skinned women" of the wealthier class who did not have to work outside. They remembered a certain tone of both envy and contempt in their mothers' voices. There is a tendency to associate "white" skin with urban and "black" skin with rural living.

In this connection, a Japanese social psychologist who had visited Okinawa several times told us that many Okinawans become self-conscious of their "black" skin when they meet Japanese from Japan. To Okinawan eyes, the Japanese appear to have "whiter" skin and, therefore, look much more refined and urban than do the Okinawans. There used to be a general association among the Japanese of "white" skin with wealth, "black" skin with lower economic status. The younger generations, however, increasingly tend to consider sun-tanned skin as the sign of the socially privileged people who can afford summer vacations at the seaside or mountain resorts.[45]

With only a few exceptions, the women interviewed voiced the opinion that Japanese women like light-brown-skinned men, seeing them as more masculine than pale-skinned men. Many women distinguished between "a beautiful man" and "an attractive man." A beautiful man (*bi-danshi*) is white-skinned and delicately featured like a Kabuki actor. Although he is admired and appreciated almost aesthetically, he is, at the same time, considered somewhat "too feminine" for a woman to depend upon. There is sometimes a reference to the saying, "A beautiful man lacks money and might." On the other hand, an attractive man (*kō-danshi*) is dusky-skinned, energetic, masculine, and dependable. Women often associate light-brown skin in a man with a dauntless spirit, a capacity for aggressive self-assertion, and a quality of manly sincerity.

A few of the women interviewed parenthetically mentioned that a woman concerned with her own "black" skin might want to marry a white-skinned man, hoping thereby to give birth to light-skinned daughters. A few younger women in favor of white skin in a man said that a white-skinned man is "more hairy" (or perhaps hair stands out better against a light background), and hairiness has a certain sexual appeal. Other women, however, expressed their dislike of body hair on a man. Some women mentioned a liking for copper-brown skin tone. They associated this with manual outdoor labor, strong health, and masculinity, though not with intelligence. A reddish, shining face is thought to suggest lewdness in middle-aged fat men who have acquired wealth through shady activities. Such a figure stands in opposition to concepts of justice, sincerity, and spiritual cleanliness. The reddish face of a drinking man may look satisfied and peaceful to some women, though it is hardly considered attractive.

In these interviews with both men and women, the present attitudes toward Caucasian skin seem to fall into opposites of likes and dislikes depending, seemingly, upon the degree of an individual's receptivity toward or identification with Western culture. These two opposite attitudes may coexist within an individual, either appearing alternately or being expressed simultaneously. Somewhat more than half of both men and women interviewed in California and about two thirds of those interviewed in Japan considered Caucasian skin to be inferior to the Japanese from the standpoint of texture and regularity. This stereotype was among the negative attitudes expressed in the interviews.

Caucasians' skin tends to be rough in texture, full of wrinkles, spots, and speckles.

If you look at the neck of an old Caucasian woman with furrows and bristles, it reminds you of that of a pig.

When I try to visualize a Caucasian woman, she is associated in my mind with skin of rough texture and unsmooth surface. Pores of her skin may be larger than ours. Young women may have smoother skin, but older women have bad skin.

A Eurasian child will be very attractive if it takes a Japanese parent's skin and a Caucasian parent's facial structure, but the result of an opposite combination could be disastrous.

This notion concerning a Eurasian child seems to be fairly widely held among Japanese. The idea that Caucasian skin is "ugly" is also expressed in the following passage taken from the work of a contemporary Japanese novelist:

When a kissing couple was projected on a large screen in a close-up, then the ugliness unique to Caucasian female skin was magnified. The freckles covering the woman's cheek and throat became clearly visible. . . . On the fingers of a man caressing a woman, gold hairs were seen shining like an animal's bristles.[46]

Some informants who favored Japanese "white" skin but not Caucasian suggested that Caucasian skin is *not white* but *transparent:*

This may be completely unscientific but I feel that when I look at the skin of a Japanese woman I see the whiteness of her skin. When I observe Caucasian skin, what I see is the whiteness of the fat underneath the skin, not the whiteness of the skin itself. Therefore, sometimes I see redness of blood under the transparent skin instead of white fat. Then it doesn't appear white but red.

I have seen Caucasians closely only a few times but my impression is that their skin is very thin, almost transparent, while our skin is thicker and more resilient.

The Caucasian skin is something like the surface of a pork sausage, while the white skin of a Japanese resembles the outside of *kamaboko* [a white, spongy fish cake].

Some men and women commented on the general hairiness of Caucasians. American women do not shave their faces and leave facial hair untouched. This causes the Japanese some discomfort since they are accustomed to a hairless, smooth face. (Japanese women customarily have their entire faces shaved except for the eyebrows.) Some women felt that the whiteness of Caucasian men lowered their appearance of masculinity; others disliked the hairiness of Caucasian men which they thought suggested a certain animality.

Japanese who have had little personal contact with Westerners often associate Caucasians with "strange creatures," if not with animality. Caucasian actors and actresses they constantly see on movie screens and on television may be the subject of their admiration for "manliness," "handsome or beautiful features," or "glamorous look," but "they don't seem to belong to reality." "Real" Caucasians are felt to be basically discontinuous with the Japanese. As one informant said:

When I think of actual Caucasians walking along the street, I feel that they are basically different beings from us. Certainly, they are humans but I don't feel they are the same creatures as we are. There is, in my mind, a definite discontinuity between us and the Caucasians. Somehow, they belong to a different world.

Deep in my mind, it seems, the Caucasians are somehow connected with something animal-like. Especially when I think of a middle-aged Caucasian woman, the first thing which comes up to my mind is a large chunk of boneless ham. This kind of association may not be limited to me. As I recall now, once in an English class at school, our teacher explained the meaning of the word "hog" as a big pig. A boy in our class said loudly, "Oh, I know what it is! It's like a foreign (meaning, Caucasian) woman!" We all laughed and I felt we all agreed with the boy.

For most of the Japanese without much personal contact with Westerners, skin is only one of several characteristics making up the image of a Caucasian. Other components of this image are the shape and color of eyes, hair, height, size, weight of the body, and also hairiness. Japanese feelings toward a Caucasian seem determined by all these factors. Many people interviewed in Japan talked of their difficulty in discussing their feelings toward

143

Caucasian skin as differentiated from other Caucasian physical characteristics. An image of a Caucasian with white skin, deep-set eyes, wavy hair of a color other than black, a tall, stout, hairy body, and large hands and feet seems to evoke in many Japanese an association with "vitality," "superior energy," "strong sexuality" or "animality," and the feeling that Caucasians are basically discontinuous with Asians.

Positive attitudes toward Caucasian skin center on the idea that Caucasian skin is, in actuality, whiter than the so-called white skin of the Japanese and, therefore, more attractive. Two college students in California who had dated only Caucasian boys said Caucasian white skin meant to them purity, advanced civilization, and spiritual cleanliness. They felt that even white-skinned Japanese men were "not white enough" to attract them. Although there is no basis upon which to generalize, the following report by a student who had a sexual relationship with a white woman may deserve some note:

Perhaps I was a little drunk. Under an electric light I saw her skin. It was so white that it was somehow incongruent with her nature. Such a pure whiteness and this girl of some questionable reputation.

He associated the whiteness of a woman's skin with purity and chastity, and felt white skin incongruent with the woman's promiscuous tendency.

A Japanese hairdresser married to a Japanese American disagreed with the notion that Caucasian skin is "ugly." She said that Caucasian women tend to have larger facial furrows; these are more visible than smaller wrinkles, but otherwise "their skin is no better or worse than ours." She added, however:

After attending to several Caucasian customers in a row, when I turn to a Japanese lady, the change in color is very striking. She *is* yellow. It always comes to me as a kind of shock, this yellow color. Does it remind me of my own color?—I don't know. I think I know I am yellow. Do I still want to forget it?—maybe.

A sudden realization that Japanese skin color is darker when compared with the white skin of Caucasians has been the experience of several Japanese men and women in the United States:

When I stay among Caucasian friends for some time and another Japanese joins the group, I look at him, my fellow countryman, and he looks yellow or even "black" to me. This, in turn, makes me momentarily self-conscious. I mean, I feel myself different in the group.

My daughter is very "white" among the Japanese. Looking at her face, I often say to myself how white she is. As a mother, I feel happy. But when I see her among Caucasian children in a nursery school, alas, my daughter is *yellow* indeed.

It is interesting to note that Japanese who have spent time in the United States acquire the idea that Japanese are "yellow" rather than brown-skinned. Those we met in Japan, with only a few exceptions, hesitate or even refuse to describe their skin as "yellow." They know that the Japanese belong to the "yellow race" (*Ōshoku jinshu,* the technical term for the Mongoloid), but they cannot think of their skin as actually yellow, "unless," as some remarked, "a person comes down with jaundice."

Having few occasions to compare their skin color with that of other races, the Japanese apparently do not have any words available other than *black* and *white* to describe their skin. In modern Japan, *shakudō-iro* ("color of alloy of copper and gold") and *komugi-iro* ("color of wheat") are used to describe sun-tanned skin, but other words for brown and yellow are rarely employed. When I asked a thirty-year-old woman college graduate to describe the color of Japanese skin, she answered spontaneously, "Of course, it is *hada-iro* ['skin color']!" It is not known why the Japanese, after spending time among Caucasians, come to adopt the word *yellow* for their skin. This may be an attempt to adhere to common terminology, or it may be partially a continuation of a distinction between themselves and Southeast Asians, whom they consider to be darker-skinned.[47]

The informant who had told us about the "yellow skin" of her daughter was asked if she felt unhappy about her daughter's "yellowness." Her answer was an emphatic no, although she admitted that the white skin of Caucasian women is beautiful. A college graduate, married to a university professor, she suggested her solution to race problems:

I think there should be three different standards of beauty to be applied separately to three groups of people of different colors. It is a confusion of these standards or the loss of one or two of them that leads to tragedy and frustration.

Many Japanese men, especially those in the United States, admit the beauty of white skin in Caucasian women, but also point out the sense of the inaccessibility of Caucasian women. Although the feeling of "basic discontinuity" between Japanese and Caucasians found among those without much contact with Westerners may become weakened as the Japanese spend time among the whites, it may sometimes persist in this feeling of basic remoteness and inaccessibility.

Looking at the white skin I feel somehow that it belongs to a different world. People understand each other a great deal but there is something which people of different races cannot quite share. It sounds foolish and irrational, I know, but somehow this is the feeling I have, looking at the white skin of a Caucasian woman.

White skin suggests a certain remoteness. When I went to Mexico, where most women are not white-skinned like the American, I felt more at home seeing them. I felt more comfortable.

Sometimes I feel that the white skin of the Caucasians tells me that after all I am an Oriental and cannot acquire everything Western, however Westernized I might be. It is like the last border I cannot go across and it is symbolized by the white skin. Is this my inferiority feeling toward the white people—I often wonder.

An extreme expression of such inferiority feelings about the Japanese skin color compared with that of the Caucasians is found in *Up to Aden*, a short story by an award-winning, French-educated, Catholic author Endō Shūsaku. Written in 1954 when he was thirty years old, this is Endō Shūsaku's first literary work. In it he emphasizes the basic discontinuity between European tradition and Japanese culture, focusing symbolically upon the hero's somewhat exaggerated feelings about physical differences between a white French woman and himself. The hero, a Japanese student on his way home from France, shares a fourth-class cabin on a cargo boat with a very ill African woman. The story is a beautiful montage of what the student sees and feels on the boat until it reaches Aden and of his reminiscences of his painful love for a French girl while he was still in France. The following are several quotations from the story:

"Race does not make any difference!" the [French] girl said impatiently. "The whites, the yellows or the blacks, they are all the same!" That was what she said. Race does not make any difference. Later she fell in love with me and I did not refuse her love. Because there was this illusion that race does not make any difference. In the beginning, in love, we did not at all take into consideration that her body was white and my skin was yellow. When we kissed for the first time—it was in the evening on our way home from Mabillon where we had gone . . . dancing— I shouted almost unintentionally to the girl who was leaning against the wall with her eyes closed, "Are you sure? Are you sure you don't mind its being me?" But she simply answered, "Stop talking and hold me in your arms." If race did not make any difference, why on the earth did I have to utter such a miserable question, like a groan, at that time? If love had no frontiers and race did not matter, I should not have felt unself-confident even for a moment. In reality, however, I had to try instinctively not to envisage a certain truth hidden beneath my groan. I was afraid of it. Less than two months after that evening, the day finally came when I had to see the truth. It was in the last winter when the two of us made a trip together from Paris to Lyon. It was in the evening when for the first time we showed our skin to each other. . . . Breathlessly, we remained long in each other's arms. Golden hair had never looked to me more beautiful. Her naked body was of spotless, pure whiteness and her golden hair smoothly flowed down from her shoulders. She was facing toward a door. I was facing toward curtained windows. As the light was on, our naked bodies were visible in a mirror on an *armoire*. In the beginning I could not believe what I had seen in the mirror was really my body. My naked body had been very well proportioned for a Japanese. I was as tall as a European and I was full in chest and limbs. Speaking of the body form, I would not look inharmonious when holding a white woman in my arms. But what I saw reflected in the mirror was something else. Beside the gleaming whiteness of her shoulders and breasts in the lighted room, my body looked dull in a lifeless, dark yellow color. My chest and stomach did not look too bad, but around the neck and shoulders turbid yellow color increased its dullness. The two different colors of our bodies in embrace did not show even a bit of beauty or harmony. It was ugly. I suddenly thought of a worm of a yellow muddy color, clinging to a pure white flower. The color of my body suggested a human secretion, like bile. I wished I could cover my face and body with my hands. Cowardly, I turned off the light to lose my body in darkness. . . . "Hold me tight. We are in love and that is enough," she said to me once when we kissed at a street corner in dusk. But it was not enough that we were in love. By love only, she could not become a yellow woman and I could not become a white man. Love, logic and ideology could not erase differences in skin color. . . . White men had allowed me to enter their world as long as their pride was not hurt. They had allowed me to wear their clothes, drink their wine and love a white woman. They could not accept that a white woman loved me. They could not accept it because white people's skin is white and beautiful and because I am yellow and ugly. They could not stand a white woman falling in love with a man of such lifeless, muddy yellow color. Foolishly enough, I had not known or thought of it at all until this day [when the girl had announced her engagement to a Japanese man only to invite frightened blame and anger from her friends].

Lying down in the fourth class cabin, I watch the feverish dark brown body of a sick African woman in front of my eyes. I truly feel her skin color is ugly. Black color is ugly and yellow turbid color is even more miserable. I and this Negro woman both belong eternally to ugly races.

I do not know why and how only the white people's skin became the standard of beauty. I do not know why and how the standard of human beauty in sculpture and paintings all stemmed from the white body of the Greeks and has been so maintained until today. But what I am sure of is that in regard to the body, those like myself and Negroes can never forget miserable inferiority feelings in front of people possessing white skin, however vexing it might be to admit it.

Three years ago when I came to Europe in high spirits, and when I came through this Suez canal, I had not yet given much thought to the fact that I was yellow. In my passport it was written that I was a Japanese, but at that time in my mind Japanese were the same human beings as white people, both possessing reason and concepts. I had thought, like a Marxian, of class struggle and race conflict but I had never thought of color conflict. Class conflict may be removed but color conflict will remain eternally and eternally, I am yellow and she is white.[48]

Though it seems somewhat painful for most Japanese to be frank about it (and many of them refuse to do so), there is among Japanese intellectuals a more or less unconscious, if not conscious, ambivalence toward the world of white people. Such an attitude is understandable if one takes even a brief glance at Japan's modern history. Japan, at first overwhelmed by an apprehension of the Western world's great power, caught up with the West in an amazingly short time. Then, feeling a sense of rejection over unequal treatment, Japan appointed itself a champion of non-white Asians. In this role, it boldly tried to win a place in the company of white imperialists. Failing disastrously after all, Japan found itself receiving a "democratic education" from its American teachers toward whom it felt the greatest rivalry mixed with admiration.[49]

The diffuse ambivalence toward Western civilization may very well be focalized in the admiration, envy, sense of being overwhelmed or threatened, fear, or disgust that are evoked in the Japanese mind by the image of a hairy giant[50] who, with his great vigor and strong sexuality, can easily satisfy an equally energetic and glamorous creature.[51] Consequently, actual sexual experiences with a white woman may help some Japanese to overcome such feelings of inferiority toward Caucasians.

One of the persons interviewed remarked that his uncle once told him that during Japan's control over Manchuria many Japanese men enjoyed sleeping with white Russian prostitutes:

My uncle said, having a relationship with a white woman made these men feel different, more masculine or something. The feeling is different from that one has after having a relationship with an Asian woman.

Generally, however, Japanese men, as authors of travel books suggest, seem rather overwhelmed and discouraged by the large physique of a white woman. This is well portrayed by author Tamura Taijiō, who is known for his bold description of human sexuality. In his reminiscences on twelve women, he describes a Russian prostitute he met in Shanghai in 1934 after graduating from a university:

Her stout body of large build also overwhelmed my feelings. . . . My arms were bigger than those of an average Japanese, but hers were much bigger than mine, almost beyond comparison. When I sat next to her, the volume and weight of her whole body made me feel inferiority and think that I was of a race physically smaller and weaker than hers. . . . "Shall we dance?" the woman talked to me perfunctorily. I put my arms around her and again I was frightened. The girth of her chest was all too broad. It did not belong to the category of chest I had known from the Japanese women. It certainly was something which wriggled in an uncanny way, something which made me wonder what she had been eating everyday. . . . "Come on!" she said. Between two heavy cylinders, like logs, covered up to thighs with black stockings, which were the only thing she wore, the central part of the woman swoll in a reddish color. It was a bizarre view. . . . It was no doubt beyond the imagination of the vegetarian Japanese how the meat-diet of these women made their sexual desire burn and blaze violently and irrepressibly.[52]

In contrast to this complex of attitudes about Caucasoid racial traits, the Japanese attitudes toward the black skin and facial characteristics of Negro Americans encountered during the Occupation were generally negative, although a number of Japanese women married Negro men. The Japanese interviewed in California, being intellectuals and living in the United States, were all keenly aware of the recent racial issues. Most of them made such statements as:

I know people should not feel different about Negroes and I have no negative notions about them.

I have nothing against them. I don't think I have any prejudice against them.

These measured comments would be followed by a "but," and then would come various expressions, usually negative:

I feel resistance to coming closer to them.

It's almost a physical reaction and has nothing to do with my thinking.

It's almost like a biological repulsion.

It's the feeling of uneasiness and something uncanny.

149

These were the reactions of the Japanese to Negro features as a total *Gestalt* (eyes, hair, nose, and lips) but particularly to black skin.

I think it is simply a matter of custom or habit. We are not accustomed to black skin. I have a Negro friend, very black. I respect him as a scholar and we are close friends and yet I still feel I am not yet used to his black skin. It's something terribly alien to my entire life. It is much better now than it was two years ago when I first met him.

Coming to this country, I had not known that a Negro's palm was different in color from the back of his hand. I was playing cards with two Americans and one African student and I suddenly noticed the color of this African student's palm. I felt I saw something which I had never seen in my life. All that evening, playing cards, I could not help looking at his hands time after time. . . . I just could not get over it.

A year after my arrival, I was introduced to an American Negro for the first time. He was a very friendly person and immediately extended his hand toward me. At that very brief moment, I hesitated. No. I did not hesitate but my arm did. My arm resisted being extended forward. Like a light flashing through my mind, I said to myself, "there is no reason why I don't want to shake hands with this black man." I did shake hands with him and I do hope he did not sense my momentary hesitation. Since then I have never hesitated to shake hands with a Negro.

The idea that black skin is something novel to the Japanese and only for that reason difficult for them to get used to was also voiced by a Japanese woman married to a Negro American.

Frankly, I felt uneasy about it [black skin] in the beginning, but you see it every day, from morning to evening; there is nothing else you can do except to get used to it. I did get used to it. Especially since he was very nice and kind all the time. Once you get used to it, you no longer see it.

The same idea is stated in a novel by Ariyoshi Sawako, a contemporary Japanese author. Although written as a comment by the heroine, a Japanese woman married to a Negro, it most probably reflects the author's frank feminine reaction to Negroid features:

The Negro's facial features—black skin, round eyes, thick round nose, big thick lips—may very well look animal-like to the eyes of those accustomed only to a yellow or a white face. Living long enough among the Negroes, however, one comes to realize how human their faces are. . . . The color of the Negro skin gives one an overwhelming impression but once one gets over it, one notices how gentle their facial features are.[53]

150

Incidentally, this novel, with the English subtitle *Not Because of Color,* is of special interest for us. Ariyoshi spent a few years in the United States as a Rockefeller Fellow. She then returned to Japan and wrote this novel, in which she describes the life of a Japanese woman married to a Negro in New York's Harlem. She also depicts a few other uneducated Japanese women married to Negro, Puerto Rican, and Italian Americans, as contrasted with a highly intellectual Japanese woman married to a Jewish college professor and working at the U.N. As suggested by the subtitle, Ariyoshi seemingly wanted to emphasize that—in spite of the prejudiced opinion of many white Americans and Japanese—laziness, apathy, lack of conjugal stability, and many other inferior characteristics attributed to Negro Americans are not racially inherent qualities, but the products of their degraded social status. The author accurately describes common Japanese reactions to Negro-Japanese marriages and their offspring. The heroine's mother, learning that her daughter wants to marry a Negro soldier, says:

Our family has been honored by its warrior ancestry. Though we were not well-to-do, none of us has ever shamed the name of our family. And you, a member of our respectable family, wish to marry a man of such blackness! How shall we apologize to our ancestors? If you wish to marry an "American," that might be a different matter. But marrying that black man!

Embraced by such a black one, don't you feel disgusted? I am afraid of him. Why don't you feel strange?

When the heroine takes her daughter to downtown Tokyo, people around them loudly voice their reactions to her child with Negro blood:

Look, the child of a *kuronbo* ["black one"].

Indeed, it's black, even when it is young.

She looks like a rubber doll.

She must have taken only after her father. So black. Poor thing.

Animal Husbandry,[54] written by Ōe Kenzaburō when he was still a French literature student at the University of Tokyo in 1957, is the story of a Negro flyer on a B-29 bomber in World War II. The flier bails out of the plane when it is shot down and lands on a mountain. Caught by Japanese villagers, he is kept in a stable like an animal. Eventually some of the villagers butcher him because they are afraid.

The story describes not only the village children's fear of an enemy soldier and their association of a Negro with an animal, but also their discovery of his "humanity" and their timid affection for him. As is already clear from the title, the Negro soldier, "with bristle-covered heavy fingers . . . thick rubber-like lips . . . springy black shining skin . . . frizzled short hair . . . and . . . suffocating body odor," was often associated with an animal. For example, "The wet skin of the naked Negro soldier shone like that of a black horse."

A third story to be mentioned here is the work of Matsumoto Seichō, a widely read author of numerous mystery and documentary stories. In this short story, two hundred and fifty Negro soldiers enroute to Korea break out of Jōno Camp in Northern Kyushu one night and attack civilian houses around the camp. Many women are raped. Two other companies of American troops are called out to subdue the disturbances; most of the soldiers are brought back to the barracks within several hours and sent to the Korean front a few days later. A Japanese man whose wife had been assaulted by a group of Negroes divorces his wife and begins working at the Army Grave Registration Service, as a carrier of corpses. One day, he finally finds what he has been looking for: the corpses of two Negro soldiers he remembered by their obscene tattoos. They were among those who raped his wife. Out of his anger, hatred, and desire for revenge, the man stabs the corpses with an autopsy knife. The Negroes in this story are frequently associated with animals and also with the primitive natives of the African jungle:

The sound of drums at a village festival was heard from far. It reminded them [Negro soldiers] of the rapture of their ancestors, who beat cylindrical and conical drums at ceremonies and in hunting, and whose same blood was running through them. . . . The melody in the distance was following the rhythmic pulsing of the human body. Unavoidably it stimulated their dancing instinct and they began moving their shoulders up and down and waving their hands in fascination. They started breathing hard, with their heads tilted and their nostrils enlarged. . . . Thick sounds and rhythm of drums woke the hunters' blood in them.

Their bodies were all dark like shadows but their eyes shone like patches of white paper. . . . His white eyes shone like the inside of a sea shell but the rest of his face was black, his nose, cheeks, jaw and all. . . . His thick lips were pink and dull in color. . . . Hair was kinky as if scorched. . . . Their bodies exhaled a strong foul smell of beasts. . . . When he took off his shirt, his upper body looked like that of a rhinoceros, with rich heaps of black flesh. The skin looked almost ready to squeak when moved, like tanned leather of black color. . . . When naked, his body was swollen, abdomen hanging low. It was cylindrical like a monkey's body.[55]

Other Japanese interviewed considered that the Japanese attitude toward black skin is more than just a simple reaction to something novel. According to this view, black skin is associated in the Japanese mind with many undesirable traits; other Negroid features are also the opposite of what Japanese have long valued as desirable physical characteristics:

Blackness is often combined with death, vice, despair and other kinds of negative things. "A black-bellied man" is wicked. "Black mood" is depression.

When something becomes dirty and smeared, it gets black. White skin in our minds symbolizes purity and cleanliness. Then, by an association, black skin is the opposite of purity and cleanliness. . . . Black skin after all suggests something unclean.[56] It is not the natural state of things.

Speaking of a Japanese face, we do not appreciate such features as a pug nose, snub nose, squatting nose, goggle eyes, thick lips, kinky hair. They are despised and often made a laughingstock. They often suggest foolishness or crudity and backwardness among Japanese. What is preferred is all the opposites of these. But just think. Aren't they what the Negroes usually have?

The following report by a graduate student who had sexual relations with a Negro woman shows that guilt feeling over sexuality can become focused on the blackness of skin, conceived as dirty:

I was not in love with her, nor was she with me. It was a play. To say the truth, I was curious about a Negro, after hearing so much about them. When it was over, however, I had to take a shower. The idea shocked me because it was ridiculous but I was caught by an urge. It was almost a sudden compulsion, to wash my body off, and I did.

Unlike the Japanese interviewed in California, those who were questioned in Japan expressed their feelings toward Negro Americans and Africans without reservation. They were undifferentiatedly seen by them as "black men, with inhumanly black skin, goggle eyes, thick lips, kinky hair, strong body odor,[57] and animal-

153

like sexuality and energy." The feelings toward such an image were invariably negative. Many said that they felt indignation toward the white American discrimination against Negroes. Some were very fond of Negro musicians. Negro baseball players were well liked. And yet, as one said, their "basic feelings are repulsion and disgust toward Negro features"; these feelings were frequently justified as a "physiological reaction, which one's reasoning cannot control."

Such strongly negative attitudes toward Negro physical characteristics certainly pose problems for the mixed-blood children of Negro American fathers and Japanese mothers, although nobody has yet made a systematic study of the lives of these children in postwar Japan. Three lower-class Japanese with less than six years of primary education independently voiced an astonishing notion when interviewed; they believed that if a Japanese woman gave birth to the black baby of a Negro man, her next baby, and probably the third one also, of a Japanese father would show some black tinge on the body. In other words, in the mind of these men, impregnation of a Japanese woman by a Negro man was associated with "blackening" of her womb as though by ink, so that the second and even the third baby conceived in it would become "stained."

The type of Negro the Japanese think attractive or handsome, or the least objectionable, is a light-skinned individual with Caucasian features. For this reason, they all find Hindu Indians with their Caucasoid facial structure generally more acceptable, even though the Hindus' black skin still groups them with African and American Negroes. The Japanese are not ready to appreciate a very Negroid Negro as attractive; the newly emergent trend among the Negro Americans[58] has not yet made any impression in Japan.

The Negro in the Japanese language is either *koku-jin* ("black person") or *kuronbo* ("black ones"); the former is a neutral word, but the latter has a definitely belittling, if not derogatory, tone. According to a philologist, the origin of *kuronbo* is Colombo, a city of Ceylon.[59] In the seventeenth century, Colombo was pronounced by the Japanese as "kuronbo" or abbreviated as "kuro," probably because of the association with the word *black* (*kuro*) since the servants on the Dutch boats, identified as "people from Colombo," were actually black-skinned. The word *bo*, originally meaning a Buddhist priest's lodge and then the priest himself, came also to mean a boy or "sonny." A suffix to certain words with the meaning of "little one," such as *akan-bo* ("a little red one": "a baby") and *sakuran-bo* ("cherry"), *bo* also creates belittling or even contemptuous connotations in other words, such as *wasuren-bo* ("a forgetful one"), *namaken-bo* ("a lazy one"), or *okorin-bo* ("a quick-tempered one"). By the same token, *kuron-bo* ("a black one") carries the connotation of childishness.

Most Japanese born before 1935 first discovered Negroes by singing "Old Black Joe" and other Stephen Foster melodies in music classes at school or by reading the Japanese translation of *Uncle Tom's Cabin*. Although they might have related the lot of Negro Americans to a vague notion of injustice, such a life remained for most Japanese children a remote world. Another sort of encounter with black people, with more direct reference to their color, was evidenced in a cartoon serialized for many years in a popular magazine for children, *Adventurous Dankichi*, and in a popular song, "The Chief's Daughter," dating from the 1920's. Dankichi was a Japanese boy who put to sea one day to go fishing and, while asleep, drifted to an island somewhere in the South Pacific. On the island, Dankichi outwitted the black natives by his cleverness and ingenuity and became their king. He wore a crown on his head and rode on a white elephant near rivers inhabited by crocodiles.

This fantasy cartoon blended ideas about South Pacific islanders and primitive tribes in Africa. Originally cannibalistic and warlike, these people could become loyal though somewhat simpleminded subjects when tamed and educated. It is worth noting that this was the kind of image of "black people" to which most Japanese children of the prewar period were exposed. "The Chief's Daughter" created an image of carefree South Sea islanders with black skin who danced away their lives under the swaying palm trees.

> My lover is the Chief's daughter.
> Though her color is black
> She is a beauty in the South Seas. . . .
> Let us dance, dance under the palm trees
> Those who don't dance, no girls will care to marry. . . .

In 1958 and 1959, there was a sudden fad for a small plastic doll called *Dakko-chan* ("a caressable one"). It was a jet black and very much caricaturized Negro child of about one foot in height when inflated; its hands extended in such a way that it could cling to a person's arm or a pole. It was so widely sold that almost every house had one, and the manufacturers could not keep up with the demand. A great many teen-agers as well as younger children carried it around with them on the streets. It was, indeed, a cute little doll, but it did not help the Japanese form an image of a more dignified adult Negro.

V

Since a very early time in history, the Japanese have valued the skin color they consider "white."[60] The Japanese "white" skin is, above all, *unsun-tanned* skin, while Mongoloid skin is, in actuality, very sensitive to the tanning action of the sun. Japanese, particularly the women, tried hard to remain "white," jealously guarding their skin from exposure to the sun. An old Japanese expression observes, "In the provinces where one can see Mt. Fuji, one can hardly see beautiful women."[61] The districts traditionally known for their white, smooth-skinned native beauties are, consequently, Izumo, Niigata, and Akita. These are all located on the Japan Sea coast where in long, snowy winter weather one rarely enjoys sunlight. Conversely, where one can see Mt. Fuji, one also enjoys a warm Pacific climate year-round and a certain continuous sunshine which can tan unguarded skin.

Mainly due to modern Japan's contact with the Western world, the Japanese became aware of the "white" skin of the Caucasians, "whiter" than the "whitest" skin of the Japanese. This could cause disappointment when they compared themselves with the Caucasians, whom they sought to emulate by guided modernization programs of industrialization, as well as in spontaneous leisure-time fads and aesthetic pursuits. During the earlier contact, the charm of the Caucasian white skin was counterbalanced by reactions to light-colored hair and eyes, and body hair—distasteful traits in terms of Japanese aesthetic standards. Under the post-World War II impact of American culture, a preference for Western facial structure and hair style brought the Japanese sense of physical aesthetics ever closer to that of Caucasians. The historical inferiority-superiority complex of this extremely Westernized Eastern nation seems today to reflect mixed attitudes toward Caucasian skin. There is the notion that Caucasian skin is "ugly" in texture and quality, thus maintaining a Japanese skin supremacy, while at the same time admitting the better appearance of the refined Caucasian facial structure.

Up to the present, the color of Negroid skin and other physical features find little favor in Japanese aesthetics. One may argue that it is simply because the Japanese are not accustomed to black skin; but one can also contend that "blackness" has been symbolically associated in the Japanese mind, as elsewhere, with things evil or negative and that the image of a Negro hitherto created in Japan has been that of a primitive, childish, simple-minded native. Relatively little note has been taken to date of the emergence of a new Africa under its modern leaders.

It remains a curious fact of Japanese identity that there is relatively little kinship expressed with any Asian countries other than China, toward which present-day Japan feels less and less cultural debt. Japanese eyes, despite cases of plastic surgery, may keep their Oriental look, but through these eyes Japanese see themselves as part of the modern Western world conceptualized in Western terms. Some Japanese wish to change their physical identity from that of a Japanese to something else, but are countered by a vague sense of resignation that such a change is not possible.

Still in search of their national identity,[62] the Japanese are experiencing some difficulties in maintaining and protecting the standards of Japanese beauty and handsomeness from the onslaughts of standardized images produced by the Western cinema. Preoccupied with changing standards, the Japanese may be slow to note a new convergent perception of beauty entering the West, which includes traditional Japanese aesthetic standards in art, architecture, and even in Mongoloid physical beauty. Physical attractiveness is gradually losing its unitary cultural or racial basis in most societies. Art or beauty cannot be maintained in a fixed, single standard. Each changes with the diversity of experiences.[63]

REFERENCES

1. The word for skin in contemporary Japanese is either *hifu* or *hada*. *Hifu* is more or less a technical word and is used less frequently in daily conversation than *hada*, which is the abbreviation of *hadae*, originally meaning "vicinity of surface." *Hada* is also used figuratively in expressions such as *hada o yurusu*, a woman "permitting her skin" to a man when she gives herself to him. *Hada* is also used in the sense of temperament or disposition, as in *hada ga awanai*, the skin of two individuals does not fit due to the incompatibility of their characters. A dashing or gallant man may be described as a man of *isami hada* ("braced-up skin") and a research-

minded man as a man of *gakusha hada* ("scholarly skin"). In describing one's skin color, the word *hada* is used more often than *hifu*, as in such expressions as *hada no shiroi hito* ("a white-skinned person"). A more common practice is to use the word *iro* ("color"), as in *iro no shiroi onna* ("a white-colored woman").

2. S. Noguchi (ed.), *Koji Kotowaza Jiten* (Dictionary of Old Sayings and Proverbs; Tokyo, 1963), pp. 40-41.

3. Face powder, which in the Japanese is *o-shiroi* ("honorable white"), was invented, according to some legends, by one of the ancient wise kings of China, Shou of Yin, Wen of Chou, or Mu of Ch'in. Actually, graves of the early Han period (202 B.C. to about A.D. 25) have given up to archaeologists numberless lacquered vessels and metal boxes containing face powder, rouge, and other toilet preparations. Face powder, together with rouge, came to Japan via Korea in the third or fourth century. In 692, a Japanese monk named Kansei, or Kanjō, succeeded in making face powder from lead and was commended by the Court and presented with "fifty lengths of cloth." A powder of glutinous rice and of millet was also used as face powder. Another substance, applied in liquid form, came from the floury seeds of the jalap plant (*o-shiroi-bana*). See T. Ema, "Keshō no hensen" (History of Toiletry), *Nihon Fūzoku Shi* (History of Japanese Customs), Vol. 4 (Tokyo, 1959), pp. 52-78; U. A. Casal, "Japanese Cosmetics and Teeth Blackening," *The Transactions of the Asiatic Society of Japan*, Third Series, Vol. 9 (May, 1966), pp. 5-27.

4. *Beni*, made from the safflower and of a good but not too luminous red, was used as rouge. It was applied with a soft, short, round brush somewhat over an inch in diameter. It was distributed rather evenly with but slight shading. A more concentrated preparation, *kuchi-beni*, was rubbed on the lips with the third finger, which is still referred to as the *beni-sashi-yubi*, or "rouge-applying finger." The lower lips, rather fleshy with most Japanese, were from early times partly covered by white powder, and the rouge was applied so as to make them appear smaller. See Casal, "Japanese Cosmetics and Teeth Blackening."

5. According to Casal, the blackening of teeth, called *nesshi* in the Japanese, is not found in China. The practice more than likely came from Malayan-mixed people on islands to the south, since teeth were blackened by various people in Southeast Asia and Polynesia. During the Heian period (794-1185), girls generally adopted the custom of teeth-blackening at puberty. From the twelfth century, court nobles dyed their teeth. In the time of the Regents, *de facto* rulers of Japan from 1200 to 1333, followers of the Regents looked upon teeth-blackening as a sign of loyalty to their lords. The custom of teeth-blackening and removal of natural eyebrows lasted until 1868, the beginning of modern Japan. Among the court nobles it appears to have been compulsory. This would seem to be implied in a decree issued on January 30, 1868, stating that nobles were "no longer obliged to paint their teeth black and remove their eyebrows." By March, 1868, the Empress had decided that "henceforth her teeth and eyebrows will be allowed to remain as nature formed them," thereby setting an

example to the nation. The blackening was done with a preparation based on iron acetate and known, therefore, as *tesshō* ("iron juice"). One way of making it was to place iron filings in a small pot with Japanese wine and juice of the snake gourd, letting the mixture simmer near the hearth or exposing it to the sun in summer. Another was to plunge a glowing, red piece of iron into a small portion of rice wine diluted with water, and after five or six days to skim off the scum and keep it in a cup near a fire until warm before adding powdered gallnuts and iron filings for further heating. The resulting dye was applied to the teeth with a brush of soft hair or feathers. See Ema, "Keshō no hensen"; Casal, "Japanese Cosmetics and Teeth Blackening."

6. T. Adachi, *Yūjo Fūzoku Sugata* (Customs of Courtesans; Tokyo, 1956); T. Endo, "Josei to Keppatsu" (Women and Their Hairdos), *Nihon Fūzoku Shi*, Vol. 12 (Tokyo, 1959), pp. 69-102.

7. Murasaki Shikibu, *Genji Monogatari* (Tokyo, 1958), pp. 232, 294.

8. Murasaki Shikibu, *Nikki* (Tokyo, 1957), pp. 182, 184.

9. Sei Shōnagon, *Makura no Sōshi* (Tokyo, 1957), pp. 262, 269.

10. Akazome Emon, *Eiga Monogatari* (Tokyo, 1957), pp. 49, 51.

11. Ema, "Keshō no hensen," p. 65.

12. Adachi, *Yūjo Fūzoku Sugata*, p. 246.

13. T. Ema, *Nihon Fūzoku Zenshi* (Complete History of Japanese Customs), Vol. 1 (Kyoto, 1925), pp. 170-75.

14. Yoshida Kenkō, *Tsure Zure Gusa* (Tokyo, 1958), p. 92.

15. Adachi, *Yūjo Fūzoku Sugata*, p. 248.

16. Ibara Saikaku, *Kōshoku Ichidai Onna* (The Woman Who Spent Her Life at Love Making; Tokyo, 1949), p. 215.

17. Ibara Saikaku, *Kōshoku Ichidai Otoko* (The Man Who Spent His Life at Love Making; Tokyo, 1958), pp. 84, 92.

18. Tanishi Kingyo, *Geisha Yobiko Dori*, quoted in R. Saito, *Edo no Sugata* (Views in Edo; Tokyo, 1936), p. 97

19. Tamenaga Shunsui, *Shunshoku Ume Goyomi* (Tokyo, 1951), pp. 76, 95, 108.

20. Yanagi Rikyō, *Hitori Ne* (Lying Alone), quoted in Adachi, *Yūjo Fūzoku Sugata*, p. 144.

21. During the early part of the Tokugawa period, when the center of culture was in Osaka and Kyoto, and Edo was still very much a frontier, the Kyoto-Osaka custom of women thickly painting their faces and necks white did not reach Edo. Edo women, instead, tended to be proud of the natural smoothness and shine of their unpainted skin, and they used powder very sparingly. After the early-nineteenth century, however, under the influence

of Kyoto-Osaka culture, the make-up of Edo's women became thicker. See
R. Saito, *Edo no Sugata*, p. 223; Y. Ikeda, K. Hara, *et al.*, *Sei Fūzoku*
(Sexual Mores), Vol. 1 (Tokyo, 1959), p. 229; R. Nishizawa, *Koto Gosui*
(Noon Nap in the Imperial Capitol), quoted in E. Mitamura, *Edo Jidai
Sama Zama* (Various Aspects of the Edo Period; Tokyo, 1929), p. 460. Edo
women also came to paint their lips and fingernails pink and red. See
S. Fujioka and K. Hiraido, *Nihon Fūzoku Shi* (History of Japanese Customs;
Tokyo, 1900), p. 133. Blackening women's teeth remained as an initiation
ceremony at the age of thirteen or fourteen among the warrior class, but a
woman of the commoner's status blackened her teeth and removed her
eyebrows when she was married. See Ema, *Nihon Fūzoku Zenshi*, p. 179.

22. Ema, "Keshō no hensen," p. 70.

23. K. Hanasaki (ed.), *Ehon Edo Keshō Shi* (Notes on Edo Toiletry, Illustrated; Tokyo, 1955), p. 66.

24. E. Mitamura, *Edo no Onna* (Women of Edo; Tokyo, 1956), p. 28.

25. *Ibid.*, pp. 33-38.

26. The word *kuroi* ("black"), used to describe the swarthy skin of the
Japanese, is also used to designate more black objects such as black charcoal
or black smoke.

27. B. Smith, *Japan—A History in Art* (New York, 1964).

28. The differences in hair color between the Portuguese and the Dutch were
mentioned in a document reporting the arrest of a Portuguese missionary
who tried to enter Japan illegally after Christianity had been banned: "His
hair is black and not red like that of a Red-haired. His eyes are not like
those of the Red-haired but similar to ours. His nose, however, is big and
high and certainly different from ours." See *Nagasaki Yawa* (Night Stories
of Nagasaki), ed. S. Nishikawa, in *Nanban Kibun Chō* (Rare Stories About
Southern Barbarians), ed. S. Mishima (Tokyo, 1929), p. 46.

29. It seems that the Japanese had various wild ideas about the Dutch living in
Dejima, Nagasaki. A Japanese physician, Ōtsuki Gentaku, who studied
Dutch medicine and, more generally, Western technology, wrote a book to
inform readers of foreign life and customs (ranging from wine and bread
to making mummies) and to correct their misconceptions. In this book the
author refers to public misconceptions that the Dutch have no ankles
(seemingly assumed because the Dutch wore shoes with heels), that their
eyes are those of beasts, that they lift one leg like a dog to urinate, and
that they know a variety of sexual techniques, and are given to taking love
potions. The author declares that these beliefs are all laughable nonsense.
See G. Ōtsuki, *Ransetsu Benwaku* (Enlightenment of Misconceptions in
Regard to the Dutch), ed. Shigeo Ōtsuki (Tokyo, 1911), p. 9.

30. Morishima Chūryō, *Kōmō Zatsuwa* (Chitchats with the Dutch), ed. R. Ono
(Tokyo, 1943), pp. 54-55, 92.

31. Ōtsuki, *Ransetsu Benwaku*, p. 16.

32. Shigeo Ōtsuki, "Kinkai Ibun" (News on the Seas Around), *Nanban Kibun Chō*, pp. 217, 225; K. Nara (ed.), "Aboku Shinwa" (News from America), *Nanban Kibun Chō*, pp. 11, 15; N. Kishi (ed.), *Jūkichi Hyōryū Ki* (Story of Jūkichi's Drifting; Tokyo, 1930), p. 51.

33. E. Mitamura, *Edo Jidai Sama Zama*, p. 460.

34. Smith, *Japan—A History in Art*.

35. Lane is pronounced *Rei-en* in the poem and two Chinese characters are used to stand for the sound; one means "cool" (*rei*), the other "charm" (*en*). As there are other characters with the sound of *rei* (for instance, one character means "beauty"), the writer's choice of the particular character with the meaning of "cool" may reflect his feeling toward Miss Lane, that is, he might have felt that she was charming but somehow distant and inaccessible.

36. T. Osatake, *Bakumatsu Tōzai Fūzoku Kan* (The East and West View Each Other's Customs in the Mid-Nineteenth Century), *Nihon Fūzoka Kōza*, Vol. 7 (Tokyo, 1929), pp. 37, 42, 44, 54, 58, 141.

37. E. S. Sugimoto, *A Daughter of the Samurai* (London, 1933), p. 131.

38. T. Tobushi, *Yōshō Shidan* (Historical Stories of Prostitutes Whose Customers Were Foreigners; Tokyo, 1956), pp. 103-24. Adachi, *Yūjo Fūzoku Sugata*, p. 258; T. Nakayama, *Ai Yoku Sanzen-nen Shi* (Three Thousand Years of Love and Lust; Tokyo, 1935), pp. 339-42.

39. T. Wakamori, *Nihon Fūzoku Shi* (History of Japanese Customs), Vol. 2 (Tokyo, 1958), pp. 740-50.

40. J. Tanizaki, *Chijin no Ai, Selected Works of Tanizaki Junichirō*, Vol. 4 (Tokyo, 1950), pp. 30, 58, 59, 140, 183.

41. The writer failed to discover when the traditional preference for narrow eyes in a woman gave way to the new preference for round eyes with double-folded eyelids, which the Japanese must have learned to value from the Western aesthetics. There is a Japanese saying, "A woman's eyes should be bell shaped, and a man's eyes should be like thread," indicating the preference for round big eyes in a woman but for rather narrow eyes in a man. The time of the origin of this saying is unclear to us. Natsume Sōseki (1867-1916), one of the greatest novelists of modern Japan, seems to be among the earliest admirers of the charms of double-folded eyelids in women. For instance, in his first novel of 1907, he describes one of the heroines: "Itoko with white, soft and full fingers and cute eyes with double-folded eyelids." He certainly mentions the whiteness of the girls: "White in color, born in the shadow of a setting moon, she was named Sayo"; "Fujiko's white face shone under her black hair." Natsume Sōseki, *Gubijinsō* (A Field Poppy), *Zenshū* (Collected Works), Vol. 4 (Tokyo, 1963), pp. 74, 112, 119. One evidence of the Japanese woman's strong desire to acquire double-folded eyelids is the popularity of a small tool, widely advertised in the 1930's and 1940's. In shape it somewhat resembles an American eyelash curler, and it helps single eyelids to fold into a

double crease. If such "folding" is repeated time after time, the eyelids, it is
believed, will eventually become accustomed to a double fold. Sales of this
instrument were revived after the war.

42. The following section is based on a series of informal interviews, the first,
in Spring 1965, with twenty-two Japanese men and women in Berkeley,
California (graduate students, visiting scholars, their wives, one woman
married to a Japanese American, another woman married to a Negro
American; their ages ranged from 28 to 50; their stays in the United States
varied from two to over ten years); the second, in Fall 1965, with thirty-six
men and women in Tokyo and Kobe, Japan, who had varied ages, and
educational and socioeconomic backgrounds. The second group shared one
common factor: They had never been abroad; they had had little or no
personal contact with Caucasians and Negroes.

43. It seems that Japanese men, especially over forty years of age, tend to be
concerned more with the skin texture of a Japanese woman than with the
measurement of her bust and hips, while the Western men will first think
of the "shape" of a woman rather than her skin texture. We might say that
the Japanese man's sexual aesthetics is traditionally "surface-oriented,"
while the Western man's is "structure-oriented." Mishima Yukio, an author
known to Western readers through English translations of many of his
works, paid attention to the texture of the skin when describing healthy
physiques of diving women. "His mother had well sun-tanned rich thighs
which did not show even a wrinkle, and their abundant flesh shone almost
in amber color. . . . She had skin which could never be called 'white' in
color but constantly washed in waves, it was smooth and tight. . . . Every
woman diver's breasts were well sun-tanned and had no mysterious whiteness, and did not show veins underneath the skin. The sun, however,
nourished a translucent, lustrous color like honey in their sun-tanned skin."
Mishima Yukio, Shiozai (Sound of Waves), Mishima Yukio Selected Works,
Vol. 14 (Tokyo, 1954), pp. 64, 67, 120. It should be noted, however, that
among the younger generation the "structure-orientation" is replacing the
"surface orientation."

44. In summer 1965, Mainichi, one of the leading newspapers, serialized
a column called "Charm School," which gives advice to women readers on
how to increase and keep their feminine beauty. The column of August 2,
with the caption, "blessed are those white in color," read, ". . . as the
proverb says, white color covers seven defects, and a woman with white
skin looks beautiful even if she is not endowed with an attractive look.
Healthy white skin is more charming than expensive accessories. How can
you become a white-colored beauty? You should be careful not to expose
your skin directly to the ultraviolet rays in sunshine. . . . Never forget to
carry a parasol when you go out on a summer day, and to apply to your
face 'foundation.' . . . It also helps to take orally Vitamin C, and to use
milky lotion and cream containing Vitamin C. 'Packing' with flour or rice
powder, mixed with several drops of hydrogen peroxide, a spoonful of
olive oil, a tablespoonful of powdered milk, and a few drops of lemon
juice, also has whitening effects." Another example of the Japanese women's

preoccupation with "white" skin may be assumed from the advertisement of a medicated face shampoo, named "Rozetta Pasta," supposedly effective in whitening skin and removing pimples, spots, freckles, and wrinkles. The advertisement, which frequently appears in newspapers, in magazines, and on television screens, shows an illustrated conversation between Kuroko-san (Miss Black) and Shiroko-san (Miss White). An advertisement for Rozetta Pasta published in *Asahi*, another leading newspaper, on August 14, 1965, read: Shiroko: "I have not seen you for a while. You are as black as ever." Kuroko: "Speaking of color, you have become very white recently. Is there any secret? I am so black that I may have to use bleaching chemicals for cloth." Shiroko: "No. Don't you remember our chemistry teacher at school once said that there are two ways of bleaching, one by reduction, the other by oxidation? Bleaching by reduction does not do any harm to cloth or skin. For instance, chloride of lime bleaches by oxidation, while brown sugar, honey, and sulphur bleach by reduction." Kuroko: "But the bleaching power of brown sugar is too weak for my black skin." Shiroko: "Sulphur, when chemically processed, takes on harmless bleaching power." Kuroko: "Then, sulphur might be used for developing an effective skin lotion, I suppose." Shiroko: "Exactly! That's Rozetta Pasta."

45. In the summer of 1966, sun-bathing became fashionable among the young urban women in Japan. Those who could not afford to go to the seaside or to mountain resorts went instead to already overcrowded swimming pools in cities. These ladies also seemed to have gone swimming after sun-bathing. Newspapers reported complaints of many pool visitors that "the water became very oily from sun-tan lotion and olive oil the ladies had lavishly applied to their skin." On August 14, 1966, *Mainichi* printed a warning by various doctors that "sudden and long exposure of skin to strong summer sunlight does damage to the skin and can also cause various health disturbances such as general fatigue, or even pleura and phthisis," and "it is a questionable tendency that the young women are very eager to have their skin sun-tanned excessively."

46. S. Ariyoshi, *Hishoku* (Not Color; Tokyo, 1964), p. 204.

47. The Japanese interviewed tended to be explicit about the physical differences they believed to exist between themselves and other Asian and Southeast Asian peoples; they also tended to be rather sensitive about Westerners mistaking them for Chinese or Burmese. Corresponding differential images may exist among other nations in the Orient: three American-educated Thai women told me, independently, the stereotypes of the Asian people held by the Thais: The Filipinos, Indonesians, Burmese, Laotians, and Cambodians look physically the same as the Thais, with big round eyes with double-folded eyelids and dark skin of rather rough texture, while the Japanese, Koreans, and Chinese look undistinguishably alike, all possessing narrow eyes and lighter skin of smooth surface. The Vietnamese, they said, fall between these two groups; some look like Thais and others like Chinese.

48. S. Endō, *Aden Made* (Up to Aden), *Shin Nihon Bungaku Zenshū* (Collection of Contemporary Literary Works), Vol. 9 (Tokyo, 1964), pp. 128-42.

49. Minami Hiroshi, an American-educated social psychologist, writes: "For

the Japanese, the foreigners are not only different people of different race and nationality, coming from outside, but they are also people of higher status and stronger power, coming from above. Japanese feel shy toward the foreigners as outsiders and feel inferiority-superiority complex toward the foreigners who come from above." H. Minami, "Nihonjin no Gaikokujin kan" (Japanese Views of Foreigners), *Ningen no Kagaku* (Science of Man), Vol. 2, No. 1 (1964), pp. 14-23.

50. Japanese ambivalence toward a large body and large limbs is reflected in some proverbs: "Wisdom cannot fill up too large a body" (Big body, little wit); "A fool has big feet," or "Seeds of prickly ash are tiny but peppery" (A small man is shrewd and wise).

51. When Japanese men feel a vague sense of annoyance or discomfort at the sight or notion of a Japanese woman marrying a white man, especially an American, the feeling may be related to their unconscious understanding that a Japanese woman, by choosing a white man, is challenging their worth as men and their masculine potency.

52. T. Tamura, *Jo Taku* (A Folio of Women's Rubbed Copies; Tokyo, 1964), pp. 73, 75, 76, 78.

53. Ariyoshi, *Hishoku.*

54. K. Ōe, *Shiiku* (Animal Husbandry; Tokyo, 1963), pp. 317, 310-11, 325.

55. S. Matsumoto, *Kuro-ji no E* (A Picture on the Black Cloth), *Tanpen Senshu* (Selected Short Stories; Tokyo, 1965), pp. 70, 75-77, 81-85, 89.

56. A study of 344 men and women of Tokyo middle-class families in regard to their attitudes toward various nations showed, by means of social-distance scale, that the Negroes were among the "most distant" and "least liked"; they were often described as "dirty" and "ugly." See M. Oka and S. Izumi, "Imminzoku Mondai" (Problems of Foreign Races), *Shakai-teki Kinchō no Kenkyū* (Studies in Social Tensions; Nihon Jinbun Kagakkai [Japan Society of Humanities]; Tokyo, 1953), pp. 423-44. A similar study by Ichiei Azuma, Mihoko Seike, and Ikuyo Yamada, probation officers at Kobe and Osaka Family Court, whose data are still being analyzed, shows that of thirteen nations and races, the Koreans are the least liked by 272 men and women of working- and middle-class background. The Negroes are the second least-liked group. Stereotypes of the Negroes, however, do not seem to show the attributes such as ugly or dirty, but they are frequently described as "athletic," "jovial," and "superstitious."

57. The strong body odor, actually perceived or imagined, of a Negro and sometimes also of a Caucasian was often considered by the Japanese to be a source of their repulsion. Fujishima Taisuke, a writer and one of the classmates of the Crown Prince at the Peers School, wrote a rather depressing essay with the title "We Cannot Marry Negroes" in a widely read and respectable magazine. He emphasized the strong body odor of the African Negroes. "When I arrived at Nairobi Airport," he writes, "I felt the air was filled with a striking smell. It was body odor of the Negroes. Unless one becomes accustomed to it, it is a sickening smell, really strong." After

164

describing his other experiences with the body odor, Fujishima comes to his conclusion: "The real underlying thought upon which racial discrimination is based, I believe, is primarily derived from the physiological repulsion caused by this striking odor. All the other sophisticated thoughts and logics are justification added later. . . . Humanism is one thing, and the physiological repulsion of human being is another thing." T. Fujishima, "Kokujin to wa kekkon dekinai," *Bungei Shunjū* (February, 1966), pp. 308-13.

58. Harold R. Isaacs, *The New World of Negro Americans* (New York, 1963), pp. 90-96.

59. A document from the late 1670's says, "In the country of Inaba there was a man of seven feet height. He was from the country of 'kuro.' He had been captured at the Korean war and brought over to Japan. His color was that of soot and people called him *kuron-bo.*" See K. Ōtsuki, *Daigenkai* (Dictionary of Japanese Language; Tokyo, 1956), p. 565.

60. The thousand years' practice of whitening a face with powder in the Far East might suggest universality of white color preference or the distant result of some past cultural diffusion of early European origin. An extremely interesting subject of inquiry, it is beyond the scope of this paper.

61. S. Shiroyanagi, *Nihon Josei Shiwa* (Stories from the History of Japanese Women; Tokyo, 1934), p. 115.

62. Harold R. Isaacs, "Group Identity and Political Change: The Role of History and Origin," a paper presented at the meeting of the Association for Asian Studies in San Francisco, April 3, 1965, pp. 31-36; R. Lifton, "Youth and History—Individual Changes in Post-War Japan," *Asian Culture Studies*, No. 3 (October, 1962), pp. 115-36; A. M. Rosenthal, "New Japan—Future Beckons to Timorous Giant in Search of an Identity," *The New York Times* (June 24-27, 1963).

63. I would like to express my deep gratitude to my friend Professor Harold R. Isaacs, of the Massachusetts Institute of Technology, who urged me to write this article and gave me constant moral support. I am also indebted to my colleague Professor George DeVos of the Department of Anthropology of the University of California, Berkeley, for his valuable advice. I am also grateful to my wife, Reiko Wagatsuma, who shared with me the burden of library research and interviewing. We are indebted to our Japanese friends in Berkeley, Tokyo, and Kobe, whose kind cooperation made the latter part of this paper possible.

ANDRÉ BÉTEILLE

Race and Descent as Social Categories in India

I

ALTHOUGH THE range of ethnic diversity in India has few parallels elsewhere, palpable physical differences have, by themselves, contributed very little to the country's recent social tensions. The most significant membership groups in the society are, however, clearly ones with which the individual identifies himself by reason of birth and through sentiments of common blood and common ancestry. Such sentiments are likely to have special appeal in a society that was until recently relatively closed, and where membership in the most significant groups could be acquired only by birth. Many outside observers have echoed the view Max Weber set forward in the opening sentence of his book on Indian religion: India is "a land ... of the most inviolable organization by birth."[1]

Since the time of Manu, Hindu law-givers have attributed particular qualities to particular lines of descent. Strict rules of law and custom circumscribed intermixture of lines. To preserve the social and cultural identity of each caste, marriages not only between different castes but often those between subdivisions of the same subcaste were forbidden. This rule nourished the idea that members of the same caste or subcaste were of common blood. Indeed, Irawati Karve has tried to show that the minimal unit of endogamy within the caste system consists of a group of persons related by real ties of kinship and affinity.[2]

The sentiment of common descent is not confined to the subcaste viewed as the minimal unit of endogamy. It is often shared by a group of related castes among which no intermarriage is practiced. Thus, although the Tamil Brahmins are divided into numerous sections, there is a keen belief among them that all Brahmins belong to a single stock. This is based on the common supposition that the subdivisions of today are the outcome of fissions within an original, undifferentiated group—a supposition that may have some historical validity, at least within a single cultural region. Depending upon context and situation, the sentiment of common descent can clearly be associated with either a broader or a narrower group.

The organization of society on the basis of birth-status groups and the general acceptance of a rank order ascribed by birth gave a distinctive character not only to the absorption of alien ethnic elements into Hindu society, but also to the place they acquired in it. In the main, Hindu society seems to have grown by adding new blocks to itself, while allowing these blocks to retain a measure of autonomy and identity. Traditionally the unit of absorption has been a community rather than an individual.[3]

This process often enabled an alien community to retain its religious or sectarian identity while imbibing a variety of Indian cultural forms. No alien community could, in fact, function as a part of Indian society without acquiring some of the structural properties of castes. Many people have noticed a caste-like organization among both Moslems and Christians in India. Also, reform movements that have sought to break through the closed system of castes have themselves generally ended as castes. The Lingayats of South India provide the best-known, though by no means the only, example of this.

The discreteness of the blocks out of which traditional Indian society was built was maintained by a combination of ecological, genetic, linguistic, and other cultural factors. The localization of a community in a particular habitat came about because of the absence of easy means of transport and communication. The concentration of large tribal blocks in certain parts of the country provides a good example of this tendency. Genetic identity was maintained at least in part by the rule of endogamy. The preservation of cultural identity was made possible by the pluralistic values of Hindu society.

In the past and to a great extent in the present, the Indian's identity has been fixed in a fairly definite manner by a variety of bounded units—each characterized by not one, but a number of different attributes. N. K. Bose writes:

The map of Calcutta . . . shows a highly differentiated texture. Ethnic groups tend to cluster together in their own quarters. They are distinguished from one another not only by language and culture but also by broad differences in the way they make their living. Naturally there is a

167

considerable amount of overlap, but this does not obscure the fact that each ethnic group tends to pursue a particular range of occupations.

It can be said, therefore, that the diverse ethnic groups in the population of the city have come to bear the same relation to one another as do the castes in India as a whole.[4]

Because of this kind of clustering, social identities have been preserved to a much greater extent in India than in the more rapidly changing societies.

In the traditional system there was a close association between caste, on the one hand, and economic and political power, on the other. Each village or group of villages had one or a few dominant castes whose members exercised control over both the land and the political system. Concomitantly, there were other castes whose members were almost wholly landless and powerless; most conspicuous among these were the Untouchable castes. Sometimes the gradations of political and economic power were almost as elaborate as those of the caste hierarchy. Recent studies by anthropologists show that the conflict among castes is often a conflict over landownership.[5] Such conflicts tend to be localized, however, because the landowning caste varies from one area to another. In describing the correspondence between caste and landownership in Kerala, M. N. Srinivas writes:

At the top of the hierarchy were the Nambutri Brahmins who were noncultivating owners (*jenmi*). The "high" Nāyar castes were the noncultivating lessees of Nambutri land on twelve-year leases (*kāṇam*). The agricultural labourers, both tied and free, came from the lower castes like Cerumān and Pulayan and from the Pāṇan tribes.[6]

Even today many castes bear occupational names. In the traditional system, caste and occupation were closely associated, particularly among artisan and service groups. Thus, potters, blacksmiths, carpenters, barbers, and washermen were not only occupational groups but also hereditary castes. The specific association between caste and traditional occupation is breaking down, although a broad relationship continues to exist. Occupations are graded by traditional values in an elaborate hierarchy in which ideas of purity and pollution play a significant part. Upper castes generally avoid manual occupations, particularly those that are considered polluting or onerous. Scavengers and sweepers are still almost wholly drawn from the ex-Untouchable castes.

The close association between caste and traditions of literacy largely explains the extent to which a few upper castes came to

168

dominate the variety of urban-middle-class occupations that developed during the nineteenth century. Western education and, through it, the new occupational structure were the preserve of a few upper castes. In Madras, the civil service and the professions were dominated almost completely by Brahmins until World War I; the situation was broadly similar in Bombay. In Bengal, Brahmins, Kayasthas, and Baidyas provided a very high proportion of recruits to the new middle class. Higher education and salaried occupations are more open today, but there is still a wide gap between the castes with traditions of literacy and those without.

Western education gave an advantage not only to certain castes but also to certain regions in the country. The British first established their rule in the three Presidencies of Bengal, Bombay, and Madras, and their capitals became centers of Western education. Bengalis who graduated from the University of Calcutta spread out to other parts of the country and manned the professions and bureaucracies there. Until recently sizable sections of the upper-middle class in large urban centers in the states of Assam, Bihar, and Orissa were Bengalis. Likewise, Tamilians from Madras dominated the administration and the professions in Andhra and Mysore. Since Independence, and particularly since the establishment of linguistic states, there has been a certain amount of tension between such outsiders and the "sons of the soil."

Certain religious communities also benefited more than others. The Parsis, who are a small and highly urbanized community, became the most Westernized section of Indian society. The Christians, in those areas where their economic position was not too backward, took advantage of schools and colleges set up by missionaries. In certain parts of Kerala they now occupy the highest position in the new occupational structure. The Moslems, who are a much larger group, at first lagged behind in education, and this was to a large extent responsible for the backward nature of the Moslem middle class in relation to the Hindus, particularly at the turn of the century.

Today, no ethnic, religious, or linguistic group in India is economically homogeneous. In general, the larger the group, the more heterogeneous it tends to be. The economic dominance of any such group is almost always a local affair.

Religious and linguistic groupings as well as caste affiliations reinforce popular notions of descent in India. Each of the dozen or so major linguistic groups has a "homeland" within the country, and, in fact, the states that make up the Indian union consist essentially of people who speak the same language and share a common history. The territorial concentration of language groups gives a particular edge to regionalism in India.

Cutting across the linguistic divisions, and in many ways just as important socially, are groupings based on religious affiliation. Although the Hindus constitute over 80 per cent of the population, there are important Moslem and Christian minorities in several regions. The concentration of people following a certain religious faith in a particular social stratum or region helps to sharpen their social identity. In East Bengal (now East Pakistan) prior to the partition of India, the Hindu-Moslem conflict was greatly accentuated because the Hindus owned most of the land while the bulk of the Moslems tilled it. Again, the fact that the Sikhs not only speak a common language but are also concentrated in a particular territory has been made the basis of a demand for a separate state (which has recently been conceded).

Although units based on regional, linguistic, sectarian, caste, or lineage affiliation have played a very important part in traditional Indian society and continue to do so today, they do not exhaust the types of groups in modern Indian society. Universalistic groups—such as those based on affiliation to classes, parties, or trade unions —exist, but have, by their nature, little to do with race or descent.

II

No significant social unit in India—whether based on language, religion, or caste—is racially homogeneous; it is more common for physical and social differences to intersect than to overlap. Studies by P. C. Mahalanobis, C. R. Rao, D. N. Majumdar, S. S. Sarkar, and others[7] have shown how complex the racial pattern may be even in a limited region or sector of society. Sarkar has demonstrated that even tribal groups—generally assumed to be homogeneous—show a great deal of internal variation when examined anthropometrically and serologically.[8]

There is also a wide range of diversity in the distribution of physical types. Whichever trait one considers—whether skin color, stature, nasal index, or head form—one encounters a very broad spectrum in which almost every variation is represented. In general, physical types are not sharply differentiated but represented on a continuum. Nowhere are the somatic differences between language groups, religious communities, or castes so sharp as the differences between Negroes and whites in the United States. Along with diversity, there is a relative absence of polarity.

The high degree of overlap between adjacent segments and the absence of polarity go a long way in explaining why there has been little or no organized conflict between "racial" groups in Indian society. In spite of the rigid rules of endogamy, no meaningful social unit can be readily identified by its physical characteristics. Clear physical types do not exist in India in the shape of concrete groups as they do in the United States or South Africa. They are, rather, constructs that enable anthropologists to order their data.

Knowledge of "racial" differences and their distribution in India is, consequently, very limited. The anthropometric and serological data available do not permit one to present a racial map of the country with any confidence. Sir Herbert Risley, under whom the 1901 Census of India was conducted, made the first systematic attempt to classify the population by race.[9] In his classification, Risley tried to relate certain physical differences—in particular, those pertaining to the shape of the nose and skin color—to certain basic features of social stratification. The main racial types in his scheme of classification—Aryan, Dravidian, Aryo-Dravidian, Mongolo-Dravidian—were really linguistic or regional categories in disguise. Risley's classification was criticized, in part, because of his failure to distinguish clearly between physical and social categories.

Several classifications have been offered since, and of these B. S. Guha's seems to be the most popular.[10] Guha identified six principal racial elements in the population of India: Negrito, Proto-Australoid, Mediterranean, Western Brachycephal, Palae-Mongoloid, and Nordic, the first and last occurring only in very diluted forms, if at all. Only the Proto-Australoid and Palae-Mongoloid groups have any real correspondence with social divisions in the country, the first being well represented in the aboriginal population of Central and Southern India and the second in the people of Assam and the Himalayan foothills. The Mediterranean and Western Brachycephal types are too broad and general to have any close connection with real social divisions.

III

Sharp physical differences may exist in India, but such differences are rarely found between territorially or structurally adjacent

171

sections of the population. One could no doubt make out a sharp contrast between, say, the Kashmiri Brahmins and the Paraiyas of Madras. These units do not, however, constitute by themselves a meaningful field of social interaction. The social distance between them is spanned by many groups whose existence serves to reduce the contrasts between the two ends of the continuum.

When skin color is taken as the criterion, regional and caste differences appear to be of particular importance. The inhabitants of the Northern states—particularly Punjab, Jammu and Kashmir, Rajasthan, and parts of Uttar Pradesh—are on the whole fairer than those of the Southern states. Indeed, many North Indians have a vague prejudice against South Indians because of their dark skin color.[11] Similarly, people from the topmost castes are generally fairer than the Harijans. But there are numerous intermediate castes, and among these one frequently encounters persons who are either darker than some Harijans or fairer than many Brahmins. Further, regional and caste differences often cut across each other. People from the lower castes in North India tend to be, on the whole, darker than those from some of the highest castes in the South.

Over the centuries, environmental factors have probably evened out to some extent the physical differences within any one region. As new ethnic elements were absorbed continuously and gradually, they are likely to have undergone some change due to geographical factors and probably also to a certain amount of intermixture. It seems almost certain that some intermixture between castes through unsanctioned unions has been a pervasive feature of traditional Indian society. Only this would explain both the high degree of overlap between structurally distant segments and the very considerable measure of heterogeneity within subcastes that in theory have bred true for centuries.

A few subcastes are well known for the distinctive physical features of their members. The Chitpavan Brahmins of Maharashtra and the Saraswat Brahmins of Mangalore have not only light skins but occasionally light eyes as well. Beyond a certain point, however, it is difficult to differentiate between facts and stereotypes. Thus, the Iyengar Brahmins of Madras, though reputed to be light skinned, include a very large number of dark individuals.

Within the subcaste, a certain amount of selective breeding has no doubt taken place for centuries. A light skin color is valued almost universally. Wealthy landowning families often have a tradition of seeking light-skinned brides from among poorer members of their subcaste. It is very common to find a high concentration of light-skinned people among established landowning families. This feature is particularly conspicuous among aristocratic Moslem families in North India, which probably also contain a high component of foreign blood.

Caste and aristocratic status as determined by landownership often cut across each other. Non-Brahmin castes tend to be, on the whole, dark skinned. Where established landowning families exist among them, however, their members are often as light skinned as the Brahmins and sometimes more so. Where members of aristocratic landowning families also belong to the highest caste, they are likely to be particularly fair.

Anthropologists have made some attempts to study systematically the relationship between the physical diversity of the population and its social diversity. Sir Herbert Risley saw the caste system as providing unique possibilities for the differentiation of physical types. He considered this differentiation to be closely related to the rank order of castes.[12] In concrete terms, he argued that the social rank of a caste varies inversely with the average nasal index of its members; in other words, members of the upper castes are narrow-nosed while those of the lower castes are broad-nosed.

Risley's views have been challenged by Ghurye, Majumdar, and others.[13] A closer examination of even the limited anthropometric material at hand shows that the relationship between the two sets of factors is extremely complex and that Risley's generalization was sweeping and hasty. Even within a region, the exceptions to the correlation suggested by him are numerous. When inter-regional comparisons are made, it seems to break down altogether.

Although Risley's correlation may be untenable from the anthropometric point of view, he was no doubt correct in drawing attention to an important fact—that in India, as elsewhere, high social values are attached to certain physical traits. Among those that are valued most highly, fair skin color occupies a conspicuous position.

In many Indian languages the words *fair* and *beautiful* are often used synonymously. The folk literature places a high value on fair skin color. The ideal bride, whose beauty and virtue are praised in the songs sung at marriages, almost always has a light complexion. A dark girl is often a liability to her family because of the difficulty of arranging a marriage for her. Marriages among educated Indians are sometimes arranged through advertisements in the news-

173

papers; even a casual examination of the matrimonial columns of such popular dailies as *The Hindu, The Hindustan Times,* or *The Hindustan Standard* shows that virginity and a light skin color are among the most desirable qualities in a bride.

The caste system has given birth to a variety of stereotypes that have a bearing on social conduct, although their influence on it is less marked now than in the past. Some of these stereotypes dwell on the physical features of the different castes, the upper castes being always represented as fair and the lower castes as dark. Further, a reversal of the assumed correlation is viewed as not only unusual but sinister. A Kannada proverb cautions, "Trust not a dark Brahmin or a fair Holeya"; a North Indian proverb maintains, "A dark Brahmin, a fair Chuhra, a woman with a beard—these three are contrary to nature"; and another North Indian proverb runs, "Do not cross a river with a black Brahmin or a fair Chamar."[14]

In spite of much evidence to the contrary, the belief that some castes are fair and others dark is very widespread, particularly in South India. During fieldwork in a Tanjore village, I lived among a very orthodox section of Brahmins. The Tanjore Brahmins have an overweening pride in their relatively light skin color. My hosts often remarked that since I looked like a Brahmin, they had no very strong objection to my living among them. Once I jokingly told one of my hosts that when I came next, I would live among the Kallas— a fairly low but influential Non-Brahmin caste—and pass myself off as a Kalla. He scoffed at me, saying, "Nobody will believe you— you are not black like those fellows."

Refinement of features of the kind that is valued by the Tanjore Brahmins is probably the outcome, in part, of a certain style of life. In the rural areas the Brahmins generally lead a sedentary existence and are not exposed to sun and rain to nearly the same extent as the average non-Brahmin peasant. I found that one of the Brahmins in the village where I lived could often identify a Kalla or a Harijan by his looks. The same Brahmin pointed out, however, that a Kalla friend of his, an educated lawyer from a neighboring town, looked quite different from the Kallas in the village. He was refined enough to pass for a Brahmin. Perhaps there is room for a cultural theory of appearance that goes beyond the conventional anthropometric indices and probes into these subtle differences of carriage and expression which have such an important bearing on social interchange.

In a society where purity of descent is palpably associated with

174

diversity of physical type, features that do not correspond to the ideal must be accommodated. Among South Indian Brahmins, a dark girl has a low value in the marriage market. At the same time, a dark Brahmin girl will always (or almost always) be preferred among them to a Non-Brahmin girl, however fair. Wherever physical differences cut across caste lines—as they frequently do—the latter are assigned far greater weight in almost every institutional sphere.

While there is clearly a preference for light skin color in almost all sections of Indian society, it is difficult to say exactly how far this preference influences social action. The most concrete expression of it is to be found in the choice of marriage partners. The choice of a fair bride (or groom) must, however, be made within limits that are strictly defined by considerations of other kinds.

In certain parts of North India, Moslem women are often very light skinned and have features that are positively valued. Nevertheless, a Moslem bride, however fair, would not normally be acceptable in a Hindu household. Likewise, a Kashmiri bride would not be acceptable in a Tamil Brahmin household in spite of her very light complexion. Thus, physical features of a particular kind are only marginally important, other things (or, at least, certain other things) being equal. Fair skin color has, for instance, much greater weight in choosing a bride than a groom. In the case of the latter, other qualities such as wealth, occupation, and education play an important part. A dark-skinned son is not so much of a liability to a middle-class family as a dark-skinned daughter, for he can more easily acquire other socially desirable qualities.

The caste system in India has often been compared with the system of Negro-white relations in the United States. Recently there has been some argument as to whether the American system can be viewed as a caste system. In a comparative study of "caste" in India and the United States, Kingsley Davis differentiates sharply between what he calls "racial" and "non-racial" caste systems:

A non-racial caste system, such as the Hindu, is one in which the criterion of caste status is primarily descent, symbolized in purely socio-economic terms; while a racial system is one in which the criterion is primarily physiognomic, usually chromatic, with socio-economic differences implied.[15]

Davis rejects the view that race has very much to do with the caste system as it operates in India today.

The hypothesis that the Hindu system began on a racial basis is unproven. Even if true, however, it does not alter the fact that today this system is for the most part purely a matter of descent rather than race, symbolized in socio-economic terms.[16]

Davis has drawn attention to an important difference, but his formulation of it is not wholly satisfactory. "Race" and "descent" do not refer to mutually exclusive categories; in fact, their connotations overlap to a very considerable extent. One can argue that descent is a social category, whereas race is a biological category. This is, however, a distinction the anthropologist makes to facilitate analysis of a certain kind. It is not clear how much such a distinction helps in the analysis of native categories of thought in which both descent and race are socially defined.

IV

The ideas of descent and race are inseparably combined in the concept of *jati*.[17] Although the word *jati* is understood by most Western sociologists to mean "caste," it often has a much wider connotation. In the Bengali language (and in some other North Indian languages as well), it not only signifies caste, but also comes closer to the meaning of "race" than perhaps any other word in popular usage. Basic to both race and caste is the idea of common descent from which, in fact, the Sanskrit word *jati* derives its root meaning.[18] This word is applied not only to "race" and caste, but to practically every closed group (such as a linguistic or religious community) that is believed to be based, however loosely, on common descent.

Anthropologists have in recent years made significant advances in the understanding of social structures through the analysis of the meanings of indigenous category words. E. E. Evans-Pritchard's analysis of the Nuer word for "spirit"[19] and E. R. Leach's analysis of the Trobriand word *tabu*[20] offer cases in point. The term *jati* is a basic category word in most of the Indian languages. An analysis of its different meanings and their relationships is likely to offer certain valuable insights into the principles of Indian social structure.

The caste system evinces several levels of differentiation. To those who participate in it, these levels have something basic in common.[21] The idea of "community" attaches to them all, although not with the same degree of intensity. Consequently, the word *jati* (and frequently the English term *caste*) is, according to the context, applied to a group of castes, a caste, a subcaste, or a subdivision of a subcaste. The term *jati* may even be extended to cover the entire Hindu community when it is viewed as a unit in opposition to other units of a like order. In Bengal, for instance, it is common to use the word *jati* (or, rather, the colloquial form *jat*) to differentiate not only between Brahmins and Shudras but also between Hindus, Moslems, and Christians.

In one important sense, the difference between Hindus and Moslems is of the same kind as that between Brahmins and Shudras, or between various sections of Shudras. Hindus and Moslems (or Christians) together form a system that is not very different from the caste system. The idea of *jati* provides a clue to the understanding of the similarities between the two. A person who has lived in a multicaste Hindu village in, say, Tamilnad will be struck by the many features that this village shares in common with the composite Hindu-Moslem villages still found in many districts of Bengal. In a Tamil village Brahmins and Non-Brahmins live in separate residential areas. Each unit is differentiated from the other by certain peculiarities of dress, food, speech, and ritual, and each generates a feeling of community.

Similarly, in a Bengal village, Hindus and Moslems live apart and are differentiated from each other by distinctive social practices and by a consciousness of community. Hindus frequently refer to the entire Moslem community by the term *jati* even as they refer to Untouchables and Tribals by the same term. In the villages in which I lived in Bengal I frequently asked people about the *jatis* present, and the list generally included—in addition to Brahmins, Sadgopes, and Aghuris (the Hindu castes)—Moslems, Harijans, and Adivasis.

In the urban areas, too, it is common for people to use the word *jati* to differentiate Hindus from Moslems. In many instances, the word "Hindu" has been entered against the information relating to caste in a census or questionnaire. If there is so much confusion even among educated Indians regarding the true referents of religion, caste, or sect, I suggest it is because the social organization of these different kinds of units has something fundamental in common.

In areas where there is a concentration of Christians, as in Kerala, the Christians often operate as caste-like units in relation to Hindu castes. Members of smaller religious denominations such as Jains, Kabirpanthis, or Brahmos are not only viewed as *jatis* but

177

frequently enumerated as castes. (The English term *caste* has generally a narrower referent than the word *jati* or its regional variant.)

The word *jati* thus refers not only to subcastes, castes, and caste groups, but also to religious communities. In some North Indian languages, it may refer, in addition, to a linguistic group that is a unit at once broader and narrower than a religious community. The Bengalis, for instance, commonly use the term *jati* to differentiate between themselves and people from other regions such as Oriyas, Assamese, and South Indians. There are stereotypes relating to linguistic groups as well as to castes, the former being generally derogatory.

Linguistic differences are sometimes expressed directly in a caste idiom. Adrian Mayer has shown that differences between subcastes in Central India are often based upon regional (that is, linguistic) affiliation. "Subcastes are mostly based on provincial distinction; they will be the Malwi, the Gujarati or the Mewari subcastes, coming from the parts of India bearing these names."[22] Throughout Peninsular India the principal cleavages among Brahmins derive from two factors: sectarian affiliation and linguistic origin. An immigrant group that comes from a different linguistic region is generally fitted into local society, but the fact that it is of a separate stock is never entirely lost sight of.

The word *jati* may thus be applied to units based on race, language, and religion as well as to castes in the narrower sense of the term. These different kinds of identity are easily confused as is illustrated by a common remark I used to hear in Bengal where I grew up. It would be said of a person: "He is not a Bengali, he is a Moslem (or Christian)." The speaker was, of course, a Bengali Hindu, and the person spoken about a Bengali born in a different religious community. The remark illustrates that in certain contexts the Bengali Hindu views himself as the Bengali *par excellence* and others as being different. It does not mean that he cannot in other contexts view the Bengali Moslem as being of the same stock as he himself.

Differences in religion, language, and caste give rise to tensions and conflicts of various kinds. A noticeable feature of recent Indian politics is the predominance of what is generally referred to as "communalism." Communal politics has many forms, one or another of which has been ascendant at different times. In its original use the term signified primarily the politics of religious communities and of Hindu-Moslem relations, in particular. Later the

178

meaning was extended to cover "regionalism," "casteism," and "tribalism."

Many Indians would deny the primacy of the communal element in Indian politics and argue instead that communalism—whatever its form—can be readily reduced to more basic economic conflicts. Communalism was no doubt heightened by the manner in which the British transferred power to the Indians, but its structural basis had deep roots in Indian society. The record of the conflict between Hindus and Moslems from the creation of the Muslim League in 1906 through the violence and bloodshed of 1946-47 to the partition of the country in 1947 is too well known to bear detailed repetition. The one point that requires emphasis here is that the Muslim League, basing its political program on the Two Nation Theory, maintained that Hindus and Moslems were different by religion, culture, and race. They consequently urged that the only rational course the British could adopt before leaving was to divide the country between the Hindus and the Moslems. The Indian National Congress under Gandhi, on the other hand, maintained that Hindus and Moslems formed inseparable parts of a single community and that partition would be suicidal to both.

That the Muslim League finally won its case and the country was partitioned does not, of course, prove the objective validity of its claims as against those of the Congress. Still, the events that took place in the country just before and after its partition do show how powerfully men can be moved by appeals to "community," "blood," a common way of life, and a common destiny.

As many had foreseen, the partition of India did not settle the Hindu-Moslem question. India still has a Moslem population of over 50 million people. The Muslim League not only survives as a watchdog of their political interests, but is on occasion even used by the ruling party for its electoral program. Moslems in India continue to preserve their social and cultural identity as do many other groups based on religious and other "communal" criteria. The case of the Moslems is, however, somewhat unique. Many of them have social and ideological links with Pakistan, and also perhaps a vague hope of finding a better life and a more secure home across the frontier. While Moslems in India may not always live with the feeling of belonging to an alien race, on occasion such feelings are not only aroused but become the source of violence and bloodshed.

The Hindu-Moslem conflict provided the pattern of communal politics in North India, but in the South this was provided largely by the Non-Brahmin movement. Kerala and certain parts of Andhra are the only areas in South India that have organized Moslem minorities. It is perhaps no accident that the Non-Brahmin movement was never quite so important in these areas as in Madras and Mysore. That the conflicts between Hindus and Moslems and between Brahmins and Non-Brahmins are examined within the same framework does not, of course, mean that they are in all ways similar or that they are mutually exclusive.

The Non-Brahmin movement was formally launched in 1916 with the issue of a Manifesto and the formation soon afterwards of the Justice Party with its headquarters in Madras. The movement's principal objective was to protect the interests of the Non-Brahmins in education, employment, and political life against domination by the Brahmins. It achieved considerable political success within a short time and provided a meeting point for influential Non-Brahmin leaders from all over South India. In fact, a distinctive feature of the first phase of the Non-Brahmin movement in the South was its success in cutting across linguistic divisions and uniting in a common cause against the Brahmins people speaking Tamil, Telugu, Kannada, and Malayalam.[23]

Soon after the formation of the Justice Party, its leaders began to make representations to the British government for a share in the affairs of the state proportional to their population in it. They argued that the Madras Presidency was dominated by a small Brahmin oligarchy, that Brahmins and Non-Brahmins were different by race and culture, and that unless the British government intervened no way could be found of reconciling their divergent interests. In the words of the Memorandum presented by the Non-Brahmin delegation to the Joint Parliament Commission in Britain in 1919:

Their customs and manners are essentially different, and even in the matter of food, the two classes differ widely. Their interests are often not identical. Over and above all this, there is the fundamental difference which goes to the root of the whole problem—*the two people belong to two different races.*[24]

Before long, the political agitation of the Justice Party was transferred to the social plane by the Self-Respect movement which emerged in the mid-twenties under the leadership of the Non-Brahmin ex-Congressman E. V. Ramaswami Naicker. This movement urged Non-Brahmins to rid themselves of the social and economic domination of the Brahmins, and it gathered strength during the 'thirties. In the 'forties Naicker created the Dravida Kazhagam, a militant organization that openly preached a racialist ideology and made the "Aryan" Brahmins their principal target. A certain amount of violence was used against the Brahmins who lived for some time under fears that seem to have been greatly exaggerated. Indeed, I have heard Tamil Brahmins refer to themselves (rather melodramatically) as the Jews of South India.

The Non-Brahmin movement had deep economic roots, as its leaders were the first to point out. In general, the Brahmins enjoyed a comfortable economic position as landowners, government officials, and members of the professions. Still, economic differences frequently cut across caste boundaries, and the Justice Party counted in its ranks the biggest landowners in the Presidency.[25] The unique position of the Brahmins in South Indian society is, in fact, based upon differences that are far more pervasive than the purely economic ones. Nowhere else in the country are they so sharply differentiated in speech, dress, and appearance from the rest of the population as in the South. These differences, along with the traditions of their North Indian origin, lent themselves easily to the myth that the Brahmins were "Aryans," living on the toil of the "Dravidian" masses.

Regionalism is today viewed as perhaps the most serious threat to the national unity of India. The demand for a separate Dravidian state has close historical links with the Non-Brahmin movement, and was first put forward in an organized way by the Dravida Kazhagam. Its principal proponent today is the Dravida Munnetra Kazhagam (D.M.K.), the largest opposition party in Madras. Although the leaders of the D.M.K. claim to speak for all the four South Indian states, the party's following outside Madras is very limited.

The four Southern states—Andhra, Kerala, Madras, and Mysore —share a number of distinctive features that mark them out from the rest of India. The unity of the South is cultural as well as geographical; the South Indian languages belong to the Dravidian family, whereas those of the North are Indo-Aryan. The confusion of linguistic and racial categories, which was such a common feature of the earlier ethnology, has no doubt contributed to the popular belief in the existence of a separate Dravidian race with Peninsular India as its homeland. This belief has been worked into an elaborate mythology by the Dravidian movement in its campaign for a separate political status for the four South Indian states.

Leaders of the D.M.K. lose no opportunity to demonstrate the threat to the "national" identity of the South. This national identity has been created largely out of a history and ethnology to which fact and fancy have contributed in about equal measure. It is kept alive by the repeated assertion of the historical, cultural, and racial identity of the Dravidian people. As M. G. Ramachandran, the noted film star and D.M.K. leader, wrote in *Homeland,* the official organ of the party:

The Dravidians, constituting of [*sic*] the Tamils, Telugus, Malayalees and Kanarese are a distinct race. They have a common linguistic origin. . . . Their food habits are alike. They think alike, live alike, do alike and act alike.[26]

Characteristically, the D.M.K. has also sought to justify its separatist demands on grounds of economic and political domination by the North. Economic development has been unequal in different parts of India, and the North appears to have benefited more than the South. This, however, is hardly the whole story. There are states in North India that are backward in relation to Madras or Mysore. Tamilians complain that commerce and industry in their state is often controlled by outsiders, but the principal threat as they view it today is of "Hindi imperialism." The imposition of Hindi as the national language is likely to turn the tables on the South Indians who have so far used their superior knowledge of English to maintain a fairly comfortable position in government and other services.

India's tribal population, over 30 million people, enjoys a certain special legal and political status in the country. The tribal population is by no means homogeneous, but sharply divided regionally, culturally, and racially. In the past, the tribes were not only fragmented, but lent themselves to slow, continuous absorption into Hindu society. This tendency has today been reversed to some extent, being replaced in part by a conscious effort to create and organize a separate tribal identity in order to achieve certain economic and political objectives.[27]

The roots of pan-tribalism go back to the nineteenth century, although the passage of the Government of India Act of 1935 helped to give it a much more organized form. By creating separate Scheduled Areas for the tribal people, the British helped to sharpen their social identity and to strengthen the feeling that they had a different political destiny from the other Indians. Most tribal people seem always to have had an ambivalent attitude toward the Hindus under whose shadow they lived. On the one hand, there was a desire to emulate their superior material techniques and more sophisticated cultural forms; on the other, an attitude of suspicion, bitterness, and even hatred toward them on the ground that they were aliens and exploiters. The Hos, one of the major tribes of Chota Nagpur, use the word *diku* (a corruption of *dacoit,* meaning "brigand") to refer to the Hindus who are their neighbors.

In the Chotanagpur area of Bihar which has a large concentration of tribal people, the Jharkhand Party was organized to put forward the demand for a separate tribal homeland. Pan-tribalism has developed its own symbols and mythology. The very words used by the tribal people to characterize themselves (*Adivasi,* "original inhabitants"; *Adimjati,* "original race") have a strong connotation of folk appeal. Attempts have been made to recreate a largely imaginary past in which the purity and vitality of tribal life have not been sapped by aliens from the plains. It is probable that tribal separatism has drawn part of its inspiration from the work of Christian missionaries. A belief current among the tribal people of Chotanagpur is that they are the descendants of one of the lost tribes of Israel.

V

The groupings discussed here have very little correspondence with race in the technical sense of the term. But sociological analysis is concerned not so much with the scientific accuracy of ideas as with their social and political consequences. Physical anthropologists are now gradually coming to discard the term *race* itself and to use in its place such "neutral" terms as *population* or *breeding unit,* but the sociologist cannot afford the luxury of confining his analysis to value-neutral categories. He must penetrate the core of the fundamental values and categories of a society to reveal their meanings—however vague and contradictory—and to show how they govern and direct social action.

Fundamental categories such as race or *jati* are often inherently ambiguous. This ambiguity enables people to use the idea to invoke different—even conflicting—loyalties in different situations. Thus, it may be invoked to unite Bengali Hindus and Moslems against the Assamese, and, in a different historical context, to divide Hindus from Moslems in Bengal.

Although the word *jati* has perhaps a wider referent than the English term *race,* in popular usage *race* has a very broad referent

183

ANDRÉ BÉTEILLE

indeed. To speak of a "Dravida-jati" would appear to be no more
unreasonable than to speak of a Semitic race or a Slavonic race.
The idea of an Aryan race has been invoked by political movements
in both India and Europe, but, ironically, almost diametrically opposite values have been placed on it.

REFERENCES

1. Max Weber, *The Religion of India, Hinduism and Buddhism,* trans. H. H.
Gerth and Don Martindale (Glencoe, 1958), p. 3.

2. Irawati Karve, *Kinship Organization in India* (Poona, 1953).

3. N. K. Bose, "The Hindu Method of Tribal Absorption," *Science and Culture,* Vol. 7, No. 7 (October, 1941), pp. 188-94.

4. N. K. Bose, "Calcutta: A Premature Metropolis," *Scientific American,* Vol.
213, No. 3 (September, 1965), p. 102.

5. Bernard S. Cohn, "The Changing Status of a Depressed Caste," *Village
India,* ed. M. Marriott (Chicago, 1955); Dagfin Silversen, *When Caste
Barriers Fall* (New York, 1963).

6. M. N. Srinivas, "Social Structure," *The Gazeteer of India,* Vol. 1 (New
Delhi, 1965), pp. 511-12.

7. P. C. Mahanlanobis, "A Revision of Risley's Anthropometric Data,"
Samkhya, Vol. 1 (1933), pp. 76-105; C. R. Rao and D. N. Majumdar,
Race Elements in Bengal (Bombay, 1960); D. N. Majumdar, *Races and
Cultures of India* (Bombay, 1958); S. S. Sarkar, *Aboriginal Races of India*
(Calcutta, 1954).

8. Sarkar, *Aboriginal Races of India.*

9. Herbert Risley, *The People of India* (Calcutta, 1908).

10. B. S. Guha, "Racial Elements in the Population," Oxford Pamphlets on
Indian Affairs, No. 22 (Bombay, 1944).

11. See, for instance, *Seminar,* No. 23 (July, 1961), pp. 10-11.

12. Risley, *The People of India.*

13. G. S. Ghurye, *Class, Caste, and Occupation* (Bombay, 1961); Majumdar,
Race Elements in Bengal.

14. Quoted in Risley, *The People of India,* p. xxviii.

15. Kingsley Davis, "Intermarriage in Caste Society," *American Anthropologist,* Vol. 43 (1941), pp. 386-87.

16. *Ibid.,* p. 387n.

184

17. Thus far I have tried to keep close to the technical or anthropological meaning of the term *race*. But this meaning is itself ambiguous and has undergone much change in the last few decades. Many physical anthropologists regard the idea of race as having outlived its utility in scientific analysis. Be that as it may, this idea, however vaguely held, continues to exercise a powerful influence over the human mind. I, therefore, turn to a consideration of the categories that correspond most closely to "race" in popular Indian thought.

18. The word *jati* is derived from *jan*, "to give birth to."

19. E. E. Evans-Pritchard, *Nuer Religion* (Oxford, 1956).

20. E. R. Leach, "Concerning Trobriand Clans and the Kinship Category Tabu," *The Developmental Cycle in Domestic Groups*, ed. Jack Goody (London, 1958), pp. 120-45.

21. I have discussed the different meanings of the word *jati* in relation to the caste system in "A Note on the Referents of Caste," *European Journal of Sociology*, Vol. 5 (1964).

22. Adrian C. Mayer, *Caste and Kinship in Central India* (London, 1960), p. 13.

23. André Béteille, "Caste and Politics in Tamilnad," forthcoming.

24. Quoted in G. V. Subba Rao, *Life and Times of Sir K. V. Reddi Naidu* (Rajahmundry, 1957), p. 46.

25. Béteille, "Caste and Politics in Tamilnad."

26. *Homeland*, May 28, 1961.

27. André Béteille, "The Future of the Backward Classes, the Competing Demands of Status and Power," *Perspectives. Supplement to the Indian Journal of Public Administration*, Vol. 11, No. 1 (1965), pp. 1-39.

LEON CARL BROWN

Color in Northern Africa

In Africa, roughly one person in five is white, and the vast majority of these whites are by no means "settlers" who have come to Africa during the last three hundred years. The white population emigrating from Europe in modern times, by the most generous estimate no more than four million people, is concentrated in the southern part of the continent. By contrast, those African lands washed by the Mediterranean to the north contain a long-established, non-European white population of at least 58 million.

Northern Africa is and has been throughout recorded time the great border zone where white ends meeting the area where black begins. In other parts of the world, vast migrations have created important juxtapositions of the two colors, as in the United States, Brazil, and South Africa. In Northern Africa, native whites and native blacks have confronted each other since the beginning of history. If there are lessons to be learned about the ways in which men of various times and cultures have reacted to differing skin colors, then Northern Africa is one of the most important places to look.

Leaders in the states of Northern Africa all speak today, with greater or lesser intensity, of a common African-ness. They contend that Africa is and always has been color-blind. The moral foundation of this assertion can only be applauded and encouraged, but is it historically valid? Has color played so marginal or even insignificant a role in the North African's vision of his neighbors to the south? Is the present cry of a common African-ness that transcends color differences based on more than an act of will, however laudable, on the part of the ruling elite?

Only one part of this complex subject can be assayed here—how the native, predominantly white populations living in the northern part of Africa have regarded the blacks to the south.[1] The question to be posed is, in fact, even more circumscribed—to what extent does color seem to have been a determining factor? Antipathies or sympathies based on language, religion, ways of life, or common enemies will be considered only as they bear on the immediate question of color.

There is considerable complexity and diversity in Northern Africa, or what some French geographers have called *l'Afrique blanche*. These many differences pale, however, when Northern Africa is compared with its neighboring regions to the east (the Middle East) or the south (Black Africa), so much so that it even seems warranted to speak of its great uniformities: Northern Africa is overwhelmingly Moslem in religion and has been for centuries; it thus presents a deep-rooted historical continuity. Arabic, the major language, provides a *lingua franca* for the entire area, including the large native Berber-speaking populations of Morocco and Algeria. It is the sole native language serving as the vehicle for a learned tradition. Such basic items as architecture, economic organization, habits of dress, and cuisine all indicate that this is a single cultural area. In the parlance of many present-day Africans, this is Arab Africa or—to be a bit more exact at the price of ponderosity—this is Arabo-Berber, Moslem, overwhelmingly white Africa.

Separating Northern Africa from Middle Africa is the world's largest desert land mass, the Sahara, which extends across the continent from the Atlantic to the Red Sea, broken only in the east by the Nile River. The extent to which the Sahara has served as a barrier between Northern and Middle Africa is still debated, but one possible measure available to the untrained eye is perhaps not lacking in significance. As one moves southward along the Nile Valley into the Sudan, there is, despite the river's many cataracts, a subtle change from white to black in the skin pigmentation of the people. The break between white and black is sharper in central and West Africa. It is safe to say that the Sahara has been somewhat more of a barrier than the Nile Valley.

There has, however, been caravan trade across the Sahara since antiquity. It is also undeniable that Islam—numerically the most important world religion represented in Black Africa—came from the north, with the exception of the influence exerted from the Arabian peninsula across the Red Sea directly on parts of East Africa. In fact, to schematize the matter, Middle Africa has been a "receiving" cultural area vis-à-vis the North in much the same way as North Africa (especially Northwest Africa) has received from the Middle East. (The parallel could be extended: Each of the "receivers" has placed its own stamp on the ideas it has borrowed and has resisted political domination from the outside source area.)

The Sahara does not provide for Africa the same kind of clear-cut boundary that the Rhine or the Alps constitute in Europe. Rather, it is a great buffer zone or—to adapt Owen Lattimore's phrase—it is the inner African frontier for both Northern and Middle Africa.[2] The nomadic life the Sahara fosters stands in marked contrast to the sedentary existence found to the north or the south. The nomads have always confronted both black and white sedentary peoples with a not dissimilar set of challenges and problems.

The Sahara itself has been the great arena where white and black have met and fought. Black peoples first inhabited the Sahara, but were slowly pushed southward by white nomads. Today, the oases of Southern Tunisia, Morocco, and Algeria reveal black populations ranging from as low as 3 per cent of the total population to as high as 75 per cent.[3] As one moves toward the Senegal and the Niger, the population tends to become more mixed between white and black. In the Sahara are also found lingering examples of what amounts to a slave caste exemplified in the domination of the black *haratin* by the Berber Touareg. To this day a fear of the "Moors" on the part of the blacks and the persistence of slavery have been noted in what is now Southern Mauretania.[4]

The Sahara is a zone unto itself. The white-black relationships there form a fascinating subject. It cannot be assumed, however, that behavioral patterns and outlooks found in the Sahara are applicable to the population of Northern Africa living in non-desert regions. The ideas and prejudices of white Sahara vis-à-vis the black man have, of course, influenced the settled areas of the North, but they have not necessarily been decisive. Many other factors have also been operative.

This conception of the Sahara as a vast inner frontier separating Northern Africa from Middle Africa serves to clarify the nature of white-black encounters in Northern Africa. There have always been blacks in Northern Africa. The blacks have never, however, really represented a group or nation and, consequently, they have

188

never constituted a threat to the non-Saharan Northern Africans. Such a confrontation between nations with all it entails of elemental human striving for security took place only in the Sahara and, along somewhat different lines, in the upper Nile Valley. The blacks arrived in Northern Africa as detribalized individuals, usually as slaves. Raymond Mauny has estimated that during the Middle Ages at least twenty thousand blacks were sent each year from West Africa into North Africa, or at least two million per century.[5] Even so, such a number coming not as a tribe in migration but as random individuals soon to be scattered over Northern Africa could easily be absorbed and even ignored.

The wide Sahara made it unthinkable that the blacks would flee or by any other means return to the "land of the blacks," which is the meaning of the Arabic word *Sudan*. Furthermore, no black nation in Middle Africa ever posed a physical threat to the states of Northern Africa. White nomads, such as the Almoravides of the eleventh century, have threatened Middle Africa and even disrupted kingdoms just as the nomads from the Sahara have done in the North. The Moroccan expedition into West Africa at the end of the sixteenth century that overthrew the declining Songhay empire furnishes a major illustration of a threat, both political and military, moving from north to south. There are, however, no examples of a threat moving in the opposite direction.

Perhaps this distinction between the inner African frontier zone (the Sahara) and the rest of Northern Africa suggests a modification of the earlier point made about the unique white-black relationship in Northern Africa. It might be more accurate to see the confrontation of *native* white and *native* black as having taken place only in the Sahara and the upper Nile Valley. Concomitantly, the white-black relationship in the rest of Northern Africa would seem disturbingly like that in the United States. A minority of detribalized blacks, almost all of whom were brought in as slaves, occupies the lowest socioeconomic rungs in the social ladder. Not only are they unable to return to their native lands, but they are also in no position to demand consideration or respect. They lack both sufficient cohesion within the domestic society and physical proximity to native black societies that might champion their cause.

Yet, as anyone familiar with society in Northern Africa will immediately recognize, the white-black relationship there is not comparable to that in the United States. The key to understanding

189

the question of color in Northern Africa lies in discovering what makes for this difference.

It is tempting to speculate that the all-too-human tendency to discriminate according to easily discernible differences is mitigated in societies which have always had some blacks living amidst whites. The black man in Northern Africa was never a strange, unknown being—not to be judged by existing mores and, thus, more readily treated as if he belonged to a different species.

The most famous historian and thinker of Moslem North Africa, Ibn Khaldūn (1332-1406), reserved his most pejorative comments for those blacks about whom the Northern Africans had no firsthand knowledge.

To the south of the Nile [Niger] there is a Negro people called Lamlam. They are unbelievers. They brand themselves on the face and temples. The people of Ghana and Takrur invade their country, capture them, and sell them to merchants who transport them to the Maghrib. There, they constitute the ordinary mass of slaves. Beyond them to the south, there is no civilization in the proper sense. There are only humans who are closer to dumb animals than to rational beings. They live in thickets and caves and eat herbs and unprepared grain. They frequently eat each other. They cannot be considered human beings.[6]

The idea that white-black familiarity in Northern Africa bred not contempt but a certain feeling of common humanity should be kept in mind as one of several possible independent variables serving to explain the color pattern there. It is at best, however, a shaky hypothesis, as the centuries-old caste system in India would immediately suggest.

Some observers would stress the role of Islam in breaking down distinctions based on color. This position raises as many problems as it answers. Christianity and Islam are quite close on the questions of slavery and racialism. Both arose in a historical context that included slavery. Although both attempted to restrict the institution, neither categorically forbade it. Furthermore, each began among a single ethnic group and moved quickly, not without tensions and problems, into a universal appeal to all races. The undeniable progress of Islam in Africa can be compared to that of Christianity among the European barbarians. This indicates the futility of attempting to explain Moslem or Christian successes in terms of certain distinctions between the two religions.

An examination of the actual economic and political roles played by the blacks in Northern Africa will be both more demonstrable and more useful. Here a crucial difference immediately emerges. The slave relationship of the Negro in the modern Western world was always closely linked to the plantation system— the exploitation of large numbers of unskilled slave laborers in vast agricultural projects. There has been nothing comparable to the plantation system of slavery in Northern Africa (excluding the Sahara) since the Islamic period began in the seventh century.[7] The blacks who came as slaves were employed as domestic servants, concubines, artisans, or porters. In the famous case of the *Abid al Bukhari* organized by Morocco's Mulay Ismail, who reigned from 1672 to 1727, they formed an elite praetorian guard that for several decades held the balance of power in Morocco. The Negroes brought in as slaves from West Africa thus played for a brief time a military role similar to that of the Turks in the rest of the Arabo-Islamic world.

The economic and social position of the black man in Northern Africa best explains many aspects of the white-black relationship there. Observers, always unanimous about the cruelty and severity of the trans-Saharan slave traffic, have remarked on the humane treatment of the black slave in Northern Africa. Nothing could be more natural. The slave was not chattel to be sent into the fields. Rather, he often lived with the family. Master-slave relations were face-to-face. The concubinage that took place was socially accepted, the children of such union being fully recognized and free.

Humane treatment of blacks, slaves, or people of slave origins is one thing, but social mobility quite another. One can cite the important, if short-lived, political role of the *Abid al Bukhara* as kingmakers in seventeenth- and eighteenth-century Morocco, or dip into history to recall that a Negro, Kafur, was *de facto* ruler of Egypt during the mid-tenth century. It might even be noted that Moroccan Sultan Mulay Hasan, who reigned from 1873 to 1894, had a Negro mother. Even so, isolated examples of this sort throughout the centuries illustrate only a slight change in the marginal position of the blacks in the various societies of Northern Africa.

There was, however, never anything approaching segregation based on color. North African cities, like those of the Middle East, were and still are to some extent characterized by a degree of residential and occupational segregation. There are, for example, the Jewish tailors, the Mzabite grocers, and the dockers of Tunis

from a specific Southern Tunisian village. These distinctions, however, lack clear-cut implications of social rank. Miscegenation, always socially acceptable, has been practiced in the best of families. The institution of black concubinage was most developed,
for example, in old, settled, upper-bourgeois families in Fez. Levi-
Provençal, in his classic study of Moslem Spain, has observed:

> Thus in the ninth century, just as in present-day Morocco, there was no
> lack of mulattos in the Muslim aristocracy and bourgeoisie among
> whom—they must be given this credit—color prejudice has never ex-
> isted, no more in the Middle Ages than today.[8]

No "color bar" developed in Northern Africa. The spectrum of
black-white relationships is explainable in class, not caste, terms.

Among the proverbs and maxims of Moroccan country people
collected by Westermarck, the following relate to color:

> A fertile negress is better [as a wife] than a sterile white woman.

> For lack of a relative I call a negro ['abd] my mother's brother. (Said by
> a woman who could find no husband in her own race.)

> A charcoal and it will give me fat to eat.[9]

All reveal a strong prejudice against the black man and the implication that he would usually be close to the bottom of the social
rankings. At the same time, the folk wisdom testifies that there is
nothing taboo about the black person; intermarriage is at most a
mésalliance. In several other proverbs a close connection is drawn
between the jinn and the Negro, black people being regarded as
unlucky. These can in large measure be explained by a major
common factor. The black man in Northern Africa is a detribalized
individual in a society where the extended family and tribe have
been the matrix of all human intercourse. In Sudan, the lighter-
skinned offspring of mixed Egyptian-Sudanese marriages is a muwallad, a term often used in a slightly pejorative sense even
though Arabo-Moslem Sudan in many ways acknowledges the cultural leadership of Egypt. This illustration suggests the extent to
which color itself is relatively marginal in Northern Africa.

A different form of prejudice is reserved for a small minority
that, unlike the muwallad and most blacks, is cohesive and even
clannish. For example, the Nubians living along the Nile in Upper
Egypt and Northern Sudan are forced by an inhospitable environment to send many men north into Egypt and south into the
Sudan for work that will support those staying behind. Nubians
dominate certain occupations such as domestic service, but many

also achieve high positions in government and administration. As one Nubian once joked, "We are either cooks or cabinet ministers." Nubians are, in fact, subjected to about the same type of prejudice as the Mzabites of Algeria, Soussi of Morocco, and Djerbans of Tunisia, all industrious clannish folk obliged to emigrate seeking work. Of interest here is that the Nubians, although not Negroid, are darker than the Egyptians of lower Egypt and lighter than the "average" Sudanese. The Mzabites, Soussi, and Djerbans are all whites living among whites. The prejudice is similar in all cases; the color difference—where it exists—is clearly incidental.

Another basic index for determining the significance of color in Northern Africa is the terminology employed. There is no vocabulary comparable to the vast number of words, both technical and colloquial, found in English to convey subtle differences of pigmentation. In fact, the most common word for a black person in Arabic is *'abd* which means "slave" and has no etymological link with color whatsoever. In the same way, the word *khadim* ("servant") eventually came to mean Negro or more particularly a Negro woman. *'Abd* is of course pejorative, but its tenuous link with color can be illustrated by a now almost legendary story the Sudanese tell. A Northern Sudanese nationalist leader made an impassioned speech in the pre-independence Legislative Assembly extolling the brotherhood that existed between the peoples of North and South. Yet, when a Southern leader rose to speak and apparently had some trouble expressing himself, the Northerner turned to a friend and demanded irritably, "What is that *'abd* trying to say?" Both the *'abd* in question and the Sudanese Arab were quite black.[10]

The word *guinea*, presumably taken from the Berber, was as early as the fourteenth century translated by Europeans to mean "black" or "Negro." In suggesting a Berber etymology, Vincent Monteil notes that the presumed Berber word simply means "dumb" or "unintelligible."[11] This would be comparable to the Arabic expression *'ajam* applied to all non-Arabic speakers regardless of color or other distinctions. (Compare this with the English usage of *barbarian*.)

The different aspects of white-black encounters in Northern Africa suggest a basic pattern: Northern Africa has always been aware of the black man, but he has not been seen as playing an especially important role. The prejudice that has always existed and still exists is best expressed in terms of class, not caste. The

193

Northern African is accustomed to seeing the black man at or close to the bottom of the socioeconomic scale. While Northern Africa is not color-blind, it is hardly color-conscious. In many of the most fundamental social relations, the Northern African is more likely to distinguish and discriminate on the basis of religion, language, or way of life than on the basis of color. In Northern Africa, there is nothing taboo about color.[12]

In 1870 Egypt's Khedive Ismail asserted that his country "does not lie in Africa but in Europe." In 1952, Jamal Abd al Nasir affirmed in his autobiographical *Philosophy of the Revolution,* "We are in Africa. The people of Africa will continue to look to us, who guard their northern gate, and who constitute their link with the outside world."[13]

Abd al Nasir can justly claim credit as the leader of Arab Africa who "discovered" the political potential lying dormant in the rest of Africa. (Another African "first" was his early support of the Algerian F.L.N.) Before that time, the several states of Northern Africa were concerned with their domestic problems, with the colonial or former colonial power, and with their fellow Arab states —more or less in that order. Tunisia's Bourguiba conceded as much with his usual candor in a 1959 public speech, "Owing to the expansion of our foreign activities in the last few years, we have come to realize our profound feelings of solidarity with the African continent."[14] And in his speech to the Tunisian people before leaving to participate in Ghana's independence celebration in 1957, Bourguiba asserted, "I am going on Sunday to a distant country, in the heart of Africa. . . . I am going to Ghana in order to emphasize the importance of a decisive event for the African continent and also to get acquainted with this country."[15]

Since the 1950's there has been a significant move toward an African identification on the part of Arab Northern Africa.[16] As early as 1955 the Egyptian radio began broadcasts in Swahili,[17] and since the mid-1950's Egypt has become the headquarters for a variety of exiled African nationalist groups, a function which post-independence Algeria has shown some interest in sharing with Egypt.

As late as the first Conference of Independent African States, in Accra in 1958, Morocco, Tunisia, and Libya had no formal diplomatic contact with Black Africa. There has been no such slighting of Black Africa since that time. All the states of Northern

Africa participate in the Organization of African Unity, and the Algerian-Moroccan border dispute of 1963 was mediated through the O.A.U. instead of the Arab League. All the states of Arab Africa have been intimately involved in Congo affairs. Tunisia and Morocco sent troops to the U.N. forces in the Congo, and later Algeria and the U.A.R. became strongly committed to the forces under Gbenye resisting Tshombe.

During the same period, the amount of space devoted to Black Africa in the journals, books, and broadcasts of Northern Africa has increased immeasurably. In November, 1957, the Egyptian information service began publication of *Nahda Ifriqiya* (*African Awakening*), an Arabic-language journal with only occasional articles in English or French. Such an official publication in Arabic and the numerous popular books and pamphlets, many of which have also been officially encouraged, strongly suggest that the U.A.R. is concerned not only with playing a major role in Black Africa but also with fostering an African-consciousness at home.[18]

Nor is it accidental that the influential Tunisian weekly *Action* became in 1960 *Afrique-Action* (now *Jeune-Afrique*), or that the Tunisian government has published in Arabic, English, and French an impressive, lavishly illustrated, and obviously expensive book entitled *New Africa*.

These attempts at achieving a *rapprochement* with Black Africa can be understood and analyzed on several different levels. Idealism, self-interest, and even the nebulous but nevertheless very real factor of desiring to follow the current fashion all play their part. The Egyptian scholar Boutros-Ghali has managed to convey in a succinct statement most of the major elements:

It must not be forgotten that sixty-six percent of the Arab community and seventy-two percent of the Arab lands are in Africa. Thus Africanism is a defense in depth for Arabism, a source of solidarity, a new opportunity for the Arab world situated as it is between Europe and Black Africa. It is destined to bring white and black races together in harmony of mutual interests.[19]

This orientation in Northern Africa and its obverse—the response from Black Africa growing out of or transcending such ideas as Pan-Africanism and *négritude*—have an important bearing on the question of color. Most obvious is the impressive claim by present-day statesmen and opinion-molders in North Africa that color is inconsequential. Even if the causes for such a stance can be explained completely in terms of self-interest and *raison d'état*, this remains a significant development. It implies that certain changes in the international diplomatic order have motivated the whites and blacks of Africa to work together.

If this is, however, the major motivation behind the present Northern African efforts in Black Africa, then the new development is unlikely to put out very hardy roots. There are just as many tangible matters of self-interest and *raison d'état* pulling Northern Africa in the opposite direction. Most important and most menacing as a potential issue between white Arab Africa and Black Africa is the problem of the Southern Sudan where almost four million non-Arabic-speaking non-Moslems live more or less under the "colonial" control of their more advanced Arabo-Moslem neighbors.

The moral case is not nearly so clear-cut as either protagonist would claim. The Southern Sudan, one of the most primitive areas in Africa, is badly in need of some variety of outside tutelage. The Northern Sudanese administration, however, has left much to be desired. It has been marked by a general lack of sympathy and understanding, in the worst cases shading into contempt. If this Suda⁻ se issue becomes a general African concern, it could polarize into an Arab (and thus white)-Africa versus Black-Africa problem. Even though the Northern Sudanese are also quite black, their cultural identification is thoroughly northward to Egypt and the Arab world. When the common enemy of Northern and Middle Africa was outside imperialism, it was no great strain, diplomatic or visceral, for them to work together. Should, however, the Northern Sudanese leadership need diplomatic support in the Southern problem, it will play upon the basic themes of Arab unity and Islamic solidarity. The choice will no longer be so easy for Northern Africa, especially for Egypt which just over a decade ago was actively campaigning for unity of the Nile Valley.

Northern Africa's attempts to line up diplomatic support in Black Africa for extra-African issues such as the Arab-Israeli conflict have also proved to be of limited utility. At the May, 1963, conference of African chiefs of state in Addis Ababa, representatives from Black Africa clearly warned Abd al Nasir against pressing for an anti-Israeli resolution. Harry B. Ellis has reported the substance of their argument:

"We are friendly with Israel," the Negro presidents had told him in effect. "You are not. That is your business, but do not inject a personal note into Addis. If you do, you will split Africa in two. You will carry white (Arab) Africa and we will carry black Africa. We will never forgive you for splitting Africa this way."[20]

The Moroccan claim to Mauretania is another potential cause of friction. Heretofore, white Africa has been reluctant to support Morocco in this issue. If tangible interests are, however, the sole criterion, this position could change at any time.

Even the easy diplomatic successes in Black Africa often leave a legacy of future trouble. Nowhere did Egyptian propaganda efforts find more receptive ground than among the fervently Moslem Somalis, whose African identification is in any case somewhat limited. On the other hand, Somali territorial claims pose a threat to Ethiopia and Kenya.

All of these cases indicate how easy it could be for Northern Africa to reawaken the old fears and charges about the "Arab slaver"—even inadvertently—simply by supporting such groups as the Somalis, the Northern Sudanese, and those in Mauretania more inclined to throw in their hand with Morocco.

Perhaps the major obstacle likely to frustrate Northern Africa's efforts is an excess of initiative, which can quickly appear as a threat or, at the very least, as an undesirable nuisance to the newly-independent states of Middle Africa. Especially is this the case with Egypt and Algeria, whose sense of mission is easily translated into activist policies of intervention. The long, bitter struggle for independence probably conditioned the present Algerian leadership to an acceptance of direct action, violence, and a somewhat simplistic Manichaean outlook on the world. It remains to be seen whether the experience of peace and independence will soften the Algerian position.[21]

The Egyptian tendency is one that the American should recognize as all too familiar. A shrewd French journalist once labeled the Egyptians as the Americans of the Middle East, and he might well have added Africa. Needless to say, this was not intended as a compliment to either party. On the diplomatic level there is some truth in this jibe. The Egyptian leadership and the intellectual class often manifest a very American moralizing enthusiasm in international affairs, coupled with a certain insensitivity to the feelings and opinions of others. The Egyptian leadership is, consequently, susceptible to the grave error of a modified latter-day white man's burden in Africa. It is worth recalling in this context that Abd al Nasir's statement "We are in Africa" was followed immediately by a sentence likely to raise eyebrows in all of independent Black Africa: "We will never in any circumstances relinquish our responsibility to support, with all our might, the spread of enlightenment and civilization to the remotest depths of the jungle."[22]

This brief listing of problems or potential disputes likely to divide Northern and Middle Africa suggests that the lofty slogans about African cooperation transcending differences of color could well come to grief. If the outcome is decided by the objective interplay of tangible interests—as presently conceived by the participants—then the steady cultivation of "African-ness" is far from assured.

Yet, much more than simply power politics and short-term considerations of interest are involved in the present relations between Northern and Middle Africa. It has become almost trite to expatiate on the ideological revolution taking place in Africa—a change in world-view at least as intensive as the concurrent waves of romanticism and nationalism in nineteenth-century Europe. These new ideas do, indeed, cut across national, religious, ethnic, linguistic, and color lines in all of Africa. The young intellectuals in the entire area share to a remarkable degree a framework of ideals and political goals.

This prevailing mentality among African intellectuals—white and black—is potentially of great consequence for creating a solid base of African identity and genuine white-black cooperation. No attempt to understand the present or to predict the future pattern of white-black relations in Africa is adequate unless weight is given to this new factor, perhaps the most important single independent variable in the entire equation.

A long step backward in time is necessary for a proper understanding of the present intellectual class in Northern Africa. For roughly one hundred and fifty years, the rulers in these countries have been wrestling with the "impact of the West" and with the problem of changing in order to stand effectively against a technically superior, more dynamic Europe. The ensuing great upheaval, which has radically changed the bases of society and economy, tended to be formulated in ideological terms as a battle between the alien, intrusive new and the native, religiously-sanctioned old. This impulse was so strong that the would-be reformers and adopters of European techniques were obliged to argue that their plans really involved a return to the pure religious and social organizations of old which had been corrupted in the intervening centuries.

By the mid-twentieth century, however, the many changes that have taken place in Northern Africa—and in the world—have rendered obsolete even the old ways of arguing the issue. Change, far from being suspect and thus requiring some form of dissimulation, is now eagerly embraced. Among the young intellectuals a certain defiance of the old is *à la mode*. No one of this class argues about how much "Westernization" can be injected without destroying something vital to the indigenous. Rather, change and innovation, whether they be economic planning or female emancipation, are seen as a force from within.

All this involves the forging of new identities. As the new intellectual class in these countries would see it, no one can identify with the traditional society. This would be to abandon any attempt to create a new order. Nor can one echo the sentiments voiced by the Khedive Ismail in the last century about belonging to Europe; this would imply a rejection of the entire *raison d'être* for the nationalist struggle and the assertion of independence.

This goes a long way in explaining the emotional attraction of the 1955 Bandung Conference, the Algerian identification with Cuba, and more generally the concept of the "Third World." Even the boldest visionary is, nevertheless, aware that ideas are better nurtured in a familiar environment. Africa is, after all, one continent. There are genuine historical links between Northern and Middle Africa upon which to build. Furthermore, cooperation within Africa does not involve exchanging one outside mentor or master for another, as would be the case in escaping Western imperialism only to join the Communist bloc. Rather, Northern Africa and Middle Africa can work together as equals. If anything, and here arises the danger of a certain paternalistic attitude already noted in the case of Egypt, Northern African intellectuals would feel that they might be in a position to guide and help the new societies of Middle Africa.

Seen in this light, there is an added attraction in the proposed cooperation. Because it would be between whites and blacks, it would fill the psychological need to assert moral superiority over a former dominator. To this extent the claim that there is no racial discrimination in Africa can be yet another way of proclaiming —and justifying—independence.

This type of attraction to Black Africa is perhaps most impor-

LEON CARL BROWN

tant in Northwest Africa. Intellectuals there are more in need of
alternative identifications. In Algeria, Tunisia, and Morocco, for
example, to emphasize what in every way is the more natural connection with the Arab East raises problems. The Arabo-Moslem
identification is the main refuge of the most conservative, even
reactionary, elements of the society. To stress connections with
the Arab East only gives additional leverage to these elements at
home. At the same time, the Maghrib leadership is somewhat dubi-
ous about the Eastern Arab performance, less emotionally involved in the Israeli question, and—most important—resentful
of the Eastern Arab's unconscious air of cultural superiority.[23]

It should be emphasized that the ideological attraction to
Black Africa on the part of Northern Africa is antithetical to the
spread of Islam and related matters such as the number of Black
Africans studying in Northern African religious institutions. Northern African emphasis on the common tie of religion can only
be disruptive in Black African countries where there are other
important religious groups or where Islam itself is a minority religion.[24] Also, the leadership in countries such as Senegal and Guinea
has domestic problems with religious conservatism (for example,
with the religious brotherhoods) comparable to those Northern
Africa experienced a generation or so earlier. For this reason, the
Northern African intellectual must choose. He cannot win a response from his Black African counterparts by stressing both
common religious ties and a common ideology devoted to radical
change and creating new societies.[25]

On the level of ideological and, perhaps equally important,
psychological needs, there is considerable impetus pushing the
Northern African intellectuals toward a closer identification with
Black Africa—and thus toward the creation of a series of bonds
that would indeed be color-blind. This tendency could easily become submerged by the combination of immediate disappoint-
ments and distractions, but when set in the historical perspective of Northern Africa's relations with Black Africa, the prospect
that Northern Africa can show the world a somewhat better example of white-black harmony should not be dismissed.

During the Bizerte crisis in 1961, President Bourguiba received
a delegation of foreign students studying in Tunisia who had come
to offer their sympathy and support. When introduced to a young
student from Senegal, Bourguiba quickly moved on from Tunisia's
present troubles to ask about the young man's home country.

"How are conditions in Senegal? Are things on the move? That's the most important thing." The white Tunisian and the black Senegalese were speaking in French, but perhaps they were speaking the same language in a more meaningful sense as well.

REFERENCES

1. The labels "white" and "black" are deliberately used in a loose, non-technical sense. "Black" as used here is not necessarily synonymous with Negro. It might well indicate Nubian, Ethiopian, or Fula, just as "white" might refer to Berber, Arab, or Egyptian Copt.

2. Cf. Owen Lattimore, *Inner Asian Frontiers of China* (Boston, 1962).

3. Robert Capot-Rey, *Le Sahara français* (Paris, 1953), pp. 167ff. Blacks account for about one fourth the population in the Djerid of Southern Tunisia; as much as three fourths in the Draa Valley of Morocco; but less in the Algerian oases. They represent 4 per cent of the population in Ghardaia; this figure increases as one moves southward. In these estimates Capot-Rey is using "blacks" (*noirs*) to include all "people of color," confining "Negro" to those "belonging to the Sudanese group."

4. Vincent Monteil, *L'Islam Noir* (Paris, 1964), p. 255.

5. Raymond Mauny, "Tableau geographique de l'Ouest africain au Moyen Age,"*Memoire IFAN #61* (Dakar, 1961), p. 397. As late as the nineteenth century, Buxton gave as a conservative estimate that twenty thousand Negro slaves were transported per year from Black Africa to Northern Africa and Arabia by the "desert trade." Cf. T. F. Buxton, *The African Slave Trade* (London, 1839), pp. 46ff.

6. Franz Rosenthal, trans., *Ibn Khaldūn's Muqaddimah*, Vol. 1 (New York, 1958), pp. 118-19. At other times, however, Ibn Khaldūn generalizes about the "blacks." "Therefore, the Negro nations are, as a rule, submissive to slavery because [Negroes] have little [that is essentially] human and have attributes that are quite similar to those of dumb animals, as we have stated." *Ibid.*, p. 301.

7. By contrast, the Arab-black relationship in Zanzibar developed more nearly as a form of plantation slavery and resulted in a pattern of white-black relationships that is radically different from the situation in Northern Africa.

8. E. Levi-Provençal, *Histoire de l'Espagne musulmane*, Vol. 3 (Paris, 1953), p. 178. On the other hand, William Shaler, a careful observer who served as American consul in neighboring Algiers in the 1820's, suggested a variant pattern. After noting the mild character of slavery in Moslem society and the relative ease of emancipation, he wrote, "From the small number of mulattoes in the Algerine population, it would appear that a prejudice exists against the colour here, as in the United States, and

probably from the same cause, namely, its slavish origin." William Shaler, *Sketches of Algiers* (Boston, 1826), p. 69.

9. Cf. the indexed references to "Negro" in E. Westermarck, *Wit and Wisdom in Morocco* (London, 1930) and also in his *Ritual and Belief in Morocco* (two volumes; London, 1926).

10. In telling this story to a small group of English and American friends, a Sudanese conveyed the sense of the original Arabic by translating, "What is that nigger trying to say?" Several of those hearing the story reacted with confusion or embarrassment. Unconsciously, we native English-speaking people considered the word *nigger* solely in terms of color. It consequently appeared that our Sudanese friend, obviously a black man by standards of the society that first used the term *nigger*, was either confused or enjoying a subtle irony at our expense. Actually, his translation was very perceptive even if not literally correct. *'Abd* and *nigger* are specific examples of a generic phenomenon—group prejudice. He was acutely aware of group prejudice, but nothing in his experience as a Sudanese inclined him to emphasize skin pigmentation as a major desideratum.

11. Monteil, *L'Islam Noir*, p. 63. It should never be forgotten how much we are all conditioned to see what we expect to see. There is strong evidence that Europe—and, by extension, the New World—has simply equated black with African perhaps to the point of being disoriented without that familiar sign. It is intriguing to speculate on why the first English translator of Leo the African added the word *tawnie* (apparently on his own whim) to Leo's description of the Moors. Nor should black Othello be forgotten. We must not assume that Africans themselves have—or have always had—the same stereotypes or prejudices.

12. A creditable amount of scholarly material on the several socioeconomic aspects of life in Northern Africa does exist, but there appears to be none that deals directly, or even primarily, with the role of the non-Saharan black man. Even the casual observer can soon detect a certain pattern, although he will not be able to buttress his impressions with statistics and detailed monographs. A disproportionately large number of black men are likely to be found, for example, working as unskilled laborers at a construction site or on a work-gang building a highway. Also, several who have had the opportunity to discuss such matters with village women have noted a tendency to favor the fair child over the dark.

The ill-defined and often ignored position of the black man in North Africa has been interpreted as indicating greater social mobility and less group resistance along color lines than prevail in white-black relations in most of the world. Such an interpretation may be too optimistic—a kind of over-reaction to the more clear-cut segregation pattern that characterizes white-black relations in the English-speaking world. Although we are inclined to feel that the muted optimism suggested in this article is justified, the more pessimistic conclusions of Messrs. Pitt-Rivers and Fernandes concerning the color problem in Brazil, Central America, and the Andes raise disturbing questions that might well be applicable in part to Northern Africa as well.

13. Jamal Abd al Nasir, *Egypt's Liberation—The Philosophy of the Revolution* (English translation; Washington, 1955), pp. 109-10.

14. Cited in the *Advancement of Africa*, selections from Bourguiba's speeches translated into English by the Tunisian Secretariat of State for Information (Tunis, n.d. [1960?]). The title of this official Tunisian publication is a significant indication of the changed attitude.

15. *Ibid.,* p. 41 (italics added).

16. This has been less true of Libya.

17. Jacques Baulin, *The Arab Role in Africa* (Baltimore, 1962), p. 41.

18. For example, such popular books as Abd al 'Azīz Rifā'i, *Tatawwur al 'Alāqāt al 'Arabiya al Ifriqiya* (The Development of Arab-African Relations; Cairo, n.d. [1962?]); 'Abduh Badawi, *Shakhsiyāt Ifriqiya* (African Personalities; published by the Egyptian Ministry of Culture and National Guidance); and Ihsan Haqqi, *Ifriqiya al Hurra, Bilad al Aml wa al Rakhā* (Independent Africa, Land of Hope and Prosperity; Cairo, 1962). More serious books include Muhammad 'Abd al Fattah Ibrahim, *Ifriqiya min al Sinighal ila Nahr Juba* (Africa from Senegal to the Juba River; Cairo, 1961); Rashid Barawi, *Mushkilat al Qara al Ifriqiya al Siyasiya wa al Iqtisadiya* (Political and Economic Problems of the African Continent; Cairo, 1960); and Abd al Malik 'Audah, *Al Siyasa wa al Hukm Fi Ifriqiya* (Politics and Government in Africa; Cairo, 1959). In 1956 Cairo University introduced a new subject—"African Problems"—to its curriculum.

19. Boutros Boutros-Ghali, "The Foreign Policy of Egypt," *Foreign Policies in a World of Change,* eds. Joseph E. Black and Kenneth W. Thompson (New York, 1963), p. 328. This point about how much of the Arab world lies in Africa is mentioned also in Boutros-Ghali's introduction to Abd al Malik 'Udah, *Al Siyasa wa al Hukm Fi Ifriqiya.*

20. Harry B. Ellis, "The Arab-Israeli Conflict Today," *The United States and the Middle East,* ed. Georgiana Stevens (Englewood Cliffs, N. J., 1964), p. 113.

21. Algerian diplomacy appears to have become much less interventionist since the overthrow of Ben Bella in June, 1965.

22. Abd al Nasir, *Egypt's Liberation,* p. 110. In the Egyptian journal *Nahdat Ifriqiya* (*African Renaissance*), which began publication in November, 1957, is found the following, "Everyone now realizes how decisive the influence of the Arab world has been on the African continent and how much Africa has responded to its liberating call. Indeed, this should not come as a surprise. Centuries ago, the Arabs already represented civilization, progress, and knowledge to the Africans." Cited in Baulin, *Arab Role in Africa,* p. 31.

23. In 1963 the author asked a group of traditionally trained Algerians who

had been active in the Algerian Association of Ulama their opinion of Algeria's foreign policy on its African connection. The question was deliberately slanted to make a favorable response more likely, but all he received was slightly embarrassed laughter. This group's arena of cultural identification is decidedly confined to the Arabo-Moslem world.

24. For example, Moslems represent the following percentage of total population: Guinea, 45 to 80 per cent; Senegal, 79 per cent; Chad, 44 per cent; Nigeria, 40 per cent; Ethiopia, 25 per cent; Ghana, 3 per cent; Congo, 2.5 per cent. These estimates are subject to considerable variation. The above figures are adapted from the summary of several sources found in J. C. Froelich, *Les Musulmans d'Afrique Noire* (Paris, 1962), p. 360.

25. The continued spread of Islam will be of immense importance in shaping Black African society, but there is little evidence that this will be accompanied by a commensurate extension of Arab influence. A thorough examination of all aspects of this question is found throughout Monteil's *L'Islam Noir*. See also Ibrahim Abu-Lughod, "The Islamic Factor in African Politics," *Orbis*, Vol. 8, No. 2 (Summer, 1964) for a very suggestive distinction between Arab and African Islam.

COLIN LEGUM

Color and Power in the South African Situation

I

COLOR IS the sole determinant of power in South Africa. This distinguishes the *apartheid* republic from all contemporary societies in which serious race problems are encountered. South Africa's power structure is specifically designed to ensure that total power remains exclusively in the hands of three million whites. It not only provides for the whites' security, but also enables them to retain their position of economic and social privilege over a colored majority of thirteen millions. Security and the maintenance of privilege are held to be inseparable.

Contrary to the dominant political tendencies throughout modern societies, differences in race and color in South Africa are consciously and methodically emphasized to buttress the *status quo*. Racial and color prejudice and discrimination are embedded in the country's power structure.[1] The irrational force of prejudice is harnessed to the rational purpose of maintaining a system of discrimination to ensure the survival of a *status quo* based on color.[2]

White South Africans are among the most economically and socially privileged communities in history, but their privilege depends wholly on their ability to retain political power exclusively in their own hands. Power and privilege always go together, and it is pointless to appeal to a privileged society to abandon its power knowing that in so doing it will condemn itself to the loss of its privileges. No privileged society—white or black or brown—has ever voluntarily surrendered its privileges at one fell swoop. The greater the privileges of the society, the greater the incentive to rally to their defense. In South Africa's case, defense of white privilege is further strengthened by the white community's fear that not only their privileges but their entire security would be placed in jeopardy if they surrendered or lost power. It is futile to argue over whether they are right in holding such fears; the point is they do, and most strongly. Moreover, on objective grounds no one can honestly say that such fears are entirely groundless. After the kind of treatment black South Africans have received over three centuries, why should one suppose they will behave any better than white South Africans? One hopes they will behave better, and indeed there is evidence from the tolerant and generous attitudes displayed by African leaders like Chief Lutuli, Robert Mangaliso Sobukwe, and Nelson Mandela that they might. Will, however, the rising generation of revolutionary African leaders have much incentive, or reason, to adopt tolerant attitudes when all they have ever known has been bitterness, frustration, anger, and humiliation? To ignore this potential danger is surely a great mistake. All white South Africans clearly have a personal stake in maintaining the *status quo*. Only the most farsighted perceive the inherent fallacies in a political system that demands increasing coercion in defense of existing privilege and that progressively isolates the republic within the international community.

This general statement about the nature of South Africa's political system exposes the fallacy of the belief that color discrimination can be abolished, or even diminished in a meaningful way, without in fact jeopardizing the entire power structure. Therefore, when defenders of white supremacy argue that any political concessions made to the colored majority must inevitably lead to the abdication of white power, they more correctly reflect the realities of the situation than those advocates of gradualist reform who think it possible to diminish prejudice and discrimination without necessarily undermining the entire structure on which white supremacy rests. These two attitudes mark the division between the major white political parties—the ruling Afrikaner National Party, which holds to the view that there must be no relaxation of white power, and the United Party, which favors economic concessions and some measure of social and political reform.

II

There have been periods in South Africa's history when white supremacy was not tantamount to white tyranny; this is no longer so. It is valid to describe the present political setup in the republic as a white tyranny in strictly non-pejorative terms for two reasons: First, the ideology of the ruling party is based on the belief that total control over the sources of power must be retained in the hands of an exclusive group distinguishable only by their color; and second, the belief that this objective justifies any coercive means necessary to secure it.

An eighteenth-century Dutch governor reporting on the attitudes of the early settlers said: "They describe themselves as humans and Christians, and the Kaffirs and Hottentots as heathens; and by believing in this they permit themselves everything." Although present-day white attitudes are usually expressed in a more sophisticated way, this assessment remains an adequate description of the general attitude of the white electorate in whom all constitutional power resides. Only those deemed by law to be, and officially registered as being, white are allowed to participate in government (whether as voters, legislators, administrators, or judges); in the armed forces; in controlling positions within the economy; or in labor organizations. This distribution of power is exercised through an elaborate system of laws, based solely on color and specifically designed to debar Africans, coloreds,[3] or Asians from free political or labor associations, free movement, free speech, free ownership of land and property, free access to education. This authoritarian construction of laws is taken to the ultimate extreme of refusing to recognize that Africans have a legal right to live anywhere in the country, and that Africans resident in urban areas may not have wives or families living with them except under certain prescribed conditions. An Orwellian position is reached when a married woman living in Reserves *may* be permitted to visit her husband in urban areas for a period of up to fourteen days for the specific purpose of conception. The exercise of even this privilege is vested in the hands of white bureaucrats answerable not to the Courts or to Parliament, but to the Minister of Bantu Affairs alone.

South Africa is, of course, not the only tyranny in the world. It is not even the only racial tyranny. What distinguishes it from other tyrannies, however, is that it is a white tyranny that exists in the African continent in the middle of the twentieth century. It is this paradox that holds the seeds of race war.

III

White supremacy, with its roots in the seventeenth century, was converted into white tyranny after World War II in response to internal pressures by an increasingly educated and articulate African elite who reflected the "colored awakening" in the rest of

207

the world. White South Africans came to feel that the *status quo* was in danger. Suspicions of the "sickly liberalism" of the segregationist policies of Field Marshall Smuts turned into open hostility. Feelings of uncertainty about the future were translated into demands for clear-cut policies and uncompromising leadership to "turn back the black flood." So long as the white society had felt itself securely based, it was willing to consider ways of easing traditional segregationist practices—especially in industry and education, though not in the franchise. Once, however, it began to feel its security challenged, it moved rapidly away from compromise toward policies offering to defend the traditional "white *laager*."[4]

The condition of a *laager* society is essentially paranoidal. Rooted in circumstances of persecution, it survives by persecuting those it fears. South Africa's "*laager* mentality" is not an isolated phenomenon; it is an essential characteristic of every frontier society. South Africa's modern frontiers lie, however, on the Limpopo River beyond which stretches a "hostile" black continent. At its back it has always felt the solid support of the Western world of which, historically, the white society regards itself as an outpost in the African continent. After World War II the *laager* felt itself threatened by two complementary developments—the weakening influence of its traditional Western ally in Africa and the strengthening of its "black enemy" through the rise of independent African states and their new role in international affairs, especially in the United Nations. The *laager's* reaction to these developments moved the center of white political power much farther to the right of the predominantly English-speaking United Party. This reaction secured Afrikanerdom[5] its first electoral victory in the immediate postwar elections in 1948. Over the next nineteen years its strength continued to grow steadily through four subsequent elections.

IV

The victory of Afrikanerdom highlights another facet of the South African dilemma. Unlike other "settler communities" in the continent, South Africa's is substantial in numbers. It has enjoyed a long tradition of independence from the metropolitan colonial countries, and has created a characteristic indigenous national group —the Afrikaners—with its own language, culture, and history. It owes no allegiance to any other country; its roots are firmly planted in African soil. For such a society, survival means survival in Africa. There is no easy line of retreat by emigration as was the ultimate course open to other settler communities. Its total involvement in and commitment to Africa is a stubborn reality. The South African situation, therefore, differs markedly from that of other colonial situations in that an acceptable settlement must fulfill two fundamental requirements: the establishment of representative government involving colored emancipation; and the guaranteeing of white survival in an independent African state with the present *herrenvolk* stripped of its power.

Attempts to find ways of dealing with these problems have produced a number of irreconcilable sets of proposals. That of the African Nationalists—supported by other colored groups and by white liberals—is for undiluted majority rule with the white minority adapting itself as best it can to a politically nonracial society with guarantees of equal rights of citizenship. A second approach offered by the major white-opposition groups is for gradual evolution, but without proposing either a time-scale or a concept of what kind of society it wants South Africa ultimately to become. This approach assumes that economic forces will compel increasing racial integration within the economy, and that economic integration will, in time, diminish rigid color differences and thus eventually make possible acceptable political compromises. A third approach is the traditional white policy that rests essentially on the presumption of white *baaskap*—the "white man boss." A fourth approach—an important variant on the theme of *baaskap*— is the Verwoerd policy of Separate Development.

The adoption in 1947 of the policy of *apartheid* by Afrikanerdom appeared at first sight only to provide a more programmatic approach to the maintenance of *baaskap*. As originally conceived, *apartheid* was defined as "a policy which sets itself the task of preserving and safeguarding the racial identity of the white population of the country; of likewise preserving and safeguarding the identity of the indigenous peoples as separate racial groups, with opportunities to develop into self-governing national units; of fostering the inculcation of national consciousness, self-esteem and mutual regard among the various races of the country." It endorsed "the general principle of territorial segregation of the Bantu[6] and the whites." This broad statement of principles disguised a much deeper division of opinion within Afrikanerdom. On the one side stood the dominant group, reflecting the wishes of the mass of the white electorate, which interpreted *apartheid* as a way of enforcing *baaskap*. This was the attitude of the first two *apartheid* prime ministers, Dr. D. F. Malan and Mr. J. G. Strijdom. This was not, however, the attitude of the other side led by the third prime minister, Dr. H. F. Verwoerd.

V

Verwoerd was in many ways a radical thinker. He was the first influential white politician to originate a fresh approach to South Africa's color problems. His starting point was the acceptance of "the scientific fact" that Africans are not inherently inferior to whites. Hitherto only liberals in South Africa had held this view. Verwoerd's thinking led him, however, to the opposite conclusion from that of the liberals. Whereas they argued that the potential equality between races justified the notion of an integrated multi-racial society, he argued that this fact only increased the danger to white survival. Another of Verwoerd's radical conclusions was that while "many derogatory things were said about black national-ism in particular, world history showed that the desire of a group or nation to become free could not be frustrated forever." If the whites were justified in not wishing to be dominated by blacks, the blacks were equally justified in wishing not to be dominated by whites. This reasoning led him to the decisive step of rejecting the policy of white supremacy or *baaskap*.

These ideas were obviously heretical to the majority of white South Africans. Verwoerd's psycho-political skills warned him not to put forward his new ideas boldly in the political arena. In-stead, they were carefully rehearsed among small groups of Afrikaner intellectuals and Dutch Reformed Church leaders and set out in a calmly reasoned way in *Has the Afrikaner Volk a Future?*, written by one of Verwoerd's closest colleagues, G. D. Scholtz. The logical conclusion drawn from this radical rethinking was that white South Africa's future lay in territorial separation, or even in complete partition. When, however, this proposal was launched publicly at a congress of the Dutch Reformed Church in 1951, both Malan and Strijdom (Verwoerd's immediate pre-decessors) denounced it as politically unrealistic.

While some of Verwoerd's colleagues insisted that the logic of partition must be preached from the rooftops, he recast his ideas into a policy of Separate Development that would provide for the creation of seven autonomous Bantustans within the "historical boundaries" of the Native Reserves. These cover only 13 per cent of the country. In this way he sought to allay the fears of the whites that they might have to lose a part of their present land to make territorial separation feasible.

Verwoerd's new proposals split the Afrikaner intellectuals. Those of his former supporters who believed uncompromisingly in genuine territorial partition were greatly strengthened when Verwoerd's own planning team—the Tomlinson Commission—reported in 1951 that even under optimal conditions the proposed Bantustans would be incapable of absorbing the existing African population, let alone its natural increase. By 2000 A.D. there would be ten million Africans instead of the present seven million in the "white areas" of the country. Thus "white South Africa" would continue to become blacker.

Verwoerd was, however, not to be stopped. Having rejected territorial separation except as "a very long-term objective," he stubbornly clung to his plan to establish seven viable Bantustans that, in time, could become independent states within a new "South African Commonwealth."

The practical difficulties in getting his ideas implemented were made even harder by his failure to persuade his own party either to provide the finances for the schemes needed to get the Bantustans going or to accept the eventual objective of allowing them to evolve into independence. So far only one Bantustan—the Transkei—has been launched, and its results have been depressingly negative. Verwoerd knew, perhaps better than any other white political leader, the danger of allowing the vested interests of his white electorate to obstruct radical changes within the *status quo* which, at least nationally, could be held to offer a promise of some equity to the colored majority. Yet, even though he was intellectually the outstanding Afrikaner of his day and politically by far the most powerful, he failed to influence his own Afrikaner people to understand and accept the kinds of constitutional changes he believed essential for white survival.

VI

The nub of the dilemma that faced Verwoerd—that faces any radical South African reformer—can be simply stated. Effective political power lies in the hands of a white electorate. The voting power of this electorate is so distributed as to give a predominant voice to the Afrikaner voters in the platteland.[7] These voters—

educationally the most backward in the white community—stand to lose the most from any fundamental change in the present political setup. They, therefore, constitute the strongest bulwark against change in the country.

Their stubborn opposition to change has been frequently discussed in Afrikaner newspapers. Here is one typical editorial comment from *Die Transvaler*[8]:

It is a tragedy that there are still so many whites who have not the vaguest idea about the change in Africa and who do not realise the need for adaptation. . . . Are the whites prepared for this degree of adaptation, or do they place their economic interests higher than their survival as a people?

Despite the inspired leadership of Verwoerd, the electorate has shown thus far no sign of a willingness to sacrifice immediate economic interests for longer-term survival. Their inflexible attitude, even against proposals made by their own most trusted leaders, makes peaceful change impossible to foresee, especially since the degree of sacrifice posed by the concept of Verwoerd's territorial partition is relatively minor compared to that which would be involved in an abdication of exclusive political power over the whole country. The electorate has shown no evidence of being prepared to countenance even that much.

While resisting change, the white electorate has strongly supported the build-up of the country's security and military strength in the belief that the white minority can, in the long run, defend itself effectively from internal sabotage and external pressures. In the nineteen years of *apartheid* rule the republic's internal situation has changed dramatically from a predominantly nonviolent political society to an increasingly violent one. Until 1960, the year of Sharpeville, the colored nationalist movement, traditionally led by the African National Congress, held to belief in the necessity of nonviolent methods of opposition. This is no longer so. Violent opposition is now one of their accepted methods of struggle. Although the first waves of sabotage were easily crushed, more sophisticated movements relying on violent methods are in the making. For example, an undisclosed number of South Africans—probably exceeding one thousand—are being trained in African and Communist countries for an armed liberation struggle.[9] The first active group of trained guerrillas began to operate in Ovamboland in the north of Southwest Africa in 1966. In October of that year the first white South African died in his home at the hands of armed guerrillas.[10] The violent change in the political climate is illustrated by the introduction of the "Sabotage Act"[11] in 1963; by the enactment of eighteen different kinds of detention and banishment orders; and by a series of Draconian measures depriving the courts of their normal functions as typified by the notorious "180 Days Detention Law," which enables the police to hold suspects in solitary confinement for as long as they think necessary.

It is clearly a mistake to minimize either white South Africa's capacity for resistance or its determination to resist. Still, although the whites have the will and the capacity to impose their great power, they do not possess sufficient moral authority over the colored majority to enable them to enlist their willing co-operation. They can rule, and they do; but only by force. On the other side, the colored peoples are able to challenge white authority, but lack the power to break it despite their superiority in numbers.

Such a situation offers no possibility of changing South Africa's existing power structure peacefully. The whites have power without authority or consent; the non-whites have the potentialities of power, but without the possibility of realizing them by peaceful means. This raises two major questions: How much violence will accompany change when it finally comes, and will this violence assume the proportions of a race war? Since conflicting forces within South Africa hold the country in political deadlock, the answers to these two questions must lie largely with the role of external forces.

VII

The African states are committed to the destruction of white supremacy. In terms of foreign policy, this is Africa's top priority. National priorities cannot, however, always be fulfilled; even the super-powers sometimes find that their power is insufficient to fulfill their priorities. Nevertheless, the failure to achieve a specific priority should not be interpreted as an abandonment of the priority or a weakening of the resolve to meet it. African leaders are aware of their weakness and of the consequent difficulties it poses for them. This is best illustrated by extracts from a statement made by Tanzania's President Nyerere about the Rhodesian confrontation, but applicable with even more force to South Africa:

In considering the future it is necessary to face up to Africa's weakness. By itself Africa does not at the present time have either the military force or the economic resources to defeat the Smith regime alone. It

213

is necessary for Africa to find and use allies. The Communist Powers, for their own purposes, are sympathetic with Africa's position in Rhodesia. But their active military support, even if it were forthcoming, would introduce the Cold-War conflict into the heart of Africa. While the possibility remains of Africa's objective being achieved without direct Cold-War confrontation in the heart of Africa, we should aim at avoiding such confrontation. This means that, for the time being, we have to exert all our efforts to get the Western Powers themselves to act.

What of the role of the international community as represented by the United Nations? On December 15, 1965, the General Assembly drew the attention of the Security Council to the threat to international peace and security posed by the situation in the Republic of South Africa. Under Chapter VII of the Charter, the General Assembly resolved that action was essential in order to solve the problem of *apartheid.* The voting on this resolution was significant. Eighty nations voted in favor, only two (South Africa and Portugal) voted against, and sixteen abstained. The Security Council itself subsequently endorsed a resolution describing the situation in the republic as likely to "disturb" world peace.

Because the power of the United Nations rests on the willingness of its members to contribute to making its decisions effective and, ultimately, on the contribution of the super-powers, its effectiveness is determined by world power and power politics. Since the Russians have repeatedly voted in favor of direct U.N. intervention in South Africa, the crucial missing factor in mobilizing the U.N. behind its existing political commitments on South Africa is that of the Western powers.

Economic and strategic interests are usually given as the two reasons for the Western powers' failure to commit themselves to more effective action against South Africa. At present, strategic interests are of very little account; economic interests are undoubtedly important, but only in Britain's case are they crucially important.

There are, however, two other factors inhibiting Western action. First, the major Western powers have not yet become convinced that the objective of transferring power in South Africa, more or less peacefully, can be achieved through international action. It is, of course, easier to argue the case for international action than to guarantee its successful outcome; few governments can be expected to commit themselves to huge enterprises without being reasonably convinced that the objectives are realizable. Here, perhaps, is the major area of weakness in the case of inter-

214

national interventionists. The ability to demonstrate more convincingly the effectiveness of international action could make a major contribution toward reducing Western inhibitions. But this alone would not be enough. The Western powers are reluctant to act because of a second major factor—they do not yet believe their national interests to be directly involved in what is happening in South Africa.

No major power—white, black, or brown; Communist, capitalist, or nonaligned—has committed its resources to a warlike enterprise purely out of moral conviction. Nations undertake the use of force, military or economic, only when their national interests are threatened or can be greatly enhanced. So long as the West's national interests are not actively threatened by the situation in South Africa, it cannot be supposed that any of the major Western powers will favor U.N. intervention in support of enforcement action under Chapter VII.

The major Western powers may be ready to intervene in South Africa once the situation in Africa as a whole produces a direct threat to their national interests. By then the situation might well have become not an incipient but an active threat to world peace. Unfortunately, such a situation will arise only when violence begins to occur on a large and mounting scale and involves the rest of Africa. Violence of such dimension might well set off a race war before the U.N. could act. It would certainly embitter relations between the races in South Africa to an extent that would make it more difficult, if not impossible, to reconcile the races after power had passed from white hands.

Nobody stands to gain anything by violence on this scale. Yet opponents of *apartheid* are left without any alternative. They cannot produce peaceful change within South Africa's existing power structure, and Western policy is unwilling to unlock U.N. power until a situation of violence makes actual a threat to world peace and to Western national interests.

VIII

The foregoing analysis of the situation in South Africa leads to the following broad conclusions:

Power inside South Africa cannot be transferred peacefully to the majority.

The transfer of power will result from the application of force either inside the republic or by external forces, or perhaps by a combination of both. Such external forces might be collectively applied by the Organization of African Unity and its allies, or by the U.N.; or they might be applied by Communist countries in support of national liberation movements.

Collective action through the U.N. will only become possible when the major Western powers are willing to support it; this depends on whether an actual threat to world peace already exists, or whether their national interests are being actively threatened.

Pressures to change the direction of Western policies can only come from the African states and from the exercise of force by the opponents of *apartheid* inside South Africa. This is the crucial dilemma created by the policies of the South African government and the Western powers.

Whatever the means and whatever the time-scale, it is now clear that South Africa is set on a collision course. It is, moreover, the only area in the world where color is so bitterly and stubbornly engaged that it threatens to entangle the world community in a race war—unless prophylactic action becomes possible.

REFERENCES

1. Although this essay deals only with the color aspect of racial prejudice, the exploitation of prejudice between "Boer and Briton" has been an important feature of South African history.

2. It is not helpful, therefore, to point to countries like, say, Brazil as offering useful lessons for South Africa. In Brazil the historical process—though slow and still very far from complete—has been working in precisely the opposite direction from South Africa's for the better part of a century.

3. *Coloreds* in this context refers to the 1,200,000 South Africans of mixed racial origins.

4. In South African history the *laager* was a circle of wagons, their wheels bound by thick thorn branches, within which the frontiersmen gathered their families. This served as a fortress from within which they could concentrate their fire on the unmounted black *impis* before they could come within *assegai*-throwing range.

5. Afrikanerdom is the systematic expression of an exclusively Afrikaans-speaking political, cultural, and social movement committed to preserving its uniqueness by establishing its hegemony over the whole country. Its political instrument is the Afrikaner National Party.

6. Bantu is the official white terminology to describe the African peoples. *African* is rejected as an imprecise and "liberalistic" term.

7. The rural areas.

8. This newspaper was founded, and at one time edited, by Dr. Verwoerd.

9. Today, South Africa's security system and army ranks with the strongest among the minor powers of the world. Annual military expenditure now runs to almost $500 million, more than six times as much as the 1960 allotment.

10. After the reported capture of fifty-six "terrorists" in Ovamboland, the South African Commissioner of Police, General J. M. Keevy, disclosed that "a special unit has been established to safeguard South Africa's northern border. This unit has been trained in guerrilla warfare and is equipped with helicopters, two-way radios, provisions, vehicles and arms. The establishment of such a unit has become a necessity since terrorist activities were intensified in Ovamboland and other northern frontier territories." (*Rhodesia Herald*, December 12, 1966.)

11. General Law Amendment Act.

E. R. BRAITHWAITE

The "Colored Immigrant" in Britain

I AM a colored immigrant.

In spite of my years of residence in Britain, any service I might render the community in times of war or times of peace, any contribution I might make or wish to make, or any feeling of identity I might entertain toward Britain and the British, I—like all other colored persons in Britain—am considered an "immigrant." Although this term indicates that we have secured entry into Britain, it describes a continuing condition in which we have no real hope of ever enjoying the desired transition to full responsible citizenship.

Immigrant groups have for many centuries been a familiar and important part of the British community. Mostly refugees from persecution in other European countries, they entered Britain and settled in one of the London boroughs (usually Stepney). During a few generations, they were gradually absorbed into the host community. Irrespective of their countries of origin or the religions which they practiced, all these groups were white-skinned. They could, if they chose, fade without difficulty into the "white" background.

The colored immigrant is and seems likely to remain the exception. His high visibility is a constant reminder to Britons of his earliest relationship with them—slave to owner, subject to sovereign, conquered to conqueror, and man to master. The history of Britain is a record of struggle against invasion or the threat of invasion from usually more numerous enemies. In time this has effectively conditioned the Briton to believe that he is by nature a higher, nobler breed of human, demonstrably worth at least two Germans, three Frenchmen, four Italians, six Spaniards or Portuguese, and an infinite number of those who are outside the "white" enclave. This belief, supported and strengthened with every territorial acquisition, served to prevent anything but minimal social contact with the subject peoples governed and administered in those territories, the majority of whom were colored.

Most colored immigrants in Britain are Indians, Pakistanis, or West Indians. I am a West Indian. To many Britons, the term *West Indian* hints of perpetual sunshine, sandy beaches, swaying palms, calypso, rum, and cricket. It conveys nothing of the real nature of that complex of islands in the Caribbean or of the people who inhabit it other than their amazing persistence in seeking exposure to the climatic and social rigors of life in Britain. A West Indian is, in fact, a unique phenomenon. He is a composite of the effects of enforced and negotiated transplantation from Africa (as slaves) and from India (as indentured labor), and of infusions of blood and culture from China, Lebanon, Europe, and America, all finally coerced and conditioned into irrevocable Britishness.

Britain became the focus of cultural, educational, and professional interests, the Mecca for all those who could afford the long and expensive journey. Any discriminatory treatment the visitor or student experienced was readily overlooked in the larger pleasure of being "home" and generally enjoying the equality of treatment that a British passport promised.

In two world wars, many volunteered for service with the British Forces. Probably encouraged by the prevailing mood of tolerance, friendliness, and unity in the face of a common threat and influenced by the prospects for well-paid employment and further education and training, many decided to settle in Britain. Settling into the community without difficulty, they comported themselves in a way that attracted no unfavorable attention or comment. They even acquired property among the large, Victorian terraced houses that became available for purchase around London.

These new settlers were relatively few in number, and mainly young, intelligent, and articulate men. Before long, however, the popular acceptance of the uniformed colored serviceman who would one day vanish into the exotic nowhere whence he came gave way to incipient irritation with the colored civilian who spoke and behaved like a Briton and expected to be treated like one. This irritation increased when colored men sought and found British girl friends, sweethearts, and wives, when they began competing on equal terms for a variety of technical jobs.

The British had welcomed these colored comrades-in-arms; colored brothers-in-law were quite another matter. Their resentment grew and expressed itself in a wide variety of proscriptions affecting the colored men and the white women who associated with them. Accommodation became difficult, and this gave rise to the unfortunate process of whites moving away from the immediate proximity of coloreds, who quickly snapped up all property that became available. Concentrations of colored persons began to appear, chiefly in the Brixton, Stepney, and Notting Hill districts of London. These helped to focus popular irritation and dislike.

The British were being challenged for the first time in history to prove on home ground their right to the reputation for justice, fairness, and human decency that they enjoyed as a feature of their overseas administration, and, concomitantly, they also found themselves confronted at home for the first time by people who, color apart, believed themselves to be equally British. Their general reaction was to close ranks and to isolate the intruder in every way possible.

As the pace of Britain's postwar reconstruction accelerated, so did the demands on available manpower. An acute shortage resulted which even an increasing flow of migrant labor from Ireland could not meet. As an experiment, certain private and government-sponsored schemes were instituted for importing selected West Indian personnel for certain essential services. Some industries followed suit. Important considerations were that the West Indians were English-speaking and good dependable workers.

Before long the word spread throughout the islands that well-paid employment was ready and waiting for anyone who could arrange his own passage to Britain. What had been an organized trickle of selected scores or hundreds now became a disorganized flood of thousands—many of them illiterate peasants and others, in spite of their claims, completely unskilled according to British standards and even lacking the basic educational requirement necessary for training in new skills. They did possess, however, strong backs, willing hands, and a deep, conditioned faith in British decency and fairness.

In spite of the increasing and vocal popular unease at this flood of immigrants, there appeared no clear, positive policy relating to their entry, no planned dispersal to anticipate and avoid local saturation, and no orientation schemes to ease the confrontation between the host community and the newcomers, many of whom had literally mortgaged themselves to make the journey and were bewildered and hurt by the open rejection and dislike that greeted them. They flocked to depressed areas in which earlier arrivals had already established themselves. Unscrupulous landlords, white and colored, were quick to appreciate the prospect of a rich harvest and mercilessly exploited the newcomers' frustration and misery.

Predictably, the demand for unskilled and even semiskilled labor disappeared with this sudden excess of untrained and untrainable personnel. More and more the newcomers were unemployable and had no choice but to join the lengthening queues for national assistance. The sight of these lines of miserable black men served only to harden popular feeling against the immigrants. They were blamed for being unemployed and battening on a generous welfare state, for living in the overcrowded ghettos into which popular discrimination had circumscribed them, and for accepting the menial jobs that indigenous whites could now afford to despise. Even the early arrivals had their troubles. Those who, through training and qualification, gave evidence of responsibility and leadership soon found the paths to promotion securely closed against them. White colleagues refused to accept them at any but the more inferior levels of employment. Obligatory union membership was of no consequence. The black man, not regarded as an equal, would not be accepted as such no matter how industrious or clever he proved himself to be.

As if to underline this hardened attitude, jobs advertised in the daily newspapers and labor exchanges frequently carried the qualification "no colored," which in time was abbreviated to "N.C." When it is remembered that labor exchanges are government offices, the implication is inescapable that the British government either deliberately subscribed to such discriminatory practices or preferred to ignore them.

The plight of the West Indian was unenviable. None of the islands had yet attained independence, so, according to law, West Indians were British and entitled to equal treatment with other Britons. In fact, they enjoyed fewer rights than aliens. Although full members of the union associated with their jobs, they were forced to accept a ruling that, in the event of recession, they would be the first to feel its effects irrespective of length of service, status, or proficiency. The cost of accommodation, either through rental or purchase, was higher for them than for any member of the host community; loans and mortgages were more difficult to acquire.

Against all these and other pressures, the West Indians offered no collective protest. They had no common voice and developed no representative leadership. The old inter-island suspicions and distrusts continued. Furthermore, there was very little contact between these immigrant workers and either the professional elite or the students. The students, on the one hand, were too preoccupied with their own problems to be concerned with the plight of the illiterate masses, and the sophisticated professionals, on the other, kept a discreet distance. They desired no contact that might adversely affect their own tenuous positions.

Although racial prejudice operated actively against West Indians in nearly every social and economic situation during this period of West Indian immigration into Britain, it was generally cloaked in self-conscious evasions and excuses, expressed in vague, inconsistent terms, and even denied when challenged. No one would openly admit to racial bias; the complainant would himself be accused of hypersensitivity or, at best, of failure to understand clearly an easily explainable situation. The colored person was obviously not wanted as tenant, guest, or client in boarding houses, hotels, and restaurants. This was never unequivocally stated, but an interesting range of devices was employed to keep him out. Although he would not be denied entrance to a restaurant, no attempt would be made to serve him, or, alternatively, the service would be so crude and clumsy that he would eventually leave. Hotels were invariably full, much to the receptionist's sincere regret, and the advertised vacancy in the boarding house would just have been taken or reserved.

In spite of this state of affairs, the sudden and dramatic interracial explosions at Nottingham and the Notting Hill district of London during the autumn of 1958 seemed to take many Britons by surprise. With the notable exception of the government of the day, every articulate section of the community joined in protest and condemnation of the events and the Fascist organizations they claimed were responsible for provoking them. No one was willing to believe that Nottingham and Notting Hill were merely the first eruptions indicative of a deep, extensive social malaise, of which racial prejudice and discrimination had become dangerously significant aspects. The slogan "Keep Britain White" daubed crudely on walls and hoardings became a familiar sight.

Perhaps as a reaction to the Notting Hill-Nottingham outbreaks, there followed a period of easement—as if there were an unspoken but widespread conspiracy of protest against the un-Christian, un-British harassment of colored persons.

This period was short-lived. Before long, other less violent demonstrations against colored persons were reported in many parts of the country. Protests against unrestricted immigration increased in pressure and volume, involving every level of social and political interest. Even the church took a hand. Priests in some of the areas most affected preached sermons on the moral and spiritual degradation which, they claimed, overtook their flocks in the wake of the large influx of black sheep; schoolmasters complained of the problems created in schools by the presence of immigrant children; politicians either echoed the popular demands or were careful to say as little as possible against them.

Finally, in 1961, the Conservative Party Conference debated the question in such clear, uncompromising terms that the government, with some show of reluctance, introduced the Commonwealth Immigrants Bill, avowedly to control the entry of all Commonwealth immigrants, except the Irish who at that time represented the largest part of the immigrant labor force.

In response to urgent appeals from the leaderless immigrants, the Prime Ministers of Jamaica and Trinidad flew to London to make representations to the government on behalf of the immigrants against the Bill. This was not merely a matter of speaking up for their nationals; it was also in defense of what, for them, was a vital economic reality. On the one hand, the heavy exodus from the West Indies meant a welcome easing of the chronic overcrowding in the islands; on the other hand, the flow of contributions from the immigrants back to relatives and friends represented a source of urgently needed sterling. These appeals were of little consequence, however, in the face of overwhelming popular demand for some form of control.

The passing of the Bill heralded a change of mood and a progressive drop in the level of tolerance. Pretense has all but disappeared, and illiberal attitudes are publicly expressed with pride and an air of respectability. It may even be said that prejudice has become commercially profitable, especially in political terms. This was unmistakably demonstrated during the 1964 General Election and since in several by-elections. Certain politically ambitious persons, quick to recognize the popular preoccupation, unashamedly based their campaigns on the explosive issues of color and immigration, exploiting them to great political advantage and success.

223

The words *color* and *immigrant* became the most emotionally loaded words in Britain, especially when used in deliberately suggestive association with the vexed questions of rising unemployment, housing shortages, overcrowded schools, disease, prostitution, drug addiction, and a host of other social ills. The West Indian became the bogeyman. If he was not openly blamed for all these ills, oblique references achieved the same purpose.

During the 1964 General Election, the Conservative candidate for Smethwick, Peter Griffiths, distributed literature in which the following paragraph appeared:

I shall press for the strictest possible control of immigration. We British must decide who shall or shall not enter our country. So vital a matter cannot be left to other Governments. Overcrowding and dirty conditions must be ended. There must be no entry permits for criminals, the unhealthy or those unwilling to work. Our streets must once again be safe at night.

If *color* and *immigration* became the most emotionally loaded words in Britain, and color the most dominant single emotional factor, both the major parties must be held equally responsible. The Labour Party made a great show of opposing the Bill. They said there was no social or economic justification for the control of immigration, and argued that its passage would give the green light to every racist interest and element in the country. Such statements, however, were in sharp contrast to the conduct and attitude of the vast majority of Labour Party supporters. Although the Labour Party is supposedly committed to the ideal of the brotherhood of the working man, racial tension is strongest between the British "working man" and his colored counterpart. Many immigrants, especially West Indians, have long been associated, either directly or indirectly, with Socialist influence through trade-union membership in their home countries. They believed that the same interest shown by the British Socialist movement in devising means to lessen the inequalities and improve the condition of workers in countries outside Britain was shared by all British Socialists, and that it would be reflected in the conduct of all other working men. In this they were wrong, and their disappointment took the form of complete refusal to seek membership in any political party. They could trust neither the Conservatives, whose policies were often openly racist and anti-immigrant, nor the Socialists, whose claims to brotherhood and unity were not borne out nor supported where they mattered most, at the grass-roots working level.

This dilemma was pointedly illustrated by the Socialist Ben Tillett in a speech at Tower Hill, London, when, in reply to a question from a West Indian heckler, he said, "Yes, you are our brothers, and we will do our duty by you. But we wish you had not come to this country."

The colored immigrant's withdrawal from political activity has inspired a spate of criticism of what is called his lack of political interest. The immigrant, especially the West Indian immigrant, is in fact a highly political person, as is testified by the wide and sometimes violent interest that characterizes every type of election in his native islands. There he is personally involved with both those seeking election and the issues. This interest and involvement is in no way dependent on his literacy, social status, or economic position. He might not be able to read or write, but he can listen to, hear, and understand the various presentations of the pertinent issues; he makes his "mark" with satisfaction and pride.

In Britain he is discouraged from experiencing any identity or involvement because, very often, he himself is the issue. The casting of his vote is unlikely to relieve his predicament. In many cases he registers on the electoral roll, then refuses to exercise his registration in mute protest against the prevailing situation. Especially in constituencies with an appreciable immigrant population, campaigning politicians of all parties are fully aware of these dormant votes and would welcome some reliably safe means of harnessing them. No politician, however, has shown any wish to risk his political life for such doubtful stakes. The Conservative image that emerged from the 1964 General Election too clearly bears the marking of racial bias, while the sharp lessons of Smethwick and the Leyton by-election are enough to discourage any Socialist candidate from any obviously pro-immigrant activity.

It has even been suggested that a colored candidate in a "safe" constituency would fulfill the dual purpose of harnessing these idle votes and providing urgently needed immigrant representation. This suggestion has been resisted most by the immigrants themselves. Because they are viewed in Britain as second-class persons, they believe that any political representative emerging from their ranks is unlikely to be viewed or treated differently at any level of representation. They argue that, irrespective of the party to which a member of Parliament belongs, he has and should recognize the responsibility for representing his whole constituency. It should follow that the same candidate who mounted his campaign on the issues of color and immigration, must, upon election, accept the responsibility for listening to and representing the views and interests of those immigrants who reside in his constituency. Failure in this would be a gross neglect of duty.

Against all present trends to the contrary, the West Indian immigrants believe that before long the balance of voting power that their presence in certain key constituencies represents will force politicians into the open. Immigrant support will unhesitatingly be given not to the candidate who sponsors any immigrant cause, but to the one who recognizes the immigrant's rights and responsibilities as a contributing citizen and who is determined to promote and secure the best possible conditions for all, without reference to color or race.

Many West Indians show a remarkably clear and unbiased appreciation of their position and the political factors that surround it. They are sufficiently political to appreciate that, in the field of politics, any circumstance which might within reason be exploited for political gain is fair game, especially at election time. They know that their contribution to Britain's postwar recovery has been positive and significant, though this is never admitted and rarely mentioned. They are convinced that Britain, along with the United States, must come to terms with a multiracial society. In spite of all their harassment, the West Indians believe they must be patient. This, in my view, is an example of that very conditioned Britishness referred to earlier.

If, at the moment, the colored immigrant takes little active part in politics, this is more than compensated for in other areas of interest. The oft-repeated claim that the immigrant represented serious competition for available employment is gradually being borne out. The first heavy waves of entrants were unskilled laborers who filled the ranks of unskilled "hewers of wood and drawers of water." But as is generally the case with immigrant groups wherever they appear, they set great store by the available opportunities for education and training, if not for themselves, then for their children. Despite the overcrowded conditions in which they lived and the antipathetic atmosphere surrounding them, the men sent for their wives and families. Many of the children who came over were either under school age or young enough to benefit from their introduction to the earliest levels of English education. Soon they were moving up through the grammar and technical schools to the colleges and universities.

Their progress was not easy. Apart from some problems of language and previous educational background, they were resented for being different in color and in social habits. Parents resented the presence of these newcomers in the same classes as their own children. Even teachers complained that colored children lowered a school's educational and social standards because they were mentally slower and less capable than the whites.

Some educational authorities attempted to assuage popular feeling by recommending separate schools. This received little general support, perhaps because even the most zealous bigot could appreciate the unfortunate social result that would accrue from any project so strongly reeking of segregation. Prejudice and discrimination could somehow be rationalized; segregation was an absolutely different thing.

Many colored children who successfully moved upward through the educational system to collegiate and university qualifications were then faced with the problem of employment outlets. Proscriptions operated against them in many fields, including police and Customs work, banking, and retailing in the major department stores, to name but a few. Following the normal processes of population increase, more and more colored children will be entering British schools. Fewer and fewer of them will have any handicaps of language or association with other educational standards or methods. Born in Britain, they will have been entirely familiar with every aspect and nuance of English education from their earliest years. They will be, therefore, even more likely to challenge the higher levels of professional employment. They are free to a large degree from much of the pressure that springs from divided loyalties. Even though they have been reared under the full influence of conflicting social and cultural attitudes, they are fully invested with the questing, thrusting restlessness and ambitiousness of youth. They are determinedly resentful of any circumstance that would impose "immigrant" status on them. They consider themselves British not by adoption, but by birth and heritage. There are many indications that they will not humbly submit to any harassment or restrictions that their color might incite or attract.

The widest complaint and criticism of the immigrants center on their accommodation, which is often described as overcrowded, dirty, and unsanitary. Viewed from outside, it would appear that these descriptions are fully justified. Most groupings of immigrants are located in and around old, disreputable property, usually large Victorian semidetached houses which have passed their best days. Once intended for gracious occupancy by one or two families, they have been divided and subdivided to exploit every foot of habitable space, often at the expense of basic sanitary requirements, and are rented at exorbitant prices to immigrant individuals or families.

During my employment in England, first as schoolmaster and later as welfare officer, I visited many of these houses. From the outside they invariably presented a most disreputable appearance because the landlords were disinclined to incur any avoidable expense, and the occupants themselves were concerned only with the rooms they occupied. Often these houses were in sections already earmarked for demolition and clearance, so the landlords considered that any monies spent on amenities or presentation were monies wasted. Within the rooms themselves, however, an amazingly high standard of order and cleanliness usually existed, considerably at variance with the shabby, filthy exteriors.

Peasant people who have been accustomed to owning little or nothing often develop a compulsive need to possess if they find themselves in circumstances where ownership is possible. The same is true of the colored immigrant. Many of them enter Britain with the fixed idea of earning, saving from their earnings, and then returning home to buy a plot of ground, a house, a shop, or some other thing that would give them the pride and satisfaction of ownership.

All the immigrants in Britain are not peasants, however. Some West Indians were from middle-class backgrounds—civil servants, engineers, clerks, teachers, policemen, and others. All were attracted by the prospect of better earnings in Britain and were willing even to change to more manual labor for the higher wages offered. For them the tiny rooms in overcrowded houses were to be borne as staging posts on the way to better things. They lived quietly and frugally against the day when they could purchase their own house, preferably with a small garden, and once again revert to the middle-class pattern of life they had known. Perhaps part of their plan would materialize.

In most parts of Britain, it is difficult for a colored person, irrespective of his social status, employment, profession, or financial position, to find accommodation outside those sections that are already abandoned to immigrant invasion. In some neighborhoods, restrictive covenants against colored persons are rigidly enforced; in others, there is tacit agreement that no house owner will sell to a colored person. As soon as a colored purchaser appears, the asking price is immediately forced upward to the point of discouragement. The same situation obtains if a colored person seeks to make the purchase through real-estate agents, many of whom share the prevailing prejudices against persons of color and either steer them away from the more desirable areas or inveigle them into paying excessively for the privilege of moving out of the ghettos

In order to circumvent the covenants and restrictions, house purchases are sometimes arranged through an interested and friendly third party—the colored person neither appearing nor being mentioned until after the transfer of title is signed and the monies are paid. The reaction of the neighbors to this device has sometimes been to offer to buy him out; that failing, they isolate him and his family by a wall of silent disapproval. This kind of racial exclusion is not only practiced by private individuals. It occurs in large housing developments. There are instances of similar discriminatory practices by local councils against colored persons wishing to buy houses in some of the new satellite towns.

House purchase is probably the only means by which the colored person can hope to escape the misery of ghetto life. Most housing authorities, both Socialist and Conservative, consider it their first duty to satisfy the urgent needs of indigenous Britons in preference to immigrants. The housing programs are all so far behind current needs that they are unlikely ever to catch up. In a few instances, West Indians have formed themselves into housing societies in order to acquire some large houses not scheduled for clearance. They redevelop them into self-contained flats and flatlets according to approved council standards and then rent them to their members on terms designed to ensure a high standard of maintenance and accommodation.

I was involved in the initial planning and creation of one of these housing societies. I well remember how difficult it was for these persons from different West Indian islands to overcome their prejudices and distrust of one another to the point of agreeing to work together, especially since their hard-earned money was involved. Although they all wanted to be free of the expensive, sparsely furnished, and uncomfortable accommodation they rented, they were very reluctant to take any action themselves to improve their own circumstances. After nearly two years of patient persuasion and introduction to every phase of the organization of their society, they were able to take it entirely into their own hands. It was exciting to observe that, though none of them had had more than an elementary education, they were eventually able to accept the responsibility of office, meet and discuss the financial aspects with a local bank, learn about the issue and sale of bonds and about the mechanics of official registration and recognition of their society. There was one surprising development. Although all the founder-members were West Indian, they insisted that membership should be open to anyone and that this be reflected in the name chosen for the society and in the constitution governing it.

This development was completely unexpected. It seems to indicate that, in spite of his experience of prejudice and discrimination within the British community, the West Indian has not yet assumed a hardened, embittered attitude. Exposure to the British in their own bailiwick has, perhaps, not yet destroyed his conditioned Britishness and willingness to be friendly. This disinclination to bitterness and violence except under dire provocation is only a phase in his adjustment to the vicissitudes of life in an unfamiliar, hostile environment, and will eventually give way to another, less tolerant attitude.

It is worth mentioning that no white person has, to date, sought membership in this housing society. The members believe that there is substantial local resentment of the society by white persons who are themselves inadequately housed, but are either too unprovident or too secure in their dependence on state housing to initiate similar action. When I inquired whether any attempts had been made to act on the society's constitution, the members replied, "It's not for us to ask them."

There exists no exact geographical frontier between the West Indian and the host community; each maintains a large degree of social isolation. There is an almost total absence of dialogue between them. Most Britons dislike foreigners; the dislike is greater in the case of black and, therefore, inferior foreigners. That the black foreigners are British or, later, Commonwealth subjects in no way modifies the dislike. Added to it is the resentment that the black foreigners are allowed into the country "to crowd us out of our homes, to take our jobs and our women, monopolise our social and welfare services," and the jealousy at the West Indian ownership of houses, cars, and other creature comforts.

That this dialogue is absent is all the more striking because all the prerequisites for it are present—propinquity, a common language, and wide similarity of customs. Attempts to bridge the gap have either failed completely or been only moderately successful. Interracial clubs were formed, but usually either the West Indians or the British stayed away. When they did come together, the clubs gradually developed an entirely West Indian flavor, probably in testimony to the more vital or dominant element. Investigation has disclosed that in nearly every case these clubs were the brain-children of dedicated white persons anxious to improve the racial situation; they founded the clubs at their own expense, then invited the colored to join them. They either ignored or were totally unaware that people under pressure are prone to be wary of the good intentions of others and to suspect some hidden purpose or motive. Furthermore, the West Indians were never consulted on the projected structure, locale, or activities of the clubs, and, therefore, had no feeling of really belonging.

The churches also failed to establish any positive interrelationship. In the West Indies, the church generally plays an intimate and active part in people's lives, providing spiritual and moral counsel and sustenance for the adults and education and guidance for the children. Most of the schools of the West Indies owe their beginnings to the activities of a missionary group or religious order that laid the solid educational foundations on which the later governmental programs have been established. In many island communities, the church was the center of all social and cultural activity. The influence of the priest spanned and sometimes dominated the period from birth to death. Perhaps because most of the priests, nuns, and missionaries were British, the immigrants naïvely expected to experience in Britain the same sincere, close contact with the religious shepherd and the same friendliness and brotherhood among the flock. For many of them, it was a severe shock to be treated with cool indifference on first exposure to the church in England. They often suffered the humiliation of being scorned in church itself. As one disillusioned dock worker said to me, "They exported all the Christianity to us in the West Indies. All they've got left is Christendom."

There is no dialogue where they work. Apart from a few friendships, the groups work together without mixing. They go their separate ways for meals and at the end of the work period. The West Indian must always be wary, avoiding any great show of enthusiasm or ability that would attract unwelcome attention. Sometimes his ability or latent potential for leadership and responsibility is noted by those in positions of higher authority, but there is always the danger that any attempt to reward him with promotion would be met by resistance and even strike action. While white workers might recognize or even admit that their colored colleagues are no less intelligent and able than themselves, they still consider them inferior. Except in a few rare instances, they refuse to accept them as foremen or supervisors, or in any position that suggests or presumes authority.

There is no dialogue in the trade unions. Though members, the West Indians know that they enjoy no equality of representation and have no voice in union affairs. Their presence at union meetings is not encouraged, and few of them appear. A regular feature of the Annual Trades Union Conferences is the total absence of colored delegates although the West Indian labor force alone is nearly a quarter of a million persons.

This unhappy state of affairs is true today, but there are rumblings which suggest that changes are on the way. These changes will be initiated by the West Indians themselves. The majority of them migrated to Britain from countries still under colonial rule, but which have now become independent. Even more important is the increasing preponderance of colored faces—some of them belonging to men who have themselves experienced the tensions and pressures of life at a lowly level in Britain—at each annual Conference of Commonwealth Prime Ministers. These leaders seem set to redress the balance of power in the determination of Commonwealth issues. This determination has been conveyed to the colored immigrant and has given him a new and different image of himself.

Hitherto he has been prepared to accept the lowly jobs and to retreat quietly at the end of each day into the fastness of his enforced ghetto. Avoiding any direct confrontation with the hostile community, he has suffered the jibes, epithets, and accusations with remarkable forbearance. Except for the notable occasions of Nottingham and Notting Hill, any counteraction was usually initiated by others on his behalf. Even in those cases, his unified resistance and aggressiveness quickly evaporated as soon as calm was restored. Some hint of the new mood may be drawn from the

West Indians' reaction to the recent appearance of Ku Klux Klan crosses and threats; they quickly served notice in clear terms of their intention to retaliate and promptly. One severe drawback has been the absence of leadership, but this may soon be rectified, especially from the ranks of the young men and women either born into the situation or introduced into it at a very early age.

At present the air is troubled and thundery with bias and tension. Every change in the delicate balance of the political structure promises a worsening of the situation. The government, fully aware of this and probably deeply conscious of its own contribution to and responsibility for the situation, is at the moment seeking to introduce legislation against racial discrimination and incitement. But such legislation is not enough. Example is always better than precept. There are many areas within the government's direct sphere of influence that could be used effectively to support the precepts of legislation. Applicants to the police force, the senior Civil Service, the Bank of England, and the Customs are still confined to those who are "British by birth," a qualification that is exercised to exclude colored persons who are "British by birth."

While attending a conference at the University of Aarhus in Denmark, I met and got into conversation with a colored youngster who spoke excellent English, but with such an intriguing accent that I was foolish enough to ask if he were West Indian. With a look of what may have been pity or scorn or a mixture of both, he replied: "I am a Dane."

Perhaps the day will come when some of the dark-skinned youth of Britain will be able to say, with equal pride, "I am a Briton."

KENNETH LITTLE

Some Aspects of Color, Class, and Culture in Britain

THERE ARE no accurate means of gauging the size of the colored[1] population in Britain, but it is probably in the neighborhood of one million. According to one estimate, based on the 1961 Census, colored people of Commonwealth origin numbered approximately 820,000 at the beginning of 1965. They included 430,000 West Indians, 165,000 Indians, 100,000 Pakistanis, and 125,000 from West and East Africa as well as other countries in the "new" Commonwealth. The great majority of these people live in London and in the towns and cities of the Midlands, the northwest, and the northeast of England. Their situation is the result of a complicated set of factors deriving in large part from the nature of the British social structure.

Most of the immigrants concerned have arrived in Britain since the early 1950's. There have been from the time of World War I small groups of Africans, West Indians, Somalis, and Arabs who married or consorted with native women, but these mixed communities were confined almost entirely to the dockland areas of Liverpool, London, Cardiff, Manchester, North and South Shields, and Hull. They were isolated from the main stream of national life and their affairs attracted only local attention. Nor did the presence of university students from the then colonial countries arouse public interest. Moreover, in the years immediately after World War II, very many more continental European workers than British colonials came into England. Between 1955 and the middle of 1962, however, nearly half a million colored immigrants arrived. This sudden increase from an annual trickle of a few thousand to more than 40,000 in both 1955 and 1956 made "race relations" a matter of political importance. Previously, the Colonial Office and the British Council (an unofficial agency) had dealt with whatever problems arose, including the welfare of overseas students. Up to that time, except in some seaport cities, in certain cosmopolitan parts of London, and in the university towns, only a small proportion of the British population had any experience of colored people as fellow workers, friends, or neighbors.

This absence of personal contact makes it difficult to assess the psychological background, especially as knowledge of and interest in the colonies were extremely small. In a social survey conducted in 1948, for example, a quarter of the informants thought that the colonial countries were mostly inhabited by white people. Hardly any were able to suggest the name of a colony that had recently maoe advances toward self-government. Investigation also showed that a number of stereotypes of colored peoples, both favorable and unfavorable, were held. This evidence led Professor A. H. Richmond to suggest that the English population fell into three broad groups of roughly equal size: One third was tolerant of colored people, one third was mildly prejudiced, and one third extremely prejudiced. This conclusion was challenged by another observer who considered that the proportion of the population that could be regarded as severely prejudiced was much less than one third. Only about half of the informants in both investigations, however, had actually "come across" a colored person. A better guide is perhaps provided by the reactions of a sample of land-ladies in London ordinarily in the habit of letting rooms to students from abroad. In response to a routine inquiry, 82 per cent of these people said that they would be willing to accept students from the "white" Dominions and the United States, and 70 per cent were willing to take "continental Europeans." Only 26 per cent would take "lightly colored non-Europeans," and only 10 per cent would accept Negroes. This investigation also showed that in order to obtain accommodations a colored person might have to pay more than would be asked of a white student.

These sociological data as well as wider evidence make it plain that prejudice and discrimination on grounds of race existed on quite a wide scale long before the colored immigrants arrived in large numbers. This point is very important, but it is necessary to take cultural factors into account as well. In the first place, although some of the immigrants possess an academic education and industrial skills, most of them are drawn from a rural or semirural proletariat.

This, in the case of the West Indians, involves a background of slavery, poverty, and frustration that has left a distinctive mark on their working habits, family organization, religious practice, and attitudes to authority. West Indians share the same language, religion, and citizenship as the British host society and lack any distinct and separate culture of their own. In some respects, however, this common heritage is more apparent than real because there are some important divergencies and incompatibilities between contemporary British and West Indian social and cultural patterns.

Family life, for example, is frequently unorthodox by British standards. In many cases, an immigrant with a wife and family in the West Indies takes a woman to live with him in England. If she "makes a baby" for him, he may contribute spasmodically toward its keep. Other men move about in search of work, setting up unstable unions in quick succession. The unstable unit usually consists of a man and woman living together for a period of weeks or months. There may be one baby who is not necessarily the child of the present male partner, but the latter usually treats him as his own, at least while the pair are cohabiting. In the West Indies, such unions might have been based on ties of neighborhood, friendship, or common interests. In England, they are often the result of fortuitous encounters on the migrant ship, at railway stations, and during the woman's subsequent search for work and, above all, for cheap lodgings.

There are also instances of what in the West Indies would be termed "faithful concubinage." This differs from the unstable union mainly in duration, but is sometimes legalized later on by marriage. In addition, an egalitarian type of family based on formal marriage is found, particularly among the younger and more ambitious working-class immigrants. In the egalitarian unit, both partners contribute financially and share responsibility and authority for the children. In such a family, children may be sent to the family of one of the partners in the West Indies.

Very many of the Pakistanis and Indians have come straight from peasant villages, and quite often their domestic arrangements are similar to those at home. A Pakistani woman, for instance, is expected to observe the *purdah*. Since she rarely goes out alone or with women neighbors, her husband does all the shopping as he sees fit, and household goods are delivered to the door. In the home, the husband never enters the kitchen for it is taboo to him. He, the wife, and the children eat their meals separately. She has complete control domestically, but the husband must approve any decision affecting a member of the family. His own friends are all outside the house, and there is little companionship between man and wife. He keeps his interests and activities to himself and does not tell her of his movements. Formality is also observed in day-to-day activities within Indian households. The women wash, cook, and clean in places reserved for them, or at separate fixed times.

Sometimes the women must adopt English clothes; this is usually done in order to get a job. Even then, however, they retain their traditional dress on all social occasions and within the community. The Sikh women, for example, wear the *salwar-kamiz* (baggy trousers topped by a loose shift and stole), and some wear the *sari*. They use Indian cosmetics and scents and have a conception of personal adornment quite different from that of the host society and, indeed, from that of fashionable Indian women. So much importance is attached to the wearing of Indian clothes that many women do not take a job if they are required to accept Western dress.

Quite often, neither the men nor the women have much knowledge of English when they arrive. The men generally learn as much as is required to earn their living, but the women have generally not felt the need. They live among Indians, constantly speak their own language, and even do most of their shopping at Indian-run grocery shops. At supermarkets a few words are usually enough, and when necessary they can rely on their children for help.

The Asian migrants, in general, are also distinguished very clearly from the host society through religion. The Sikhs have established a number of temples, and the Moslem communities use both mosques and private houses for their devotions. One of the latter groups consists of Arabs from Yemen who live together in houses inhabited by men from the same village or clan. Each group is organized for its domestic needs, and its members cook and dine together. The organization of such a house centers on the *masgid*, a room set aside for prayers and equipped with copies of the Holy Qur'an, books on catechism, hymnbooks, rosaries, and joss sticks. During the weekends, public holidays, and the annual summer holidays, the *masgid* also serves as a center of social and recreational activities. All such houses are also fitted with washing facilities specially designed for ritual ablutions.

Cultural differences, therefore, are not superficial, especially as the attitude toward the host society varies. The West Indians, for instance, regard themselves as Westerners. Their aspirations are set in the direction of Western civilization. They have, in this respect, what one observer has called a "white bias."

The white bias includes a cultural bias towards a nineteenth century colonial version of British culture. This has been strengthened by a long period of English-oriented education, during which generation children learned about the rivers of England and King Alfred and the cakes, or wrote essays on how to build a snowman at Christmas and the production of beet sugar. They also learned from liberal minded and nostalgic English teachers and ministers that they were members of a proud Empire or Commonwealth of which Britain was the centre and "mother country."[2]

Consequently, most West Indians would like to enter more into British society. They are disappointed when they are shunned, and they are confused because West Indian values and patterns differ from the British. In the sphere of religion, for example, the orthodox Christian church acts as a binding force in West Indian society by bringing together in a single congregation members of various social classes. West Indian worshipers get a feeling of warmth and community with fellow worshipers that stretches over color divisions. This feeling is sometimes rudely shaken among migrants in Britain. They expect to find the same sort of fellowship in the country in which their church originated.

The background of race relations and racial consciousness is also vastly but subtly different. In the West Indies, the lighter-skinned person quite often considers himself to be on a higher social plane than a person of darker color. His lighter skin marks him out in general terms as a member of a wealthier and more socially favored group. He is color-conscious, therefore, as well as race-conscious, and acutely so, for two reasons. Prejudice and discrimination mark him out not only as a member of an inferior race, but also in certain circumstances as a member of an inferior social class. The West Indian resents obvious manifestations of prejudice in the belief that both his social status and his race are being impugned. These rather subtle distinctions between light and dark and their implications are neither known nor appreciated in England.

The position of the Asians, on the other hand, is quite different. They come from well-established civilizations in which they are deeply rooted by religion, and most of them belong to homogeneous communities at home with which they are constantly in touch. Indeed, quite often most of the Indian families settled in a given English city can be traced to one district of the Punjab, or even to a dozen or so neighboring towns and villages there. Thus, a newly arrived family comes into a ready-made Indian community, sets up a household that is a faithful imitation of the one it had at home, and usually prefers to be surrounded by its own kinsfolk or village kin. In this way, a microcosm of the life of the Indian village is transplanted to England.

The stabilization of life appears to have gone further among the Indians than among the Pakistanis. Nevertheless, although a larger proportion of the Pakistani immigrants are bachelors or men who have traveled without their wives, the social and cultural patterns are basically similar. The most common social grouping is the all-male lodging house, which frequently consists of kinsmen with a resident landlord from the same village. The main social activities are centered on informal gatherings of acquaintances in friends' houses, smoking the *hookah,* exchanging news and problems, listening to tape-recorded love songs, and week-end visits to Pakistani film shows and to the Mosque. Indians also have their own cultural institutions, including the showing of Indian films, that bring Indians together as a group and serve to remind them of their common ties and of the moral values of Indian society.

There are signs that a proportion of the Indians is disposed to settle and that the younger generation attending school is assimilating English habits and customs. On the whole, however, Asians tend to hold themselves aloof from British culture. They meet and interact with British people as fellow workers, employers, and customers, and they try, by avoiding all areas of racial conflict, to live harmoniously with their British neighbors. They want to be given the same economic opportunity as any other citizen; they do not seek to be socially accepted. They are in England primarily to work and to live their own lives.

The cultural position of West Indians, Pakistanis, and Indians has been stressed because from the local people's point of view these immigrants are not "British." Not only their racial appearance but their different styles of life, dress, and behavior mark them as foreigners. For many British people, "foreigner" denotes a category of person who has no place in one's own society. Although he is not to be treated with hostility, it is considered best to regard him with suspicion and to keep out of his way. This aversion to

239

and avoidance of outsiders does not operate only in relation to colored immigrants. In recent years, xenophobia has included opposition to Polish, Italian, and other Europeans brought into the United Kingdom to work under government schemes. The objections voiced were generally economic, and it was with the greatest reluctance that the trade unions eventually accepted these workers. Unions, too, often insisted that in the case of unemployment foreigners should be dismissed first. Although hostility is displayed toward the colored immigrant, almost identical complaints have been made at various times about the Jews and even about the Welsh, the Scots, and the Irish. In each case there has been an unfavorable stereotype of the "intruders"; the only difference is that the colored individual, as Professor Michael Banton has pointed out, apparently represents the furthest removed type of stranger. The darker the color, the more likely the exclusion. Support for this suggestion is given by the study of landladies' attitudes cited earlier.

An alternative, though not unrelated suggestion, is that "color" has negative value in the British social class system. When investigating the attitudes of women undergraduates in one of the Oxbridge colleges, Sheila Webster used a social distance test. She found that the girls roughly divided the world into two main categories: P.L.U. (People like us) and the others, those unlike us, outside our social sphere, those who are N.O.C.D. (Not our class, dear). Color or, rather, color plus the physical features that often accompany it (prognathism, a flat wide nose, thick lips, and kinky hair in the case of the Negro) appeared to be the cue for a high degree of social distance. It was the supreme symbol of "unlikeness." Even more significantly, the stereotypes relating to "lower-class people" and to Jews, Indians, and Negroes were almost the same. Stereotypes common to all four groups included dirty, lustful, sensitive, lazy, superstitious, immoral, unreliable, and "very clever if allowed to get ahead."

The social unacceptability and inferiority of "color" is undoubtedly strengthened because immigrants usually live in the more dilapidated parts of town. To a considerable extent they occupy accommodations in areas that the more respectable elements of the white working class are leaving or have already left. Immigrants live in such areas, in part, because owners of property in better residential districts sometimes refuse to rent or sell to a colored individual even when he is obviously in a position to afford it.

Tenants may be offered a lease that expressly prohibits their sub-letting to a colored person. As in the United States, the explanation offered is that a colored family in residence would lower the economic value of the other houses in the area.

Nevertheless, only a small proportion of those who arrive as labor migrants are both able and willing to pay for expensive accommodations. Many Pakistanis, for example, are disposed to save as much of their earnings as possible. They do not regard where they live as a permanent home and, consequently, are prepared to put up with unsalubrious and overcrowded conditions provided they are cheap. Since each newly arrived Pakistani or Indian tends to gravitate toward his countrymen, the number of colored people on particular streets naturally increases.

Moreover, there is a general shortage of houses in Britain, and immigrants are unlikely to qualify for newer buildings provided by the local authority. The latter, usually allocated on a points system, are awarded for deficiencies in accommodations currently occupied, size and state of family, and, above all, length of time on the waiting list. The five- or ten-year period that is often insisted upon effectively prevents the immigrant from obtaining a council house or flat. In the meantime, he may be allocated a "patched house," a slum awaiting demolition, or he may find rooms in a lodging house where the landlord will ask no questions and show no prejudice if his tenant pays the rent.

In some cases, immigrants find their own temporary solution to the problem of living space by buying up large dilapidated, short-lease properties that no longer have any investment value for British buyers. As a result a newcomer no longer faces the ordeal of a door-to-door search for accommodations or the possible snubs of white landladies. He can be fairly sure of finding some sort of living space with relatives or fellow migrants from the day of his arrival. In other cases, the entrepreneur is white. In either event, the proprietor, having borrowed money, needs to use his property intensively in order to earn rent. He, therefore, divides it into separate apartments or flats and rents to a number of families at the same time. Multioccupation has certain consequences because the tenants—whether they are immigrants or not—feel no responsibility for the passages or for the house as a whole. The landlord does not care because he has only a short lease and may even base his whole enterprise on the assumption of the house's total loss. Fifteen inhabitants generate more garbage than five, although the

Salvage Department does not increase the scale of its services. Nor does the landlord concern himself with how the rooms are used.

These conditions are characteristic of sections of Birmingham, which has the second largest colored population in the country. English and Irish as well as immigrants inhabit the area in question. Nevertheless, for the most part, it is the latter who live there. Sharing this part of the town with the flotsam and jetsam of the host society, they do not belong to Birmingham as a whole, but, as Professor John Rex has put it, to the marginal world of its twilight zone.

The variety of factors and circumstances makes it difficult to generalize about relationships between the immigrants and the native population. In the 1958 disturbances, colored groups in the Notting Hill district of London and in Nottingham were physically attacked. Displays of racial antagonisms in London and elsewhere have ranged from the daubing of fiery crosses and racist slogans on walls to the throwing of petrol bombs and the firing of guns at colored individuals. In many of the smaller towns and local communities, on the other hand, the newcomers seem to have reached a reasonable stage of accommodation at work and in housing. On the whole, they are accepted as fellow residents, and in churches, schools, places of recreation, and public houses. Still, most local people avoid closer informal social contacts, and most immigrants do not participate actively in local political, civic, or trade-union activities.

The development of such a situation has been described in detail in Sheila Patterson's study of Brixton. After 1948, this part of London became an unofficial reception center for many of the Caribbean migrants who were arriving. By 1958, West Indians owned several hundred houses in the area and were letting furnished rooms to their compatriots, most of whom were law-abiding people. Most South London employers seem to have had misgivings about hiring colored workers on the grounds of strangeness, unpredictability, and possibly low working ability, but a sizable number of industries that require a large semiskilled or unskilled labor force agreed to try them out. Quite soon, however, most of these avenues had been explored. Although a few employers who had tried West Indian workers were well satisfied, the majority were unenthusiastic. It was said that the colored men required more supervision than other workers; that they were prone to make exaggerated claims about their skills and to expect far higher wages than they were worth; and that many were touchy and had a chip on their shoulder about color. Nor did the reiteration by so many West Indians of their intentions to return home after a year or so help their case. It gave employers a valid reason for regarding them as temporary workers whose interests should be considered after those of settled local workers ("our own people," in the common phrase). Local workers complained that the colored men made poor comrades. A high trade-union official told Sheila Patterson:

The West Indian is a worse outsider than most. Often he doesn't smoke—he doesn't stand his round of drinks in the pub after work—he may work too hard and he doesn't know or bother to learn the factory gossip or protocol of behavior or use accepted forms of swearing.

After some acute experiences of unemployment, however, the West Indians ceased to regard their jobs as expendable. As a result, West Indian turnover fell and their punctuality improved. Many employers who had formerly criticized the West Indians' nonchalant attitude and high mobility came to regard them as more reliable than most other workers in this respect. In addition, West Indians appeared to be talking less about their "get-rich-quick" intentions and their imminent return home. By 1960, in fact, the evidence in Brixton was that many employers were coming to accept West Indians as part of the local labor force.

Bradford, a city of over 295,000 inhabitants and the center of the British woolen industry, is another place where relations, largely characterized by avoidance, have been peaceable in the ten years since the main immigration started. About one fifth of the male labor force in the local mills is immigrant, predominantly Pakistanis. The great majority work in unskilled and semiskilled occupations, but a small group—considered by other Pakistanis to have a higher status—works in public transport and forms about a third of the platform staff (drivers and conductors) employed by the municipal undertaking. Apart from these groups, there are some proprietors of shops and businesses, and a very small number of professional men among the immigrants.

This occupational structure is not atypical of the situation as a whole. By and large the immigrants have found ready employment whenever there has been a call for labor in semiskilled and unskilled capacities; professional and white-collar employment, however, tends to be another matter. In a recent investigation some white and colored grammar-school dropouts were sent to try

243

for jobs advertised in banks, insurance companies, and similar establishments. The white youngsters were usually offered the job or were told it was still vacant after the colored boys had been sent away. Also, recent experiences at youth-employment offices in London showed a tendency to a general pattern whereby white youngsters were almost five times more likely to get skilled jobs than were colored. In one such area half the available jobs listed at a busy youth-employment office were barred to colored youngsters, "N.C." for "No Colored" appearing on the cards of 52 firms out of 147. Whitehall said that "N.C." should not appear on records, but things looked different at the grass roots. Some firms would take exceptional individuals; others, more liberal, were cutting back to stiffer quotas because they were being saturated with colored applicants and were afraid of getting a name as a "colored shop"; still others were staffing whole departments, usually those with the heaviest and dirtiest jobs, with colored workers.

Apart from the recently arrived immigrants who, on the whole, are economically poor and uneducated by British standards, there also exists a small minority of colored individuals whose general position is different. This group, which is fully assimilated to local conditions, includes British-born men and women of mixed parentage. Some of these people are well-known actors and actresses on stage and television, while others have made their mark in the civil service or in business. In addition to more than seventy thousand students from the Commonwealth countries, there are African, West Indian, Pakistani, and Indian members of the professional class, usually practicing medicine. Most of these men are temporarily employed in hospitals under the National Health Service, but a number are permanent residents and have British or European wives.

The latter families generally have plenty of friends and acquaintances, and there is no apparent restraint on the grounds of color in this middle- and upper-middle-class section of society. Contacts are made and friendships established through membership in various left-wing associations opposed to South African *apartheid* or in the course of professional work. In other cases, the white and the colored individuals concerned have met while the former was employed as a civil servant or as a university teacher in the latter's country. In social groups of this kind, use of the term *colored* is eschewed. Non-European people as well as non-European personalities are referred to as far as possible by their nationality. Although the parties concerned probably share a number of personal and intellectual interests, this practice implies a certain self-consciousness where "race" and "color" are concerned.

The social as well as the cultural gap between the well-educated colored person and his less literate, economically poorer compatriots is very wide. A number of West Indian, Indian, and Pakistani professional men sponsor ethnic associations, sit on interracial committees, and perform a political role as spokesmen and intermediaries in connection with the affairs of their particular ethnic group or nationality. But most of the well-educated colored, including the students, have as few personal relationships with working-class people, colored or white, as their counterparts in the white middle and upper-middle classes.

They naturally condemn racial prejudice in all its forms and generally deplore any legislation that appears to restrict immigration on grounds of color. Individual views in this connection are vociferously expressed and receive support from the more politically minded and militant rank and file among the immigrants. In particular, the organization known as CARD (Campaign Against Racial Discrimination) has actively sought, by publicizing cases of alleged discrimination, to bring pressure to bear on the British government. No doubt, the average well-to-do colored person sympathizes with these efforts. There are few signs, however, that he is disposed to join a crusade—except in special circumstances—on behalf of colored people in Britain. His attitude seems to be that pressure is best exerted at the government level by the Commonwealth countries taking action themselves.

Obviously, a great deal more should be said about the latter political aspect, including the British government's own side of the case. One would need to explain in some detail the position of Labour Party spokesmen both before the passing of the Commonwealth Immigration Bill in 1962 and during the financial crisis and other difficulties since Labour's advent to power. Mention should be made in this connection of the recent enactment of laws that include machinery for investigating allegations of discriminatory practices. There is also a Minister for Immigration to whom a National Committee for Commonwealth Immigrants reports. This Committee's task is to promote "integration" in various ways, and its sub-committees provide the government with specialist advice on housing, education, and other matters. It also helps to advise the municipal bodies of the various towns and cities where

245

immigrants reside. Also, in addition to the work of the churches, there are numerous voluntary associations, including interracial councils and committees, that offer guidance and information and organize educational and language classes for adult immigrants.

In short, Commonwealth immigration is now a matter of great concern not only to the municipal bodies directly involved, but to the three major political parties. Although the racial issue was soft-pedaled at the last General Election, in the event of a severe spell of unemployment it is likely to enter party politics to a fairly considerable extent. There may be an increasing attempt to air on public platforms racist dogma that until now has been disavowed by nearly all parliamentary politicians; as yet, the extremist groups whose principal slogan is "keep Britain white" have little influence. But unfortunately the electorate has been encouraged to count heads and to think of colored immigration primarily in terms of numbers. Even in official circles little apparent attention has been paid to the sociological issues that lie beneath the surface of what is oversimplified as a black-white confrontation.

Basically these issues derive from an urbanization process. Immigrant individuals and families have entered a society with standards of life and education materially and technically much in advance of their own. Adaptation is also rendered difficult by the different sets of expectations on both sides and by the conflict between much of the newcomers' behavior and the bourgeois values of the host society. The latter include such things as a settled home life based on legal marriage, a degree of companionship between man and wife, an absence of extramarital relations, a tidy house, punctuality in personal as well as business dealings, and restraint and impersonality in most social relationships outside the sphere of kinship and close friendship. Their lack of conformity to these norms marks the immigrants as foreigners, and their darker complexion and other physical characteristics enhance their unlikeness. Most of the recent immigrants lack education, work in manual and unskilled occupations, and occupy the more dilapidated and less respectable parts of the town—all criteria, in British eyes, of low social status. Color, class, and culture, thus, work together to exclude the immigrant from better working-class and middle-class society.

Nevertheless, a section of the colored population is being assimilated into life in Britain. For practical purposes, they have assumed the cultural appearance of British people by conforming, at least outwardly, to local ideas of acceptable social behavior. They act, speak, and generally conduct their domestic and other affairs in ways that are barely distinguishable from the native community. For these immigrants, racial differences cease to be such an important symbol of unlikeness, and the way is paved for in-group membership. With the psychological effect of color minimized, there is scope, at least within the context of face-to-face relationships, for the attainment of a "normal" social identity based upon ordinary class criteria and personal interests. The colored individual will have the opportunity of making white friends and acquaintances on the basis of such things as the kind of house he lives in, his general manner, his education, the nature of his job, and whether he owns a car.

As far as the future is concerned, a very great deal will depend upon how matters are dealt with administratively, including the question of special social services for the immigrants. Very many of them clearly prefer to have their own institutions, particularly in religion, and their own social clubs and associations. Public amenities are another matter, however, because the immigrants live under basically the same economic and housing conditions as the white population of the same neighborhood. It would seem, therefore, that the best way to facilitate "integration" is to treat the difficulties of the areas concerned as a common problem. Where social centers, welfare organizations, and schemes for housing are needed, they are best provided with a view to envigorating the total life of the community and not merely its colored section.

At the same time, there is also scope for colored leadership because the future course of events depends, in part, upon the immigrants' own intentions and on whether they regard themselves as permanent settlers. Their general desire, undoubtedly, is for social equality, but it is idle to expect a sympathetic reception unless some sections are prepared to accommodate themselves more deliberately to British conditions and notions of what is "right" behavior. This includes dealing more effectively with the small but socially significant criminal elements, especially men who live off the earnings of white prostitutes. If the West Indian immigrants want middle-class people as neighbors, they must adopt middle-class ways themselves.

The government's obligation, on the other hand, is to persuade the public that relations with people of different races and color are a normal part of human experience. Possibly this lesson could be driven home effectively by more stringent legislation that would prohibit discrimination in all public places as well as strengthen the law relating to racial incitement. There have been frequent official hints that the government would be willing to move in this direction, and it is also being urged by the Society of Labour Lawyers to include in the Act discriminatory housing, employment, insurance, and credit practices.

On the educational front, a good deal has been done locally to overcome the linguistic difficulties of the adult immigrants as well as their children. The reorientation of public attitudes has been slow, however, despite the efforts of the National Committee and of voluntary bodies. Interest in race relations as an academic subject has increased in the universities, although specific courses are offered in only two or three departments. There is particular need for considerable expansion in this field in the colleges that train schoolteachers. It also seems desirable that other important cultural media, such as the B.B.C., take a more deliberate part in this educational process. Some of the Corporation's programs have provided excellent lectures, but the absence of a constructive and systematic approach is symptomatic in some respects of the official attitude.

In Britain, race relations are a sensitive theme, and one avoids as far as possible digging too deeply into such matters.

REFERENCES

1. The expression *colored* is used very loosely in Britain; its popular application is wide enough to include almost any person who is apparently not of European origin. It tends, therefore, to denote not only African and New-World Negroes, but Arabs, Indians, Pakistanis, Chinese, North Africans, and so on.

2. Sheila Patterson, *Dark Strangers* (London, 1963), p. 225

C. ERIC LINCOLN

Color and Group Identity in the United States

> Mary had a little lamb
> Its fleece was white as snow
> And everywhere that Mary went
> That little white lamb could go.
>
> Mary had another lamb
> Its fleece was black, you see
> They thought he was a "you-know-what"
> And hung him from a tree.[1]

In the United States where the enduring problem in social relations is between whites and Negroes, skin color is probably the most important single index for uncritical human evaluation. It is paradoxical that this is so, for color is notoriously unreliable as a tool for determining any substantial qualities of an individual, particularly his "race." And it is with race that the question of color is ultimately concerned. Despite this obvious unreliability, color is made to function as a cultural index for racial determination whenever it is conceived of as a valid external symbol of supposedly intrinsic qualities. The presence or absence of these qualities determines whether a person belongs to an "inferior" or "superior" social group, and whether his life chances are circumscribed or maximized in terms of his group membership.

In social relations in the United States, color is often read as a signal to denigrate, to discriminate, to segregate. It takes on the characteristics of a cultural norm, so much so that a complex of rewards, punishments, and the strictest taboos have grown up around it. American children, both Negro and white, very early develop behavior patterns and adopt value systems based on color, and American adults are seldom free from its connotations. That a racial determination on the basis of color can only be approximate and for a limited spectrum of individuals at best does not

seem to impair its credibility as a legitimate index for human evaluation. Nor does it seem to diminish the apparent *need* for identifying persons by race. On the surface this would seem to indicate
that America's cultural concern about color is essentially nominal. The need to make decisions on a racial basis is perhaps psychologically atavistic, a tribal anachronism rooted in the dim past
when everyone not a member of the tribe threatened its well-
being.

Thousands of Negroes "pass" permanently into the white race
each year. This cannot be effectively prevented so long as there
are interracial unions, with or without benefit of law or clergy.
Thousands of others pass whenever it provides social or economic opportunities not readily available outside the majority
group. Reliable estimates on the basis of three hundred and fifty
years of miscegenation and passing suggest that there are several
million "Caucasians" in this country who are part Negro insofar as
they have Negro blood or Negro ancestry.[2] Since there are few
Negro Americans who do not have some white blood, the continuing preoccupation with racial identification by color would seem to
be of little reward—the more crucial facts having already been
established by a countervailing proclivity.

Nonetheless, American society has troubled itself considerably
to detect by various supplementary devices—sometimes refined,
but more often of a cruder sort—what may be undetectable to the
uncritical eye. It thus reaffirms its apparent need (and the quality
of its commitment) for the establishment of racial identity as a crucial factor in social intercourse. A generation ago when strict segregation followed identification, some of the night clubs, hotels, and
other places of entertainment and public accommodation in Chicago and other cities hired "spotters" to point out light-skinned
Negroes who sought to pass for white and enter the segregated
establishments. Since the operating premise of the white proprietors was that "one coon can recognize another," the spotters were
always Negroes, some of whom were themselves light enough to
pass. The system broke down during the depression years when
few Negroes, light-skinned or otherwise, had enough money to
bother about trying to spend it in places where they had to run a
color gantlet. Having nobody to spot, the "spotters" felt their jobs
in jeopardy and began to ask their friends to come by occasionally in the interest of the survival of the profession. The whole
sordid arrangement collapsed when the supply of friends of "pass-

able" skin color ran low, and the ersatz "Caucasians" became darker and darker with hair that was fuzzier and fuzzier. Reduced to spotting the obvious, the spotters were soon dispensed with.

This absurd practice demonstrates the near pathological obsession with race and color Americans have exhibited. It is *e pluribus unum*—one out of a multitude. In the illustration given, those most anxious about color and identity were Caucasian, which is to say, white. But in a well-known southern city a leading Negro church for years discouraged the attendance of would-be worshipers who were darker than a *café au lait* stripe painted conveniently on the doorjamb of the sanctuary.

In its American manifestations, the fundamental problem of color and group identity derives in large measure from the desire of the established white hegemony, particularly the former slave-owning class, to distinguish itself by all means available from the blacks, who, whether as slaves or freedmen, had little status and no power.[3] As long as the vast majority of the blacks were of unmixed African descent, the problem was minimized. Their distinctive visibility made their racial origins unmistakable. In fact, the very first significance of color was the early development of a rationale in the colonies that made it possible to hold a black bond-servant for life, to make him a slave, while a white bondservant could be held only for a term of years.[4]

From the date that blacks could, as a matter of course, be held in legal servitude for life, color became an important index of race and, hence, of prestige and status.[5] A ban against inter-marriage was immediately instituted. Theretofore, intermarriage between black bondsmen from Africa and white bondswomen from England and Ireland had been common. Social acceptability was measured in terms of class, which could be transcended, rather than in terms of race, which was immutable. In the context of a distribution of status and power that implied the freedom of all white men and the susceptibility to chattel slavery of all Negroes, color became the visual rule of thumb for the assignment of "place" or status.

It is no less ironic for all its inevitability that Negroes, who were (and who remain) the prime subjects of color discrimination, adopted color as an index of social worth. They made the evaluative modifications necessary to suit their peculiar condition as a color caste undergirding an otherwise class-oriented society.

In the process of establishing a "democracy" in the New World, colonial Europeans did not contemplate the inclusion of Negroes (nor Indians for that matter) in the ruling caste. As American social and moral philosophy evolved through an agonizing assessment of economic preferments and political demands, consensus arose that the issue of color and caste implied in Negro slavery should be excluded from the founding documents of the emergent democracy.[6] For the British founders and the succeeding generations of Euro-Americans, the issue of color was without complication once Negro slavery had become institutionalized. Indeed, the issue of political status transcended the issue of color. All white men were free; all black men were slaves (with the exception of "free" Negroes who were in a sort of limbo in between).[7] Unlike the complicated experiments of slaveholding countries that sought to match a hierarchy of privileges with a spectrum of color, America's color-caste arrangement was inflexible. There were but two recognized categories of color: "white" and "colored." "Colored" was the common designation for any person having any Negro ancestry whatever—no matter how "light" or how "dark" his skin color, and irrespective of any quantity of "white blood" less than 100 per cent. The term *mulatto* was loosely used in commercial parlance to refer to a slave of mixed blood in any degree, but it had no political, social, or legal meaning. From the perspective of the white ruling caste, *all* Negroes of *any* color were of a lower caste. The question of color as a matter of identity was to have substantial meaning only to Negroes.

In the search for an identity based on color, the Negro reacted (and perhaps is still reacting) to a status first ascribed to him by the white man and then perpetuated in a self-fulfilling prophecy. The white man rationalized the Negro's peculiar fitness, even his God-willed destiny, to be a slave and then enslaved him. The Negro in his yearnings to be free and equal, and everywhere observing that blacks were in servitude and whites were free, mistakenly equated whiteness as a necessary corollary to freedom, and blackness as the inevitable concomitant to bondage.

> Aught's de aught
> Figger's de figger. . .
> All fo' de white man
> And none fo' de nigger.

Even the experience of emancipation, a rather qualified freedom, did not significantly change the black man's awe of the mystery of whiteness.

There is not, to my knowledge, any history of pre-colonial color-consciousness among the various African tribes whose descendants make up the Negro population in America. If color-consciousness was *not* a factor in their social relations, two hundred and fifty years of slavery, and another hundred years of marginal involvement in the pervasive, ubiquitous culture of a white, European society have created a color-consciousness that has become such a factor. In a sub-society alienated so completely and with such finality from its parent culture and its traditional spectrum of values, a modified adoption of the cultural values of the host society would seem to be predictable.

At the uncritical stage of their yearning for equivalence, the powerless and the disinherited find attractive whatever is associated with the peculiar mystique of the group in power. This was true of the Jews, the American colonists, and probably of every other subject people. The slave affects the style of his master; the student, the language of his teacher. Whether the quality affected or yearned after is germane to the status associated with it is unimportant so long as it is *thought* to be by those impressed by it. In America, the white man was unchallenged in his power. His grand style bespoke wealth and learning. Negroes were powerless, poor, and ignorant. Indeed, both races commonly supposed that an unmixed Negro was incapable of education, to say nothing of mastering the intricacies of politics or economics.

If the secret of the white man's success lay in his color, it stood to reason that the closer to being "white" a black man was, the more likely he was to have power and status. This reasoning was reinforced by the slave-era tradition of making household servants of the slave master's mulatto offspring, thus securing them in positions of relative privilege *vis à vis* the unmixed field hands. Frequently, the law permitting, a conscience-stricken master would free the half-white fruit of his cabin dalliances when they reached majority, or he would provide for their freedom in his will.

Thus, a substantial proportion of free Negroes were mulattoes. The various literary and mutual-aid societies, and sometimes churches formed by "free persons of color"[8] often disdained the admission of free Negroes with dark skin. When the slavocracy was destroyed and all Negroes were elevated to a single legal status, the Negro group—as a sub-society—already had an emerging class arrangement based on color within a nether caste also defined by color. The mulattoes were at the top of the lowly heap.

They maintained their position as a class within the caste until after World War II when values like wealth, education, and profession reduced the mere possession of a light skin to relative insignificance.

Yet to say that color is dead as an aspect of racial psychosis would be to lay prematurely to rest a troublesome syndrome likely to defy interment. Quite apart from its elemental concern with status and power, color as a cultural value has continuing significance for aesthetics and for personal identity. The prevailing conceptions of what or who is beautiful vary widely between native Africans and their Afro-American counterparts. The white ideal of feminine pulchritude, though less stressed than formerly, is still the archetype for the overwhelming majority of Negro American women and the persistent choice of Negro men. Cosmetic preparations for lightening skin and straightening hair represent a multi-million-dollar market among Negroes not favored with Caucasoid features. Among the less affluent and more credulous, urine rinses for the face and "mammy-leg"[9] presses for the hair contribute to the unending search for some approximation of the white ideal.

To the intense delight of a street-corner gathering, a Negro punster described the ideal woman in exaggerated terms reflecting the Negro's preoccupation with color:

> She got to be *white*, Jack—
> 'Cause white is right
> Both day and night!
> She got to be *old* and white,
> 'Cause if she's old
> She's been white *longer!*
> She got to be *big* and white,
> Cause if she's big
> She's much *more* white!
> But listen, Jack—
> If she just can't be *white*
> Then let her be real *light brown!*[10]

A college jester put it this way: "A light woman is your passport to Negro society. I'd rather give a light woman plane fare to St. Louis than to tell a tack head[11] what time the train leaves!"

During the uncertain years of World War II, "passport parties" were actually held as pranks on some college campuses. To attend such a party, male escorts were made to pay (unknown to their dates) a color tax based on the complexion of the girls they escorted; the money thus raised made up a pot to buy refreshments. Any girl as fair as a secretly agreed upon "Fairy Queen" was designated a "Natural Passport"; she and her escort were admitted without charge. The color of the male was inconsequential. That college youths could face the color issue squarely enough to joke about it is probably indicative of its declining importance as early as two decades ago, but is no less indicative of its pervasiveness.

The problem of negative associations with blackness goes deeper than aesthetics. American culture associates Negroes with darkness, an extremely negative quality. In the innocent and painful prattle of Negro children heard a scant generation ago, *"Black is evil!"* was a retort intended to account for behavior one disapproved of in a playmate.[12] In the rural areas, black people were frequently associated with sorcery and voodoo.[13] Everywhere black people were pitied, for deep in the soul of even the whitest Negro was an erosive *self*-pity, even a self-hatred that gnawed at his vitals, questioned his manhood, and excused his failures in a way he did not want them to be excused. There was something inherent in being black that marked a man; something sinister that mocked a man.

The crucial question has always been the question of identity. Who *is* this Negro whose identifying characteristic is his color and what is his status in the world? *Whence does that status derive?* Is he African—an involuntary expatriate? Is he, in fact, "just a nigger"—a monster, blackened by God, broken in servitude, and inherently incapable of human excellence? How should he designate himself? By what name should he identify himself before the world and serve notice of what he conceives himself to be?

There has been little unanimity in the Negro's search for his identity. The Negro slaves came from many tribes and many cultures. Even though the experience of slavery reduced them all to a common denominator, it did not fuse them into an ideological unit. Only attractive ideas and persuasive leadership could do that; the nature of slavery in America left little room for the development of either.

The confusion of identity is vividly expressed in the names by which Negroes have chosen at various times to designate themselves: "persons of color," "colored people," "Negroes," "colored Americans," "Black Anglo-Saxons," "Americans," "Afro-Americans,"

"Afra-Americans," "Negro Americans"; and, more recently: "black men," "black Americans," "black people." Widely used by white writers, but commonly rejected by Negro intellectuals and black nationalists is the term *American Negroes*. This eristic term allegedly carries the stamp of something "made in America" and is the inverse of the designations commonly applied to other ethnic groups—"German Americans," for instance.[14] "That we are called 'American Negroes,'" a prominent Negro writer has said, "is a concession of courtesy on the part of our Caucasian brothers. In translation, 'the American Negro' can only mean 'our nigger.'"

Despite some improvements in the Negroes' position as a major ethnic group pressing for a larger share of the common values of the society, the question of color and identity has in some sense become more involved and more intricate than before. There have been changes in the way Caucasians and Negroes see each other, and profound changes in the way Negroes see themselves. These newly developing attitudes have not always found mutual acceptance, nor are they necessarily consistent with one another. The de-escalation of color as an index of social standing in the Negro sub-society immeasurably strengthened and unified the factions previously contending for leadership and prestige. Forced to more diligently prepare themselves, the descendants of the less-favored field hands of plantation days have at least caught up. Today, education, wealth, high social status, and leadership are distributed fairly evenly across the color spectrum of the Negro community.

If anything, the light-skinned Negro is at a disadvantage. In the old days, color meant (at least nominal) privilege, for it bespoke the presence of the master's blood. Today, as the Negro develops an increasing appreciation of his own accomplishments and shares vicariously the accomplishments of other non-whites, the premium on "the master's blood" is signally diminished. Anyone whose light skin color is thought to be of recent derivation is exposed to a degree of censure and disapproval not known in former times.

As far as the larger society is concerned, the presence of white blood in a Negro does not bridge the chasm between castes any more today than it did formerly. In personal relations, Caucasians have, since the plantation days, usually been less threatened by blacks who were thought of as "knowing their places" than by mulattoes or "yellow niggers" who were always suspect. This white attitude can be explained in part, of course, by guilt feelings deriving from a covert recognition of kinship, which could never be openly admitted without violating the strictest taboos. But there was also the deep-seated belief that too much white blood transformed the stereotyped docile, accommodating Negro into a dissatisfied, potential trouble-maker. Hence, enduring bonds of affection and qualified respect frequently developed between whites and darker Negroes, a felicitous relationship from which light-skinned Negroes were generally excluded. In quite recent times, this tradition has undergone some interesting changes that reflect the inconsistencies of a color differential.

When civil rights legislation first required the employment of Negroes in major industry, wherever possible the "instant Negroes"[15] hired were of very fair complexions. Negroes serving as clerks and saleswomen in department stores or as route salesmen were frequently mistaken for white by their customers and sometimes by their co-workers. This was, of course, precisely what their employers had hoped for. In hiring Negroes who could "pass," they complied with the law without appearing to have done so. They thus reduced the supposed threat of customer and white employee reaction against being served by or working with Negroes. This policy was discontinued in favor of hiring highly visible Negroes and placing them in the most conspicuous assignments when compliance officials could discover no change in hiring policies, and Negro leaders protested that their followers wanted to "see their people on the job without having to look for them."

There are signs that the civil rights movement as a supporting thrust to a certain degree of Negro "readiness" in terms of education, accomplishment, and demonstrated potential has successfully breached the wall separating Negroes and whites into two castes. The breach is certainly not general, but for the first time in American history, Negroes enjoy some degree of lateral mobility. There is *some* social movement across color lines. Perhaps the sudden recognition of this fact contributed in no small degree to the amazing "pull-back" on the part of large numbers of whites who had been heavily involved in the civil rights movement so long as it was limited to civil rights—and concentrated in the South. The white retreat would seem to buttress other evidence that white America in general, despite some fits and starts, is not yet ready to accept Negroes on equal terms so long as they remain

Negroes. Arnold Toynbee's observations of thirty years ago are still valid:

The . . . [Negro] may have found spiritual salvation in the White Man's faith; he may have acquired the White Man's culture and learnt to speak his language with the tongue of an angel; he may have become adept in the White Man's economic technique, and yet it profits him nothing if he has not changed his skin.[16]

A few, select, individual Negroes have been able to approach the American main stream with varying degrees of marginality. In doing so, they run the inevitable risk of becoming as alienated from the nether culture from which they came as they are likely to remain in reference to the culture they seek to enter. But change *is* occurring.

Even as the machinery of caste is being dismantled and discarded, the color-caste psychology persists. It is not difficult to understand the continuing frustrations of the black masses. A universal system of *apartheid* has, in effect, been exchanged for a selective system of *apartheid*. This may be progress, but it is not progressive enough to satisfy the present-day needs of the black millions who are still beyond the pale. The color computer has been programmed to extend to selected Negroes of high accomplishment selected categories of privileges previously withheld from all Negroes. An "integrated" society in which the common values of that society will be freely accessible to the general population regardless of color has not been realized, nor does it seem to be rapidly approaching.

Taking no comfort from what they perceive as an *entente cordiale* between the white establishment and the Negro leadership class, the black *lumpen proletariat* seethes with hostility and resentment. Despite modifications of law and practice produced by the efforts of the civil rights movement, the black masses are unimpressed because they are unaffected. Critical selectivity functions at the top; the tortured masses at the bottom feel no tremor of change.

The Great Society has spent millions of dollars in the interest of the poor and the disinherited. In doing so, the government created yet another clique of petty bureaucrats and interposed them between the people and the help they need. By day the black ghetto is resplendent with sleek, fat professionals—Negro and white—striving mightily to re-mold the people in images they reject and despise; by night—the professionals having fled home to the suburbs—the people gather on the street corners to con-template the probabilities of black power, or the ecstasy of long, hot summers. Despite the ministrations of the professionals, the people are as hungry, as unemployed, and as hostile as before.

As their frustrations multiply, the black masses become more and more alienated from the larger society and from the tiny Ne-gro middle class that hopes to cross the chasm eventually and to enter the American main stream. The problem of color and iden-tity takes on crucial meaning in this context. The term *Negro*, which has for so long aroused mixed emotions even among those who accepted it, has for the militant[17] masses become an epithet reserved for the Negro middle class, particularly those suspected of desiring to be integrated into the white society.

Neither the traditional black nationalists nor the advocates of "black power," which is a new form of militant black nationalism, accept integration as being either possible or desirable under existing conditions. Integration is interpreted as a one-way street. It means to those not impressed by its possibilities the abandon-ment of traditional values and styles of life on the off-chance of be-ing accepted by a group "which never appreciated you for what you were, and resents you for what you are trying to become." Stokely Carmichael declares:

Integration . . . speaks to the problem of blackness in a despicable way. As a goal it has been based on complete acceptance of the fact [*sic*] that in order to have a decent house or education, blacks must move into a white neighborhood or send their children to a white school.

This reinforces, among both black and white, the idea that "white" is automatically better and "black" is by definition inferior. This is why integration is a subterfuge for the maintenance of white supremacy.[18]

To the black masses, the Negro integrationists and integrationist leaders seem to take on the characteristics of "collaborators with the enemy," and need to be labeled distinctly as such. Hence, the black militants have resurrected the connotation of "Negro" as being a thing, a puppet, a creation of the white man, finding it peculiarly applicable to the Negro middle class and its leadership.[19]

Like the Garveyites and the Black Muslims before them, the new black militants—particularly those in the Student Non-Violent Coordinating Committee—do not see themselves in the image of the white American. They dress unaffectedly and wear their hair *à la mode Africaine*—combed, but unstraightened. They refer to themselves and to all other non-integrationist-minded

259

black Americans as "black people." The term is deliberately chosen as a symbol of racial polarization. It intends to imply the solidarity of the black masses, here and abroad; to disavow any necessary commitment to white values or deference to the white establishment; to distinguish the masses from the integrationists; and to exploit new feelings of black nationalism and *négritude* that have taken hold in the Negro community since World War II. It answers, at least for the time being, all the important questions of identity and color. Many middle-class Negroes, remembering the negative stereotypes formerly associated with blackness, cannot bring themselves to speak of Negroes as "black people." Neither can many whites for that matter.[20] The stereotypes die too hard.

The new SNCC strategy aims at organizing a power base from which black people can influence decisions within the existing political arrangement without being subject to review by white monitors. Implied is a fundamental rejection of reliance upon the white man's integrity, a point to which all black nationalist groups must come by definition. The synonym for black nationalism is black ethnocentrism, and ethnocentrism always implies a suspicion of some other peoples' integrity, their values, and their truth.

In the conventional interpretation of human confrontation, belief is always preceded by doubt. Not so with the Negro in America. He believed first and has but lately learned to doubt. It is a tragedy that doubt was even necessary, since the faith he had required so little to fulfill. But America is now forever beyond the point of naïveté and innocence, and is unlikely to pass that way again. The lessons that have been learned cannot be forgotten, and there are new teachers to interpret old experiences. Elijah Muhammad justifies his all-black Muslim organization on the grounds that "You can't whip a man when he's helping you," thus surreptitiously but unequivocally identifying the enemy as the white man. The SNCC rationale is more adroit. SNCC wants its white supporters to work among prejudiced whites "who are not accessible" to its Negro agents. The net result is the same: the effective removal of white individuals, however well-intentioned, from sensitive strategy and policy-making areas where racial loyalties may jeopardize the pursuit of the black man's program.

Traditional black nationalism has been oriented toward separatism—or, at best, toward a pluralistic society. The "black-power" syndrome recognizes the substantial existence of a plural society already and intends to capitalize on it. Like the integrationists, SNCC wants power within the existing political structure, but unlike more moderate organizations, SNCC is impatient with indirect power and suspicious of contingent or shared power. "Black power" is conceived as palpable, manipulatable, black-controlled power that carries with it a sense of dignity for black people and a feeling of security from white caprice. An organized, voting black minority with a substantially unified ideological orientation could conceivably produce such power. Whether it can be produced on the basis of color alone is debatable.[21]

The question is not whether black people are capable of leadership and self-direction or of making the sacrifices that may be needed. They have demonstrated their capabilities in all these areas, and more. The more fundamental question is whether color alone is a unifying force sufficient to weld together in a monolithic (or, better, monochromatic) sociopolitical movement a black minority exhibiting an immense spectrum of needs, wants, desires, and intentions based on conflicting systems of value. The question of identity has not been resolved. Color alone does not answer satisfactorily the questions about the self one needs to have answered as the basis for intelligent decision-making about oneself and others. Negroes in America still do not know who they are. Not having resolved this elemental problem, they approach all other problems in human relations with predictable ambivalence and uncertainty. That is why they fight bravely in the far off places of the world, march peacefully in Washington, and die cravenly in Mississippi and Alabama. This, too, is why they sing "Black and White Together" by day, and "Burn! Baby, Burn!" by night.

The Negro's experiences in America have produced in him a mass social neurosis that can only become more morbid as the frustrations of trying to cope with the problem of color and identity are intensified by education and increased marginality at the top of the social pyramid, and by increasing poverty and the concomitant loss of personhood at the bottom. Involuntary servitude did not shatter the psyche of the Negro. He could overcome servitude—slavery if you insist—just as countless other peoples of different races and cultures had. Slavery was not a unique experience. Still, although it existed for centuries in Africa as well as elsewhere, nowhere but in America was it accompanied by such devastation of personality. It was not the slavery *per se*, but the pitiless obliteration of the history and the culture of a people, the deliberate distortion of that history and culture. It was the casual pollution of a race without the compassion and responsibility of acknowledgment. It was, above all, the snide rejection of the Negro's claim to be "American." Less deserving people from all over the world could come to America and claim that identity so long as they were white. The Negro could never claim it because he was black.

The trauma of this rejection polarizes the color crisis between the races and keeps alive the anxieties of identification and color within the Negro sub-group. Charles Silberman is probably right: "Consciousness of color is not likely to disappear unless color itself disappears, or unless men lose their eyesight."[22] But consciousness of color, like consciousness of kind, is not a reasonable basis upon which to project a system of group relations. Nor has it ever been.

REFERENCES

1. From "Joe Jipson," *The Autobiography of a Southern Town;* an unpublished manuscript by C. Eric Lincoln.

2. Sociologist Robert P. Stuckert of Ohio State University estimates: "Over 28 million white persons are descendants of persons of African origins"— about 21 per cent of the Caucasian population of the United States.

3. In a larger sense, the problem of color and identity in America is related to the general ascendancy of the West, which is to say white Europeans, since the fifteenth century, and the subsequent colonization of Asia, Africa, and the New World. In his book, *Caste, Class and Race* ([Garden City, N. Y., 1948], p. 346), Oliver Cox makes the signal observation that "since the belief in white superiority—that is to say white nationalism— began to move over the world, no people of color have been able to develop race prejudice independent of whites."

4. See John Hope Franklin, *From Slavery to Freedom* (New York, 1947), p. 70ff.

5. This was first practiced in Virginia in 1661; Maryland followed in 1663. A Virginia law of 1670 fixed the status of Negroes and Indians respectively by decreeing that "all servants not being Christians" (that is, not being "white") coming into the colony by sea, "shall be slaves for their lives." Those "coming by land" (Indians) could be bound for a term of years.

6. The Continental Congress refused to accept Thomas Jefferson's draft of the Declaration of Independence which included a strong indictment of Negro slavery and of the English Crown which was allegedly responsible for the establishment and continuation of slavery in the colonies. It is significant that once free of British rule, the colonies continued slavery on their own, although there was always dissent against the practice.

7. "His color" says Wade, "suggested servitude, but his national status secured a portion of freedom." Richard C. Wade, *Slavery in the Cities* (New York, 1964), p. 249.

8. A term normally meaning "colored"—that is, "Negro."

9. A sort of cap made from a woman's stocking, the "mammy-leg" is much used by males and females to hold the hair in place during informal hours at home. They are sometimes seen on children and teen-agers on neighborhood streets.

10. Lincoln, "Joe Jipson," *The Autobiography of a Southern Town.*

11. A slang term for a dark woman with crimpy hair.

12. In Boston, the author was once physically attacked by a white child with no other explanation than, "I don't like you because you're black!"

13. A belief possibly reinforced by once popular "jungle" films and stories; but possibly a recollection of a fragmentary cultural experience having to do with tribal religious rites or witchcraft.

14. The implication, say the critics, is that the Negro has no prior nationality or culture, that he is in fact a creation of the white man, "something made in America." Only the Indian should have "American" placed before his ethnic name, it is argued.

15. Negroes hired in token numbers merely to comply with the law.

16. Arnold J. Toynbee, *A Study of History*, Vol. 1 (London, 1935), p. 224.

17. The greater portion of the black masses can still be classified as "quiescent," although they are certainly more susceptible to sporadic activities than ever before.

18. Stokely Carmichael, "What We Want," *The Boston Sunday Herald*, October 2, 1966.

19. In conversation, the word may be sarcastically pronounced with excessive stress on the first syllable ("NEE-gro"), recalling readily to the in-group mind the slurred pronunciation of some Southerners that renders the word "Negra," which to sensitive ears is a covert way of saying "nigger."

20. In a graduate seminar on minority relations, a young white student protested to a Negro classmate: "Why do you call yourself 'black'? I could never call you black. There is something not right about it. Besides, I think you're a nice guy." "You can't call me 'black,'" the Negro student answered, "and that is your guilt. I can call myself 'black,' and that is my freedom."

21. Malcolm X saw color as the only possible basis of unification. He attempted to eclipse the problem of white ancestry so obvious in many Negroes, himself included, by declaring: "We are all black, different shades of black, and not one of us means any more to a white cracker than any other one."

22. Charles E. Silberman, *Crisis in Black and White* (New York, 1964), p. 166.

263

JULIAN PITT-RIVERS

Race, Color, and Class in Central America and the Andes

AMONG ITS many *fiestas*, the Hispanic world celebrates one with
the name of "El día de la raza" (which is what is called Columbus
Day in the United States). Why it should be so called remains
something of an enigma. It was inaugurated in Spain in 1917 to
encourage friendship with Latin America, but its name has been
changed there to "El día de la Hispanidad"—in the cause, more
suitable to present times, of extolling Spanish culture rather than
Spanish genes. The old name still remains, however, in Mexico and
in other countries. The *fiesta* might, more consequentially, have
been called "The Day of Race Relations" rather than of "The Race,"
for it celebrates the day on which they may be said to have commenced.

For the Spaniards, the celebration evokes the age, long since
eclipsed, when they conquered half the world; it pays tribute to the
egregious stamina of their ancestors. But Mexicans tend to think it
refers to the Aztec race; the Monumento a la Raza in Mexico City is
composed of a pyramid surmounted by an Aztec eagle.[1] In other
countries, some people think it refers to the Spanish race, but it
seldom evokes for anyone the name of Columbus, whose race remains a matter of dispute to this day.

Quite apart from the mysteries surrounding The Day of the
Race, the concept of *race* itself is unclear in Latin America.
My concern here is not with what anthropologists mean by
race, but only with what the people of Latin America think
the word means when they encounter it in their daily speech.
By minimal definition, it refers to a group of people who
are felt to be somehow similar in their essential nature. El Día de
la Raza is above all a patriotic *fiesta*; it expresses national unity,
the common nature of the whole nation. As such, it is certainly
worth celebrating, especially in countries where racial differences

pose such grave moral and social problems on other days of the year. It is in keeping with this interpretation that the *fiesta* should be a comparatively modern innovation coinciding with the growth of national and social consciousness.

The word *race* is, of course, also used to mark differences of ethnic identity within the nation. Sometimes awareness of any implication of heredity is so slight that a man can think of himself as belonging to a race different from that of his parents. The word clearly owes little to physical anthropology but refers, however it may be defined, to the ways in which people are classified in daily life. What are called race relations are, in fact, always questions of social structure.

Ethnic classification is the end product of the most elusive social processes that endow not only words but feelings and perceptions with a special significance. The varied definitions of *race* have no more in common than the fact that they say something about the essential and indelible nature of people. Hence, for all its ambiguities, the notion of race possesses a prime claim upon the solidarities that bind men into social and political alliance.

Approaches to the study of race relations have varied considerably. Certain theories constructed out of the commonplaces of the traditional popular idiom attribute culture to "blood." Moral qualities, like psychological characteristics and intellectual aptitudes, are thought to derive from heredity, since the "blood" is what is inherited. The social order depends, by implication, upon genetic transmission, since the capacities and the character that fit people for a particular status are acquired by birth.

This view leads to the conclusion that social status should be hereditary and derive from the nature of persons. The system works well enough because the totality of a person's descent is not only hard to know in a genetically homogeneous population, but also quite easily falsified. Birth produces the expectation of excellence. Recognized excellence demonstrates the presence of dis tinguished forebears who may not have previously been claimed. "Blood will out!" In operation the system confirms its premises. Thanks to its flexibility, the facts can be made to fit; the reality of social mobility can be reconciled with a belief in the determinism of birth.[2]

Where descent can be inferred from appearance, such a theory finds itself constricted. Plebian origins do not "show"; colored origins do. Putative descent can no longer be invoked to validate the reality established by the social process, but the real ancestors come to light in the phenotype. "Bad blood" explains moral and intellectual defects, but in those who show visible signs of having it, these can be expected in advance. Moral qualities are no longer inferred from status; rather, status is accorded on the basis of physical qualities that can be seen, and these, then, determine the nature of persons. Birth decides not merely opportunity but fate. In a homogeneous society the possession of a prestigious ancestor entitles a man to claim status. Once blood is a matter of ethnic distinction, however, its purity becomes the subject of concern. The attribution of an impure ancestor destroys status. Blood exchanges a positive for a negative significance. Preoccupations with "purity of descent" take on a racial connotation and bring an adverse value to miscegenation (a word which by the unhappy fortuity of its spelling becomes misconstrued today to imply that racial prejudices have a scientific background). The result is a color bar, prohibiting social mobility and enforcing ethnic endogamy.[3]

When blood is considered the determinant of culture, racial differences between peoples can be used to explain all else, even military and political fortunes. Purity of blood becomes the key to national success. The most distinguished literary expression of such ideas is that of Gobineau. By zeal and industry rather than by any great originality of mind, he succeeded in elevating the social prejudices of a petty noble of the mid-nineteenth century to the status of a philosophy of history. If Gobineau committed what Claude Lévi-Strauss has called the "original sin" of anthropology,[4] later anthropologists have committed other less spectacular sins in their attempts to grapple with the problems of race relations—or, more often, they have sinned by default in not attempting to grapple with them at all.

The "diffusionist" theory offered such an evasion. Viewing race relations in terms of culture contact, this theory concentrated upon establishing the origin of the cultural traits of different peoples to the neglect of their present social function. The preoccupation with the transmission of culture between different ethnic groups, rather than with reciprocal modes of behavior, left this branch of anthropology with little to say about the problems of race relations. This is particularly important in Latin America, where in the past a great many anthropologists have devoted their labors to the discovery of the cultures of pre-Hispanic times on the assumption that they have been preserved among the Indians of the present. This archaeological orientation has meant that, until recently, in spite of the quantity of professional work done in Latin America, few accounts have been concerned with race relations as such. Concentrating on the passage of cultural traits rather than on the social structure through which these traits passed, the anthropologists tended to deal with only one side of the ethnic division and touched only incidentally its relationship to the other.

The Marxist interpretation of race relations has been of the greatest importance in stressing their economic aspects and in giving them a dynamic dimension. It has clarified in particular the stages of colonial development. But if the proponents of the "acculturation theory" have neglected the society within which acculturation took place, the Marxist sociologists have tended to neglect the significance of culture by treating race relations simply as a special instance of class relations carried over into a colonial setting.

The same reproach cannot be leveled at the American urban sociologists whose awareness of the factor of culture and whose feeling for its nuances have brought a high level of excellence to their ethnography. But, as Professor Everett Hughes pointed out a dozen years ago (and it is still true), they have been inclined to conduct their analysis within the framework of their own values and reformist desires. For want of a comparative field of reference, they have tended to overlook the wider significance of their data.

Studies of race relations by political thinkers have seldom given sufficient weight to the course of feeling that lies behind political events or to the dynamics of a changing consciousness and the formation of fresh solidarities. Politics has been called the science of the possible. Time and again it has turned out to be, where racial issues were concerned, the science of what was once possible but is so no longer.

A study that straddles the frontiers of established disciplines requires consideration from such varied viewpoints. It must above all achieve a synthesis of the cultural and the social aspects. The detail of the ethnography must be integrated in an overview of race relations in space and time. The preliminary condition of such an enterprise is a clear description of the systems of ethnic classification at the local level and a recognition of their social sig-

nificance. Charles Wagley was making this point when he coined
the phrase "social race."[5] He went on to point to the importance of
knowing how the terminology varies, for this matter is filled with
confusion. Not only do the words used vary from area to area and
from class to class, but the conceptions to which they correspond
also change, and the criteria on which the system of classification
is based vary in relevance. It is difficult to say what is an Indian,[6]
but it is scarcely easier to say what is a Negro.

Terminological inconsistencies complicate from the outset discussion of race relations in Latin America. Indeed, there is not
even agreement as to whether or not a "problem" of race relations exists in Latin America. The nationals of these countries often
deny the existence of racial discrimination. They claim from this
fact a virtue that makes them, despite their supposed economic
and technological underdevelopment, the moral superiors of their
northern neighbor, whose "inhumanity" toward colored people
they deplore. Moreover, this opinion is held not only by Latin
Americans themselves, but by outside observers, the most eminent
of whom is Professor Arnold Toynbee, who speaks of the Latin
American's freedom from race prejudice.[7]

This point of view, in many cases a way of expressing criticism of the United States, is also held by many patriotic
American citizens, including especially some who are "colored"
and whose testimony, if firsthand, might be thought to suffice.[8]
Nevertheless, it is not by any means held universally and is sometimes regarded as a myth. Certain critics, both national and foreign, maintain that race is as important in Latin as in North
America, once it is admitted that in addition to differences in the
form discrimination takes, there is a major difference: The race
that is penalized is the Indian rather than the Negro. Neither of
these points of view appears correct.[9] Both are confused as to the
nature of the question. Yet by examining the observations upon
which they are based and how they have come to hold sway,
one can understand better the role ethnic distinctiveness plays in
ordering the society of Latin America.

"Segregation" as it is found in the United States does not exist
in Latin America. "Color" in the North American sense is not
the basis of a classification into two statuses to which differential
rights attach. Segregated schools, public facilities, transport, or
restaurants do not exist in Latin America. The Negro is not formally distinguished at any point. While many institutions are de-

voted specifically to the Indians, the definition of Indian in this regard is not based on physical criteria. Moreover, neither color nor phenotype has sufficed in the past to debar men from prominence in the national life, as the long list of Negroid or Indian-looking men of eminence in Latin American history shows.[10]

Intermarriage is not regarded with horror. Among the upper classes and in many places among the population generally, it is, however, considered denigrating to marry someone much darker than oneself. This is so, for example, in Barranquilla, Colombia, where the greater part of the population is more or less Negroid. The idea of physical contact with darker races is nowhere considered shocking, nor is it regarded as polluting by the whites. Dark-skinned people are thought to be more sensual and therefore more desirable sexually. This is not the expression of a neurotic fear of sexual insufficiency but an accepted and openly stated commonplace. Pale-skinned people of both sexes are thought to be more frigid and proud, and less warmhearted. Mistresses tend, consequently, to be more swarthy than wives, whose pale skin indicates social superiority.

The immense majority of the population from Mexico to Bolivia are well aware of their mixed ancestry. "A touch of the tarbrush" can, therefore, never mean total social disqualification. "We are all half-castes," Mexicans commonly remark, pointing to their forearm to show the color of their skin. Still, they sometimes go on to stress that only a small percentage of their blood is Indian. National unity demands that to be truly Mexican they must have some Indian blood, but social aspirations require that they should not have too much. Color is a matter of degree, not the basis of a division into black and white.

In consequence, physical characteristics cannot be said to be socially insignificant; their significance is only different. Physical traits never account for more than part of the image that individuals present. These images are perceived in terms of what they can be contrasted with; there is no color problem where the population is homogeneous in color, whatever that color may be. Social distinctions must then be made according to other criteria. From one place to another, in greater or lesser degree, physical traits are qualified by cultural and economic indicators in order to produce that total image which accords a social identity.

Arnulfo Arias, a former president of Panamá known for his "racist" policy, is credited with the proposal to exterminate the

Negroes. In a country whose capital city is predominantly Negro, he nevertheless retained sufficient popularity to be a close runner-up in the presidential elections of 1964. This is no longer curious when one realizes that the term *Negro* refers only to the population of Jamaican origins. Imported for the construction of the canal, these people have retained their English tongue and their Protestant faith. Language and religion are the significant qualifiers of color in the definition of *Negro* in Panamá.

In Barranquilla, Colombia, color is qualified by other social factors, and the term *Negro* confined to the slum-dwellers of the city. In the modern housing developments where no one is to be seen who would not qualify as a Negro in the United States, one may be told: "Only white people live here." The definition of *Negro* varies from place to place and, of course, from class to class. A man may be defined as Negro in one place, but simply as *moreno, trigueño, canela*, or even white in another. A man who would be considered Negro in the United States might, by traveling to Mexico, become *moreno* or *prieto*, then *canela* or *trigueño* in Panamá, and end up in Barranquilla white. The definition of *Indian* presents a comparable problem once the word no longer refers to a member of an Indian community. Different places and classes use different criteria.

Skin color is merely one of the indices among physical traits that contribute to a person's total image. It is not necessarily more significant than hair type or shape of eye. The relative evaluation of different physical traits varies. The Reichel-Dolmatoffs record of a village in Northern Colombia:

Distinctions are made mainly according to the nature of the hair and of the eyes and to a certain degree according to stature. Skin color, the shape of the lips or nose, or other similar traits are hardly taken into account. In this way, a person with predominantly Negroid features, but with long and wavy hair is often considered a "Spaniard." On the other hand, an individual with predominantly Caucasoid features and a light skin, but with straight black hair, slightly oblique eyes and of small stature, is considered an "Indian."[11]

The social structure is divided, primarily according to place of residence, into two segments—Spanish and Indian. This dichotomy, while employing a strictness which the Reichel-Dolmatoffs regard as exceptional in Colombia, allows no place for the category "Negro."

The system of classification makes what it will of the objective

270

reality of the phenotype. The forces of the social structure utilize the raw material of phenotypical distinctions, building out of it the social statuses into which people are classified.

It has sometimes been said that the difference between Anglo and Latin America is that in the former anyone who has a drop of Negro blood is a Negro, whereas in the latter anyone who has white blood is a white.[12] The first statement is approximately true, but the second is emphatically not so. The concept of "blood" is fundamentally different in the two and has, in the past, varied from one century to another.

In Latin America, a person with non-white physical traits may be classed as white socially. A trace of European physique is, however, quite insufficient in itself to class a person as white. Although Indians with pale skin and European traits or gray hair may be found sporadically throughout Latin America, they are considered to be no less Indian on this account. In any market in the Andes one or two can usually be seen, and the *indio gringo* ("fair-skinned" or "blond" Indian) is a recognized type in parts of northern Peru. There is nothing anomalous in this description. "Indian" is not, in the first place, a physical type but a social status. The Indian is distinguished not by genetic inheritance but by birth in, and therefore membership of, an Indian community and by possession of that community's culture. This is all that is needed for the definition of an Indian, though Indians normally look "Indian." The word *Indian* has, therefore, come to mean "of Indian descent"; it is used of persons who no longer occupy Indian status, but whose physical resemblance to the Indians implies descent from them. Since Indians are the "lowest" or least "civilized" element of the population, the word in this sense means "low class." It can also be used to mean "savage," or "uncivilized," or "bad" in a purely figurative way—equivalent, say, to that of *canaille* in French. *Negro*, on the other hand, denotes a physical type that commonly carries with it the general implication of low class, but culture is usually quite subsidiary to the definition.[13]

Racial status in the United States, defined in terms of "blood" and identified purely by physical appearance, divides the population into two halves within which two parallel systems of class differentiation are recognized. In Latin America, appearance is merely one indicator of social position. It is never sufficient in itself to determine how an individual should be classed. The discrimination imposed on the basis of "color" in the United States has sometimes been called a "caste" system and has been contrasted with class systems. This distinction is impossible in Latin America where color is an ingredient of total social position, not the criterion for distinguishing two racial "castes." A policy of segregation on the basis of color would, therefore, be not merely repugnant to Latin Americans but literally impossible.

Even in Panamá where the bulk of the urban population is Negro and the "oligarchy," as the traditional upper class is called, entirely European, the notion of segregation is repulsive. A member of the Panamanian upper class concluded a bitter criticism of discrimination in the United States with the remark: "After all, it's a matter of luck whether one is born black or white." It remained to be added, of course, that in Panamá it is nevertheless bad luck to be born black and good luck to be born white.

At the time of the race riots in Oxford, Mississippi, Hector Velarde, a distinguished critic, took the occasion to deplore racial discrimination in the United States in an article in a Peruvian newspaper. Why can the North Americans not learn from us the virtue of racial tolerance? he asked. He went on to illustrate his argument with the usage of the word *negrita* as a term of affection. *Negrita de mi alma* was an expression used toward a sweetheart, he said. Indeed he did not exaggerate, for *negrita* and *negra* are both forms of address that imply a certain intimacy or informality (as a diminutive the former carries the implication of a potential sexual interest the latter lacks). Velarde did not mention the Indians (who are very much more numerous in Peru than the Negroes). If he had, it would not have helped his thesis since *Indian* is never used in an equivalent fashion, though *cholo* ("civilized Indian") and *zambo* ("half-caste") are both used as terms of affection among comrades.[14]

The implication of racial equality that he drew from his examples invites precision. Such terms do not find their way into such a context because they are flattering in formal usage, but precisely because they are not. Intimacy is opposed to respect; because these terms are disrespectful, they are used to establish or stress a relationship in which no respect is due. The word *nigger* is used in this way among Negroes in the United States, but only among Negroes. Color has, in fact, the same kind of class connotation in the Negro community as in Latin America: Pale-skinned means upper class. Hence *nigger*, in this context dark-skinned or lower class, implies a relationship that is free of the obligation of mutual respect. Velarde's example, consequently, shows that color is an indicator of class, not a criterion of caste.

Those who find no racial discrimination in Latin America take the United States as their model. They point out, correctly, that there is no color bar and that race riots do not occur. (Indian risings are a matter they do not consider.) On the other hand, those who do find racial discrimination in Latin America are concerned with the fact that there exist high degrees of social differentiation that are habitually associated with physical traits and frequently expressed in the idiom of "race." They justify their view by the racial overtones given to social distinctions. In Latin America, these critics are commonly persons of left-wing sympathy who see racial discrimination as a bulwark of class distinction and, evading all nuances, they equate the two. Taking more easily to the emotive aspects of Marxism than to its dialectic, these would-be Marxists end by finding themselves as far from reality as those colonial legislators who once attempted so vainly to control the legal status of individuals on the basis of their descent. Because there is no color bar but rather a color scale that contributes only partially to the definition of status, they are pushed to an implied definition of race that is worthy of Gobineau. They speak of "racial hypocrisy" to explain why certain people claim a "racial" status to which their phenotype would not entitle them if "race" were really a matter of genes. This "false race-consciousness" is false only by the standards of a theory that would obliterate the historical evolution of the past four hundred years. History may validate these theorists if the Chinese interpretation of Marxist-Leninism acquires authority, and the class struggle, transposed to the international plane, becomes a matter of race.

The contrary opinion is usually held by persons of right-wing views. They regard class distinctions as either unobjectionable, insignificant, or at least inevitable. Once they can cite examples of people of upper-class status who show marked traces of non-European descent, they are satisfied that there is no racial discrimination in their country. (This conviction accords with the liberality of their nature and the official creed of their nation.) They are content that there is no problem if there is no "discrimination" as in the United States.

In the first case, the distinctiveness of class and color must be denied; in the second, the association between the two. The first theory ignores the individual instance; only the statistical aspect counts. The exception is evaded lest it disprove the rule. The second theory takes as significant only the chosen individual instance, overlooking the existence of a statistical norm. Indeed, no one is boycotted on account of his phenotype if his class standing is secured by the other criteria that define high status. In such a case, infrequent as it may be in Panamá, color may properly be said to be a matter of luck in the sense that it is a contingency that carries little of the weight of social definition. Economic power, culture, and community are what count.

The disapproval that Latin American visitors to the United States feel of the segregation they find there is not unconnected with the disrespectful attitude they are likely to inspire as Spanish speakers. They know that as Hispanics they are judged socially inferior in many places. Visitors from the United States, on the other hand, are often highly critical of the treatment the Indians of Latin America receive. This strikes them as much more reprehensible than the treatment of the Negroes in their own country, who have indeed much greater opportunities to improve their economic position and who, as domestic servants, are treated with more courtesy and consideration by their employers than the Indians of Latin America—a fact not unconnected with the shortage of domestic servants in the United States. Moreover, the treatment of Indians appears all the less justifiable to these visitors because Indians are not the object of discrimination throughout the greater part of North America.

Thus, comfortably blinkered by the assumptions of their own culture, each nation sees the mite in the other's eye.

In the United States one does sometimes find strong sentiments of hostility toward Indians in areas surrounding their communities; the same is sometimes true in Latin America of the Negroes (however they happen to be defined there). If Indians are not generally subject to discrimination in the United States nor Negroes in Latin America, it is in the first place due to their numerical weakness. In both countries, they pose local, not national, problems. There is roughly one Indian to fifty Negroes in the United States; in Latin America, the inverse disproportion would be greater even if one were to include only those recognized as Negro. Such a comparison can be taken no further than this, however, since the nature of social distinctions is different in the two lands.

The Indian's predicament in Latin America can be likened to that of the Negro in the United States in only one way: Both provide a major national problem at the present time. There the resemblance stops. Not only is the nature of race relations fundamentally different in the societies that evolved from the English and Spanish colonies, but Indians and Negroes are different in their physical appearance and cultural origins. They are different above all in their place within the structure of the two societies, and have been so from the very beginning of colonial times. The Indians were the original inhabitants of the land; their incorporation or their refusal to be incorporated into colonial society hinged on the existence of Indian communities with a separate culture and a separate identity. The Negroes came in servile status and were marketed as chattel to the industrialized producers of sugar and metals. Cut off from their fellows, they soon lost their language and their original culture and became an integral part of colonial society.[15]

The Negro's status was within colonial society. The Indian's was not. To the extent that the Indian abandoned his Indian community and changed his culture, he lost his Indian identity. While the status of Negro refers to phenotype and attaches to individuals, Indian status refers to culture and attaches to a collectivity. One might speak of individual versus collective status, with all that these imply in terms of social structure. Consequently, while phenotypical differences are irrelevant to the definition of the Indian—hence the *indio gringo*—they have importance in according an individual status once he becomes "civilized." They establish a presumption as to descent, and this is an ingredient of class status. Paradoxically, the genetic background is important only in social distinctions between persons who are recognized as belonging to the same "non-Indian" race; not in the distinction between them and the Indians. "Race" is a matter of culture and community, not of genes, though class is connected with genes.

The problems of race relations in North America and Latin America are, therefore, fundamentally different. One concerns the assimilation of all ethnic groups into a single society; the other, the status distinction between persons who have been assimilated for hundreds of years but who are still distinguished socially by their appearance. The two are comparable only at the highest level of abstraction. One may wonder, therefore, whether the word *caste*, which is so often used in reference to the status distinction between Indians and *mestizos* (or *ladinos*) in Latin American society is not something of a misnomer. It carries quite different implications in Latin as opposed to North America. It would appear that it comes into the sociological literature about Latin America on the basis of several different and all equally false assumptions which will be dealt with elsewhere.

While the value of color is somewhat similar within the Negro community of the United States and the Hispanic section of Latin America, the Negro community is separated by a *caste* distinction from a socially superior element defined by phenotype; the Hispanic population of Latin America is distinguished by language and customs, beliefs and values and habitat from an element it regards as inferior, which does not participate in the same social system and, for the most part, far from wishing to be integrated into it, desires only to be rid of the *mestizos* physically. For this reason, the aims of Indian rebellions are the opposite of the aims of race riots. The former would like to separate once and for all the two ethnic elements; the latter are inspired by the resentment at the existence of a separation. Indians rebel to drive the intruders out of the countryside; Negroes riot in towns when they are not accorded full civic privileges.

The ethnic statuses of modern Latin America vary in number from the simple division into Indian and *mestizo* found in Mexico north of the Isthmus to the four tiers of highland Peru which include *cholos* and *blancos*: (*indio, cholo, mestizo, blanco*). These "social races" have much in common with the class distinctions of stratified societies. Woodrow Borah has even maintained that the ethnic distinction in Mexico is no more in essence than a matter of social class. This view raises a further problem in those areas where a regional ethnic consciousness emerges, for example among the Tlascalans, Isthmus Zapotecs, and the wealthy, educated Indians of Quetzaltenango in Guatemala.

Admitting that the class structure of Latin America carries ethnic overtones, how is this structure affected by class differences being thought about largely in the idiom of "race"? Such a view implies that classes are different in their essential nature. If the concept of "social race" teaches us to think about race in terms of social structure, we should also have a concept of "ethnic class" to remind us that class systems no longer function in the same way once class has phenotypical associations. Processes of selection come into operation that cannot exist in a homogeneous population however it is stratified.

This observation leads to a conclusion that does not altogether accord with that of Professor Wagley[16] who states: "At least, theoretically, it is only a question of time until such populations may be entirely classed as mestizo by social race and social differentiation will be entirely in terms of socioeconomic classes."[17]

In terms of his thesis continued racial intermixture produces in Latin America, unlike North America, a blurring of the distinctions among different "social races." This would be true enough, if time could be trusted to produce phenotypical homogeneity, but it ceases to be so once one introduces the notion of selection into the theory. The absence of a bar on intermarriage does not necessarily produce homogeneity.

Distinctions of status are not always exhibited in the same ways. The castes of India are held apart by prohibitions on physical contact and commensality, and by endogamy. Feudal Europe accorded no importance to the first two and little to the third. The division of labor implied by any social distinction can bring people into either direct co-operation or segregation, depending upon the range of their ties and the basis of their "complementarity." If their status difference is assured in one way, it may prove indifferent to any other basis of distinction. For this reason the intimacy to which servants were admitted by their masters was greater in an earlier age when social distinctions were more clear-cut.

Physical differences can never be obliterated, but whether they, rather than cultural or social differences, are regarded as significant is a matter each social system decides for itself. It is for this reason that the value accorded to physical appearance varies so greatly from place to place and class to class in Latin America. But the significance of phenotype also varies greatly according to context. Political or commercial alliances are not the same as alliances through marriage. Their products are of a different order. Profits are colorless, children are not. Hence, phenotype may not matter in commercial dealings, but it is never more important than in marriage.

In Latin America today the grandchildren of a rich man who looks Indian or Negroid always appear much more European than he is himself. Color is an ingredient, not a determinant of class. It can, therefore, be traded for the other ingredients. It is not something that can be altered in the individual's life, but it is something that can be put right in the next generation. For this reason, the wives of the well-to-do tend to look more European than their husbands. In the lower classes, paler children are sometimes favored at the expense of their more swarthy siblings; their potential for social mobility is greater.

Individual motivations are ordered to produce conformity with an ideal image of ethnic class. This tends to reinforce the original image. Moreover, demographical factors reinforce this conformity in other ways—through the immigration of Europeans into Latin America and the existence of a pool of unassimilated Indians on the land. Indians are constantly abandoning their Indian identity and becoming integrated into the nation. This process is not unconnected with the current flight to the cities, for you lose Indian status once you settle in the city.[18] The result is a continual influx of persons of mainly Indian physique into the proletariat. At the same time, the immigration of Europeans into these countries has been very considerable in the last two decades, and these Europeans have almost all been absorbed into the upper classes. For demographic reasons, the correlation between class and color is increasing rather than diminishing.

Moreover, the significance of this correlation is also increasing under modern conditions. (It would be rash to say that it will go on increasing in the future, for the structure itself may well change to offset this effect.) The expansion of the open society at the expense of the local community changes the criteria whereby people are defined socially. Where known descent establishes status, color may carry little of the weight of social definition, but the descent must be known. It must be known whose child you are if you are to inherit the status of your father. If you have exchanged your local community for the big city, your descent becomes a matter of conjecture; you can no longer be respected because of your birth despite your Indian features. If you look Indian, it will be concluded that you were born of Indian parents. Thus, in the open society, appearance takes over the function of descent in allocating social status. In a world in flux, the fact that appearance cannot be dissimulated recommends it above all other indicators. Clothing, speech, and culture are losing force as indicators of status in the context of expanding cities, but color is becoming ever more crucial.

Although these same conditions might create an increase in social mobility that would tend to reduce the phenotypical correlation of class, it appears that the opposite is happening today. If the classification into social races is losing its precision, the ethnic aspect of class is coming to have increased importance. The social structure is changing and with it the criteria of social classification. Under modern industrial conditions, much of Latin America is moving from the systems of social race that flourished in the communities of yesterday to a system of ethnic class adapted to the requirements of the open society of tomorrow.

REFERENCES

1. There is also a celebration on that day in front of the memorial to Columbus.

2. Sociologists have recently asserted that social mobility is as great in the traditional societies of Europe as in the U. S., which pays homage to the ideal of social mobility. The anomaly is quite superficial: Nobody has ever acted in accordance with an ideal notion of this type. It provides not a rule of conduct but only a basis for validating an achieved position. It is as easy to claim to be a self-made man as to claim not to be. The former claim appears to be as often untrue in the contemporary U. S. as the latter was in Victorian England.

3. The desire of the European aristocracy to maintain endogamy required a man to be able to quarter his arms and thereby prove his noble descent in both lines for four generations. Class status was treated as if it were a matter of race, as the term *breeding* implied. But, in the absence of any phenotypical indications, the margins of doubt were very great, and genealogists were entrusted with the task, performed in simpler societies by the memories of the elders, of bringing history into line with present social relations. Only in Renaissance Spain, because of the Moorish and Jewish populations of the Peninsula, did purity of blood relate to any ethnic distinction. This distinction was a social and religious one rather than a matter of phenotype. In fact, the differences in color among the different religious communities appear to have been negligible. The Moslems were mainly of Berber stock and, as such, very similar to the Iberians, if somewhat darker than the descendants of the Visigoths. Contrary to what is often imagined, there was no "color problem" in ancient Spain.

4. Claude Lévi-Strauss, *Race et Histoire* (Paris, 1952), p. 5.

5. Charles Wagley, "On the Concept of Social Race in the Americas", *Actas del 33 Congreso Internacional de Americanistas* (San José, 1959). Reprinted in Dwight B. Heath and Richard N. Adams, eds., *Contemporary Cultures and Societies of Latin America* (New York, 1965).

6. Woodrow Borah, "Race and Class in Mexico," *Pacific Historical Review*, Vol. 23, No. 4 (November, 1954); Julian Pitt-Rivers, "Who Are the Indians," *Encounter* (September, 1965).

7. "In Latin America happily this racial distinction is not important and this is very much to Latin America's credit." Arnold Toynbee, *The Economy of the Western Hemisphere* (Oxford, 1962), p. 4. "Here is a country [Mexico] whose population is racially diversified yet is socially and culturally united. . . . I can only hope that the Latin American and Islamic freedom from race prejudice is the 'wave of the future.'" Arnold Toynbee, "The Racial Solution," *Encounter* (September, 1965), p. 31.

8. For example, Robert S. Browne, *Race Relations in International Affairs* (Washington, 1961), p. 22: "South and Central America have in some places developed veritable interracial societies." The qualification is vital.

9. Juan Comas reviews some of the more scholarly versions of the two views in "Relaciones inter-raciales en America Latina, 1940-60," *Cuadernos del Instituto de Historia, serie antropologica*, No. 12 (Mexico, 1961).

10. Paez, Morelos, and Alamán looked Negroid; Porfirio Díaz, Juarez, and Melgarejo looked Indian. This can be verified from contemporary evidence. In modern popular literature and schoolbooks they are sometimes quite literally "whitewashed."

11. G. and A. Reichel-Dolmatoff, *The People of Aritama* (Chicago, 1961), p. 138.

12. See, for example, Albert Sireau, *Terre d'angoisse et d'espérance* (Paris, 1959), p. 22.

13. The situation in Panamá, referred to above, is exceptional. It derives from the influx of a large number of persons of different language and culture. Some slight difference in style of speech is attributed to Negroes in certain regions.

14. The same is true in Ecuador. N. E. Whitten, *Class, Kinship and Power in an Ecuadorian Town* (Stanford, 1965), p. 91

15. This loss of language and culture does not hold for parts of the West Indies and Brazil. Aguirre Beltran maintains that elements of African culture have survived in Mexico. This is true in the case of certain details of material culture and musical style, though it might be more exact to call these Caribbean rather than African. In any case, they have long since ceased to be recognized as such. See, Aguirre Beltran, *Gonzalo: La Poblacion Negra de Mexico, 1519-1810* (Mexico, 1946), p. 96.

16. If I disagree with Professor Wagley ultimately with regard to the prospects

of the future (about which wise anthropologists refrain from speculating), I do not wish to obscure my debt to Professor Wagley's thinking on this subject nor to deny homage to his admirable essay. But I would not write about this subject at all if I did not think there remains something more to be said.

17. Wagley, "On the Concept of Social Race in the Americas," p. 540.

18. Only exceptionally, as in the Isthmus of Tehuantepec or Quetzaltenango, can a man become integrated while retaining an Indian (or is it a pseudo-Indian?) identity. Then region replaces community as the defining unit.

FLORESTAN FERNANDES

The Weight of the Past

BRAZIL LIVES simultaneously in a number of historico-social epochs. Some scenes recall the relations of the colonizers and conquerors with the natives; others abound in the turbulent activity of an industrial civilization with all the characteristics—both national and foreign—associated with it. Against this backdrop, ethnic or racial relations and the significance of color in human life manifest themselves in different ways. The Brazilian racial dilemma may be characterized most succinctly by the situation of the Negro or mulatto in the city of São Paulo. Although the percentage of Negroes and *métis* in São Paulo is among the lowest in the urban centers of Brazil, the city is significant for other reasons. On the one hand, it is situated in the last region in Brazil where slavery played a constructive role in the long cycle of economic prosperity that began with the production and export of coffee. On the other hand, it was the first Brazilian city that exposed the Negro and the mulatto to the vicissitudes of life that are characteristic of and unavoidable in a competitive economy in the process of expansion. It, therefore, permits one to analyze objectively and under almost ideal conditions why the old racial order did not disappear with the abolition and legal interdiction of the caste system, but spread out into the social structure that emerged with the expansion of free labor.

Racial Inequality and Social Stratification

The Brazilian racial dilemma, as seen from the example of São Paulo, has its origins in phenomena of social stratification. The major historico-social transformations that have taken place since the 1800's have benefited only the white population. Their world has been profoundly changed by the economic expansion and social progress that originated with the production and export of coffee and was afterwards linked to accelerated urbanization and industrialization. The world of the Negroes has remained essentially outside these socioeconomic processes.

The disintegration and the end of slavery did not immediately modify the relative positions of the racial groups in São Paulo's social structure. Legally the caste system was abolished; in practice, the Negro and the mulatto population did not rise above the social situation they had known earlier. Instead of entering *en masse* into the social classes that were in the process of formation and differentiation, they found themselves incorporated into "the plebs"—as if they were destined to become a class socially dependent and condemned to a disguised "caste condition." The asymmetric model of traditional social relations that assured white supremacy and Negro inferiority found in São Paulo the material and moral conditions to survive intact.

São Paulo's geographical and socioeconomic development is not typical of other Brazilian cities, for the latter owed their expansion to the early exploitation of slave labor. It was not until the last quarter of the nineteenth century that São Paulo underwent the changes that transformed it into a city comparable to the other urban agglomerations of Brazil. Only after coffee started being produced in the western part of the province and exported in increased quantities did São Paulo, in fact, cease being a rural area and begin to enjoy economic prosperity.

That São Paulo participated only belatedly in Brazil's colonial economy worked to the disadvantage of the Negro and *métis* population and the emancipated slave. The beginning of São Paulo's economic expansion coincided with the influx and concentration of an increasing number of immigrants of European origin and with a crisis in the system of slavery itself. Few Negroes and mulattos were able to take advantage of the facilities that would have been available to them under different circumstances and that would have permitted them to become artisans or merchants. With the abolition of slavery, they were drawn into the least desirable and low-yielding occupations, inasmuch as the most interesting occupations were taken over by and became the monopoly of the immigrants.

The movement on behalf of the abolition of slavery and the whole process of the disintegration of the system of slavery appeared—as was inevitable—to be a revolt of the whites against slavery and the seignorial order. These institutions interfered with the socioeconomic development of the prosperous regions of the country and stifled the expansion of capitalism. The abolitionist movement, even though seemingly inspired by humanitarian motives, marshaled in actuality against the impediment to social and economic interests that slavery represented.

The Negroes and the mulattos were merely an "object" and a "mass for maneuvering" in the revolt. They could give expression to neither their deep-seated aspirations nor their immediate needs. With rare exceptions, they were relegated to a secondary role. What may be termed the "abolitionist conscience" was more than anything else the patrimony of the whites. They led, organized, and, at the same time, contained the revolt within the limits defined by the preponderant race.

In the acute stage of transformation, the control of the process passed into the hands of the most conservative elements, who were anxious to take charge of the social, economic, and political interests of the large landholders. They not only refused to indemnify the landholders for the financial losses they had suffered as a result of abolition, but also totally ignored the problem of applying measures that would assure a minimum of protection to the slave or the freedman. They focused their principal effort on elaborating a policy that would guarantee the rapid replacement of slave manpower. At the close of the Empire and the beginning of the Republic, governmental policy was, consequently, directed primarily toward encouraging immigration by all possible means.

The Negroes took no active part in the "bourgeois revolution." Its development centered on two types of persons: the coffee producers and the immigrants. The sociological and economic position of the coffee producers underwent a vast change along with the economic growth stemming from the coffee trade and the expansion of the cities and towns. The immigrants tenaciously seized upon every opportunity in the new country and forced the Negroes out of the few worthwhile positions they had been able to obtain in the skilled trades and in small-business activities. The victims of a negative process of selection, the Negroes had to be satisfied with what came to be considered "Negro service"—uncertain and degrading work, as hard as it was badly paid. While prosperity favored all other elements of the population, they struggled with very great difficulties in holding—or even obtaining—the humblest and most undesirable positions.

The Negroes had not been prepared in advance—either as slaves or as freedmen—for the socioeconomic role of independent workers. They had neither the technical training nor the mentality and discipline of a wage earner. Having formerly had no status in the social order, the Negroes were unable to evaluate correctly the nature, obligations, and limitations of a work contract. They suspected that a labor contract was a trick intended to enforce slavery by other means. They felt that if a man sold his muscles and his work, he was selling himself.

Seeing and feeling themselves free, the Negroes wanted to be treated like men or, as they saw it, like those who were masters of their own lives. A fatal lack of adaptation on the part of the Negroes and mulattos resulted. The attitude and behavior of the ex-slaves, who conceived of their freedom as being absolute, irritated white employers. The Negroes assumed that since they were "free," they could work when and where they pleased. They tended not to show up for work whenever they had money enough on hand to live for a while without working; they especially did not like to be remonstrated with, warned, or reprimanded.

On the pretext that they were "free" and that "slavery was a thing of the past," they wanted a kind of independence entirely incompatible with any system of employed labor. This misunderstanding could, of course, have been gradually corrected. Since there was, however, a comparative abundance of labor owing to immigration, the employers were intolerant of the Negroes and mulattos. They did not attempt to understand them, considering them irresponsible and too difficult to handle outside slavery.

The abundance of qualified labor available as a result of intensive immigration led to a rapid change in the thinking and the attitude of employers, even in the choice of field workers. The Negroes had formerly been considered the only possible field labor, at least for the kind of work previously done by slaves. The employers had been comparatively tolerant of the Negroes' defects and had a real desire to help them improve as much as possible. As it became evident that the Negroes could be replaced—even quite easily in the more prosperous areas—and that the replacements were more intelligent and more efficient, this indulgence on the part of employers disappeared. The Negroes, consequently, passed without transition from the category of privileged workers to that of third-class laborers at the very same time that they were increasing their own demands and becoming more exacting. Almost automatically, they were relegated to the lower edge of the productive system—to undesirable, poorly paid, and socially degrading occupations.

Slavery had despoiled the Negroes of almost every vestige of their own cultural heritage. It allowed them only a very limited share in the social order. They developed their personality under the shadow of a slave or ex-slave status. Abolition thrust them into the "freeman's world" without the social and institutional resources that would have enabled them to adapt themselves to their new position in society. They were ignorant of, and thus could not practice, any form of organized life normally enjoyed by the white people—including family life and all forms of cooperation and mutual assistance based on the family. In order to make real use of his rights as a free man, it would have been necessary, first, for the Negro to shed his second nature—formed during the times when he was a slave or a recently freed slave—and to assimilate the social customs that constituted the white man's world. This lack of a definite sociocultural background was an insurmountable handicap for the Negroes who settled in São Paulo, a city whose rapid growth and great industrial development caused intensely keen competition among all classes and strata of the social order.

The Negro population became extremely mobile after the abolition of slavery. Negroes and mulattos migrating to the city found room as best they could by huddling into the caves and the overpopulated sections of the metropolis. Many Negroes, poorly adapted to city life, moved toward the interior of the state of São Paulo or toward the parts of Brazil where they had first lived, most often the northeast and the north. In general, the movements into and away from the city balanced one another, but there was a definite concentration of rural population in an urban area.

Ill-adapted to urban life by nature and lacking the mental or moral qualities necessary to earn wages and to meet economic competition, three quarters of the Negro and mulatto population lived in a hand-to-mouth way. They crowded into hovels—those caves cannot be called anything else—and there was actually not room enough for them all. The abandonment of children, the sick, and the old, unmarried mothers, alcoholism, homeless wandering, prostitution, occasional or organized crime—all these were the normal results of a human drama unprecedented in the sociological history of Brazil.

The only members of this population assured of earning a wage were the women, who could always find work as household servants. The women immediately became the support of the family groups. They provided the living either entirely or partially for the home, supplying the men with money for food and clothing and even for their minor expenses. The idleness of the men, at first due only to circumstances and endured as a kind of dignified protest, soon became transformed in many cases into an ill-disguised and sociopathic form of exploitation of one human being by another.

Under these conditions, the Negroes had nothing on which to base any hopes for the present or for the future. The future took on, in fact, a still more negative aspect because the white people looked upon this situation, and explained it, from a racial standpoint. Reading about these people in the newspapers or observing scenes of depravity, they accused the Negroes themselves of being responsible for their condition since they had no ambition, did not like to work, were naturally inclined toward crime, prostitution, and drunkenness, and incapable of controlling themselves without the domination of the white people. The tragedy of the Negroes' condition had little emotional effect upon the whites. They did not exercise any direct or indirect social control to improve that condition. The victims became, consequently, ever more degraded by common consent.

The Negroes and mulattos did not have any organized methods that would have enabled them to lift themselves out of that phase of degrading collective life. Nor could the city authorities do anything since they lacked social services comprehensive enough to solve such serious human problems. Demoralization went hand in hand with material degradation. The Negroes abandoned themselves to their fate with a feeling of profound frustration and an apathy they could not overcome. A defeatist state of mind took possession of them and made them think that "the Negro was born to suffer," "a Negro's life is like that," "there is no use trying to do anything about it." The only point on which the Negroes would not yield was on their stubborn desire to remain in the city.

No human group could support with total inertia a situation like that faced by the Negro and mulatto population in São Paulo. Before long, a few timid attempts to protest and to defend themselves began to appear and to grow in importance. These attempts became more substantial between 1925 and 1930 and began to bear their first fruits. A Negro press started a campaign to make the Negroes conscious of the racial situation in Brazil and of the "abandonment of the Negro." Organizations joined in the campaign to lend practical effectiveness to the "Negro protest." For the first time in the history of the city, Negroes and mulattos joined together to protect the economic, social, and cultural interests of the race. They sought to create forms of unity and of organized social activity that would result in the re-education of the Negro, the progressive increase of his earnings and his standard of living, his participation in the political activities of the community, and, consequently, the possibility of his becoming a real citizen according to all social standards.

These social movements succeeded, however, in attracting only a small fraction of the Negro and mulatto population of São Paulo. The Negroes' conformism, apathy, and dependence on white people prevented the successful conclusion of these attempts to affirm Negro independence. By exposing the dominant racial ideology, however, these movements set up a counter-ideology that enlarged the Negroes' zone of perception and consciousness of the racial reality in Brazil. Moreover, by stressing certain basic trends of equality, they encouraged the Negroes to wave the flag of racial democracy and to demand a fair share of the earnings, the standard of living, and the prerogatives of the other classes of the community. As these claims were manifested in a peaceful manner, they did not lead to any measures of racial segregation and did not provoke any tensions or racial conflicts. To that extent, they were constructive from the social point of view. They disseminated new ideas about the Negroes, gave a new dimension to their method of solving problems, and constituted an effort to assimilate the social methods and to profit by the economic facilities enjoyed by the white people. They answered exactly the requirements of the competitive economy and revealed themselves to be the only means by which the colored population of São Paulo was attempting to adapt itself collectively to the historico-social demands of the times.

These movements and the objectives toward which they were directed did not meet, however, with any constructive reaction on the part of the white people. The latter remained indifferent to them, raising a wall of incomprehension that deprived the movements of their practical effectiveness. Moreover, the more influential circles, with their traditionalist attitudes and judgments, considered the social movements arising from the Negro community to be a danger and a threat—as if it had been these movements that had introduced the racial problem into the country.

When the "New State" was set up, these movements were legally prohibited and the principal organization that appeared during this period, the Brazilian Negro Front, was suppressed. With the disappearance of the New State, between 1945 and 1948, there were some attempts to reorganize the protest. All failed completely because the Negroes who were reaching a higher level in society preferred a selfish and individualistic strategy for the resolution of the Negro problem. Lack of machinery for racial unity deprived the Negro community of the loyalty and altruistic support of the rare elements that arose from it. The contribution that the social movements could have made to the modernization of the traditional system of racial relations was repressed and nullified. The adaptation of that system to the historico-social situation prevalent in the city now depends, if no change takes place, on the slow and indirect effects of the gradual assimilation of Negroes and mulattos into the present social order.

In the period immediately following the abolition of slavery, the economic facilities of São Paulo were monopolized by the white people of the former dominant classes and by the immigrants. A census conducted in the city in 1893 clearly demonstrates this. Of 170 capitalists, 137 were Brazilians (80.5 per cent); 33, foreigners (19.4 per cent). Of 740 property owners, 509 were Brazilians (69 per cent); 231, foreigners (31 per cent). In certain of the leading professions that had traditionally been controlled by the local elite, there were few foreigners. This was the case, for example, with the judges and lawyers. In professions more closely connected to technical progress, foreigners appeared in significant proportions. There were, for example, 127 Brazilian engineers to 105 foreign; 23 Brazilian architects to 34 foreign; 10 Brazilian surveyors to 11 foreign; and 274 Brazilian teachers and professors to 129 foreign. Among those listed as "personnel of the industries," immigrants appeared to be the privileged workers.

Unlike the agricultural occupations, in which the native element predominated (1,673 Brazilians or 68 per cent as compared with 783 foreigners or 32 per cent), urbanization actually amounted in the other sectors to Europeanization, as shown by the following important examples: 5,878 natives (41.6 per cent) in domestic service against 8,226 foreigners (58.3 per cent); 774 natives (21 per cent) in manufacturing activities against 2,893 foreigners (79 per cent); 1,481 natives (14.4 per cent) in skilled trades or handicrafts against 8,760 foreigners (85.5 per cent); 1,988 natives (18.9 per cent) in transportation and affiliated occupations against 8,527 foreigners (81 per cent); 2,680 natives (28.3 per cent) in commercial activities against 6,776 foreigners (71.6 percent). The average for these activities shows that 71.2 per cent of the jobs were held by foreigners.

Since other sundry information shows that the participation of the Negro was very low in percentage, especially for skilled or semiskilled work, there is an indirect but very significant indication that the later economic development of the city corrected only negligibly the Negroes' economic participation. In fact, it was not until after 1935, with the intensification of internal migration, that the need for manual labor increased greatly the employment possibilities of the Negro and mulatto population. Even this change was more a matter of quantity than of quality. A larger number of Negroes succeeded in earning a living wage, although at the more unskilled and badly paid types of work.

A census taken in 1951 shows that the activities of Negroes were beginning to reach a level that could have existed at the time of abolition had it not been for the competition provided by the immigrants. Sample statistics, selected at random among men and women, show that 29 per cent of the Negroes and mulattos were working in skilled trades and 21 per cent were employed in domestic service. The following figures of the percentage of Negroes employed in specific activities give a clear idea of the situation: 9 per cent in public service, including principally ushers or court messengers, servants, and bookkeepers; 8 per cent in industry, mostly skilled or semiskilled work; 7 per cent in office work, including a small number as stenographer-typists, file clerks, and bookkeepers; 4 per cent in business, a few of them employed as salesmen or heads of sections. On the whole, the picture has changed, but not greatly. The Negroes, still in a very unprofitable situation in the scale of occupations, have little possibility to advance or improve themselves in the near future. In this connection, figures from the census of 1940 should be noted. By collecting only the most significant indications, the following table could be established:

Distribution According to Employment Situation of Men and Women,
Age 10 and Above—City of São Paulo—Census of 1940

Situation	Whites	Negroes	Mulattos	Orientals	Totals
Employer	15,261	51	72	342	15,726
	97.04%	0.32%	0.46%	2.17%	100%
Employed	323,997	15,114	10,925	2,317	352,353
	91.95%	4.28%	3.10%	0.66%	100%
Independent	74,448	2,051	1,595	1,577	79,671
	93.44%	2.57%	2.00%	1.98%	100%
Member of	4,644	80	56	565	5,345
Family	86.88%	1.50%	1.05%	10.57%	100%
Situation	4,393	356	325	44	5,118
Unknown	85.83%	6.96%	6.35%	0.86%	100%
Percentage of	1,203,111	63,546	45,136	14,074	1,326,261*
the Population	90.71%	4.79%	3.40%	1.06%	100%

* Including individuals whose color was not given.

In spite of the pessimistic conclusions that must be drawn from
these statistics on the whole, the changes that had taken place are
significant. The Negroes and the mulattos had succeeded in obtaining reliable sources of earnings, regardless of the employment
situation in which those earnings were obtained. This enabled
them to integrate themselves into the employment structure, creating, thereby, a situation favorable to the gradual acquisition of the
social techniques formerly the monopoly of the white people.
Moreover, the Negroes and the mulattos had simultaneously
reached a level, as regards the classification of occupations and
competition with the white man, that opened to them certain
possibilities of vertical mobility from the sociological standpoint.
"A part of the system," the Negroes and mulattos could struggle
to elevate themselves, to improve their position in the system. Although still not very strong, the colored elite or the colored middle class stood forth as a new reality and would have a chance to
increase continuously if socioeconomic conditions continued as they
were.

Prejudice and Discrimination in Racial Relations

Insofar as the integration of the white race into the system of
social relations is concerned, only the class system fully applies in

São Paulo. In the case of the Negroes and mulattos, however, both the caste and the class systems combine in variable forms. Archaic influences are always free to act and to cause them to live over again to a large extent a racial order that should no longer be more than a relic of the historic past. This configuration of the caste and class systems favors the persistence and, under some aspects, the renewal of the traditionalist and asymmetric model of racial relations. This model maintained itself practically intact in São Paulo until about 1930—that is, for a half century after the abolition of slavery. Even today one cannot say that the abolition is irreversible or that the old model is entirely obsolete. It still clings to the past in part and is continually strengthened by the extreme inequality in the economic situation and the social destiny of the two races.

The final disappearance of the old model of racial relations will not become historically concrete in São Paulo until the entire Negro and mulatto population reaches class situations equivalent to those enjoyed by the white population. The old model will not disappear until the competitive social order is freed in the economic, social, and cultural fields of the distortions that result from the tendency to concentrate income, social privilege, and power in the hands of a single race. Generally speaking, the Brazilian racial difficulty resides more in the lack of equilibrium between racial stratification and the current social order than in specific ethnocentric and irreducible influences.

Prejudice and discrimination appeared in Brazilian society as unavoidable consequences of slavery. The Catholic mores condemned the enslavement of man by man. They imposed upon the master, moreover, the fundamental obligation of providing the slave with religious instruction and faith, making slave and master equal before God. In order to escape or neutralize such obligations, the masters resorted to an extravagant sociocultural rationalization that converted slavery into an apparently pious and merciful relationship. The slave was assumed to be a brutish, pagan, and animal-like creature, dependent for his existence and survival upon the responsibility so generously assumed by his master. The condition of being a slave became inseparable from total degradation, both biologically and psychologically.

These rationalizations, so painfully demanded by the religious mores, were strongly reinforced by arguments borrowed from Roman law, which did not recognize the slave as having the status of a person and conferred almost unlimited power upon the master. Uniting these two tendencies, the prejudice against the Negroes and their descendants, the half-breeds or mulattos, took the form of a moral sanction from the social standpoint. A person's status was thought to be transmitted by the mother (*partus sequitur ventrem*). Racial marks or features played a secondary role in this context, since they merely served to show ostensibly, as if they were a stigmata, those who were in the degrading and infamous situation of having been a slave and later a freed slave. This prejudice became racial, however, by the contingency of the slaves' biological origins.

Discrimination, in its turn, was considered an institutional condition made especially necessary by the relations between master and slave, and by the corresponding social order. Since the basis of the distinction between master and slave rested upon the social situation (and consequently upon their respective positions), discrimination was established mainly as a means for the social separation of coexisting racial categories. It determined the relationship between master and slave living closely together. Words, gestures, clothing, housing, food, occupations, entertainment, ambitions, rights, and duties—everything was subjected to a process that transformed cohabitation and coexistence into total separation, rigid and irremediable, of the two social categories which were at the same time two different races.

Because the slaves formed the bulk of the population, a majority that could become dangerous and uncontrollable, they were rated as enemies of the public and private order. To keep slaves under the master's yoke, increased violence in repression, discipline, and control was considered necessary. The bodily substance of the slave was ignored as being part of a "person." It became an inflexible habit to put the slave in his place and to keep him there, to force him with violence or gentleness to obedience and passivity.

Prejudice in Brazil served to confer legitimacy upon morally outlawed behavior and institutions, while discrimination served to regulate the coexistence and cohabitation between the races by a truly inflexible code of ethics intended to maintain the economic, social, and cultural distance existing between master and slave. From their most distant origins, prejudice and discrimination had two aspects: one, structural and dynamically social; the other, racial. On the one hand, master and slave were in close relationship,

293

but opposed to each other as social categories. Both prejudice and discrimination were basically linked to the structure and operation of a caste society in which racial stratification corresponded to principles of economic and sociocultural integration in the social organization. On the other hand, the masters were of the white race, and, for the sake of their interests and their social values, they exercised a social domination that was at the same time a racial domination. This applied conversely to the slaves who were, by selection, Negroes or mulattos.

Social stratification presupposed, therefore, a racial stratification that it covered and concealed. Because the one was inherent in the other, the existence of a basic parallel between color and social situation could be admitted. The history of São Paulo illustrates the different and successive steps of this parallelism—from the final disintegration of the old system to the formation of a class society. Leaving aside the age of slavery, one faces three clear-cut periods. In the first, the transitional phase, the traditionalist and asymmetric model of racial relations remains unchanged. The second shows what occurred when the social rise of the Negro caused a break in the parallelism between color and the social situation. The third poses the question of the probability or improbability of this parallelism being incorporated into the class system, which would mean the absorption of racial inequality into an expanding competitive economy.

The first period can be illustrated by what happened in São Paulo between 1888, the date of the abolition of slavery, and 1930. Under living conditions that excluded the Negro and mulatto population almost entirely from the active economic life of the city, this population remained essentially in a status equivalent to that of the freedman or ex-slave in the slaveholding and seignorial social order. The traditionalist and asymmetric model of racial relations maintained itself almost completely in the new historico-social situation, as if the change in the legal status of the Negroes and mulattos were not to be reflected in their social prerogatives. The traditionalist model of racial relations was, however, not the only die-hard process. The entire social structure on which it was based, the racial ideology that gave it its meaning, and the social customs that it fulfilled remained intact.

These facts are truly significant from the sociological point of view. They bring out two essential truths. First, changes affecting the integrated model of the social order are not necessarily reflected directly, immediately, and deeply upon racial relations. Where traditionalism persists in Brazil, it is inevitable that the parallel between color and social situation should be more or less vigorously maintained, even if the human beings concerned deny that reality. Secondly, prejudice and racial discrimination do not appear as historical by-products of the legal chain of the social status of the Negro and the mulatto. On the contrary, the persistence of this prejudice and discrimination constitutes a phenomenon of cultural backwardness. The old social regime's attitudes, behavior, and values concerning racial relations are maintained in historico-social situations in which they are in open conflict with the economic, legal, and moral foundations of the prevailing social order. In this connection, the manifestations of racial prejudice and discrimination have to do neither with the competition or rivalry between Negroes and white people nor with the real or possible aggravation of racial tensions. They are the expression of mechanisms that actually perpetuate the past in the present; they represent the continuation of racial inequality as it prevailed under the old caste system. Wherever traditionalism remains intact in racial relations —even if the contrary tendency is announced—it implies a tacit survival of the parallelism between color and social situation.

The second phase deserves still greater attention. Under certain circumstances, Negroes and mulattos could emerge from their condition in the slaveholding and seignorial society. It was necessary, however, for them either to be incorporated into the legal nucleus of the white family that granted them its favor or to be accepted as the protégés of that family. In such a case the individual would to some extent lose his racial identity and acquire the social identity of the family to which he owed his freedom. It cannot be claimed, as many have thought, that an alternative of this kind amounted to a complete and definite correction of color by social situation. Although the sphere in which the colored person was accepted and could act in the white environment was sometimes quite large, he had to know how to keep up appearances, how to remain in his place, and how to practice toward his white benefactors a policy of sympathetic appeal and unconditional obedience.

These were cases of social upgrading that could actually be called social infiltration. By favoring a talented mulatto or a remarkable Negro, this process of social elevation deprived the colored population of its elite in a continuous and inexorable manner. Moreover, because it concerned only a small number of persons, this mechanism did not help to change the racial situation or to alter the white man's conception of the Negro. The individuals selected for their particular gifts were considered to be the exception that confirmed the rule. Their abilities did not benefit their race, but were thought to result from the influence or the psychobiological and social heritage of the whites. People would say in speaking of them: "He is a Negro with a white soul," "he is black only on the outside," "he is white on the inside," or "he doesn't seem to be a Negro at all." On the other hand, if they failed in any way or showed an unexpected weakness of any kind, people would say: "I told you so," "when a Negro doesn't mess things up on his way in, he will do it on his way out," "once a Negro, always a Negro," "what could you expect of a Negro?" The substantial possibilities for employment and increased earnings and for social elevation offered in a competitive economy—especially during the last twenty years—have, however, made it possible for many of the so-called colored elite or colored middle class to reclassify themselves socially without recourse to white patronage for vertical social mobility.

Confronted by the "New Negro," the white man finds himself in a confused and ambiguous position. The "New Negro" is already a relatively complicated human being. His mentality has adapted to the times and to city life. He is not afraid to compete freely with the white man, and, above all, he intends to succeed in life at all costs. Refusing to live with poor Negroes, he breaks the material bonds or the moral ties that united him and his original environment. He does not want to live on a low scale and does not respect the unity that would make the rich Negro a defenseless victim of his needy friends and relatives. He despises the careless Negro whom he considers the cause of the degradation of the race; he opposes social movements of a protest character, maintaining that these movements could stimulate illusions among the Negroes and animosity among the white people. He assimilates the white mentality, exaggerating and taking the white man as a model for his ambitions. He often practices a naïve but severe kind of puritanism that he thinks will protect him from criticism and purify him from any external cause of moral degradation. He deliberately cultivates refinement and amiability not only to tone down his attitude of self-assertion but also to express himself, his thinking, and his evaluation of human importance. Furthermore, he will not listen to any white people who attempt to put him in his place by applying the traditional model of race relations. If he yielded on this score, he would lose all gains he had so far achieved. The "New Negro" appears to be the chief human agent in modernizing racial relations in the city of São Paulo. He is, in fact, the active and constant expression of the rejection of the traditional manifestation of racial prejudice and discrimination.

Three essential conclusions can be derived from a study of the "New Negro." First, when the Negro breaks with the stereotyped conditions and the dissimilated proprieties of the past and gain a social position by his personal merits, his wealth, or his prestige, the polarization that served to camouflage the parallelism between color and social situation inevitably disappears. The lines of resistance to color itself then appear in comparatively clear-cut profile. Prejudice and racial discrimination are unmasked. Restrictions that seemed in a confused way to be linked to social situation manifest themselves in terms of color alone. Moreover, when the white man finds himself in competition with the Negro, he is finally obliged to resort, more or less openly, to attitudes and behavior that are incompatible with the tradition of dignity and to appeal to ethnocentrism or racial intolerance as a medium of self-defense.

Secondly, an opposite reaction is also clearly made manifest, although in an apparently more superficial and less prevalent form. White people who really believe in tolerance and equality seek to protect this "New Negro." They defend him against indirect pressure and encourage him to realize his ambitions. Their attitudes may be more or less ambiguous or insincere, and they may have a distorted concept of racial reality. Still, these white people do declare their hostility to the Pharisees of prejudice and racial discrimination in disguise. At the same time, they try to lend a helping hand to the deserving Negro, as they express it, even if they are not always successful. In this way, following the advent of the "New Negro" and as a result of the strength of his personality and his success, some sectors of the white population have committed themselves more deeply to a modernization of the existing standards and customs of racial relations.

A third aspect is that the Negroes themselves do not react in a uniform way to the success of the "New Negro." Friends and relatives on the same social level may be enthusiastic and offer sympathy and moral help, serving as a kind of sounding board and a source of encouragement to the Negro concerned. But evil tongues are often at work even in his own social environment. His pretensions and accomplishments are sneered at or ridiculed. Negroes, especially those of a lower social level, are just as apt to react to his achievement with resentment as with satisfaction. Success ultimately leads to social elevation, and that results in a break with his former circles. This is why relatives and friends are anxious and, by a strange reaction of affection, condemn those they love.

Aside from relations of personal character, success is pointed to with enthusiasm. The most prevalent feeling is that what one Negro can do, another Negro can also do. A kind of folklore is built about the Negro who makes his way in the world and who serves as an example to encourage others who have the same ambitions. Nevertheless, the heroes of this folklore abandon their old environment, isolate themselves from their origins, and endeavor laboriously to forge the prestige of the "good Negro" who has a social situation and who is "somebody." This more or less characteristic reaction separates the leading Negro figures from the environment of the great colored masses and induces them to ignore the vital importance of movement, which could succeed in accelerating the democratization of racial relations.

The third problem places before one an enigma. It is impossible to know how Brazilian racial relations will evolve in a distant future. It seems probable that dominant trends will lead to the establishment of an authentic racial democracy. In the immediate future, however, certain repeated events cause one to fear the success of these trends. A spontaneous socioeconomic development was the real cause of certain significant changes in Brazil. Up to the present time, this development has, however, obviously been insufficient to bring about an adaptation of the social order, inherited from the past, to the demands of the class society. In many social environments, there exists a very clear-cut tendency to accept and to practice old discriminatory procedures. Some people are afraid they will lose their social standing by "accepting the Negro"; others accept the Negro only under conventional circumstances and reject him when it is a question of a true friendship or communion of sentiments. Still others defend certain archaic positions at all costs and reject any possibility for the Negro to reach positions of management or leadership. Mixed marriages meet with almost insurmountable resistance as things now stand.

Facts of this kind show the danger that is beginning to appear. The concentration of income, social privilege, and power in the hands of one single race, the weakness of the efforts that could be capable of correcting the necessarily negative efforts of this concentration, and ethnocentric and discriminatory attitudes may facilitate the gradual absorption of the parallelism between color and social standing into the class system. There is no doubt about the existence of this threat. The worst aspect of it is that only a fully conscious and organized effort can successfully fight against it.

Under present conditions, it is very unlikely that this kind of reaction on the part of society could be definitely established. What is vital for the white sectors of the population is not the fate of racial democracy but the continuity and the rhythm of expansion of the competitive social order. Democracy at the political level does not even appear to them to constitute a problem. Negro and mulatto circles, for their part, do not possess the elements that would enable them to spread and generalize a state of mind necessary for a conscious, systematic, and organized defense of racial democracy. The poor sectors lack the appropriate means; the successful Negroes or "colored elite" either do not feel the necessity of this defense or do not consider it advantageous to compromise themselves for such objectives, which concern the future of the community rather than their own personal situation. Racial democracy is, consequently, abandoned to its fate without having any champions to defend it as an absolute value. If in the formation and spontaneous development of social classes racial inequality were confused with the inequality inherent in the competitive social order, racial democracy would then be fatally condemned and would continue to be nothing but a beautiful myth, as it is now.

Men and the societies they form do not always modernize themselves entirely. Archaic elements and factors sometimes continue to exist and to have an active effect long after their own historical period. They exercise negative influences on the development of personality, of culture, and of society itself. This seems to be the case with São Paulo, even though it is the most modern and the most highly developed city in Brazil. It is still held in the clutches of the past in the field of racial relations. It has plunged in an indecisive way into a period of transition that is being indefinitely prolonged, as if the Negroes had to wait for the spontaneous advent of a second abolition[1] in order to become the equals of the whites.

These aspects of reality raise two major problems. One concerns the kinds of men who "make history"—the social classes from which they arise, and the economic, social, or political interests and the concepts of ideology, nation, or race to which their leadership is applied. In São Paulo these men have been of very diverse social origins. They represent, respectively, the former privileged classes or their descendants, the immigrants or their descendants, and selected elements among the national migrating populations. All have had the same deeply rooted desire to enrich themselves, to achieve success, and to exercise power. For them, the ideal values of the competitive social order have had no charm. They have been content to make use of those values as a means of achieving their own success in a rational, rapid, and sure manner. They have "made history," but they have neither known nor cared about the people and their human problems. They have banished equity from their cultural horizon. They have had, therefore, no perspective from which to form an appreciation of the human tragedy of the Negro —or other tragedies just as poignant and as worthy of "history-making action." The Negro ceased to count in the process of discovery—as if he were excluded from the common social life. And, even worse, democracy, which constituted the legal and political foundation for the competitive economy and at the same time was its only means of moral control, actually ceased to be the source of inspiration for those who were "making history."

The other problem concerns modernization, particularly its repercussions in the field of racial relations. It is very difficult for modernization to reach balanced proportions and to be extended thoroughly to all levels of organized social life. Modernization goes hand in hand with the relative power and vitality of those groups that are interested in certain sociocultural changes. It progresses in accordance with their ability to establish these changes definitely in the course of history. Although the city of São Paulo underwent a rapid transformation in its urban physiognomy and in its economic organization, it remained more or less a prisoner of the past in other fields, including those of human relations and the development of its institutions. This is especially true of its racial relations, which have revealed themselves to be an astonishing and dangerous pool of stagnation.

In order to change this situation, the human groups directly concerned must become conscious of the situation and make an organized effort to change it—as has happened in other spheres of social life that have become rapidly modernized. The Negro himself must launch the initial challenge provoked by the Brazilian racial problem. He must achieve one immediate objective—a more

300

equitable share in the benefits of the competitive economy. He must strive for a long-term objective—the building of real racial democracy in the community. If he strives toward this goal, he will lead the white people of the various social classes to defend this cause, on which a balanced operation and development of the competitive economy largely depend.

In this perspective, the extent to which the modernization of racial relations is linked to the faculty of rationalization and to the capacity for social action of certain human groups can be better understood. So long as the Negro is limited by the racial ideology set up by the white people and governed only by the desire to "belong to the system"—that is, to identify himself as much as possible with the white people themselves—he will remain historically neutral. He thus becomes the principal victim of an invisible chain that results from the weight of the past. He becomes incapable of measuring up socially and positively to the demands of the present. He does not assert himself as strongly as he could in the shaping of his own future in humanity.[2]

REFERENCES

1. An expression found in the writings of racially nonconformist Negro intellectuals.

2. Interested readers will find in the following two works the empirical foundation and the interpretation of the sociological considerations developed herein, together with further bibliographical references to other publications on the subject: Roger Bastide and Florestan Fernandes, *Brancos e Negros em São Paulo* (Whites and Blacks in São Paulo; São Paulo, 1959); Florestan Fernandes, *A Integracao do Negro a Sociedade de Classes* (The Integration of the Negro in a Class Society: São Paulo, 1964).

DAVID LOWENTHAL

Race and Color in the West Indies

Myths and Realities

"NOTHING HAS ever really gone right in the West Indies in the half millennium since Christopher Columbus saw it. . . . No just or rational cause has ever really prospered there."[1] This condemnation stands in sharp contrast to the general American impression of that region. It was applied, in fact, only to the island of Hispaniola; but the gulf between scholarly analysis and public images is similar for all the islands. Oscar Lewis's *La Vida* characterizes Puerto Rican slum life as hell. But this exposé will alter few tourist stereotypes.

To Americans the Caribbean usually evokes ideas of colorful felicity. It is seen as a realm of tropical delight only occasionally troubled by social upheaval. The U. S. Marines and the resort hotel have exorcised or domesticated the ghosts of the Conquistadors, pirates, and slave traders. Of the massacres of Arawaks and the tortures of Africans no vestiges remain; the crack of the whip and the whish of the machete are drowned out by the thump of steel bands and the lilt of calypso.

Central to this image is the notion that West Indians enjoy harmony and practice tolerance among manifold races, colors, and creeds. In the outside world, Caribbean race relations are often termed exemplary. Local governments industriously promote this impression to attract foreign investments, to emphasize social progress, and to vaunt their achievements. Guyana, once the "Land of Six Peoples," now proclaims it is "One People, One Nation"; Trinidad's coat of arms reads "Together We Aspire, Together We Achieve," and the ruling party's slogan is, "All o' we is one"; Jamaica proclaims "Out of Many, One People," and the island's Five-Year Independence Plan insists that "racial integration, in our society, is not merely an ideal; . . . it is in fact a part of life."[2] "Nowhere in the

302

world," asserted Jamaica's premier in 1961, "has more progress been made in developing a nonracial society . . . in which color is not . . . psychologically significant."[3] Color is most emphatically denied by a West Indian journalist: "Long dead are the days, when the ruling class was white; the working class, the down-trodden the black. . . . The privileged class and the underprivileged class . . . are no longer separated by race, but by the distinction of their ability to better themselves."[4] Any instances of discrimination are apt to be blamed on visitors from abroad who "bring with them prejudices they acquired in societies less tolerant."[5]

By contrast with the rigidity of race relations in South Africa or the United States, those in the West Indies are indeed free and pleasant. But the rosy image of multiracial harmony has been challenged by a distressed and newly articulate lower class, by West Indian students, and by some popular leaders. "The myth of social and racial integration has been pretty nearly exploded," writes a young Jamaican nationalist. "The accepted passport to preferment seems to be a physical appearance as near to that of the average European as possible."[6] And a Guyanese finds "more race prejudice in the West Indies than anywhere in the world. . . .The Negroes hate the Indians, the dark-skinned people hate the light brown people. . . . They're hopeless."[7]

Local misgivings are confirmed by scholarly inquiries. A survey of race relationships in Martinique and Guadeloupe reports grave antagonisms between white entrepreneurs and colored laborers, local white interdiction against intermarriage, and racial categories that parallel those of class. A study of social stratification in Trinidad depicts a society little resembling the popular conception of easygoing, egalitarian interracial mingling. The light-colored elite and the black peasantry of Grenada are shown to inhabit worlds not remotely alike.[8] Studies of other islands reveal similar circumstances.

Nowhere in the West Indies does racial discrimination have the sanction of law, and social exclusion based on color, once the rule, is now much moderated. But color distinctions correlate with class differences and govern most personal associations. They are frequently voiced to derogate the darker among the people. Touring the Caribbean, a Trinidad-born novelist remarked "how deep in nearly every West Indian, high and low, were the prejudices of race; how often these prejudices were rooted in self-contempt; and how much important action they prompted."[9]

Recent events arouse the concern that in some respects West Indian race relations have actually deteriorated. In British Guiana, the riots and incendiarism of the past decade originated in racial fears and resentments. In Martinique, the immigration of Algerian whites touched off serious race riots. In Jamaica, the distress of slum dwellers explodes now in black nationalism, now in political-party violence, and now in assaults against Chinese shopkeepers who serve as scapegoats. Racial feelings are particularly inflamed where political independence and economic development benefit relatively few while throwing the misery of the many into sharper relief. "If there was justice and equality for us black people," argued a Jamaican, "there wouldn't be so many of us starving while white people in Stony Hill are feeding their dogs with beefsteak. . . . The white people's dogs live better than the black man in this country."[10] A political leader maintains: "The black man eats the least, wears the least, owns the least, prays the most, works the most, suffers the most and dies the most."[11] There is no doubting the truth of these propositions. Jamaica can still be summed up in the familiar lines, "If you white, you all right; if you brown, stick around; if you black, stand back."[12] The differences are less taken for granted than they used to be, but that makes them no easier to endure.

As the more blatant features of prejudice fade away, other aspects come to the fore. "The colour discrimination which still persists in this island is not of any real importance," a Barbadian editorial concludes, "but it is embarrassing."[13] Some Barbadian social clubs still exclude dark people, and the government itself was accused of bias at entertainments where, a black legislator complained, "you see a sprinkling of the population that looks like myself and then you see a whole mass of the [white] minority."[14] In Jamaica "there are still upper class whites who talk and think about damned niggers, and throw their children out of the house for marrying people with a touch of colour."[15] And an editorial contends that "many people in Jamaica still boast that they have never entertained a negroid person in their homes."[16] On the other hand, some insist that they have always been color-blind. "Now that racialism is under fire and in retreat," observes a Trinidadian, local whites "profess a lofty scorn for it and are terribly pained when you so much as refer to it."[17] Yet Negroes who try to practice the multiracial integration they preach may be "castigated as 'having a preference for mixing with white people.' "[18] It is not surprising that the former Chief Minister felt it necessary to explain that "Jamaica has a very complex . . . social structure which very few people understand. . . . We're only beginning to unify it."[19]

Finally there is isolation. Even in the smallest West Indian community, people of different colors may scarcely know one another.
Back home after a few years' absence, an old lady told me: "It was
sad to walk out in the street and not to recognize anyone. We
never met the colored people when we were children, and I never
did learn to distinguish between them." All she had learned was
their color. This is what many people still know best, however little
else they know about their neighbors.

Yet neither facts nor opinions about race and color in the West
Indies are easy to verify. Answers to direct questions are often misleading. Although a formal questionnaire indicated that color mattered little in Puerto Rico, off-the-record talks showed it was acutely
felt in personal relationships, especially among the middle and upper classes.[20] In the British, French, and Dutch islands even the
most informal and relaxed queries, if at all explicit, are answered
with cautious circumspection. As a West Indian friend warned me,
"West Indians like to say that color no longer matters to them. They
know very well that this is not true—though it is more true than it
used to be. But they will not like to admit it to an outsider or to
have it suggested to them by anyone else, particularly by an American." Even when posed by insiders, questions about color may meet
with hostility. "Why don't [you] leave it alone?" responded one
student a Jamaican interviewed on the subject. "That way people
would be less conscious of it and the problem would solve itself."[21]

A great many West Indians, in short, are highly sensitive about
matters of color. As one observer put it, to "talk about 'the colour
question' or 'race relations' is to pick a way through thorns while
walking on eggshells, as even the commonest adjectives of description appear to bear allusive barbs." But to ignore the subject is no
solution, for "too great a circumspection . . . may also arouse hostility."[22] A visitor found that "the mere mention of colour on the
part of the stranger is liable to put the average Guianese on the
defensive," while "the effort of avoiding pitfalls can result in a
stiltedness that may in itself be considered indirectly insulting."[23]

Some West Indians in fact regard the public airing of color
complaints as a sign that they matter less than before. Formerly,
writes a Jamaican, "you seldom if ever heard talk and protest about
this colour thing, . . . for when something is accepted—accepted so
deeply that to drag it up to the surface would be unbearably pain-

ful—nobody talks about it. . . . It's only when the pain gets less, when you see an end to it just round the corner, that you dare to drag it into the open and face it. That's why we talk about it endlessly in Jamaica today. For we are, today, nearer to beating it than anywhere else in the world."[24]

Historical Background

Race relations in the West Indies today seem especially benign by contrast with the past. Ethnic distinctions have mattered more and longer there than in any other part of the New World. A local leader terms it "the first area in the world which saw the emergence of this modern problem of race relations and the contact between the so-called 'advanced' and 'backward' peoples."[25] On Caribbean sugar estates, European masters exerted absolute control over the lives of African slaves and Asian indentured laborers. The impact of plantation slavery elsewhere in America, from Brazil to Maryland, was less pervasive. West Indian physical landscapes, social structures, and ways of life are in great measure plantation by-products. In order to raise sugar, "the flora, the fauna, the economy, and the people were all at various times imported into empty islands, and spread out there like butter on waiting slices of bread."[26]

Such conditions, especially Negro slavery, were most marked in the British, French, and Dutch West Indies, and my focus is principally on these non-Iberian realms. Here live twelve million people in fifty separate societies ranging in size from Haiti's five million to tiny islands of a few hundred. They include Jamaica, Trinidad and Tobago, and Barbados, which have gained independence from Britain within the past five years; a string of eight semidependent British colonies stretching from the Virgin Islands southward through the Leewards and the Windwards; the French islands of Martinique and Guadeloupe, which in 1948 ceased to be dependencies and became *départements*, integrated in theory but not assimilated in fact with the rest of France; six islands, headed by Curaçao, comprising the semiautonomous Netherlands Antilles; and a miscellaneous remnant—the American Virgin Islands, the Caymans (British), and San Andrés and Providencia (ruled by Colombia but inhabited by folk of Jamaican stock and English speech). Other islands in this Iberian sea are British Honduras in Central America, and in South America the three Guianas: Guyana, which gained independence from Britain in 1966; Surinam, associated with the Netherlands in the same fashion as the Netherlands Antilles; and French Guiana, like Martinique and Guadeloupe, a *département* of France. The Guianas have little contact with neighboring Brazil or Venezuela, but have histories and ethnic compositions similar to those of the Caribbean islands; they are in most ways that matter "West Indian."

Within the non-Iberian Caribbean there is contrast enough. But there are also certain basic similarities among these territories, styles of life that set them apart from Latin America. Spanish and Portuguese ideas and behavior about race, slavery, freedom, and equality differ sharply from those of other Europeans in the New World (though the differences have been exaggerated by apologists on both sides). Their ethnic histories are likewise different. Although Indian bondage was an important feature of colonial Latin America, slavery there seldom played the pervasive role that it did in the British, French, and Dutch islands, where African slaves preponderated. Where slaves were the largest element in the population, racial issues have been most dominant.

These lands have other common features significant for race relations. Because the Indians were early exterminated, the only enduring contacts have been among European, African, and Asian newcomers. Other countries have minority problems, but in the West Indies the "minority" is a numerical majority, and the whole flavor of affairs derives from that fact. Whites are a small and diminishing group, almost everywhere less than 5 per cent of the population; non-whites comprise more than nine tenths of the inhabitants of all but a few tiny islands. In other parts of the world where Europeans are few—West Africa, India, Southeast Asia—indigenous ways prevail. But in the West Indies there are practically no indigenes; the circumstances of slavery allowed little African culture to survive, and many inhabitants recognize no tradition other than the European. Most of the area has thrown off formal colonial rule but remains linked to London, Paris, and Amsterdam by political, economic, cultural, and emotional bonds. "Despite their new status," writes an observer in Trinidad, "history, to them, is still what happens elsewhere—in Europe or America. Never here."[27] That is the crux of the West Indian condition.

In the West Indies as nowhere else in the New World, Europeans met native Americans only to annihilate them—the Spanish "falling first upon their knees and then upon the Indians," other Europeans not even bothering with the first fall. Columbus and his fol-

lowers thought of little but gold. Because the islands failed to satisfy this obsession, they abandoned them. Their North European
successors outdid the Spanish in treating the islands only as the
sources of fortune and the seats of enterprise. Few thought of the
West Indies as home or forged any bonds between land and society. The ties between Spanish and Indian in Mexico and Peru,
the familial obligations of slaveholders on Latin American haci-
endas, had no Caribbean counterparts.

The Dutch, French, and English organized the islands as purely
commercial enterprises with greater energy and success than had
the Spanish. For gold, the North Europeans substituted sugar; for
Indian labor they substituted African. As with the Indians, it
seemed easier to work Negroes hard and replace them with newly-
bought slaves than to look after them and encourage them to re-
produce. The Negro was a replaceable machine.

The European also was a machine, a machine for making money.
The wealthy West Indian planter was a stock figure of the
eighteenth century, but the money he made flowed back to London,
Paris, and Amsterdam. The West Indian "Great House" was great
only by contrast with the slave huts and barracks; Europeans
thought them bleak barns, barely adorned and poorly furnished.
Many affluent estate owners never set foot on the islands. Those who
did well there lost no time returning to Europe. In the West Indies
they rarely cultivated the art of living, as opposed to gaining a livelihood. For Europeans, the islands existed only to be exploited.
Government officials, lawyers, doctors, and clergy appointed to
West Indian posts regularly farmed them out to substitutes.

Because the islands were seldom considered fit to live in, most
of them failed to develop a true elite. "In British West Indian . . . society," a local historian writes, "a man became a member of the
élite only when he qualified as a potential absentee. . . . 'Colonial
élite' was a contradiction in terms [to men] . . . whose means permitted them to be élite rather than colonial."[28] No wonder colonial
officials complained about the inadequacies of resident West Indian
whites. Except for Barbados and, perhaps, Martinique, most men of
intelligence and enterprise had gone "home"; those who remained
had no qualifications but their white skins. Educated colored men
were barred from the elite first by law and later by prejudice. Many
West Indian societies were, in effect, truncated structures. Their
natural leaders were either in Europe or proscribed by color. They
were dominated, instead, by European castoffs and remittance men

concerned only to maintain an oligarchy that was their sole compensation for exile.

The elite steadily withdrew its stake as well as itself. After four generations on the island of Nevis, the Pinney family sold out to resume their place in England "as if they had never been out of the county."[29] But "seen through West Indian eyes, against the background of the derelict island today, it is as if they had never been in Nevis."[30] Whites who did stay on gradually withdrew into endogamous isolation. In the seventeenth century white Barbadians proudly defied imperial rule. Today a Barbadian writes me: "We whites are all dreading the very thought of independence. Ah well, this has been brought by the lack of interest that the white people have shown in the island for years."

Whites long considered themselves the only inhabitants of the West Indies. Even those who baptized, punished, or slept with their slaves viewed them as property, not as people. To be sure, the conditions of slavery and the treatment of slaves varied with the nationality and religion of their owners, the nature of the economy, and the numerical balance between slave and free, black and white. Thus the Dutch were reputed crueler slavemasters than the French, the Protestants than the Catholics, sugar planters more demanding than coffee growers, and so on. But these differences were neither substantial nor consistent; the lot of West Indian slaves was everywhere much alike. In terms of work routine, nourishment, confinement, and punishment they were worse off than any others in the New World. It was considered a condign punishment to be sent there; George Washington sold a slave to the West Indies because "this fellow is both a rogue and a runaway."[31] The paucity of whites made repression more savage than in Brazil or in the American South.

The West Indian sugar plantation used up slaves at a rapid rate; only continual imports from Africa could meet the planters' needs for labor. In addition to deaths on the Middle Passage, slave mortality in the West Indies probably approached 20 per cent a year. About five million Africans were brought to the British, French, and Dutch Caribbean; yet in the mid-nineteenth century, when slavery ended, the Negro population there was less than two million.[32]

Between the millions of slaves and the dwindling thousands of whites, a third class came to occupy an increasingly prominent position. This was the "free colored" group—manumitted slaves who were often the offspring of white men and slave women, or their descendants. At the end of the eighteenth century the free colored comprised from 5 to 20 per cent of various West Indian populations; by the time of emancipation they outnumbered the whites.

The free colored were distinguished from the slaves not only by freedom but by color. Most of them were free, in fact, because their fathers or grandfathers had been white. They were by and large intermediate in shade—mulatto, quadroon, octoroon, and other gradations between white and black. Many free persons were black, and many slaves were colored, but the preponderance of mulattoes among free non-whites and of blacks among slaves shaped a shorthand view that lumped all free persons together as "colored" and all slaves as "black." Most important, whites recognized the free colored as superior both to slaves and to free blacks, and gave them privileges according to their shade. Within the free-colored group itself, rank and privilege largely depended on closeness to white features and ancestors.[33]

Like colored West Indians, many light-colored Americans felt themselves superior to Negroes, but they failed to establish their identity as a separate group in the social hierarchy. American Negroes who came into contact with West Indian color stratification were struck by the difference. Many features help to explain it. In the West Indies the free colored took occupations vacated by whites, whereas in the United States the two competed for jobs. West Indian slaves so greatly outnumbered whites that the latter viewed free-colored people as allies in case of slave insurrection— indeed, many of the free colored were slaveholders. In the United States, where whites were everywhere numerous, colored men were seen more as leaders of slave revolt than as buffers against it.

Sexual relationships between white men and colored and black women in the West Indies, especially where white women were few, were openly countenanced; whites customarily had colored mistresses, white fathers regularly placed their colored daughters as concubines, and few colored girls were available for marriage with colored men. White fathers not only recognized their colored children, but often educated them in Europe and left them large properties. In the American South, by contrast, relationships between white men and colored women were usually clandestine.

Greater familiarity with colored people led West Indian whites to make fine color distinctions that seemed pointless to Americans, who lumped all folk of African descent together as Negroes. Moreover, being Europeans, white West Indians took a stratified social order for granted and regarded the separate identity of the free colored as a means of consolidating their own control over the hierarchy. In the United States, on the contrary, egalitarian ideals made the existence of free-colored people an embarrassment even to whites who disliked slavery; Americans tended to regard Negroes, whether slave or free, black or colored, as equally inferior.

The balance among the three elements of West Indian society was strained, however, as the free-colored group grew in numbers and affluence. In Saint-Domingue, rivalry between the free colored and white immigrants from France was so bitter in the late-eighteenth century that both groups ignored warnings of slave revolt and were overwhelmed by it. In the British and Dutch territories, barriers between white and colored remained high; up to the eve of emancipation, law as well as custom discriminated against the free colored. A small racial minority exercised absolute power over social institutions that everywhere discriminated against all non-whites.

Yet within two generations race and color virtually vanished in the eyes of the law. Between the Haitian revolution of 1791 and the emancipation of 1863 in Surinam, all West Indian slaves (outside the Spanish islands) were freed and all legal disabilities against non-whites eliminated. The transition took place in various ways and at various tempos. In Haiti, where slaves and free colored had suffered the most galling restrictions, the revolution reversed the hierarchy; surviving whites were forbidden to own land and mulattoes were penalized by blacks. The British West Indian transition was more orderly, slave-law reforms leading to free-colored civil rights, ex-slave apprenticeship, and final emancipation between 1823 and 1838. Suffrage was limited on the basis of property, not race; juries no longer excluded black and colored men; schools were open, at least in theory, to all. A pure European background remained the best road to colonial fortune, but governments no longer systematically denied advancement to colored people. And if whites still barred others from their doors and their daughters and their clubs, they mingled with them freely in the market place and the local legislature, linked by a community of interests.

Nevertheless formal freedom availed most West Indians little in the face of customary discrimination. Indeed, emancipation intensified color prejudice. In the absence of slavery, race assumed paramount importance in social issues. Even the most zealous emancipationists had not expected the freed slaves to gain early

311

equality with their former masters. Failure to create an instant utopià and the supposed decline of the West Indian economy were cited as evidence of Negro inferiority, unfitness for self-rule, and hereditary ineducability. West Indian whites, still in local control, reduced the scope of Negro freedom by means of vagrancy laws, by coercive rental and wage arrangements that tied tenancies to plantation duties, and by state-subsidized indentured immigration that kept estate wages low.

"A race has been freed, but a society has not been formed," a colonial official reminded Britain in 1848.[34] For most Englishmen, however, West Indian "society" did not include the freed slaves. The English congratulated themselves on their magnanimity in paying slaveholders twenty million pounds sterling for their property. And they allotted less than 1 per cent of that sum for educating former slaves to take roles as men in a free society. "Is education what going to release this village, this island, from the tyrannies o' slavery," remarks a Barbadian in a novel. "But slavery abolished, long time!" says a friend. "One kind they abolish, but they forget to abolish the next kind."[35]

In every West Indian territory, emancipation conferred political equality; in every territory, equality was a legal fiction. Universal suffrage in the French Antilles became meaningless when centralization in Paris deprived local councils of all power. In the British islands there was no thought of a broad suffrage. Whites controlled local legislatures with a handful of "qualified"—that is, rich, educated, and well-connected—men of color; non-whites occupied only a few subordinate governmental niches. The spectre of Haiti and the conviction that Negroes were inferior reinforced white reluctance to yield any power or perquisites.

To protect West Indian Negroes against local white oligarchies, a Crown Colony system replaced most elected legislatures in the late-nineteenth century. But this was also an instrument to assure continued white control, and thus to counteract the constant decline of local white populations. Given their numbers, nothing in the law could prevent men of African descent from coming to rule, as Froude gloomily foresaw in the 1880's.[36] Under Crown Colony government, however, colored officeholders were substantially reduced in numbers; in the absence of local whites, Europeans were appointed, long after qualified colored men were available. Not until after World War II did the British West Indies advance to universal adult suffrage and internal self-rule.

In West Indian economic and social life, color until recently played almost as great a role as it had during slavery. Where sugar estates provided the only possible livelihood, as in Barbados, the Leewards, and Martinique, the former slaves remained in close subordination to a managerial elite. "When I woke up after the drunken joy of finding myself free," a Martiniquan is imagined as saying, "the hard reality that stared me in the face was that nothing had changed either for me or for my friends who'd been in chains with me. . . . The *békés* [white Creoles] still owned the land, all the land in the place, and we went right on working for them as before."[37] Where there were only a few resident whites, as in the Windwards, light-colored folk assumed the roles—and the behavior —of the whites. And where ex-slaves found ways to make a living off the estates, as in Jamaica, the Windwards, and Guiana, the physical segregation of black and white diminished daily contacts between the races. As a Jamaican summarizes the process: "The black Jamaicans tended to withdraw from the estates and to found the free peasant communities . . . ; the brown Jamaicans tended to consolidate their positions as a professional-commercial class based on the towns; the whites either abandoned the island altogether or tried [to] maintain a separate social existence." As social contacts diminished, cultural differences became accentuated, and "there persisted among the peasantry an obscure and separate development of . . . patterns of behavior and belief, art, and . . . religion."[38]

The Plural Society

Most social systems are held together by general consensus based on a widespread community of interests. But where a dominant minority and a subordinate majority have opposing interests and modes of life, the social structure is validated not by consensus but by force. This kind of society, frequently resulting from the European conquest, enslavement, or introduction of "native" populations, has been termed "plural."

West Indian slave societies were based on force, openly avowed by the slaveowners and governments and more or less resisted by the slaves. After emancipation, a few whites, many of the colored middle class, and some of the former slaves worked to build a society based on consensus and social integration. Such a society nowhere came to pass. The elite minority retained its predominance and, with imperial support, preserved the old distinctions—based now on color rather than on servitude. The colored middle class helped to sustain this hierarchy just as their forebears had during slavery. "The black race is separated from its natural leaders and remains . . . a contented and helpless mass," wrote an admiring American scholar. "The mulatto, . . . flattered by a racial designation that separates him from the peasantry and implies his superiority to it, maintains [an] . . . obsequious and respectful attitude of mind toward his superiors."[39]

The plural structure was not effectively challenged until the middle of this century. The masses endured it as preferable to a more naked display of coercion. And the middle class accepted it because it secured them against the lower and provided for a modest rate of infiltration into the upper. The modes of life, systems of belief, and springs of action of the three sections of society, especially those of the elite and the majority, remained as far apart—if not farther—than during slavery.

West Indian society is still a hierarchy of sections differing profoundly in institutional forms and behavior, culture and values. In some Caribbean lands—Trinidad, Guyana, Surinam—the presence of descendants of East Indian indentured laborers creates a still more complex and divisive situation. But almost every West Indian territory is dominated by a small white or light-colored group whose way of life is both the unattainable envy and the dreadful burden of the predominantly black majority. A growing middle class awkwardly amalgamates traits and institutions from above and below. Middle-class obsession with status based on color emphasizes sectional discontinuities and keeps the whole structure precariously balanced. Brute force and punitive repression figure less as agencies of social cohesion than they did during slavery. But gulfs in living standards and opportunities persist, and some of them are broader than they were. Political independence and declarations of racial unity notwithstanding, pluralism in many West Indian societies shows no sign of disappearing.[40]

In most respects the West Indian social order correlates with color differences, but the pattern of ranking is not everywhere the same. The plural structure has no relevance in a few islands that are racially homogeneous, and color plays little part in considerations of status on French St. Barthélemy (almost entirely white) and on British Carriacou and Barbuda (almost entirely black).

Where black, colored, and white persons coexist, their relations differ from place to place. In the French Antilles, local-born whites remain a virtually self-contained and endogamous group, excluding most French metropolitans from the elite. Black, colored, and white on small islands like Bequia, Saba, and the Saintes form segregated communities rather than ranked sections of one society. The poor whites of Barbados, St. Vincent, and Guadeloupe, the descendants of German settlers in Jamaica, and the St. Barts French on St. Thomas are not part of the elite but are close in culture and status to the black peasantry. The elite in Haiti, Dominica, Grenada, and St. Lucia is no longer white but light-colored. The colored middle class is attenuated in Guadeloupe, Montserrat, and St. Kitts. In newly independent Jamaica and Barbados whites have lost some perquisites, while in Haiti mulattoes are harassed by blacks.

The tripartite association of color with status nevertheless remains a fundamental fact of most West Indian societies. The upper section contains from 2 to 5 per cent of the population, the middle from 5 to 15 per cent, and the lower the remainder. The upper and middle groups—that is, white and colored—have many institutions in common and sometimes unite in opposing the black masses, but their springs of action and self-images differ. The top section practices a somewhat outdated variant of Western European culture and is locally regarded as the authoritative guide to that culture. The black majority's culture amalgamates elements derived from earlier European forms with some African features, filtered through the context of slavery. The middle section combines elements of both the others, usually as uneasy alternatives rather than in a viable integrated form.

Unlike as the sections are in culture and institutions, their evaluations of status and prestige are similar; almost everyone would like to be as European as possible. Basic disparities are apt to be masked by this apparent agreement. Each section professes loyalty to some national or imperial symbol, avoids manual labor, and accepts marriage as an ideal, but this coincidence of values does not show that they share a common way of life; rather, each strives to emulate the elite and discredits its own circumstances and habits. Shared values are an added source of tension because these values are beyond the reach of most West Indians.

The fact that the elite and the middle class do not want to know anything about folk culture accentuates sectional segregation. To the educated West Indian—especially if his own origins are lower class—folk beliefs are highly repugnant because they remind him of aspects of life he has been trained to avoid. Only in the past decade have elements of folk culture become respectable as national symbols. And the middle class still prefers third-rate Shakespeare to first-rate local drama, requires steel bands to play classical music, and disdains "Creole" cultural performances as fabrications for tourist consumption—as, indeed, they sometimes are.[41]

Middle-class people often profess to be more ignorant of lower-class ways than they really think they are. Those who in their homes regularly speak the local Creole or patois variant of standard English and French are apt to deny that they can even understand it,[42] and then go on to revile it as a vulgar and debasing tongue. Turning their backs on folk ways of life, as a linguist put it, "they will not talk to their own people in their own language but wish only to remain aloof in a middle-class suburb."[43]

Elite and middle-class West Indians are in daily contact with domestic servants, gardeners, and other employees. But they remain extraordinarily ignorant of the circumstances of lower-class life— which helps to explain why agricultural-extension and social-welfare work is so often ineffectual. Rural cultivators are unlikely to adopt reforms advocated by visitors whose doctrinaire theories, brown skins, and city clothing highlight their lack of local understanding and insight.[44] Just how far the classes are insulated from one another became clear in the late 1950's when the Jamaica Family Life Project hired middle-class Kingston ladies to ascertain peasant attitudes toward birth control and family size. In some country districts, project directors noted, "the advent of the middle-class Jamaican 'lady' was about as unusual as the arrival of an anthropologist to a pre-literate community." Interviewers nearly lost their lives in one community where local people misinterpreted their promises of secrecy as threats of witchcraft, and "consequently banded together and plotted the demise of the witches."[45]

The misunderstanding was mutual. Many interviewers knew so little about the countryside that they sallied forth in city shoes to communities accessible only by mule track. When they reached their destinations, they could scarcely believe that humans actually lived there. "I was very upset after this interview as the house was filthy," wrote one lady. "The mattress was stuffed with banana trash which almost suffocated me with the smell of urine. The bed was covered with flies." Crowding, dirt, and abject poverty were disturbing novelties to middle-class interviewers, who had come face to face with a class of people they had not realized existed in Jamaica.[46]

What the sections of society do know about others they usually disapprove of. Each class uses moral dogmas to justify its images. Because these dogmas are mutually incompatible, each group condemns the behavior and attitudes of the others. Thus West Indians tend to "moralize incessantly about one another's actions in order to assert their cultural and social identity."[47] The language is not didactic but censorious; no one really wants other classes to become like one's own.

Legal institutions illustrate how mutual ignorance and moral judgments reinforce West Indian sectional differences. Despite universal suffrage, the chief law-making and law-enforcing agencies reflect elite social views. One is that the lower class is innately criminal. The belief is self-fulfilling for much of the local criminal code and police action is directed against practices that are defined as criminal but are in fact customary—bastardy, praedial larceny, obscenity, obeah, marijuana. The masses see formal law as a class weapon and policemen as their natural enemies; the elite expect preferential police treatment as a matter of course. In the courts, a laborer is gravely disadvantaged by illiteracy and unfamiliarity with the law. Lack of money makes legal aid hard to get, even should he overcome his suspicion of lawyers as representatives of the elite. No wonder many people regard the law as "an alien thing, not felt as applying to their daily life because there are so many basic points at which it runs counter to their habits of thought."[48]

Religious differences further illustrate how sectional hostilities operate. Planters, European officials, and the established churches have tried since the inception of slavery to eradicate voodoo and obeah; they reprobate lower-class revivalist and pentecostal sects as the heathen, African, diabolical superstitions of unlettered savages. The middle class, emphasizing its respectability and its remoteness from African superstition, has led the campaign. Any organized slave activity was potentially seditious; any mass gathering today arouses the fears of the well-off. Response to the Ras Tafari movement in Jamaica is a case in point; wholly ignorant of the aims and creeds of this "back-to-Africa" sect, the elite and the middle class saw it only as evidence of the depravity and criminal intent of the threatening masses.[49]

Family forms exemplify the complexity of West Indian social structure and attitudes. The three sections share an ideal of married monogamy, but each approaches this ideal by a different route.

317

Many working-class West Indians feel that a man ought not to marry until he can afford to build or buy his own house, pay for an elaborate wedding celebration, and support a wife without her going out to work. Such responsibilities cannot ordinarily be met until late in life (nor do young women relish giving up their freedom). Marriage is, therefore, a consummation rather than a commencement; a couple may marry to celebrate the birth of a first grandchild. Although two out of three children in the West Indies are born out of wedlock, most people do eventually marry; four out of five British West Indians aged sixty-five or over are or have been married.[50] Thus although marriage is ultimately desirable, illegitimacy carries little stigma among the folk. But the middle class regards the high rate of illegitimacy as shameful and wicked, proof of promiscuity and immorality. Blaming the lower class for the image of colored West Indians they think Europeans have adopted, middle-class people denounce non-legal unions to show their disapproval of "African" and their loyalty to "European" forms.

The social gradient is steep, and most West Indians find the barriers difficult to cross. The very fact that people do contrast their own lot with that of others, and react bitterly to the discrepancies, evinces a community of discourse. And the minority position of the elite makes it impossible for them entirely to ignore the demands of the majority. Besides this connection, there is a color-class continuum; the social hierarchy is knit together by intermarriage, by acculturation, by assimilation.

Each territory has its own style of consensus. In Grenada, Dominica, St. Lucia, and Trinidad, despite profound cultural differences between peasant and elite, color tolerance facilitates easy contact in a wide range of milieus. In Barbados, color-consciousness and class barriers inhibit social contact, but society is bound together by common cultural features and modes of behavior, and by a parochial pride that pervades the entire community.[51] Such linkages, however, also emphasize the gulf between aspiration and reality. Law and medicine are the first occupational choices of almost all Jamaican schoolchildren and of their parents for them; practically no one chooses farming, the principal source of livelihood for the great majority. West Indian society fosters expectations among the majority that are in most cases doomed to disappointment. There is little room at the top and what room there is is largely monopolized by the existing elite.[52]

At the top, pluralism has positive utility. The successful civil servant adopts elite behavior and then maximizes class distinctions; the successful politician, whatever his origins, identifies himself with the subordinate sector and wins popular favor by stressing the exploitation it has suffered. West Indian societies perpetuate pluralism by encouraging sectional leadership. Struggles for power between popularly-elected rulers and an appointed civil service highlight the absence of consensus.

There is little evidence that the upper classes are anxious to reform this state of affairs or to be less isolated from the masses. Nor are sectional differences becoming less extreme. In 1961 Jamaicans learned that while the economy as a whole was expanding, the gap between the "haves" and the "have-nots" was growing too. Awareness of these discrepancies has also increased. The visibly impoverished are ever more numerous; the Kingston slums held 39,000 in 1958, 60,000 in 1960, perhaps 80,000 in 1964. As a Jamaican premier described the situation, "more and more jobs are being created at good pay. . . . There is more money, a greater growth of the economy. But there are thousands of people whom it does not touch. And the more they see . . . the more they ask themselves the question: 'What about little me? What about little me?' "[53]

The Dimensions of Color

Race and color do not define West Indian classes. But class grievances are mainly expressed in terms of race and color. The degree of significance varies with class. The elite take their ascription as whites for granted; color is an overt issue among them only in gross transgressions of the social code. Nor is color *per se* overwhelmingly important in lower-class communities; the interest in identifying ancestral strains focuses on lines of descent, not degrees of whiteness.[54] But in the middle class color is the crucial determinant of status, and status is the main goal in life. The degree of preoccupation is suggested in the legendary remark that "one used to be able to go to Government House and be sure that one would meet no one there who was darker than oneself." Now that black men are Governors as well as guests, some members of the middle class stay away and contemplate their light-skinned status in the seclusion of their own homes. But because the middle class articulates most inter-class contacts, such relationships are generally suffused with color-consciousness.

Physiognomy is only one of many ways of perceiving color, which West Indians rank according to appearance, ancestry, and asso-

319

ciation. Where ancestry is a matter of common knowledge, as it is apt to be in small islands, genotype may be more important than phenotype. In Grenada, for example, genealogy is a truer indicator of class than is physiognomy.[55] In territories with a less rigid hierarchy or a larger elite, birth may count for relatively less. Color also depends on the company one keeps. "I don't like too many dark people around me," the working-class Trinidadian will say, and "I want somebody [to be with] to lighten up my complexion."[56]

In the final analysis, color is a matter of culture. Whatever their actual appearance, middle-class folk tend to be considered and to view themselves as "colored," while lower-class folk are "black." The adage "every rich Negro is a mulatto, every poor mulatto is a Negro" fits West Indian society today as in the past. Family background, wealth, and education make the distinctions between "colored" and "white" almost as flexible. Many West Indians known to have colored forebears are locally accepted as white. In St. Vincent, for example, "even plainly negro folk by virtue of the mixing with the Whites in clubs and organisations are counted as pass-for Whites, or Vincentian Whites."[57] In the United States, by contrast, there is no breach in the classification for anyone known to be of even remotely African origins.

Other variables notwithstanding, appearance is far more significant in West Indian life than it is, say, in Great Britain. British differences in height, hair, and facial structure are associated with being Welsh or Scottish or upper class, but the hierarchical implications of these features are slight. To West Indians, on the contrary, attributions based on physical differences stand in the way of social unity.

Physical "color" in the West Indies is not a matter of skin pigmentation alone; it involves a constellation of traits that differentiate European and African. The most important, besides shade, are hair texture and facial structure. These three aspects of physiognomy are almost invariably combined in color attributions. Straight or wavy hair helps to make up for a dark skin; "a dark person with 'good' hair and features ranks above a fair person with 'bad' hair and features," maintains a Jamaican sociologist, but European features count for more than straight hair.[58] These features matter at every social level. Among Guyanese villagers an anthropologist finds "the tendency to see beauty in a straight nose, a skin a shade lighter, or hair which is less 'kinky' or 'hard,' [and] mothers even pull their children's noses to make them longer."[59]

Only a generation ago, an American scholar noted that West Indians were "less inclined to undertake the impossible in trying to change their features with hair straightening and bleaching processes" than were American Negroes. This was not because "the black West Indian is not ashamed of his color," as the writer thought,[60] but because he lacked the technical means to alter it. But hair straightening, unknown in the islands before the 1920's, has since become practically universal even among rural women. Bleaching creams and lotions, introduced from America during World War II, are widely used, as is peroxide. Women who fear that bleaching is bad for the skin confine themselves to using face powders and avoiding the sun. But even this has to some extent declined with the advent of a brown-skin ideal in the new West Indian nations.

Although pigmentation is not the sole determinant, it is the diagnostic trait of perceived color; group names everywhere refer to the color spectrum. Gradations between European and African concern pigmentation exclusively; hair and features are ignored. A Jamaican beauty contest a decade ago selected a dozen winners of different shades, named after trees, fruit, or flowers of analogous color.[61] Their hair and features were not mentioned.

Yet pigmentation was aesthetically the easiest barrier to hurdle. Blackness was the badge of slavery, but Europeans came to regard it without the abhorrence they professed for kinky hair and thick lips. Planters throughout the islands were attracted by brown or *café-au-lait* skins. West Indian non-whites today hold similar aesthetic values. Antillean exemplars of *négritude* who glorify African beauty single out black skins for praise, but seldom laud other "African" traits.

The ascription of "white," "colored," and "black" varies with metropolitan background and local experience. Mediterraneans of dark complexion are apt to view as "white" folk who might elsewhere be considered "colored." This difference in perception partly explains the much higher proportion of "whites" in the Spanish Caribbean than in the French and British. In Hispaniola, for example, free-colored refugees fleeing the Haitian revolution became "white" when they crossed the border into Spanish Santo Domingo. Subjective change of color, along with Iberian immigration, increased the "white" population of Puerto Rico from 46 per cent in 1777 to 76.5 per cent in 1940.[62]

In the British, French, and Dutch West Indies, identification as "white" remains relatively stable, partly because whites are few and their identities well known. But the line between "colored" and "black" fluctuates with the bias of the census-taker and the mood of the populace. The "colored" proportion of Dominica was reported as 30 per cent in 1921, 75 per cent in 1946, and 33 per cent in 1960—variations explicable only by changes in local evaluations. Jamaica exhibits similar anomalies. Between 1943 and 1960 the "colored" population of Kingston declined from 33 to 14 per cent of the total, while that of one rural parish rose from 11 to 19 per cent. A change in names doubtless played a part; Kingstonians were less chary of being called "African" in 1960 than "black" in 1943.[63]

Traditionally, however, Jamaican "samboes"—about one-fourth white—classify themselves as black rather than colored.[64] Similarly in Guadeloupe *mulâtre* is used less to refer to a person of half-white and half-black ancestry than to a fair-skinned quadroon or octoroon with straight or wavy hair. Darker folk are *câpres*, a word originally equivalent to "sambo." But Trinidadians exaggerate the true size of the "colored" or mixed population, and Martiniquans claim they have no "pure" Negroes at all—that they all have at least one white ancestor.[65]

Perhaps one third of all West Indians are mixtures of white and black—a far smaller proportion than is estimated for the so-called "Negro" population in the United States. West Indians tend to believe that in time the whole population will, through mixing, become increasingly light in color. The reverse is more likely, for both the white and the light-colored populations are declining. In Dominica and Martinique today the population as a whole is visibly light-skinned, but the evolution of most territories is probably in the direction of more blackness rather than less. Until early in the nineteenth century, the increase of colored relative to both white and black resulted almost entirely from unmarried unions between white men and non-white women. Within the past century, stricter white marital standards and a continuing decline of the white population have reduced the numbers and the privileges of their mixed offspring.

A relatively small—albeit influential—proportion of the colored population today can point to a white father or grandfather; white ancestors are generally of earlier vintage. In most territories, however, the light-colored group mixes little with black folk, marrying among themselves in order to produce offspring as light as possible. The darker children merge with the bulk of the black population. And the light-colored group suffers another type of attrition. Wealthier and better educated than most, they more readily gain professional and other positions outside the West Indies, and a larger proportion of them emigrates.

Few West Indians, in time, will not have some degree of white genetic inheritance, but for most it will be so small that in West Indian terms they will count as black.[66] The presence of small but influential white and colored remnants, however, will make it hard to forget that color is important. Any change must come from new ways of seeing, which will cease to value color according to the standard that has prevailed for three centuries.

The Burdens of Prejudice

The impact of the distinctions West Indians make is manifold, weighty, and complex. This complexity is itself a significant feature of West Indian life. Color underlies many problems even when it does not dominate them. Yet social and economic issues are often wrongly viewed as racial, and criticism of any local effort is apt to be imputed to color or to color prejudice.

Rationalizations in terms of race permeate West Indian political life. Like imperialism, prejudice and segregation make easy and convenient targets. "Race has been played up in politics to the point where it is becoming well nigh impossible for the races to freely represent each other's interests, without consideration of skin texture," asserts a Barbadian barrister.[67]

Absorption with color has parallel effects on personal relations. Inadequacies, even affronts, are passed over in silence lest they be misconstrued as racial slurs. Color-consciousness often stultifies constructive criticism and makes plain speaking impossible. Ascription of events and attitudes to color prejudice relieves one of personal responsibility. "The black man in Jamaica is lucky," comments a correspondent. "If the white man fails, he can only blame himself. If the black man fails, he can always blame colour prejudice."[68] But whites also join the hue and cry against racism. "It is not uncommon to find whites scourging themselves for the prejudices of their group before black audiences," writes a Trinidadian. "This they do by reporting outrageous statements made by members of their group, and dissociating themselves from the sentiments."[69]

Color-awareness is a corrosive and enervating preoccupation that hampers West Indian efforts to cope with other problems. And for all but the very light-skinned, it is also a form of masochism. Those who blame discrimination for every failure believe at heart that their color makes them inferior. The old white association of blackness with laziness and stupidity is accepted today by many colored and black people themselves. They are schizophrenics who consider the part of them that is "white" good and the part that is "black" bad. The frustrated aspiration of being "white" is a frequent feature of British West Indian paranoia, not to mention of everyday life. "I could never love a black man," asserts a dark colored woman. "Black and black breed picknies like monkeys. I always want my picknies to be as light as possible."[70]

Not being white, they avoid all other racial attributions. West Indian census history reflects the shifts from euphemism to euphemism, each in turn unacceptable as it accumulates undesirable connotations. "African," "Negro," "black," "colored," "Creole" are continually adopted as polite and abandoned as derogatory. In short, West Indians resist being called anything. No possible designation would flatter them; better the chaotic diversity of "Black brown yellow pink and cream/. . . Our English hymns creole proverbs/ Steel band calypso rock-'n'-roll/Anancy-stories obeah and Christ" than to be fixed in "one quick-drying definition."[71]

West Indians are as unsure of their national as of their racial identity. "They have no country of their own," wrote Trollope a century ago; they were only "a servile people in a foreign land."[72] Many remain rootless still; their willingness to sell all they own for passage money leads one observer to conclude that "tens of thousands of West Indians would prefer to live anywhere than in the West Indies."[73] A calypsonian notes, however, that the typical West Indian lacks exclusive attachment to another land:

> You can send the Indians to India,
> And the Negroes back to Africa,
> But will somebody please tell me,
> Where they sending poor me, poor me?
> I'm neither one nor the other—
> Six of one, half a dozen of the other,
> If they serious 'bout sending back people in tru'
> They're going to have to split me in two.[74]

Not truly West Indian, they are not anything else, either. Although African nationalism has kindled West Indian pride, Africa and *négritude* are not vivid memories; they are abstractions meaningful mainly to poets and visionaries. Most West Indians still reject

Africa for its associations of blackness, barbarism, and slavery. The extent of West Indian identification with an African heritage is inversely proportional to its relevance to daily life. The rural backwaters where Herskovits found African survivals in speech, folklore, religion, social organization, and family life hardly know that Africa exists; it is the light-skinned, urban, cosmopolitan West Indian who is most aware of Africa.[75]

The difference between African origins and African self-consciousness is clearest in Haiti. Peasant life and faith provide a wealth of African parallels, but interest in African culture is not to be found in the countryside but among French-educated intellectuals. The advocates of *négritude* do not really recall their African heritage; they rediscover it as an adjunct to national and racial pride. The West Indian patriot identifies not with ancient Africa, but with the Africa newly emerged from colonial bondage.

Although Eric Williams and Aimé Cesaire, among others, are fashioning a relevant West Indian heritage, it may be a long time before most West Indians enjoy being identified with Africans. Antillean Creoles mingle with Africans in Paris where both can be French, but British West Indians in London resent being taken for Africans. Even at the United Nations, West Indians reject African for European and American models to such a degree that some Africans regard Jamaica as "a reactionary black English outpost in the lap of America"[76] and term the West Indians "Afro-Saxons."[77]

Middle-class West Indians yearn instead to be Europeans. "The Antilles cannot and do not want to be anything other than French," states a Martiniquan. "They are French in spirit, in heart, in blood."[78] This is still the case in Haiti after six generations of independence. French education and manners are dear to the heart of the Haitian elite. Even though the Creole patois is the only tongue of nine tenths of the inhabitants, French remains the language of law, of debate, of polite society. While it is now politically fashionable to exalt folk speech, neither the social structure nor the aspirations of educated Haitians permit them to pay more than lip service to a creed that would deprive them of their French tradition.[79]

The British West Indies are hardly less British in sympathy and identification. Fealty, not geography, earned Barbados the name "Little England." Jamaicans and Trinidadians also take pride in Commonwealth status, ape English manners, and pursue British honors—a "socially and psychologically corrupting [system] for taming the colonial natives," as a Trinidadian describes it, that

325

"causes middle-aged 'social workers' with big bosoms and M.B.E's to say 'sixpence' instead of 'twelve cents,'" and "implies full acceptance of the ascribed role . . . [by] 'good' West Indians—yes, Sir Uncle Tom."[80]

Self-rule calls for some show of independence. Trinidad especially makes common cause with other new nations, and sees Anglophile traditions as hindrances to the establishment of a genuine West Indian identity. The West Indianization of intellectual life has, however, hardly gone beyond the publication of schoolbooks with a Caribbean focus and of a new journal that substitutes the sugar-plantation periods "dead season," "croptime," "high season," and "cropover" for the traditional seasons of the year.[81]

West Indians are, then, unhappy about their color and uneasy about their nationality. A third feature of the local scene is the isolation of white, colored, and black in exclusive social roles. The West Indian white, identified by color with imperialism and oppression, can seldom hope to win an election. No head of government can risk alienating popular support by making many white appointments. Because West Indianization is official policy in all but the French islands, there will soon be few expatriates in local governments. Yet whites, expatriate and local, dominate most economic enterprises, notably those that are subsidiaries of foreign firms. Ten *béké* families own 80 per cent of the cultivable land in Martinique.[82] In St. Vincent whites are only 2.3 per cent of the population, but they control the banks, the principal hotels, the newspaper, and practically all the arrowroot estates, St. Vincent's principal industry.[83] Thus the small group that dominates the private sector of the economy and makes most of the important economic decisions participates less and less in public affairs except on an advisory basis.

The colored middle class today controls local government and the civil service. But they have little background in political affairs, little understanding of the life of the people, and no real connection with the mainsprings of economic activity. Like the whites of earlier epochs, they remain attached to old ways of doing things out of fear and ignorance and in order to keep their social privileges. Economic development is regarded as chimerical because those who control the economy mistrust the people, and those who control the people mistrust or are wholly ignorant of economics:

One hundred and fifty years ago, when the Non-conformists told the slave-owners, "You cannot continue to keep human beings in this condition," all the slave-owners could reply was, "You will ruin the economy, and further what can you expect from people like these?" When you try to tell the middle classes of today, "Why not place responsibility for the economy on the people?" their reply is the same as that of the old slave-owners: "You will ruin the economy, and further what can you expect from people like these?"[84]

In politics, if nowhere else, the black West Indian now finds every door open; "the 'blacks' feel that they, because of their numbers, have a divine right to rule."[85] But black political leaders are often as remote from the bulk of the people as the white and colored men they have replaced. As a character in a Barbadian novel put it, "they have lots o' eddicated sons-o'-bitches down in that House o' 'Sembly and they so damn important that they ain't farting on their own people."[86] A recent survey revealed that most Jamaicans thought there were only two or three black representatives in the House, although sixteen black men, in fact, sat there. The clue to the "error" lies in the prevalent feeling that many of them were, indeed, "black, but they've got white minds."[87]

This situation endures partly because the bulk of the people are too ill-informed and powerless to secure more responsive leaders, and partly because their resentment is tinged with admiration. A self-made Barbadian is viewed with "a queer blend of pride and prejudice. . . . He managed to keep [the rural people] at a distance, so that his acts of kindness left them feeling that they had had recourse to the Almshouse. . . . On the other hand, when one looked back on how it used to be . . . it was gratifying to see an ordinary black man owning land and property and really prospering."[88]

Creoles and East Indians

There are other West Indians besides those of European and African descent. Prominent among them are the descendants of more recent immigrants from India, called "East Indians," "Hindustanis," or pejoratively, "Coolies." The rivalry between this group and black, colored, and white, collectively known as "Creoles,"[89] has sparked discord and turbulence in several Caribbean territories, reflecting tensions of a different order than those delineated thus far.

The East Indian community in the West Indies owes its origins to the need West Indian planters felt, after emancipation, for large and steady supplies of labor to work (and keep wages down) on plantations abandoned or neglected by the ex-slaves. With government support, sometimes by means of bounties and sometimes by means of force, planters induced people from Africa, Madeira, China, India, and Java to come to the Caribbean as indentured servants. Descendants of all these folk occupy distinctive roles in West Indian society today. But only those from India (and later the Javanese in Surinam) proved a success on the plantations. Between 1837 and 1917 about 550,000 East Indians entered the West Indies on contracts binding them to serve from three to five years.[90] They were then free to go home, and many did; but more of them cashed in their return passages and remained in the West Indies, at first on new estate contracts and later as small farmers on their own.

About one quarter of the Indians went to Jamaica, Martinique, and Guadeloupe, but they were not numerous enough in these islands to have much impact on either the economic or the social structure, and their descendants have drifted with little differentiation of race into the laboring class.[91] Only in Trinidad, British Guiana, and Surinam, where the demand for plantation labor was greatest, did Indians really transform the local scene. In each of these territories East Indians now account for nearly half the total population. Early marriages and stable unions give them birth rates that presage their numerical preponderance within a few years.[92]

Like the African slaves before them, East Indian indentured laborers suffered under oppressions, restraints, and punishments. These were no less harsh though the workers were formally free. They were herded together in estate barracks, inadequately fed and cared for in illness, and culturally ghettoized. For slight offenses or none, they were jailed, fined, and often forced to reindenture themselves. The planters viewed them, as they had the slaves, simply as machines for producing sugar.

Despised by blacks as well as whites, East Indians maintained a social cohesiveness that endures to this day, neither intermarrying with Africans nor adopting the ideals of Europeans. Only in this generation have East Indians begun to take much part in West Indian education, business, professional life, and politics, while the Javanese in Surinam have not yet begun to do so. East Indian family patterns, religion, and associations remain separate and different, consciously turned toward "Mother" India and away from the West Indies.

Indian ways of life in the Caribbean now bear little resemblance, however, to those in India. Despite a revival of sentiment since Indian independence in 1947, few of them speak Hindi, wear the *dhoti*, recognize more than a rudimentary vestige of the caste system, or think seriously of returning to India. Clannish, conscious of their "superiority," and uneasy about Creole political domination, they have nevertheless irrevocably cast their lot as West Indians and have assimilated much of West Indian culture and patterns of behavior.[93]

Greater or lesser similarity to Creole culture and personality would not, of itself, define the East Indian's role in Caribbean society, let alone fix his image of others or theirs of him. But the extent to which East Indians are Creolized—that is, like other West Indians—is a question that is argued with much vehemence and passion.[94] In Trinidad the image of racial assimilation is so important that the Prime Minister denounced a foreign anthropological study that stressed East Indian distinctiveness.[95]

Nevertheless, political parties are racially aligned wherever East Indians are prominent. In Guyana, where East Indian and Creole radicals originally united against the colonial regime, personal and ideological differences split the movement into racial components. The East Indian P.P.P., led by Cheddi Jagan, represents more than half the population. It is out of power owing to a system of proportional representation imposed by Britain as a requirement for Guyanese independence. An uneasy coalition between Lyndon Forbes Burnham's predominantly Creole [Negro] P.N.C. and the conservative United Front, made up of well-to-do Portuguese and mixed Creoles, now governs the country. Although each party avows a non-racial policy and parades a few candidates of the other race, ethnic affiliation has been the most important factor in the last three general elections, and house-to-house canvassers urged people to "vote race." The East Indian strength is rural, the Creole urban; the P.P.P. does not even contest Creole strongholds in the towns.[96]

In Surinam, the leading parties are all avowedly racial. Although the Creoles are outnumbered by East Indians and Javanese combined, a system of block-voting in the Creole-dominated urban areas and the failure of the East Indians (predominantly Hindu) and the Javanese (Moslem) to unite enable Creoles to control the local government. As a minority group, the East Indians seek Dutch protection against Creole demands for greater Surinamese autonomy. But these and other differences are muted by a coalition government and division of spoils and by Creole caution against the day when East Indians will be dominant.[97]

In Trinidad, most parties avow multiracial aims. Prime Minister Eric Williams is a strong advocate of assimilation, and his ruling P.N.M. cabinet includes Hindus and Moslems, as well as men of Chinese and European origins. Yet the identification of party with race is almost as complete in Trinidad as it is in Surinam and Guyana.

"There are many PNM members . . . for whom, underneath the thin veneer of their ideology, the word 'Indian' is still a word of opprobium," and who feel menaced by "the Indian threat."[98] To Indians, even more than to Creoles, race is a significant and alarming factor. In the past, Trinidad's East Indians opposed West Indian federation (which would have reduced their potential power when they became a majority in Trinidad), and they continue to oppose the P.N.M. on racial grounds. As they see it, favoritism dominates government employment, welfare, and education schemes. "Negroes," some contend, "would rather have a dishonest Negro than an honest East Indian as Prime Minister."[99] Grudging and tentative approbation by a Hindu organization was worth a banner headline in the P.N.M. party paper in 1966, which gives some idea just how fragile the interracial consensus really is.

Racial tensions are less serious in Trinidad than in the Guianas, perhaps because in Trinidad the two groups, less divided by geography and occupation, maintain better communications. But even there, a scholar friendly to the assimilationist image concedes that "the notorious clannishness of the Indian . . . will take a long time to disappear, [and] . . . the gospel of an all-Trinidadian racial solidarity remains, as yet, an aspiration rather than a reality."[100]

East Indian-Creole disputes that seem to be racial—like those between white and black—may at times be economic or occupational in origin. Laborers of both races were linked in sympathy against white and brown oppressors as recently as a decade ago in British Guiana.[101] But in most cases race alignments take precedence over class alignments. In view of the general lack of contact and understanding between the two groups, their divergent aims and disparate values will not easily be reconciled. Guyanese independence under Creole leadership has not yet resolved the inequities of employment in the police force, school system, and civil service about which East Indians complain.[102]

The racial situation in these three territories is thus strikingly different from that elsewhere in the West Indies. Stresses among diverse ethnic elements, ranked not vertically but horizontally, constitute the principal social problem in Trinidad and the Guianas. Put at the bottom of the social hierarchy by black and colored Creoles, the East Indians rejected this relegation. Instead, they regard themselves as superior to the blacks and even use white and colored stereotypes to validate this evaluation, pointing to their lighter skin, straight hair, and European features. In essence, however, they remain outside the Creole hierarchical structure.[103] Meanwhile their presence in these three countries has to some extent united white, colored, and black in a mutually protective alliance.

In summary, then, West Indian social organization ranges from fragmented Surinam, where ethnic and religious divisions are superimposed on a color hierarchy, to an almost classless Carriacou, where racial and cultural homogeneity prevails. Between these extremes, social pluralism operates to a greater or lesser degree to identify and articulate relationships among classes mainly divided along lines of color. Special circumstances in each West Indian territory serve here to exacerbate, there to attenuate, the nature and stress of class distinctions.

West Indians and the American Negro

How do these circumstances affect West Indian life, thought, and personality? One approach to such a question is to explore the differences between West Indians and American Negroes. Perhaps the most significant difference is what the names themselves imply. To most white Americans, a Negro is still a Negro first and a man afterwards; the West Indian is a man from the outset in the eyes of the community and, therefore, to himself. The word "Negro," explains a Guyanese poet, is "a label denoting a type of human being who was part of a black minority in a white majority." In America, " 'Negro' meant problem. It had no application to the people living in the Antilles, where they . . . form a black majority."[104] Within the West Indies most designations are geographical. A black or colored man from Jamaica or Martinique is simply a Jamaican or a Martiniquan; it is the white man who must establish his special identity. In the United States the opposite is the case. "Southerner" is invariably taken to mean "white Southerner"; the southern Negro is simply a Negro from the South.[105]

The West Indian may still look to Europe for his elite model, but at home he no longer has to contend with images other than his own; he has inherited the islands and is their majority voice. Despite their extreme dependence on the outside world, many West Indians are conscious, perhaps unrealistically so, of controlling their own national destiny. Their rootlessness and ambivalence notwithstanding, the close association of island identity with culture and even with race gives the West Indian a sense of personal integration rare among American Negroes.

Early recognition of formal freedom and opportunity regardless of race is a source of special pride and satisfaction to West Indians. Until recently, few colored West Indians gained pre-eminent status, and those who did were seldom dark. But the achievement of top rank by even a few black men was a safety valve for the ambitious. They could feel that their depressed status was a matter less of race than of class.

West Indian immigrants to the United States present a striking contrast to native-born Negroes. Their belief in their own worth and in their unlimited potentialities has given them a degree of self-confidence envied, resented, and emulated by American colored men. In ante-bellum New Orleans descendants of West Indian *gens de couleur*, well-educated and well-to-do, were noted for their self-respect. "In their contact with white men," one observer wrote, "they did not assume that creeping posture of debasement—nor did the whites expect it."[106] Mulatto West Indians in the 1830's inspired some northern Negroes to seek assimilation and amalgamation with whites as "men" and "people of color," not as slaves or Negroes.[107] Light-colored middle-class West Indians often de-emphasized, denied, and even escaped identification as Negroes.

Many West Indian immigrants felt superior to American Negroes because in the islands they "had come from families of high social position and had never experienced the openly racial 'jim-crow' discrimination of the United States," as a Guyanese explains.[108] "The West Indian comes to New York with a supreme advantage," writes a Trinidadian. "Unaccustomed to the social mores, . . . he goes out . . . and swings through every door." Because he is unaware that most jobs are off-limits to Negroes, "there are fewer boundaries for him."[109]

West Indian advantages are tangible as well as psychological. Most American Negroes get inferior segregated schooling, whereas West Indian immigrants either enjoy the best educational opportunities available in the islands, or are pushed to do well in school in the United States by their parents and by West Indian traditions that accord status to academic learning, in a Trinidadian's frank phrase, "as a path to another niche in the elite of skinocracy."[110]

Insular backgrounds make them ambitious also to acquire property, associated in the Caribbean with freedom, economic security, high status, and, until recently, voting qualifications. Paule Marshall's description of Brooklyn Barbadians scrimping and saving to buy brownstone houses, by contrast with their stereotype of spendthrift American Negroes who buy Cadillacs, conveys something of the West Indian passion for home-ownership.[111]

West Indian ambitions have paid off in America. Although they constituted less than 1 per cent of the American Negro population in 1930, they were 2.3 per cent of the Negro college graduates and 7.8 per cent of leaders in *Who's Who in Colored America*. In New York City, where West Indians were about one eighth of the Negro population, they contributed an estimated one third of all Negro professionals. "They are powerful in Harlem's business, financial, labor, and political worlds," noted an observer in 1954. "They are a hustling, vital people, and the influence they have on colored affairs is far out of proportion to their numbers."[112]

Not all West Indians have adjusted so successfully to American conditions. Some who would not take menial work constantly referred to the glories of the past and to their remote social standing in the islands; others expressed such extreme resentment of white discourtesies that their employment opportunities were severely limited. Still others trained as carpenters, bricklayers, or shoemakers found those occupations pre-empted by whites in the United States. But enough West Indians succeeded in America to engender an American Negro stereotype of them as "Black Jews"— in their eyes, aggressive, efficient, acquisitive, calculating, and clannish.

Thousands of British West Indians have come to the United States to make their fortunes. But they seldom break their home ties, as the scores of West Indian benevolent and social organizations testify. The islands are remembered, through a nostalgic haze that screens out the actual lot of the black majority, as places "where every human being, regardless, was a man"[113]; after a white affront West Indian parents are apt to tell their American children, "If you were at home this could not happen." French West Indians and Haitians responded similarly to American conditions. Proud of the part played by Negroes in French history, they place a high value on personal liberty regardless of color, resent and ridicule American segregation, and are sometimes critical of American Negroes for submitting to it.

Some West Indians still adhere to formal "European" nationality. Foreign passports not only emphasize their difference from Americans but give them an advantage when they run afoul of discrimination: "I am a British subject! I shall appeal to my consul!" has been a common and often an effective West Indian response.[114] The "West Indian population has checked out of the islands," one writer commented a generation ago, but "it has retained the pawn tickets."[115]

Those who remain in the islands are apt to conclude that in the United States all Negroes, however light, are doomed to permanent subordination. Even though successful Negroes in the United States are financially better off than their counterparts in the West Indies, their positions are less prestigious. Whatever mark they make, they are accepted only to a limited and grudging degree as Negroes in a white world. In the West Indies, where "Negro" leadership is taken for granted in many fields, successful black and colored men identify more easily with the whole society. The election of Edward Brooke, a light-colored Negro from Massachusetts, to the United States Senate in 1966 is a "first" about on a par with the selection of the Barbadian mulatto, Conrad Reeves, as Chief Justice of Barbados in 1884. Both are protégés of the propertied, "safe," "responsible" men to whom whites proudly point as evidence of the absence of color prejudice.

But there is another side to the picture. The lot of the great majority of West Indians does not remotely resemble the ideal. At the bottom of the social hierarchy the top is too far away to see or to enjoy, except vicariously. The success of the few who have stormed the portals of the elite has little meaning to those who struggle every day for a bare living. The black masses deem it no accident that those who are better off have lighter skins than they do, and they remember the long history of colored advance at their expense. The free-colored alliance with whites against the slaves has endured, socially if not politically, down to the present. "If the interests of the white plutocracy and the people . . . clash outright," writes an observer in Martinique, the mulatto "has no doubts as to where he stands: he's on the side of the whites."[116] And in Barbados, well known for white intransigence, a columnist avers that the situation between "gradations in the Negro sector of the community [is] far worse" than that between black and white.[117]

With the new West Indian mixed-race image, the black is still the odd man out. "If the hybrid is the norm, then the vast majority of pure blacks must be the aberration," notes a Jamaican. "The mixed blood idealization . . . is unacceptable to the lower-class blacks . . . [and] a source of great irritation to a growing body of middle-class black opinion."[118]

Black dissatisfaction has taken several forms. In Haiti, elimination of all whites after the revolution left black and colored locked in rivalry that grew fiercer with the years. It remains potent to this day; in 1966 black government officials laid Haitian unrest at the door of the colored elite now displaced from power. The cult of *négritude,* the glorification of Africa and blackness, was born in Haiti and the French Antilles, and the Martiniquan Aimé Cesaire is one of its principal and most passionate advocates. In the British Caribbean, bitterness between Negro and mulatto led to black nationalism, exemplified by the Jamaican, Marcus Garvey, who struck out against white and colored entrenched privilege on behalf of Negro masses all over the world.

Garvey was said to speak for a peasantry whose "natural leaders, both mulatto and black, have crossed the color line" leaving them "with only the rudiments of education, . . . grovelling at the bottom" of the English colonial system.[119] The crux of Garvey's appeal was his assertion of black unity and virtue. He affirmed pride in being Negro, denounced colored men who sought assimilation with whites, and taught his followers to venerate their African connection.

In Jamaica stratification was so intense that Garvey made little headway against black apathy and self-abasement. But in the United States after 1916, West Indians sparked and for a time practically dominated Garvey's Universal Negro Improvement Association. They enlisted under Garvey's banner as if "they would show these damned American Negroes what British West Indians could do."[120]

American Negro leaders, both accommodationists like Booker T. Washington and militants like W. E. B. DuBois, looked toward integration with white culture and society. At the same time they affirmed Negro solidarity in the face of white antipathy to colored men of all shades. Color differences did matter; well into the twentieth century the Negro hierarchy in most cities was headed by

descendants of free-colored folk of ante-bellum origin, and successful Negroes were—and are—usually lighter than the rest; but these
distinctions were little discussed. Unimportant to whites, they were
viewed with caution by Negroes. The very idea of color stratification was at odds with what Negroes were fighting for, and those who
did not deny its existence minimized its significance. Many leaders
were, or professed to be, surprised to discover that color shade was
important among Negroes. Garvey's blunt assault brought it into the
open for the first time and aroused tremendous response among
the darker, less-educated Negroes who had been substantially forgotten by the light-skinned leaders of "the Talented Tenth."[121]

But Garvey wrongly assumed that black and mulatto status in
the United States was akin to that in the West Indies. His appeals
to black men victimized by the West Indian color-class system
alienated Americans of mixed blood as well as black Americans who
had not been conditioned to regard mulattoes as their oppressors.
The impassable white barrier, the prejudice that operated against
all non-whites alike, then, as now, gave American Negroes a feeling
of solidarity, a sense of community regardless of shade, quite absent
in the West Indies. A constant concern about status and acceptance
is more characteristic of light-skinned West Indians, accustomed
to differential treatment by whites, than of American colored people. As a black laborer says of a colored shopkeeper in a Barbadian
village, "Biscombe can't know which side he on, man, 'cause Biscombe is a two-tone man. He have to be on both sides. That is the
way he was born!"[122]

The West Indian who is poor and black comes to America not
only to make his fortune but to break out of a system that leaves
him at the bottom no matter what he does. In the American Negro
world, by contrast, a sharecropper's son may easily become a
leader; hearing of a high place gained by a West Indian of plebian
origin, an islander in America exclaimed, "Why the very idea! I
would not speak to the fellow at home."[123] To the black laborer, class
barriers in the islands may be more galling than the white-black
barrier in America. After revisiting most of the islands, one West
Indian returned to America and remarked: "I am ashamed to say
that I choose to live in my prison."[124]

Some West Indians resign themselves to the American racial
"prison"; they gain wealth, acquire property, and explain to the
militant, "I came here to drink milk, not to count cattle."[125] Others
are satisfied to stand on their dignity as West Indians, and protest

discrimination merely on their own behalf. But contrasts between their perceptions of island and mainland conditions and between American ideals and realities impel others to speak out against injustice. Because he is an immigrant, the West Indian in the United States is more apt to be forceful and enterprising than either the native American or the stay-at-home. But his West Indian experience also makes him more sensitive and articulate than the American Negro. The islander is shocked to find colored men of high family and professional standing in the United States suffering the same indignities as Negro laborers. Accustomed from infancy to stand up for his rights, the West Indian may go on to face the issue he had ignored at home, and ask why *any* Negro should endure such treatment. A long history of fighting for self-government has conditioned the immigrants to be litigious and aggressive. Resentment against American patterns of segregation makes some of them, at least, relentless antagonists of all Negro disabilities. "The insistent assertion of their manhood" and their unwillingness "to accept tamely an inferior status" make West Indians well suited to lead American Negroes who have been trained to stay in their place.[126]

West Indian reforming zeal has taken several forms in the United States. West Indians were among the earliest, strongest, and most persistent pan-Africanists. They led Negroes into the American labor movement, notably the needle trades, the fur industries, and the longshoremen's union. And they have taken the lead especially in black nationalism. Those who followed Garvey on race pride, black solidarity, and equal rights and who rejected integration as spurious were at first mainly black, lower-class, barely literate; but in recent years West Indians who are light-colored, well-educated, or middle-class have also espoused these principles, though not always for the same reasons.

Malcolm X's father was a militant Garveyite, but the influence of his West Indian mother was also profound: "My mother, who was born in Grenada, in the British West Indies, looked like a white woman. Her father *was* white. . . . Of this white father of hers, I know nothing except her shame about it. I remember hearing her say she was glad that she had never seen him." Owing to his mother's lightness, Malcolm X was at first one of "the millions of Negroes who were insane enough to feel that it was some kind of status symbol to be light-complexioned. . . . But, still later, I learned to hate every drop of that white rapist's blood that is in me."[127]

A surprising number of Malcolm X's ideological successors, advocates of "black power," "black nationalism," or, more fundamentally, black self-esteem, are West Indian-born. SNCC-leader Stokely Carmichael came to the United States from Trinidad at the age of eleven, Lincoln Lynch of CORE from Jamaica at twenty-one, Roy Innis of CORE from St. Croix as a boy of twelve or thirteen. The disparity between the West Indian and American conditions triggered an apostolic role for each of them. "I was shocked when I came here to find that the word 'black' was almost a cuss word with the American Negroes," Innis states. "It is true that there is a lot of poverty in the islands, but we felt proud in being black and did not feel the alienations in society that you feel here."[128] As Lynch states their aims, "we need black people standing on their own two feet. . . . The white man will not respect you until you can stand eye to eye with him."[129] In Trinidad the immediate authorities— police, teachers, ministers, civil service—had all been colored, and colored as well as white lived in big mansions, Carmichael told an interviewer; consequently, "the question of the exploitation of the black by the white had not occurred to the boy."[130] In America all was different; "fourteen years of accommodating to white authority in this country has molded him into . . . the chief architect of 'black power.' "[131] These impressions of West Indian life, however, are a far cry from those of Marcus Garvey. Carmichael's feeling of identification with colored authorities stands in sharp contrast to the sense of alienation and elite oppression still to be found among the black majority.

It is easy to exaggerate both the defects and the virtues of the West Indian situation. The problems of poverty and overpopulation, of unemployment at home and closed doors abroad probably perturb West Indians more than inherited prejudices of color. Those who are relatively well off would probably concur in the judgment of a Jamaican resident that these islands "have gone farther toward working out the problems of how people of different colors can live together in harmony and dignity and respect than any other place and any other people I know." In the West Indies he has watched American Negro visitors shed the "protective shield behind which they spend so much of their lives and function simply as human beings in a world of other human beings."[132]

For West Indians who are both poor and black, the outlook—

despite self-government and the absence of formal discrimination—is less attractive. Scores of recent episodes support a judgment that self-contempt still characterizes the Jamaican masses: the parent who is glad to see her child "marry brown, and forget the roots"; the maid who would never work "for black people"; the black watchman who claims authorities told him not to let "any black people pass"; the black woman who votes for a white candidate "for no black man can help me in this yah country these days."[133]

Both the progress made and the problems remaining in the West Indies are crisply epitomized in a calypsonian's comment on the new order:

> Well, the way how things shapin' up
> All this nigger business go' stop
> I tell you soon in the West Indies
> It's please Mr. Nigger please.[134]

REFERENCES

1. Richard H. Rovere, "Bedevilled Island," *New Yorker* (November 26, 1966), p. 226.

2. Jamaica, Ministry of Development and Welfare, Central Planning Unit, *Five Year Independence Plan, 1963-1968; A Long Term Development Programme for Jamaica* (Kingston, Jamaica, 1963), p. 3.

3. Norman W. Manley, address to the National Press Club, Washington, D. C., April 19, 1961, quoted in *Congressional Record*, Vol. 107, p. 7306.

4. Orford St. John, "A New Horizon," *Public Opinion* (Jamaica), September 30, 1961, p. 3.

5. Jamaica, Report to the United Nations on Racial Discrimination, quoted in *Jamaica Daily Gleaner*, October 4, 1964.

6. "Realism and Race" by A Young Jamaican Nationalist, in "Two Views on the Problem of Race and Colour in Jamaica Today," *West Indian Economist* (Jamaica), Vol. 3, No. 10 (April, 1961), p. 6.

7. Ivor Leila, "The Changing Attitude to Mixed Marriages," *Flamingo* (London), No. 2 (October, 1961), p. 36.

8. Michel Leiris, *Contacts de civilisations en Martinique et en Guadeloupe* (Paris, 1955); Lloyd Braithwaite, "Social Stratification in Trinidad: A Preliminary Analysis," *Social and Economic Studies*, Vol. 2, Nos. 2 and 3 (1953), pp. 5-175; M. G. Smith, *Stratification in Grenada* (Berkeley and Los Angeles, 1965).

9. V. S. Naipaul, *The Middle Passage* (London, 1962), p. 230.

10. "Black Shadow Over 'Paradise Isle,'" *Newday* (Jamaica), Vol. 5, No. 6 (June, 1961), p. 20.

11. Millard Johnson, cited in S. George Minott, "The P.P.P. and Charges of Race Hatred," *Jamaica Times*, June 29, 1961, p. 9.

12. H. Orlando Patterson, *The Children of Sisyphus* (London, 1964), p. 115.

13. "Colour Bar Should Be Swept Away," *Barbados Advocate*, February 13, 1962.

14. F. L. Walcott, in the House of Assembly, *Barbados Advocate*, February 14, 1962.

15. Thomas Wright, "Candidly Yours," *Jamaica Daily Gleaner*, April 25, 1961, p. 12.

16. *Jamaica Daily Gleaner*, May 6, 1964.

17. C. L. R. James, *Beyond a Boundary* (London, 1963), p. 65.

18. Henry Forde, "Barbadians Are Hypocritical about Colour," *Barbados Advocate*, February 21, 1962.

19. Norman W. Manley, address at Social Development Conference, quoted in *Jamaica Daily Gleaner*, July 18, 1961, p. 2.

20. Melvin M. Tumin with Arnold S. Feldman, *Social Class and Social Change in Puerto Rico* (Princeton, 1961), p. 233.

21. H. Orlando Patterson, "The Social Structure of a University Hall of Residence," *Pelican* (U.C.W.I. campus magazine; Jamaica), Vol. 9, No. 3 (March, 1962), p. 30.

22. A. P. Thornton, "Aspects of West Indian Society," *International Journal*, Vol. 15 (1960), p. 113.

23. Zahra Freeth, *Run Softly Demerara* (London, 1960), p. 62.

24. Wright, "Candidly Yours," *Jamaica Daily Gleaner*, April 25, 1961.

25. Eric Williams, "The Historical Background of Race Relations in the Caribbean," Teachers Economic and Cultural Association, Ltd., *Public Affairs Pamphlets No. 3* (Port-of-Spain, Trinidad, 1955), p. 3.

26. Thornton, "Aspects of West Indian Society," p. 116.

27. Bernard Taper, "Letter from Port of Spain," *New Yorker* (October 23, 1965), p. 226.

28. Douglas Hall, "Absentee-Proprietorship in the British West Indies, to about 1850," *Jamaican Historical Review*, Vol. 4 (1964), pp. 27-29.

29. Richard Pares, *A West-India Fortune* (London, 1950), p. 332.

30. Eric Williams, *British Historians and the West Indies* (London, 1966), p. 34.

31. Quoted in W. E. B. DuBois, *Black Reconstruction in America* (New York, 1935), p. 45.

32. See Elsa V. Goveia, "The West Indian Slave Laws of the Eighteenth Century," *Revista de Ciencias Sociales,* Vol. 4 (1960), pp. 75-105; Douglas Hall, "Slaves and Slavery in the British West Indies," *Social and Economic Studies,* Vol. 11 (1962), pp. 305-18; George W. Roberts, "A Life Table for a West Indian Slave Population," *Population Studies,* Vol. 5 (1952), pp. 238-43. Slave conditions are compared in Frank Tannenbaum, *Slave and Citizen* (Vintage Books; New York, 1963); Stanley M. Elkins, *Slavery: A Problem in American Institutional and Intellectual Life* (Universal Library; New York, 1963); Marvin Harris, *Patterns of Race in the Americas* (New York, 1964); and David Brion Davis, *The Problem of Slavery in Western Culture* (Ithaca, N. Y., 1966).

33. Sheila Duncker, "The Free Coloured and Their Fight for Civil Rights in Jamaica, 1800-1830" (unpublished Master's thesis, University of London, 1959); Winthrop Jordan, "American Chiaroscuro: The Status and Definition of Mulattoes in the British Colonies," *William and Mary Quarterly,* 2d ser., Vol. 19 (1962), pp. 183-200; Elsa V. Goveia, *Slave Society in the British Leeward Islands at the End of the Eighteenth Century* (New Haven, 1965), pp. 258-59, 315-17.

34. Lord Harris, Governor of Trinidad, quoted in Eric Williams, *History of the People of Trinidad and Tobago* (Port-of-Spain, Trinidad, 1962), p. 97.

35. Austin C. Clarke, *The Survivors of the Crossing* (London, 1964), p. 24.

36. James Anthony Froude, *The English in the West Indies* (London, 1888).

37. Joseph Zobel, *La Rue Cases-Nègres* (Paris, 1955), p. 37.

38. John Hearne, "European Heritage and Asian Influence in Jamaica," *Our Heritage,* University of the West Indies, Department of Extra-Mural Studies, Public Affairs in Jamaica, No. 1 (1963), p. 30.

39. Edward Byron Reuter, *The Mulatto in the United States* (Boston, 1918), pp. 333-34.

40. J. S. Furnivall, *Colonial Policy and Practice* (London, 1948); Vera Rubin (ed.), "Social and Cultural Pluralism in the Caribbean," *Annals, New York Academy of Sciences,* Vol. 83 (1960), pp. 761-916; M. G. Smith, *The Plural Society in the British West Indies* (Berkeley and Los Angeles, 1965).

41. See Edgar Mittelholzer, *A Morning at the Office* (London, 1950), pp. 238, 242.

42. But the elite and middle-class West Indians who claim ignorance of lower-class ways commonly know even less about the masses than they themselves realize. Every Jamaican is to some extent bilingual in Creole and standard English, but educated people do not understand an estimated 30 per cent of folk vocabulary (Mervin C. Alleyne, "Communication

between the Elite and the Masses," *The Caribbean in Transition, Papers on Social, Political, and Economic Development,* ed. F. M. Andic and T. G. Mathews [Rio Piedras, P.R., 1965], pp. 12-19).

43. R. B. Le Page, "The Language Problem of the British Caribbean," *Caribbean Quarterly,* Vol. 4, No. 1 (1955), p. 45.

44. Hyman Rodman, "On Understanding Lower-Class Behaviour," *Social and Economic Studies,* Vol. 8 (1959), pp. 441-50, describes the problems involved; M. G. Smith and G. J. Kruijer, *A Sociological Manual for Extension Workers in the Caribbean* (Kingston, Jamaica, 1957), warns against neglecting them. James M. Blaut *et al.,* "A Study of Cultural Determinants of Soil Erosion and Conservation in the Blue Mountains of Jamaica," *Social and Economic Studies,* Vol. 8 (1959), pp. 403-20; and David Edwards, *Report on an Economic Study of Small Farming in Jamaica* (Kingston, Jamaica, 1961), underline the failure to make contact.

45. Kurt W. Back and J. Mayone Stycos, *The Survey under Unusual Conditions: The Jamaica Human Fertility Investigation,* Society for Applied Anthropology, Monograph No. 1 (Ithaca, N. Y., 1959), pp. 7, 9; J. Mayone Stycos, "Studies of Fertility in Underdeveloped Areas," *Human Organization,* Vol. 13 (1954), p. 10.

46. Back and Stycos, *The Survey under Unusual Conditions,* pp. 5, 23. The results of the study appear in J. Mayone Stycos and Kurt W. Back, *The Control of Human Fertility in Jamaica* (Ithaca, N. Y., 1964).

47. Smith, *Plural Society,* p. 175.

48. "The Case for Law Reform—2: The Conditions Affecting Demand," *West Indian Economist,* Vol. 2, No. 10 (April, 1960), p. 7.

49. M. G. Smith, Roy Augier, and Rex Nettleford, *The Ras Tafari Movement in Kingston, Jamaica* (Kingston, Jamaica, 1960); James A. Mau, "The Threatening Masses: Myth or Reality?" *The Caribbean in Transition, Papers on Social, Political, and Economic Development,* eds. F. M. Andic and T. G. Mathews (Rio Piedras, P. R., 1965), pp. 258-70.

50. Edith Clarke, *My Mother Who Fathered Me: A Study of the Family in Three Selected Communities in Jamaica* (London, 1957), is the pioneer study, and the voluminous literature is summarized in M. G. Smith's "Introduction" to the second edition of her book (London, 1966), pp. i-xliv.

51. "Carry on England; Barbados is behind you" ran an apocryphal cable received in London during World War I.

52. M. G. Smith, "Education and Occupational Choice in Rural Jamaica," in his *Plural Society,* pp. 196-220; G. E. Cumper, "The Differentiation of Economic Groups in the West Indies," *Social and Economic Studies,* Vol. 11 (1962), pp. 327-29.

53. Norman W. Manley quoted in "National Purpose," *West Indian Economist,* Vol. 3, No. 6 (December, 1960), p. 5. "Jamaica's Income and Its

Distribution," *West Indian Economist,* Vol. 3, No. 11 (May, 1961), pp. 4-7, describes the gap that then existed; C. G. Clarke, "Population Pressure in Kingston, Jamaica: A Study of Unemployment and Overcrowding," *Transactions and Papers, Institute of British Geographers,* Publication No. 38 (1966), p. 173, gives the population figures.

54. G. E. Cumper, "The Jamaican Family: Village and Estate," *Social and Economic Studies,* Vol. 7 (1958), p. 92.

55. M. G. Smith, "A Framework for Caribbean Studies," in his *Plural Society,* pp. 60-66, outlines the categories, and, in his *Stratification in Grenada,* pp. 158-68, correlates phenotype and genotype with status.

56. Braithwaite, "Social Stratification in Trinidad," p. 132.

57. Kenneth John, "Footnotes on Slavery," *Flambeau* (St. Vincent), No. 3 (January, 1966), p. 14.

58. Fernando Henriques, *Family and Colour in Jamaica* (London, 1953), pp. 47-48.

59. Raymond T. Smith, *The Negro Family in British Guiana* (London, 1956), p. 212.

60. C. G. Woodson, "West Indian Racial Purity Considered an Advantage" (1931), quoted in Ira De Augustine Reid, *The Negro Immigrant: His Background, Characteristics and Social Adjustment, 1899-1937* (New York, 1939), p. 228.

61. Ebony, Mahogany, Satinwood, Allspice, Sandalwood, Golden Apple, Jasmine, Pomegranate, Lotus, Appleblossom.

62. Harry Hoetink, *The Double Image in the Caribbean* (London, in press).

63. O. C. Francis, *The Population of Modern Jamaica,* Jamaica, Department of Statistics (Kingston, 1963).

64. H. G. De Lisser, *Twentieth Century Jamaica* (Kingston, Jamaica, 1913), p. 44. But see Madeline Kerr, *Personality and Conflict in Jamaica* (London, 1963), p. 101.

65. Guy Lasserre, *La Guadeloupe: Étude géographique,* Vol. 1 (2 vols.; Bordeaux, 1961), p. 324; Braithwaite, "Social Stratification in Trinidad," p. 160; Jean Benoist, "Les Martiniquais: Anthropologie d'une population métissée," *Bull. Soc. Anthropologie de Paris,* 11th Sér., Vol. 4 (1963), p. 265.

66. George Cumper, *The Social Structure of the British Caribbean (Excluding Jamaica),* Part 2 (Kingston, Jamaica, 1949), pp. 26-27.

67. Forde, "Barbadians Are Hypocritical about Colour."

68. Thomas Wright, "Candidly Yours," *Jamaica Daily Gleaner,* April 25, 1961, p. 13.

69. Naipaul, *The Middle Passage,* p. 78.

343

70. Kerr, *Personality and Conflict in Jamaica*, p. 96.

71. Mervyn Morris, "To a West Indian Definer," *Caribbean Literature, An Anthology*, ed. G. R. Coulthard (London, 1966), pp. 86-87.

72. Anthony Trollope, *The West Indies and the Spanish Main* (London, 1860), p. 55.

73. "Nationalism in the 'Sixties," *West Indian Economist*, Vol. 3, No. 7 (January, 1961), p. 7.

74. By The Mighty Dougla. (*Dougla* is a pejorative word for a person of mixed Negro and East Indian descent.)

75. M. J. and F. S. Herskovits, *Rebel Destiny: Among the Bush Negroes of Dutch Guiana* (New York, 1934); Melville J. Herskovits, *Life in a Haitian Valley* (New York, 1937); Melville J. and Frances S. Herskovits, *Trinidad Village* (New York, 1947). G. R. Coulthard, *Race and Colour in Caribbean Literature* (London, 1962), Chapters 4 and 5, traces the growth of West Indian *négritude*.

76. Rex Nettleford, "The African Connexion—The Significance for Jamaica," *Our Heritage*, p. 52.

77. Rex Nettleford, "National Identity and Attitudes to Race in Jamaica," *Race*, Vol. 7 (1965), p. 62.

78. Victor Sablé, *La transformation des isles d'Amérique en départements français* (Paris, 1955), p. 176.

79. Edith Efron, "French and Creole Patois in Haiti," *Caribbean Quarterly*, Vol. 3, No. 4 (August, 1954), pp. 199-213; Pradel Pompilus, *La langue française en Haïti* (Paris, 1961); Jacques-J. Zéphir, "Situation de la langue française en Haïti," *La Revue de l'Université Laval*, Vol. 19 (1965), pp. 701-13.

80. Adrian Espinet, "Honours and *Paquotille*," *New World Quarterly*, Vol. 2, No. 1 (Dead Season, 1965), p. 21.

81. *New World Quarterly*.

82. Gérard Latortue, "Political Status of the French Caribbean," *Politics and Economics in the Caribbean: A Contemporary Analysis of the Dutch, French and British Caribbean*, Institute of Caribbean Studies, Special Study No. 3 (Rio Piedras, P.R., 1966), p. 162.

83. Andron Wilwright, "Of Colour of Skin and St. Vincent," *Flambeau*, No. 3 (January, 1966), pp. 4-5.

84. C. L. R. James, *Party Politics in the West Indies* (San Juan, Trinidad, 1962), pp. 131-32, 136; quotation, p. 139.

85. Forde, "Barbadians Are Hypocritical about Colour."

86. Clarke, *The Survivors of the Crossing*, p. 169.

87. Public-opinion survey undertaken by Cyril Rogers, 1961. For the actual composition see Wendell Bell, *Jamaican Leaders: Political Attitudes in a New Nation* (Berkeley and Los Angeles, 1964), p. 83.

88. Millicent Payne, "The Chink in His Armour," *Bim* (Barbados), Vol. 10, No. 41 (June-December, 1965), p. 17.

89. Wally Thompson, "Creoles and Pidgins, East and West," *New World Quarterly*, Vol. 2, No. 4 (Cropover, 1966), p. 11; David Lowenthal, "Population Contrasts in the Guianas," *Geographical Review*, Vol. 50 (1960), p. 51.

90. G. W. Roberts and J. Byrne, "Summary Statistics on Indenture and Associated Migration Affecting the West Indies, 1834-1918," *Population Studies*, Vol. 20 (1966), pp. 125-34.

91. Guy Lasserre, "Les 'Indiens' de Guadeloupe," *Cahiers d'Outre-Mer*, Vol. 6 (1953), pp. 128-58.

92. G. W. Roberts and L. Braithwaite, "Mating among East Indian and Non-Indian Women in Trinidad," *Social and Economic Studies*, Vol. 11 (1962), pp. 203-40; Leo Davids, "The East Indian Family Overseas," *Social and Economic Studies*, Vol. 13 (1964), pp. 383-96.

93. Morton Klass, *East Indians in Trinidad: A Study of Cultural Persistence* (New York, 1961); Arthur and Juanita Niehoff, "East Indians in the West Indies," *Milwaukee Public Museum Publication in Anthropology*, No. 6 (Milwaukee, Wis., 1960); Johan Dirk Speckmann, *Marriage and Kinship among the Indians in Surinam* (Assen, Netherlands, 1965); Annemarie de Waal Malefijt, *The Javanese of Surinam: Segment of a Plural Society* (Assen, Netherlands, 1963).

94. Daniel J. Crowley, "Cultural Assimilation in a Multiracial Society," *Annals, New York Academy of Sciences*, Vol. 83 (1960), pp. 850-54; Morton Klass, "East and West Indian: Cultural Complexity in Trinidad," *Annals, New York Academy of Sciences*, Vol. 83 (1960), pp. 855-61; Raymond T. Smith, *British Guiana* (London, 1962), pp. 107-11.

95. Eric Williams, *History of the People of Trinidad and Tobago* (Port-of-Spain, Trinidad, 1962), p. 280. A scholar friendly to his regime charges that social scientists who doubt Trinidadian unity are merely projecting their own minority malaise (Gordon K. Lewis in a review of this book in *Caribbean Studies*, Vol. 3, No. 1 [April, 1965], p. 104).

96. C. Paul Bradley, "The Party System in British Guiana and the General Election of 1961," *Caribbean Studies*, Vol. 1, No. 3 (October, 1961), pp. 1-26; Leo A. Despres, "The Implications of Nationalist Politics in British Guiana for the Development of Cultural Theory," *American Anthropologist*, Vol. 66 (1964), pp. 1051-77; B. A. N. Collins, "Acceding to Independence: Some Constitutional Problems of a Poly-Ethnic Society (British Guiana)," *Civilisations*, Vol. 15, No. 3 (1965), pp. 1-21.

97. Thomas G. Mathews, "Political Picture in Surinam," *Politics and Economics in the Caribbean,* pp. 92-103; Peter Dodge, "Ethnic Fragmentation and Politics: The Case of Surinam," *Political Science Quarterly,* Vol. 81 (1966), pp. 593-601.

98. Gordon K. Lewis, "The Trinidad and Tobago General Election of 1961," *Caribbean Studies,* Vol. 2, No. 2 (1962), p. 23.

99. Krishna Bahadoorsingh, "What Trinidad's Leaders Believe about Race and Politics," *Trinidad & Tobago Index,* No. 4 (September, 1966), p. 40.

100. Lewis, "The Trinidad and Tobago General Election," pp. 23-24.

101. Chandra Jayawardena, *Conflict and Solidarity in a Guianese Plantation* (London, 1963).

102. B. A. N. Collins, "Racial Imbalance in Public Services and Security Forces," *Race,* Vol. 7 (1965-66), pp. 235-54.

103. See Braithwaite, "Social Stratification in Trinidad," pp. 49ff; David Lowenthal, "The Range and Variation of Caribbean Societies," *Annals, New York Academy of Sciences,* Vol. 83 (1960), pp. 789-92. Plural societies elsewhere resemble the Trinidad-Guiana situation, rather than that of the other West Indies. See Burton Benedict, "Stratification in Plural Societies," *American Anthropologist,* Vol. 64 (1962), p. 1239.

104. A. J. Seymour, "The Poetical Imagination at Work," *Kaie* (Georgetown, Guyana), No. 2 (May, 1966), pp. 28-30.

105. Thomas F. Pettigrew, "The Negro American—2," *Daedalus,* Vol. 95, No. 1 (Winter, 1966), p. 441.

106. Charles Gayarré, unpublished ms. quoted in Grace King, *New Orleans: The Place and the People* (New York, 1896), p. 345.

107. W. E. B. DuBois, *The Souls of Black Folk* (1903), in *3 Negro Classics* (Avon; New York, 1965), pp. 244-45.

108. Cheddi Jagan, *The West on Trial: My Fight for Guyana's Freedom* (London, 1966), p. 51.

109. Lennox Raphael, "West Indians and Afro-Americans," *Freedomways,* Vol. 4 (1964), p. 445.

110. *Ibid.,* p. 442. Their success is noted in Carter G. Woodson, *The Negro Professional Man and the Community* (Washington, D. C., 1934), p. 83.

111. Paule Marshall, *Brown Girl, Brownstones* (New York, 1960); and Gene Grove, "American Scene: The West Indians," *Tuesday Magazine* (November, 1966), p. 15.

112. J. M. Flagler, "Well Caught, Mr. Holder!" *New Yorker* (September 25, 1954), p. 65. The West Indian proportion of New York Negroes is

calculated from the 1930 U. S. Census, *Population*, Vol 2. Chap. 2, Table 23, p. 70, and Chap. 5, Table 2, p. 231; the estimate of West Indian professionals is from Reid, *The Negro Immigrant*, p. 221.

113. Hugh Panton Morrison, "Home Is the Hunter," *Focus: An Anthology of Contemporary Jamaican Writing*, ed. Edna Manley (Kingston, Jamaica, 1956), p. 18.

114. Reid, *The Negro Immigrant*, p. 110.

115. Quoted in *ibid.*, p. 219.

116. Daniel Guérin, *The West Indies and Their Future* (London, 1961), p. 75.

117. Mitchie Hewitt, "Yes, She's as Subtle as a Serpent," *Barbados Advocate*, February 9, 1962.

118. Nettleford, "National Identity and Attitudes to Race in Jamaica," p. 64.

119. W. E. B. DuBois, "Marcus Garvey," *The Crisis*, Vol. 21, No. 2 (December, 1920), p. 60.

120. Samuel L. Brooks, "Marcus Garvey, An Analysis," *Interstate Tattler*, quoted in Reid, *The Negro Immigrant*, p. 150.

121. August Meier, *Negro Thought in America, 1880-1915* (Ann Arbor, Mich., 1963), especially Chapters 12-14; Harold R. Isaacs, *The New World of Negro Americans* (London, 1964), pp. 133-46; and E. D. Cronon, *Black Moses, the Story of Marcus Garvey and the Universal Negro Improvement Association* (Madison, Wis., 1955).

122. Clarke, *The Survivors of the Crossing*, p. 116.

123. Quoted in Reid, *The Negro Immigrant*, p. 226.

124. *Ibid.*, p. 205.

125. Raphael, "West Indians and Afro-Americans," p. 441.

126. W. A. Domingo, quoted in Raphael, "West Indians and Afro-Americans," p. 444.

127. Malcolm X, *Autobiography* (Grove Press; New York, 1966), p. 2.

128. *The New York Times*, July 24, 1966, p. 51.

129. *The New York Times*, June 22, 1966, p. 24.

130. Robert Penn Warren, *Who Speaks for the Negro?* (New York, 1965), p. 390.

131. "Black Power Prophet," *The New York Times*, August 5, 1966, p. 10.

132. Peter Abrahams, "We Can Learn to Be Color-Blind," *The New York Times Magazine* (April 11, 1965), p. 38.

133. Nettleford, "National Identity and Attitudes to Race in Jamaica," pp. 69-70.

134. The Mighty Sparrow. See James, *Party Politics in the West Indies*, pp. 164-75.

This paper is a by-product of a work being prepared for the Institute of Race Relations (London). I am grateful to Marion Bellamy, W. Haywood Burns, Lambros Comitas, Edward Cumberbatch, Charles Hobson, Max Lowenthal, and Paule Marshall for criticisms and suggestions.

TALCOTT PARSONS

The Problem of Polarization on the Axis of Color

A NUMBER OF THEMES in this volume, perhaps especially that of Professor Bastide, seem to merit further discussion. The first concerns the sense in which color differences are "intrinsic" or "primordial," as Professor Shils uses those terms. The second is Bastide's argument about the relation of Christianity to color symbolism, particularly his remarks about Protestantism. The third is the question, discussed at various points, of how far the world system is, in fact, tending to become polarized on the axis of color—especially as this is more or less encouraged by the Communist Chinese, although Dr. Gardiner emphasizes that they have not done this clearly and consistently.

I am particularly concerned with the theme of polarization. The phenomenon of polarization—the term is, of course, relative—seems to involve two main aspects or types of factors.

Like other kinds of living systems, social systems change by, among other things, processes of differentiation. A prototype is the embryological development of multicellular organisms by the process of cell division, but similar processes are generally pervasive, occurring in the psychological, social, and cultural worlds as well as the organic. We speak of such a process as differentiation when of two—or more—subsystems resulting there is a *complementary* relation of function for the system which includes both. Thus the differentiated units differ both in structure and in function as in the very important biological case of the respective roles of the two sexes in the process of reproduction. Such a process may, however, not result in complementary parts but parts which are merely separate, with or without conflict. In this case I should speak of segmentation rather than differentiation. Segmented parts may relatively easily separate off from the parent system.

Further, there is massive evidence that by far the most important type of process leading either to differentiation or to segmentation is *binary* in character. This is to say that what at the beginning of the process was *one* structure, divides by one step into *two* and not more. There are many cases of such division in social and cultural history. Just to illustrate what is meant, I may anticipate the following analysis by mentioning two. A very old one in human social evolution is the division between upper and lower classes in a scale of stratification—for example, between an aristocracy and the "common people."[1] Whatever the complications, there has in many societies been a basic format of a "two-class" system on this basis. The second example is the one which has dominated socialist thought since the mid-nineteenth century—namely, the division between the two classes called in this literature "bourgeoisie" and "proletariat," a division based in the first instance on the structure of the producing unit which emerged in the Industrial Revolution, the industrial firm.

Binary division may conceivably result in total separation or, at the opposite extreme, in complete integration, with complementarity of function and minimal tension. The case of polarization which is the focus of interest here lies in between. It is a case where there are *two* structural components of salient importance: in the two examples just cited, "social classes." They remain, however, as elements in the same society and do not separate, but at the same time they stand for a more or less extended period in some important relation of conflict and tension toward each other.

The problem which we call that of inclusion concerns the possible and probable courses of events which follow on such a structural situation—that is, the presence of two salient structural elements in a state of tension. Such a situation may eventuate in a process of segmentation, as for example, the breaking up of the relative and tenuous unity of Western Christian society in the Middle Ages into a system of territorial, more or less "national" states. Present interest, however, centers on the case where, in spite of conflict and tension, the components remain within the same system and the trend is in the direction of some kind of tension-reducing integration.

In outlining the possibilities it is important to note that there are generally two interdependent but also partially independent dimensions involved even in polarized systems. One of these is a dimension of superiority-inferiority on some scale which involves in varying combinations elements of political power, wealth, and cultural or other prestige. The other is a dimension of qualitative difference of function, as for example, between the private sector of economic production and the governmental sector in modern societies. Both are dimensions of differentiation in the above sense.

One possible outcome is the revolutionary one, where the lower element ousts the upper from its superior position and "takes over." It is very likely then that, even if the previous upper group is thoroughly extirpated, some approximation to the previous pattern of differentiation will be restored within the remaining group. Thus, though in the present Communist societies there is allegedly no longer a "bourgeois" class, these societies are far from being undifferentiated on a scale of stratification. Though the "intelligentsia" are called members of the "working class," their actual roles, especially as what we would call managerial and professional personnel and "intellectuals," are closely equivalent to those of upper "middle class" groups in so-called "capitalist" societies. Ownership of the means of production has, to be sure, changed, but stratification much less so. The case of a previously colonial society achieving its independence, which of course was that of the United States, is an interesting combination of successful "revolution" and segmentation.

The type of outcome which primarily interests me for present purposes, however, is a combination of *internal* inclusion and upgrading and of further differentiation by virtue of which the lines which defined the earlier polarization are deprived of their salient significance. Thus the Mediterranean City States of the ancient world, both in Greece and Italy, at an early phase were divided into aristocracies and "commoners"—for example, the early Roman patricians and plebeians. By the time of full "maturity" of this form, however, the previous lower class had become upgraded to full membership in the central citizen body. By this process of *inclusion* the distinction between the two classes had virtually disappeared, though it should be remembered the citizen body was even then only a minority of the total population. Somewhat similar things can, as I shall note, be said of the process of "democratization" in modern societies.

Finally, within a system where hierarchical polarization is sufficiently mitigated, in part by relatively open opportunities for mobility, we can speak of further qualitative differentiation resulting in *pluralization*. This has been most conspicuous in modern societies, where such distinctions as those between economic, managerial, political, technical, and cultural functions have by and large not implied *generalized* hierarchical status, but the qualitative differences have tended to predominate in defining status. Furthermore, pluralization in this sense is intimately involved with a phenomenon we call *interpenetration*. This is to say that the collective structures which define the principal differentiated functions for the wider societal system are themselves differentiated internally on a cross-cutting basis. Thus some lawyers teach in university law schools and not only do others practice privately but still others perform essential services in governmental and business organizations. The lawyer in a governmental agency is therefore, at the same time, a member of the legal profession and, let us say, of the executive branch of the federal government. The common membership is a "zone of interpenetration" between the legal profession and the structure of government.

Without justifying it here, I shall assume that inclusion as an outcome of either differentiation or processes of "environmental" change presupposes some order of *common* value-commitment. Such great principles as the Christian equality of all souls before God and the Natural Rights philosophy of the Enlightenment are classical instances of the grounding of basic rights in common value complexes.

It is very common, though by no means universal, that the moral appeal for the right to be included, generally invoking the relevance of such common values, comes predominantly from the disadvantaged component of the polarized system. When it is grounded in common values, however, an assertion of "rights" necessarily stimulates *some* resonance in the superordinate group, although this is very generally complicated by formidable resistances, not only to actual inclusion, but even to the recognition that the subordinate elements have any right in the matter.

Relatively sharp polarization clearly favors conflict and antagonism in the first instance. Providing, however, other conditions are fulfilled, sharp polarization seems on the longer run to be more favorable to effective inclusion than is a complex grading of the differences between components, perhaps particularly where gradations are arranged on a superiority-inferiority hierarchy. To put cases immediately in point, I take the position that the race relations problem has a better prospect of resolution in the United States than in Brazil, partly *because* the line between white and Negro has been so rigidly drawn in the United States because the system has been sharply polarized. This draws a clear issue which is difficult to evade once it has been clearly posed, although resolution depends, of course, on a complex set of conditions.[2]

Perhaps the prominence of polarizations in Western history is a feature of the West's greatness as well as a source of its innumerable tragedies. Although polarization implies exclusiveness, at least on one side it may also set the stage for important processes of inclusion. The polarizations between Christian and Pagan, between Religious and Laity within the Church, and between Christendom and the world of Infidels are early examples. The patternings of polarization in which I am particularly interested, however, are those which have obtained since the Reformation, both within Western society and in its relations to the rest of the world.

The Reformation so drastically polarized Europe that it took a long period of Wars of Religion before the beginnings of a new integration could appear.[3] The Protestant movement, however, more or less completely overcame an ancient dichotomy internal to Christian society. For the first time since the Catholic Church was fully institutionalized, the Christian *laity* came to be fully included in a Christian community on a basis of fundamental equality with the religious elements. This was a tremendously radical innovation in the light of previous Western Christian history.[4]

The Reformation was a revolutionary movement which presumed to the leadership of Western Christendom, a position which, despite many vicissitudes, it broadly attained, although its failure to carry France after prolonged conflict greatly retarded its achievements. Particularly in Great Britain and the Netherlands, however, it achieved a new level of socio-religious organization in that a predominantly secular community—the new Nation—was set free on a new mission to organize the "world" in terms of a religious ideal. In Germany, only the territorial princes were brought into the ascetic-activistic wing of the Reform, and they were subject to peculiar limitations. In France, the outcome of the struggle left the French King his "most Catholic Majesty." So, clearly, England became, after a struggle with the Dutch, the spearhead of the movement.

Under the tension of the European developments at that time, there was perhaps a particularly strong need to draw sharp lines between the European system within which such events were occurring and the outside. The period coincided with a new confrontation between Europe and the rest of the world through the "Discoveries"

353

in which the Portuguese and Spanish took the initial lead, but were soon formidably challenged by the Dutch and particularly the English. Christians, to say nothing of Protestants, surely did not originate the slavery which underlay so much of the modern westward expansion of Europe; it was perhaps more Arab in origin than anything else. Nevertheless, as Bastide notes, slavery played an especially strong role in the Protestant complex, particularly in accentuating the line between Christian and outsider and in establishing color as the symbol of rejection from Christian religious points of view.

A decisive difference between the eastward and westward expansions of Europe was that old, established civilizations were encountered in the Orient, whereas except for the Aztec-Inca realms, only quite primitive societies were found in the Americas. Given the pressures of the European intrusion and the availability of African slaves, it is perhaps not surprising that a very large slave population was brought from Africa to the Western Hemisphere, and that the justice of subordinating the black man was more sharply asserted by English Protestants than by Iberian Catholics. There is no doubt whatever that slavery and, more generally, a sharp color line were more strongly legitimated by the Protestants than by the Catholics. This fact does not explain, however, why it was English nonconformism that underlay the antislavery movement of the nineteenth century, including Abolition in the United States, or why the Protestant Churches are so deeply involved in the American civil rights movement today.

In my opinion, Bastide is quite right that the original Protestant movement—particularly the pure Calvinist form that was especially important in France—developed a conspicuous tendency toward rigidly polarizing relationships, both within and across the boundaries of the Protestant community. Moreover, *one* of its principal manifestations was the acceptance of the symbol of color, which, as Bastide brilliantly demonstrates, played the important role in Christian history of defining the line between the membership of the potential Holy Community and the outsiders. Bastide also seems to argue that this pattern was rigidly and irrevocably set in the Reformation period, that it remains characteristic of all Protestantism today, and that only the Enlightenment has brought about any basic change. To my mind, this errs in identifying Protestantism, in general, with what we may call its "Fundamentalist" versions and grossly misinterprets many phases of post-Reformation Western history.

It is my view that the Reformation has proved the most important single fountainhead of the "modern" phase of European societal development.[5] Let us sketch a few aspects of its internal development before returning to its impact on the world outside European culture.

At the height of its "effervescence," the Reformation involved three major polarizations: Christian/non-Christian, with special reference to the "uncivilized" world of the Americas and later Africa; Protestant/Catholic; and, within the Protestant system, becoming increasingly sharp for a time, the Calvinistic version of the dichotomy between the Elect and the Damned.[6]

Such polarization may be conceived as involving a kind of Freudian "condensation" of previous dichotomous themes. The new identification of *Lay* Christians with the Religious of yore as the elite component combined with the old traditions of aristocracy. Together they placed a premium on the conception of an elite as the ostensibly Divinely appointed (though, in empirical fact, "self-appointed") agency for implementing the Divine mandate to establish the new Holy Community. This community emphatically differs from the graded "compromise" between Divine and Natural worlds in Thomism.[7]

The new elite basically renounced *both* of the more immediate bases of legitimation which had been fundamental to its predecessors. First, it was not sanctioned by the single universal church—a Calvinistic saint could not gain ordination to the religious life by authority of the Vicar of God on earth, but was "justified by faith alone." Second, it cut loose entirely from any basis of aristocracy in the prestige of hereditary status. In this sense, it was inherently a "bourgeois" rather than an aristocratic elite.

This double "cutting loose" raised acute questions about the basis of the legitimation of the new Holy Community and its leading groups. It could lie neither in the specifically Catholic form of Divine sanction assured by the supernatural powers of the Church nor in a "Natural" basis of the kind which Thomas built into the Catholic system at a lower level. It is my thesis, however, that the solution lay not in an "individualistic" version of "Natural Law," but in the conception of the Divine Mission of the total *Community*. If this was the case, it seems natural that questions concerning the normative order of the community and the constitution of its membership should have been very central.

Inherent in Calvinism, which for a considerable time comprised the dominant branch of Protestantism, was an initial polarization that, as noted, was ambiguous with respect to the problem of inclusion. In pure Calvinism, only the presumptively elect were members of the church; the presumptive "Reprobates" were subject to the discipline of the church—in which there was no "nonsense" about religious toleration—but were denied membership. In polarizing this drastic line of predestination, old Calvinism, in *one* of its versions, came to identify the line between Elect and Damned with the color line. Perhaps the most drastic case has been the Conservative wing of the Dutch Reformed Church in South Africa, although this syndrome has also played an important part in the United States, especially, but not exclusively, in the South.[8] Bastide, then, is right that this syndrome is an authentic and important product of Protestantism, and that it contributes greatly to explaining the difference between the attitudes toward color in Catholic Brazil and in Protestant North America, which is Bastide's focal problem.

This is, however, neither the whole story nor even the *main* one affecting the development in the United States, which concerns the development from the "Puritan" modifications of early Calvinism to modern "liberal" Protestantism.[9]

The "liberal" trend was toward the *inclusion* of the previous religious "lower class," the presumptive Reprobates. The doctrine of Predestination, with its rigid polarization of Elect and Damned, gave way to a doctrine maintaining the openness of salvation to all who make the fundamental commitment of Faith and "come to Christ." The "invisible" church ceased to be a "two-class" system and became an association of presumptive equals, in principle open to all who would join.[10] This type of conception was clearly incompatible with a whole series of polarizations which had been drawn in historic Christian societies. Above all, there is a critical sense in which pluralization processes "bracketed" the impact of the liberalization upon the society between the ancient polarization of aristocracy and commonness and the polarization of color.

Not only did the Reformation destroy the sacredness of the visible church and elevate the laity to the status of full membership in the invisible church, but, by destroying the relativity of the Thomistic system, it also destroyed any presumptive legitimation of the "intrinsic" (read "primordial") superiority of hereditary aristocracy over the rest of the people in Western societies. Of course, this involved a complex historic process of differentiation in human societies, but the crucial point is that, for the first time in anything but an antinomian sect, the *legitimacy* of aristocracy had been undermined.

The "ascetic" Protestant conception of the Holy Community referred to *secular* society in the sense that, though the visible church was a part of it, the "true" church was not part of it, but its invisible inspiration and legitimator. The Divine Mandate for man was to do God's Will on earth by building the good society. The ultimate source of *capacity* to contribute was believed to lie in Divine Grace, conceived of (as noted) as being accessible to all through Faith, not as dependent on the sacraments of a visible church, nor as tied to Predestined Election. Grace could in no way be identified with position in an hereditary kinship system, and hence both leadership and privilege had to be legitimated by personal qualities and achievements. The death of the aristocratic principle in Western society has been both agonizing and lingering, but it can be said that it has been clearly inevitable since the seventeenth century. England, in particular, worked out subtle compromises which, however, have been visibly weakening in our own time.

In both religious and secular senses, the ascetic Protestant Holy Community has become the basis of an increasingly pluralistic society. Not only did "the" church become invisible, but only in the early post-Reform period was a single invisible Protestant church substituted for the Catholic Church. With the development of religious liberty and toleration, which implied that adherence to a religious collectivity was basically voluntary, it came to be recognized that a modern Protestant society might include an indefinite plurality of religious associations, all equally legitimate in terms of the constitution of the secular society. This recognition has come to be known as the system of "denominational pluralism." This development, which has long been most marked in the United States because of the complete absence of an established church, later facilitated the inclusion of Roman Catholics and Jews in the American religious community.

On the secular level, two most important developments toward pluralism were both consequences of the gradual elimination of aristocracy and its counterpart, indelible "commonness." On the one hand, all commoners came to be fully included in the societal community. On the other, the possibility of there being a single diffuse basis of superiority was eliminated. The social structure, especially its occupational aspect, came to be differentiated into a variety of qualitatively different types of components, each of which performed different functions in the larger system. Hence, each was provided a different base of distinction and differential reward. Although by no means abolished, hierarchy could no longer be a basis for simple polarization of the society.

Kinship is clearly a "primordial" basis of social categorization and organization, in Shils' sense. Not only have all human societies —with only very marginal exceptions—institutionalized kinship systems, but all which have advanced beyond the most primitive stages have thoroughly linked the status of kinship units with their prestige and power hierarchies. The polarized version of such linkage is the institution of aristocracy.

I accept Shils' contention that color is also primordial. The permeation of status symbolization with that of color is impressive— as is shown by Bastide and several other contributors to this work. The relative consistency with which light color is held to be superior to dark color is also impressive, even though the exceptions are also notable (see, for example, Pitt-Rivers' discussion). In any case, it is not surprising, in the light of societal developments to be sketched presently, that a color line should loom as a possible substitute in the emerging world society for the "class" line which has been so prominent historically both in Western society and elsewhere (class here referring to the hereditary basis of aristocracy, not to social position relative to the "relations of production"). Here one must note that kinship units can be classified as aristocratic or common only *within* an already organized society. Color, however, is a sufficiently generalized basis of classification that all men, regardless of status in *any* other respect, may be subject to it.

Within this framework, let us return to the Holy Community of ascetic Protestantism as a kind of ideal type. I suggest that, having cut loose from the two historic bases of legitimation for both its identity as a social entity and its internal hierarchical differentiation, it required that a new basis of order be developed from historic components. On the new basis, it seems to have gone through two major cycles of the polarization-inclusion process before the present emergence of a major confrontation with the color problem. These were by no means confined to the ascetic Protestant area, but certainly developed most clearly there.

The new basis of legitimacy lay in the transformation of the conception of the Holy Community—which itself evolved from the early Israelitic conception of the Chosen People—into that of a society dedicated to "righteous" achievement under a *rule of law*. The conception of legal order has a long, complex history which cannot be discussed here, beyond mention that the Western heritage of Roman Law was crucial.[11] Yet, it seems well established that the Reformation, particularly in England, gave a new emphasis to developing and maintaining legal order on essentially universalistic bases, especially in stressing the rights of private individuals, independent of Church and State.[12] This linked in turn to the enormous burden of responsibility that the Protestant religious conception laid upon the individual. Law was the normative framework within which the individual was expected to do his "Christian duty" in and on behalf of the developing Holy Community. In this connection, it is striking that the crucial development of English law came to a head in the time of Justice Coke, briefly preceding the early development of Parliamentarism, and very much preceding that of political democracy.

Legal order in this new sense was the institutionalized counterpart in human society of the order of Divine Providence. It was basically "individualistic" in that the individual was placed on his own responsibility to be guided ultimately by his *conscience*, not subordinated to an authoritarian system. Since human society was composed of many individuals, their activities, no matter how conscientious, might conflict and required coordination through law.

On this background, the first major "cycle" in the above sense concerned the new type of society in the aspect of a political community. Here the process of evolution departed from the inherited "absolutism" of the early modern nation-state, particularly prominent in England with the Tudors and their "Epigoni," the Stuarts. After all, the "absolute" monarchy comprised an accentuation of the aristocratic principle, although its well-known "leveling" effect brought into question the hereditary prerogatives of all but the royal lineage itself. The English development involved a broadening of the base of aristocratic responsibility as the Crown was brought into partnership with a Parliament, which was in a graded sense an aristocratic body, that eventually subordinated it. The House of Commons, though its principal anchorage was a nontitled gentry class, could not be closed on an aristocratic basis both because of its openness to upward mobility and because some of the boroughs it represented had electorates which included considerable nonaristocratic elements. In any case, later developments opened with the Reform Bill of 1832, eventually led to the full enfranchisement of the whole adult citizenry of Britain.[13]

Thus, aristocratic presumptions of the "right to govern" by virtue of hereditary status were profoundly undermined in favor of eventual universal adult suffrage, most conspicuously in England, but much more broadly. It is to be noted that the originally excluded groups asserted *moral* claims to inclusion, and that these played an important part in this general process. In France, the excluded groups actually overthrew the aristocratic monopolists of political power and perhaps more important, of social prestige (although the monopoly had become greatly attenuated by 1789). In England, the tendency toward polarization was considerably mitigated. In any case, the typical national political community in the Western world has come to comprise the total body of citizens without reference to aristocracy of origin, however tenaciously certain special privileges of hereditary status may still be retained. Within ascetic Protestant tradition, this seems to be a "logical conclusion" of the liberal version of the Holy Community. If there is no elect within the church, why should there be any elect in the secular polity, especially on the presumptively nonlegitimate basis of biological heredity?

The type of democratic polity which thus emerged was characterized by the inclusion of the whole citizenry and became increasingly pluralistic. In its development, governmental functions were differentiated from other aspects of the societal community. This has enabled government increasingly to become an instrumentality of the plural interest groups within the society. These, however, must be—more or less successfully—integrated with one another under the law. For the individual, the role of citizen in the societal community as a whole, bearing its share of responsibility for government, has become differentiated from his involvements in various discrete "interests"—occupational, regional and local, religious, ethnic, and so forth. Unlike the older absolutism, modern democracy no longer confines political allegiance to a strict alternative between loyalty and disloyalty to the "legitimate" authority, but involves legitimized political opposition and, hence, political parties competing for the "support" of citizens.

The second "cycle" of polarization-inclusion centers at the economic rather than the political level, and concerns "class" in the economic sense rather than the "social" sense of the aristocratic-common dichotomy. Its emergence as the most salient polarization depends on a relatively full institutionalization of both legal order in the universalistic sense and political democracy. It is no accident that the principal prophet of the new polarization, Karl Marx, though a German, did his principal work in Britain and largely took for granted the British base of legal order and political democracy —however equivocally and however wrong some of his predictions from that base may have been. We may also note that this phase of development relates to T. H. Marshall's conception of the "social" component of citizenship[14]—whereas T. H. Marshall's legal (or "civil") and political components were involved in the phases just discussed.

Like practically any such case, this phase involved a complex combination of differentiation within the relevant social system and relations to elements excluded. Marx focused on the structure of the business firm, and its polarization between a proprietary element— the "capitalists"—and an element of propertyless wage labor. The status of the labor component, however, was characteristically equivocal because most wage workers were recent migrants from the countryside to the industrial centers. It was difficult to determine the extent to which their status, including the extent to which they were "exploited," derived from their positions as peasants and recent migrants. Furthermore, the "bourgeoisie" was not easy to distinguish from the older aristocracy and from "technical" and managerial personnel who were not primarily proprietors.

However problems concerning the clarity of the structural dichotomy may work out—for the long run, it has been difficult to maintain with much purity—it was marked by one critical difference from the political dichotomy just discussed. Not only was its focus economic rather than political, but it could also be generalized more readily beyond any particular nation-state. The problem of political democracy is, after all, more directly and inherently limited to the particular politically organized system which is to be governed. Various polities may or may not conform to any specific pattern, but economic-social movements of considerable ideological generality, like the international labor movement or socialist (communist) party, have been meaningless as confined to one society.[15] This distinction should not be overemphasized, but certainly economic organization at the level under consideration is more generalizable as to type than a political regime.

The socialist class definition—the Marxian version being the sharpest as well as the most influential—certainly came as close to polarizing European society as did the Reformation and the democratic movement spearheaded by the French Revolution. Indeed, there is an interesting sense in which Britain's relative "outsideness" from this disturbance was paralleled by the classic failure of the United States to polarize over the socialist issue in the late nineteenth century.[16]

Perhaps more than any other recent author, Seymour Martin Lipset has made clear that in the parts of Western industrial society outside Communist control—quite aside from the failure of the socialist movement to gain political ascendancy in any drastic sense —the polarization itself has become so attenuated that it can no longer predominate in viable interpretations of the "essential" interest conflicts within such societies.[17] From this perspective, the United States seems to be no more an anomalous case than did Britain's failure, a century and more ago, to experience a "French Revolutionary" polarization. Both cases seem to have involved main trends toward inclusion processes in the sense of this discussion. This, essentially, is what T. H. Marshall means by the development of the "social" component of citizenship.

This process of inclusion seems to have depended in turn on another process of differentiation. The directly economic interests of the "working class" have become socially problematic in the general context of distributive justice and "welfare," the broad "welfare state" pattern being the main developmental response. Essentially, this response has involved first the establishment of a "floor" level of minimum economic consumption, whether in the form of cash income or of various types of services, such as health care and education. This has now been broadening to include the requisites, in the form of capacities and opportunities, actually to implement autonomously the rights of *social* citizenship in Marshall's sense. Certainly, some considerable development of this "welfare complex" is proving to be strikingly universal among the "modern," industrial-urban societies, one which cuts across the line between the "democratic" and Communist societies. This makes it progressively more difficult for the latter to maintain their propaganda position that the leadership of the former is engaged primarily in "exploiting the working class."

Another primary component of the socialist position is clearly an emphasis on the importance of planning, especially in the context of economic development. Understandably, this emphasis is apt

362

to be most strongly asserted in the relatively "underdeveloped" societies. Among those which are both more "advanced" economically and more democratic (in the Western sense) politically, it seems that, universally, long steps have been taken away from the doctrinaire *laissez-faire* position, that central government has, in fact, been greatly strengthened. The difference between the "capitalist" and "socialist" nations, then, lies in dogmatism respecting the imperativeness of "nationalization" of *all* the critical means of production. The socialist parties of Western Europe have recently attenuated their demands in this respect markedly, tending to adopt an essentially pragmatic point of view. Of course, underlying the extreme demands has been a deep distrust of all "private enterprise," matched on the other side by distrust of government. Some sort of working relation between private enterprise and governmental function has, however, evidently been reached within most Western societies. Hence, the rigidity of the polarization between *either* capitalism or socialism (and between the interests of *either* the "bourgeoisie" or the "proletariat") has been greatly mitigated.

As in the religious and political cases, pluralization has been an essential aspect of this process of integration. A major analytical problem in this area has been perpetuated by the all-too-simple way in which ideologists, especially those of socialism, have tended to relate occupational categories to the structure of operative organization, including (but not exclusive to) the business firm. Such paradoxes appear as the tenet that a factory manager in a socialist society is a member of the "working class" (through that special subdivision called the "intelligentsia") whereas in a capitalist firm he is a "bourgeois." The most important cases which do not fit the sharp polarizations of ideology, however, are those of the modern professions. No society outdoes the socialists in their valuation of technology, but the engineers—and the scientists back of them—are surely not "proletarians" in any ordinary sense, nor are they "capitalists." It is particularly significant that the learned professions have not figured on *either side* of the ideological debates over capitalism *versus* socialism.

In terms of economic organization, there is surely a wide range of pluralistic differentiation according to function which cuts across the differences between capitalism and socialism, governmental and nongovernmental control, and the various types of formal, associational, and market organization. The plain fact is that the kind of polarization envisaged by the socialist-capitalist dichotomy cannot

363

fit the complexities of occupational and organizational differentiation and integration in the central operative sectors of modern societies. Neither the Marxian doctrine of the class struggle within capitalism nor its ideal of the status-undifferentiated "classless society" of socialism or communism can fit the realities of *any* modern industrial society.

The Marxian doctrine was originally formulated with respect to the *internal* structure of an industrial society. Its theory of "imperialism" was a secondary, derivative feature. When the Revolution failed to appear in the most advanced industrial countries as predicted, however, the theory of imperialism gained increasing prominence, so that some quarters came to believe the primary polarization to be that between exploiting and exploited *societies*, not that between exploiting and exploited classes within national societies. In the Communist versions of the theory, especially, reliance was still to be placed on the "working class" of each society, but in the predominantly underdeveloped parts of the world this was far from a proletariat of the classical Marxian type. Indeed, the history of the Chinese Communist movement, with Mao's early reliance mainly on the peasantry in sharp and bitter defiance of the orders (rather than advice) of the International (Stalin), is most instructive. Further, it seems that in these circumstances intellectuals play an even larger part than they did in the European socialist movements.

The shift to emphasis upon imperialism was, of course, very closely related to the actual international changes brought about by the rapid liquidation of the old colonial Empires. Not only could the theory of imperialism provide an ideological rationalization of this process, but it could also much more nearly approach defining a *world-wide* polarization than classical Marxian theory. Hence, its development has been linked with the emergence of a world-wide society of a type and in a sense that never existed before.

The central theme of exploitation played right into the theory of imperialism—indeed was its core—however complex the facts have been in many instances. In fact, underdevelopment has meant relative poverty on the societal level. Furthermore, the predominant economic emphasis has also been consonant with Marxian tradition. The main difficulty has lain with the central Marxian tenets of *class* conflict. It is indeed difficult for a non-Marxist to see how this tenet can maintain the centrality claimed for it.

As several papers have noted, it is not surprising that this new definition of the essential polarization should come to emphasize the color line. There was, in fact, a notable rough coincidence between the colonial or former colonial peoples and the nonwhite peoples. A principal ideological trouble, however, was that this line cut across that between the socialist and nonsocialist countries, leaving Soviet Russia and its East European satellites on the white side.[18] This situation has given the Chinese grounds for claiming the basic leadership role of the nonwhite peoples of the world in the name of the Marxian revolution.

The post-aristocratic polarizations we have discussed have followed a certain notable order. We have held that the most important impetus undermining the legitimacy of the aristocratic institutions was religious—namely, the Reformation—though economic and political factors were also very much involved. The first major post-aristocratic polarization was political, concerning essentially the status of the common people in relation to their governments. The second was primarily economic, focusing upon the class problem in the Marxian sense. It seems clear to me that this polarization is beginning to lose its force, on the one hand, because the conflict has been partly resolved by inclusion and pluralization within the advanced societies and, on the other hand, because it is being cross-cut by the problems of imperialism and color. This, then, raises the question of whether color is emerging as a new line of polarization on a world basis.

Unlike the problems of political democracy and the Marxian class conflict, color has, in common with aristocracy, a primordial component in Shils' sense. It differs from aristocracy, however, in that it is perhaps the most universalistic single criterion on which human populations can be categorized, since literally *all* men may be classified by color in relation to each other.

One primary aspect of its primordial character is that it is completely ascribed, so far as the individual is concerned; it is no more subject to change by individual achievement than the leopard's spots. This it shares with aristocratic or "common" birth. Furthermore, there is ample evidence of a formidable tendency, evident well before modern times, for lightness in color to be treated as honorific, and darkness as in some sense unfavorable—though certainly this tendency does not stand alone. Perhaps the most striking contemporary evidence is the prevalence in such predominantly dark communities as the West Indian and Negro American of a positive valuation of lightness of color—a case interestingly parallel to the anti-Semitism sometimes found among Jews.

Nevertheless, there are intrinsic difficulties in consistently polarizing world society on the basis of color, difficulties which in some respects are parallel to those inherent in the Marxian class polarity. Perhaps the most formidable difficulty is that the East Asian "yellow" peoples do not in any simple sense fit into a continuum with the European white and the African black. Though Professor Wagatsuma has shown that color plays its role within Japanese society, it has surely not been a primary basis of polarization in East Asia, nor has the "European" been nearly so sharply defined as the "white man" in East Asia as in other parts of the world.

I have suggested above that the primary historic origin of the modern color problem lies in the relation of Europeans to African slavery, as that became established along the whole Atlantic coast of the Americas from the Southern North American Colonies to Southern Brazil, very much including the Caribbean area.[19] This is certainly connected with the fact that sub-Saharan Africa remained more "primitive" than any other continental area of comparable importance once the Americas were settled by Europeans.[20] Nevertheless, it must be recognized that the color theme was first injected into the modern international system by the earlier "Imperial Powers," and that it comprised a major element in the theories with which they legitimized subjecting other peoples to the subordinate, colonial or slave, status.

I have also suggested that the pattern established in the Caribbean and the southern states of the U.S. by predominantly Protestant English groups, through initially more severe than the "Latin" pattern to the South, was in the long run more favorable to the resolution of the color problem by means of inclusion and pluralization precisely *because* it imposed rigorous polarization, a man being *either* white or colored with no intermediate category. This inclination includes the fact that, since anyone with any "Negro blood" was classified as a Negro, the rigid categorization became increasingly anomalous and morally untenable with the growth of egalitarian ideas.

For this to take effect at the level of social organization, however, it was necessary *both* for the cultural structure to change in the direction taken by "liberal Protestantism" *and* for the social, political, and economic structure to change in the direction of greater differentiation and inclusion. The change in Protestantism was thus the cultural prerequisite of the total change. The decline of aristocracy and its replacement by political democracy and by pluralism in the system of occupation and stratification, as sketched above, constitute the social prerequisites. In American terms, only so long as the South remained essentially an aristocratic society was its pattern of race relations tenable. The elaborate "Jim Crow" system, which has only recently been breaking down, may be regarded as the defensive maneuvers of a dying aristocratic system, which included a desperate attempt of the "poor white" element to attain a pseudo-aristocratic position.[21]

Surely even the issue of "dictatorship" is now largely resolved on the level at least of legitimacy, in spite of the prominence of the communist dictatorships and of the more "regressive" types found, for example, in Latin America. I have also argued that the Marxian class dichotomy is losing its force, though many would certainly contest this.[22]

The most serious possibility for the emergence of a new polarization—this time of *world*, not just European, society—is clearly the axis of color. If there is a broad continuation of the more general line of development I have attempted to sketch, the prospect is that this polarization will fail to crystallize as the major basis of division in the world. This failure is by no means a certainty, however, but clearly depends on the future operation of the inclusive and pluralizing forces which have been the principal concern of this paper.

It should be clear that in my view the polarization in terms of color is not an isolated phenomenon. Although its primordial status makes the color line in some sense "intrinsic," this does not determine how it will be interpreted or what consequences it is likely to have for the development of the world system. These problems must be seen in the context of the whole development of Western society in its relations to the rest of the world. I hope it will have proved helpful to place the color-based dichotomy in relation to four others which have been of historic importance, namely, the Protestant one of Elect and Reprobates, the broad "secular" one of aristocracy and commonness, the political one of ascribed authority versus democracy, and the "class" one of bourgeois and proletariat.

*

REFERENCES

1. Cf. my *Societies: Comparative and Evolutionary Perspectives,* Chapter 3, (Englewood Cliffs, 1966).

2. Cf. Talcott Parsons, "Full Citizenship for the Negro American: A Sociological Problem," *Dædalus* (Fall, 1965).

3. On a basis of pluralistic inclusion, incidentally.

4. Cf. Ernst Troeltsch, *The Social Teachings of the Christian Churches* (New York, 1960).

5. I have presented my view on this point most generally in *The System of Modern Societies* (Englewood Cliffs, forthcoming).

6. Clearly, the Calvinistic community utilized a special, double case of this polarization. Perhaps more stringently than Catholic society, it drew the line between Christian and non-Christian. This was certainly important in the relations between European colonists and "natives" in the New World. *Within* the Calvinistic community, however, there was also a line—that between Saints and Reprobates. Yet, it is important to note that, relative to "pagan," even Reprobates were very significantly included, but in a way quite different from that of later "liberal" Protestantism which altogether eliminated the category of Predestined Reprobate.

7. Troeltsch, *The Social Teachings of the Christian Churches.*

8. This point has been developed by J. J. Loubser in some unpublished papers. The generality of the phenomenon in American history has been documented by Leon F. Litwack in *North of Slavery* (Chicago, 1961).

9. The most massive scholarly elucidation of this development is in the extensive works of Perry Miller. A particularly important part of the English background, with special reference to the law, has been clarified in David Little's dissertation, "The Logic of Order: An Examination of the Sources of Puritan-Anglican Controversy and of Their Relations to Prevailing Legal Conceptions of Corporation in the Late 16th and Early 17th Century in England" (Harvard University, 1963). The later phases of the development in Massachusetts have been analyzed by J. J. Loubser in *Puritanism and Religious Liberty* (forthcoming).

10. This process of inclusion obviously could not have taken place without fulfillment of a complex series of conditions along the way. Cf. Miller and Loubser.

11. See Max Weber, *Max Weber on Law in Economy and Society,* ed. Max Rheinstein (Cambridge, 1954).

12. Little, "The Logic of Order."

13. Cf. T. H. Marshall, *Class, Citizenship, and Social Development* (Garden City, 1965), for an analysis of these developments in Britain; Stein Rokkan has classically analyzed the general process of extension of the franchise in

his "Mass Suffrage, Secret Voting, and Political Participation," *The European Journal of Sociology* (1961).

14. As discussed in my paper, *Dædalus* (Fall, 1965). See also T. H. Marshall, *Class Citizenship and Social Development*, Chapter 4 (Garden City, 1964).

15. *The Communist Manifesto* says, "Workers of the World Unite . . ."

16. In my opinion, the view that the United States simply opted for the "capitalist" alternative is grossly oversimplified, but this question cannot be discussed here.

17. Seymour Martin Lipset, *Political Man* (Garden City, 1963).

18. There are various further anomalies, such as the position of "white" North Africa, and that of the white components in Latin American societies. Where whiteness is associated with upper-class status, as in Latin America, the class struggle can be brought into line with the color theme.

19. Cf. Frank Tannenbaum, *Slave and Citizen* (New York, 1946).

20. The white settlement of what is now the Union of South Africa, Rhodesia, etc., may be considered another special case of the pattern that predominated in America, especially the part played in it by the Dutch who arrived in the seventeenth century. Muslim North Africa is, of course, quite another matter.

21. Cf. C. Vann Woodward, *The Strange Career of Jim Crow* (New York, 1959). In certain respects the above analysis, with special reference to the trend of development with respect to the color line, is continuous with my own recent analysis of the development of race relations in the United States. This was presented in the paper, "Full Citizenship for the Negro American?" and somewhat supplemented by my introductory contribution as co-editor, in the volume *The Negro American* (eds. Talcott Parsons and Kenneth B. Clark) (Boston, 1966).

22. This I think is the main point in Daniel Bell's thesis that we have entered the period of the "end of ideology."

NOTES ON CONTRIBUTORS

NOTES ON CONTRIBUTORS

Roger Bastide, born in 1898 in Nîmes, France, is Professor in the Faculté de Lettres et Sciences Humaines at the Sorbonne and Director of the Centre de Psychiatrie Sociale. He is the author of *Sociologie et Psychanalyse* (Paris, 1950); *Les Religions Africaines au Brèsil* (Paris, 1960); and *Sociologie des Maladies Mentales* (Paris, 1965). Mr. Bastide did research for UNESCO on race relations in São Paulo, Brazil, in 1951-52, and, more recently, on African students in France.

André Béteille, born in 1934 in Chandannagore, India, is a Reader in Sociology at the University of Delhi. He has published *Caste, Class and Power: Changing Patterns of Stratification in a Tanjore Village* (Berkeley and Los Angeles, 1965) and numerous articles in scholarly journals.

Eustace Ricardo Braithwaite, born in 1912 in Guyana, South America, is Ambassador and Permanent Representative of Guyana to the United Nations. His novels include *To Sir, With Love* (1959); *A Kind of Homecoming* (1961); *Paid Servant* (1962); and *A Choice of Straws* (1967). In 1962 he received the Anisfield-Wolf Literary Award for *To Sir, With Love*.

Leon Carl Brown, born in 1928 in Mayfield, Kentucky, is Associate Professor of Oriental Studies at Princeton University. The editor of *State and Society in Independent North Africa* (Washington, D. C., 1966), he was co-author of *Tunisia: The Politics of Modernization* (New York, 1964). Mr. Brown served with the U. S. Foreign Service in Beirut, Lebanon, in 1954-55, and in Khartoum, Sudan, from 1956 to 1958.

Florestan Fernandes, born in 1920 in São Paulo, Brazil, is Professor of Sociology at the University of São Paulo. His many publications include *Mudanças Sociais no Brasil* (São Paulo, 1960); *Folclore e Mudança Social na Cidade de São Paulo* (São Paulo, 1961); *A Sociologia numa Era de Revolução Social* (São Paulo, 1963); *A Integração do Negro à Sociedade de Classes* (São Paulo, 1965); and *Educação e Sociedade no Brasil* (São Paulo, 1966).

JOHN HOPE FRANKLIN, born in 1915, in Rentiesville, Oklahoma, is chairman of the Department of History at the University of Chicago. His publications include *From Slavery to Freedom: A History of American Negroes* (3rd ed., 1967); *Militant South* (1956); *Reconstruction After the Civil War* (1961); and *The Emancipation Proclamation* (1963).

ROBERT KWEKU ATTA GARDINER, born in 1914 in Kumasi, Ghana, is Executive Secretary of the Economic Commission for Africa. Mr. Gardiner was Officer-in-Charge of the United Nations Operation in the Congo in 1962-63, and in 1961 was appointed Director of the Public Administration of the United Nations Department of Economic and Social Affairs.

KENNETH J. GERGEN, born in 1934 in Rochester, New York, is Assistant Professor of Social Psychology at Harvard University. Mr. Gergen has three books in press: *The Self in Social Interaction*, Vol. 1; *Personality and Social Interaction;* and *The Study of Policy Formation.* He has published some thirty studies in psychology in scholarly journals.

HAROLD R. ISAACS, born in 1910, is Professor of Political Science at Massachusetts Institute of Technology. Mr. Isaacs was associate editor and correspondent for *Newsweek* from 1943 to 1950 with assignments in Washington, New York, China, India, and Southeast Asia. His publications include, among many, *India's Ex-Untouchables* (New York, 1965); *The New World of Negro Americans* (New York, 1963); and *Scratches on Our Minds, American Images of China and India* (New York, 1958).

COLIN LEGUM, born in 1919 in Kestell, Orange Free State, South Africa, is Commonwealth Correspondent for *The Observer* in London. Mr. Legum has edited *Africa Handbook* (1961, 1966); *Lumumba, My Country* (1963); *Zambia—Independence and After* (1966). He has also published *Must We Lose Africa?* (1954); *Bandung Cairo & Accra* (1958); *Congo Disaster* (1960); *A Short Guide to Pan-Africanism* (1962); and with Margaret Legum *South Africa: Crisis for the West* (1964).

C. ERIC LINCOLN, born in 1924 in Athens, Alabama, is Professor of Sociology at Union Theological Seminary. Mr. Lincoln's publications include *The Black Muslims in America* (Boston, 1961); *My Face Is Black* (Boston, 1964); and *The Negro Pilgrimage in America* (New York, in press). Mr. Lincoln has lectured widely in the United States and abroad and has contributed numerous articles to scholarly journals and magazines.

KENNETH LINDSAY LITTLE, born in 1908 in Liverpool, England, is Professor of Social Anthropology at the University of Edinburgh. He is the author of *Negroes in Britain* (London, 1947); *Race and Society* (Paris, 1952); *The Mende of Sierra Leone* (London, 1951); and *West African Urbanization* (Cambridge, 1965).

DAVID LOWENTHAL, born in 1923 in New York City, is Research Associate of the American Geographical Society and Visiting Professor at Harvard and Massachusetts Institute of Technology. Mr. Lowenthal has written *George Perkins Marsh, Versatile Vermonter* (New York, 1958), and *The West Indies Federation: Perspectives on a New Nation* (New York, 1961); he has also edited *Man and Nature* (Cambridge, Mass., 1965).

PHILIP MASON, CIE, OBE, born in 1906 in London, is Director of the Institute of Race Relations in London. As Philip Woodruff, he published *The Men Who Ruled India* in two volumes: *The Founders* (London, 1953) and *The Guardians* (London, 1954). He has also written *The Birth of a Dilemma* (London, 1958) and *Prospero's Magic* (London, 1962).

TALCOTT PARSONS, born in 1902 in Colorado Springs, Colorado, is Professor of Sociology at Harvard University. Among his extensive publications are *Structure of Social Action* (1937); *Toward a General Theory of Action* (1951); *Family, Socialization and Interaction Process* (1955), *Structure and Process in Modern Societies* (1959); and *Evolutionary and Comparative Perspectives* (1965). Mr. Parsons was co-editor, with Kenneth B. Clark, of the Dædalus Library volume *The Negro American.*

JULIAN PITT-RIVERS, born in 1919 in London, is Visiting Professor at the École Pratique des Hautes Études of the Sorbonne. Since 1957 he has taught at the University of Chicago. Mr. Pitt-Rivers has published *The People of the Sierra* (London, 1954) and as editor *Mediterranean Countrymen* (The Hague, 1964). In preparation or in press are *Social and Cultural Change in the Highlands of Chiapas* and *Race Relations in Latin America.*

FRANÇOIS H. M. RAVEAU, born in 1928 in Saintes (Charente Maritime), France, is Assistant Director of the Centre de Psychiatrie Sociale of the École Pratique des Hautes Études at the Sorbonne. Dr. Raveau, a neuropsychiatrist, is also a professor in the Faculty of Medicine of Paris. His publications include *Contribution sur le plan neuro-psychiatrique à la pathologie post-concentrationnaire* (Paris, 1962); *Pathologie mentale et adaptation chez les Africains* (Paris, 1965); and numerous articles in medical and sociological journals.

EDWARD SHILS, born in 1911, is Professor of Sociology and Social Thought at the University of Chicago and a Fellow of King's College, Cambridge University. His books include *The Present State of American Sociology* and *The Intellectual Between Tradition and Modernity.* He is also editor of *Minerva*, a quarterly review of the relations of science, learning, and policy.

HIROSHI WAGATSUMA, born in 1927 in Tokyo, Japan, was Assistant Research Psychologist at the Institute of Human Development at the University of California at Berkeley from 1962 to 1966. His writings in Japanese include *Psychology of Human Nature* (with Otoya Miyagi, Ichiro Yasuda, Yoshio Nagumo); *National Character—The Europeans, the Americans, and the Japanese* (with Takao Sofue); *For the Understanding of Love—Psychological Analysis of Marital Life;* and *Social Psychology of the Self.* Mr. Wagatsuma is presently writing with George DeVos *Japan's Invisible Race: Cultural Psychology of the Caste System.*

INDEX

INDEX

379

INDEX

in Latin America, 46, 269; in West Indies, 310
Shakespeare, William, 9, 119
Shantung province, China, 21
Sharpeville, South Africa, 212
Shepstone, Sir Theophilus, 52
Shils, Edward, viii, ix, xi, 349, 358, 365, 375
Shunsui, Tamenaga, 132
Shūsaku, Endō, his *Up to Aden*, 146
Sierra Leone, 86
Sikhs, Indian, 170; in Britain, 237
Silberman, Charles, 262
Similarity, and mutual attraction, 115–117
Sin, contagion of, 41–42, 44–45
Sino-Soviet dispute, 93
Slavery, 50–51, 354, 366; Christian justification of, 36; and Enlightenment, 45; Aristotle's justification for, 51; and Islam, 190; in Northern Africa, 191; U.S., 253–254, 256, 261–262; in Brazil, 282–286, 289, 292–294; in West Indies, 306, 307, 309–313
Smith, Ian, 213
Smuts, Jan Christiaan, 208
SNCC, *see* Student Nonviolent Co-Ordinating Committee
Sobukwe, Robert Mangaliso, 206
Social distance, British, 240, 244–245
Socialism, 362–363; African, 66, 67; British, 224, 229. *See also* Communism
Socialization, 116
Society of Labour Lawyers, Britain, 248
Somalia, vii, 87
Somalis, Moslem, 197
Songhay empire, 189
South Africa, xii–xiii, 32; and U.N., 22, 214; segregated worship in, 35; and pagan-contagion attitude, 44; battle of white supremacy, 77 (*see also Apartheid*); Indians in, 94–95; color as power determinant in, 205–216, 303; *laager* society, 208; Separate Development policy, 209–210; electorate, 211–213
South America, xiv
Southeast Asia, 18–19, 32; colonial domination of, 89
Southeast Asia Treaty Organization (SEATO), xv

South-West Africa, 22, 212. *See also* Africa
Southern Christian Leadership Conference, 55
Soviet Union, *see* Russia
Spain, 84–85
Srinivas, M. N., 168
Stalin, Josef, 364
Status, color determinant of, xiv, 251–253; by birth, 265–266; in Latin America, 271, 275–276, 278–279; in Roman law, 293; West Indian middle class, 314, 315, 319, 332
Stephen, Wallace, his "Domination of Black," 121
Stereotypes, 123–125, 333; British-held, 235, 241; and U.S. Negro, 260; in West Indies, 324; East Indian, 331
Strijdom, J. G., 210
Student Nonviolent Co-Ordinating Committee (SNCC), 55, 259, 260, 261, 338
Sudan, vii, 88, 187, 189, 192; Arabo-Moslem control in, 196
Suffrage, universal, 312, 317, 360
Sugimoto, E. S., 137–138
Sukarno, Dr. Achmed, 25
Superpowers, and Africa, 213–214
Surinam, 306–307, 311, 328; plural society of, 314; political racism in, 329–330; social organization in, 331
Symbolism, and color, ix-x, 35–37, 39–48, 52, 117–123; and Aryanization of Christ, 37–38

Tacitus, 98
Taijio, Tamura, 149
Tale of Genji, The (Lady Murasaki), 130
Tale of Glory, The (Akazome Emon), 130
Tamil Brahmins, India, 166, 169. *See also* Caste
Tanganyika, 67
Tanzania, 213
Technology, 22–23; European superiority in, 24; and internationalism, 30; Japanese, 137
Tertullian, 35
Third World, 23–24, 199
Tillett, Ben, 225
Tobago, 306
Tomlinson Commission, 211

389